MAFIA BROTHERHOODS

STUDIES IN CRIME AND PUBLIC POLICY
Michael Tonry and Norval Morris, General Editors

Making Crime Pay: Law and Order in Contemporary American Politics
Katherine Beckett

Community Policing, Chicago Style
Wesley G. Skogan and Susan M. Hartnett

Crime Is Not the Problem: Lethal Violence in America
Franklin E. Zimring and Gordon Hawkins

Hate Crimes: Criminal Law and Identity Politics
James B. Jacobs and Kimberly Potter

Politics, Punishment, and Populism
Lord Windlesham

American Youth Violence
Franklin E. Zimring

Bad Kids: Race and the Transformation of the Juvenile Court
Barry C. Feld

Gun Violence: The Real Costs
Philip J. Cook and Jens Ludwig

Punishment, Communication, and Community
R. A. Duff

Punishment and Democracy: Three Strikes and You're Out in California
Franklin E. Zimring, Gordon Hawkins, and Sam Kamin

Restorative Justice and Responsive Regulation
John Braithwaite

Maconochie's Gentlemen: The Story of Norfolk Island and the Roots of Modern Prison Reform
Norval Morris

Can Gun Control Work?
James B. Jacobs

Penal Populism and Public Opinion: Lessons from Five Countries
Julian V. Roberts, Loretta J. Stalans, David Indermaur, and Mike Hough

Mafia Brotherhoods: Organized Crime, Italian Style
Letizia Paoli

MAFIA BROTHERHOODS

ORGANIZED CRIME,

ITALIAN STYLE

Letizia Paoli

2003

OXFORD
UNIVERSITY PRESS

Oxford   New York
Auckland   Bangkok   Buenos Aires   Cape Town   Chennai
Dar es Salaam   Delhi   Hong Kong   Istanbul   Karachi   Kolkata
Kuala Lumpur   Madrid   Melbourne   Mexico City   Mumbai   Nairobi
São Paulo   Shanghai   Taipei   Tokyo   Toronto

Copyright © 2003 by Oxford University Press, Inc.

Published by Oxford University Press, Inc.
198 Madison Avenue, New York, New York 10016

www.oup.com

Oxford is a registered trademark of Oxford University Press

All rights reserved. No part of this publication may be reproduced,
stored in a retrieval system, or transmitted, in any form or by any means,
electronic, mechanical, photocopying, recording, or otherwise,
without the prior permission of Oxford University Press.

Library of Congress Cataloging-in-Publication Data
Paoli, Letizia.
[Fratelli di mafia. English]
Mafia brotherhoods : organized crime, Italian style / by Letizia Paoli.
p. cm. — (Studies in crime and public policy)
Includes bibliographical references and index.
ISBN 978-0-19-537526-8
1. Mafia—Italy—Sicily—History.   2. Mafia—United States—History.
3. 'Ndrangheta—Italy—History.   4. 'Ndrangheta—History.   I. Title.   II. Series.
HV6453.I82 S654613   2003
364.1'06'09458—dc21   2002009518

Printed in the United States of America
on acid-free paper

for Michel and Maddalena

Preface to the American Edition

The main aim of this book is to reconstruct the culture, structure, and action of the Sicilian Cosa Nostra and the Calabrian 'Ndrangheta. Not only are these Italy's most dangerous criminal organizations, but they have also profoundly influenced the mafia phenomenon in North America. It was from the Sicilian Cosa Nostra's nineteenth-century forerunners that the Italian American mafia developed, as millions of Italian immigrants settled in the United States, most of them coming from southern Italy. Significantly, the largest and most influential Italian American mafia confederation is called Cosa Nostra as well. The Calabrian 'Ndrangheta also has offshoots in the Anglo-Saxon world. In the early twentieth century, 'Ndrangheta groups were established in both Canada and Australia, and these are still active now, maintaining close contacts with their Calabrian counterparts.

In order to depict the culture, structure, and action of these organized crime groups, I consulted numerous sources, ranging from criminal cases to parliamentary hearings, from archival and other standard secondary sources to interviews with law enforcement officials, local politicians, and anti-mafia activists. The portrait given in this book, however, relies most heavily on the confessions and testimonies of former mafia members now cooperating with judicial authorities. As my introduction explains, these statements have not been accepted uncritically but have been taken seriously even when they seem to contradict the evil activities in which most mafiosi engage. Cooperating mafia witnesses are, in fact, the most direct source of information about the mafia, describing the mafia world not only from the outside but also—as one defector put it—from within.

The picture emerging from the analysis of mafia witnesses' statements supplements and amends previous interpretations of the mafia in both Italy and the United States. This will be presented in its entirety in the following pages. Here it suffices to say that Italy's mafia associations cannot be reduced to any of the most common forms of sociability in the contemporary world: they are not mere blood families, nor are they bureaucracies or enterprises. Cosa Nostra and the 'Ndrangheta are confederations of mafia groups, which are called families by their members but are distinct from the mafiosi's blood families. Though consanguineous ties are sometimes very important, especially in the Calabrian 'Ndrangheta, the bond uniting a mafia family has a fictive, ritual nature and is reestablished with the ceremony of initiation of each new member. Since mafiosi are required to regard their associates as brothers, mafia families are—at least prescriptively, if not always effectively—brotherhoods. They are, in particular, male fraternities, as women are excluded from participation.

As a nineteenth-century observer noted of Cosa Nostra's forerunners, "Mutual assistance was the basis of these associations, which were usually known as societies of mutual aid" (Cutrera [1900] 1988: 125). Unlike legitimate fraternal insurance companies, the members of a mafia family promise to help each other even in crimes and must be ready to use violence if the group requests it. No means are excluded, nor are the concrete goals and functions of mafia action predetermined or fixed over time. Since the consolidation of mafia groups in the late nineteenth century, brotherhood ties have been exploited by mafia members—and particularly by their chiefs—for the achievement of a wide variety of collective and personal goals. Though economic enrichment has become more and more important in recent decades, it has never been—nor is it now—the exclusive or even the main goal of southern Italian mafia families. Founded on a premodern bond, these organizations are functionally diffuse and have remained so up to the present. Because of their use of violence, they have had to protect themselves from state repression with increasing degrees of secrecy and have thus never participated in the process of functional differentiation that has invested Western societies from the nineteenth century onward.

Although mafia families have often been considered business enterprises, one of their key and long-underassessed functions has always been the exercise of a political dominion over the communities in which they are settled. By providing security and protection, they have often substituted themselves for the Italian state, at the same time preventing the government's effective consolidation in large portions of the Italian South.

Brotherhood ties and multifunctionality—including the claim to exert a political dominion—are the main typifying characteristics of the Sicilian Cosa Nostra and the Calabrian 'Ndrangheta, the two most powerful Italian mafia associations. As we will see in the following pages, these traits are at the same time the source of their lasting success and of their most recent difficulties.

Acknowledgments

This book is a further working of the Ph.D. thesis I defended in June 1997 at the Department of Social and Political Sciences of the European University Institute (EUI) in Florence ("The Pledge to Secrecy: Culture, Structure and Action of Mafia Associations"). A first revised and updated version of my dissertation was published in Italian in 2000 by Il Mulino under the title *Fratelli di Mafia: Cosa Nostra and 'Ndrangheta*. In the following years, I wrote the current English manuscript, further updating and refining my analysis of the Italian mafia phenomenon.

During the long gestation of this volume, I benefited from the help and support of a large number of people. In a sort of chronological order, I would like first of all to thank Prof. Pino Arlacchi (Università di Sassari). His influence on my work has been profound since the end of the 1980s, when I first attended his seminars in the Department of Political Sciences at the University of Florence. Since then he has consistently communicated his deep passion for and interest in the study of the mafia and illicit economies, inspiring my own fascination with these areas, culminating in this book.

Together with Arlacchi I served for about three years (1992–1995) as a consultant to the Direzione Investigativa Antimafia (DIA), a police agency of the Italian Ministry of the Interior that specializes in the fight against organized crime. Among other duties, I was in charge of writing the annual reports on organized crime in Italy, which were presented to the Italian parliament by the Ministry of the Interior. This was an invaluable experience, since it gave me the chance to listen to and closely analyze the "voices" inside the mafia world. There are too many people to whom I am grateful at the Direzione Investigativa Antimafia to be mentioned by name. Extending my thanks to all those who helped me, I would particularly like to mention Prefect Gianni De Gennaro, the current chief of the Italian police; General of the Carabinieri Luigi Magliuolo, who, as head of the DIA Preventive Investigations Department, was my direct contact person and was always very cooperative and affable; and Colonel of the Carabinieri Angiolo Pellegrini. Being at the time head of the DIA Reggio Calabria Operative Center, Pellegrini was a most generous host and an authoritative guide in the meanders of the Calabrian 'Ndrangheta and helped me contact prosecutors and judges and collect criminal cases. My deep gratitude also goes to Anna Maria Romano and Alessandro Pelliccia, my closest assistants in those years, who were not only very efficient in retrieving judicial, police, and other official documents but also instrumental in creating a pleasant and friendly working atmosphere.

Notwithstanding their busy schedules, many prosecutors and judges of the Direzione Nazionale Antimafia (DNA) and the courts and prosecutor's offices of several Italian cities found the time to answer my questions and explain the past and current development of the different forms of crime that they had targeted. While they are too numerous to be listed one by one, I would like to thank them all for the time they gave me and the information they shared with me.

A special mention is due to several current and former members of the Direzione Distrettuale Antimafia (DDA) of the Palermitan prosecutor's office, who were extremely cooperative in securing my access to criminal cases and shared their analyses of Cosa Nostra with me: Dr. Ignazio De Francisci (the current chief prosecutor at the Agrigento Court), Dr. Antonio Ingroia, Dr. Guido Lo Forte (adjunct chief prosecutor in Palermo), Dr. Giancarlo Caselli (former chief prosecutor in Palermo, now prosecutor general at the Turin Court of Appeals), Dr. Piero Grasso (the current chief prosecutor in Palermo) and Dr. Alfonso Sabella. My deepest thanks also goes to Dr. Salvatore Boemi, the adjunct chief prosecutor and head of the Direzione Distrettuale Antimafia in Reggio Calabria, and to Dr. Vincenzo Macrì, prosecutor at the DNA, for their precious help but even more so for their civil courage and determination in the repression of the Calabrian 'Ndrangheta, a criminal organization that is still too often underassessed by the national government and public opinion alike.

Closing the list of my sources, I would finally like to thank all the activists of grassroots anti-mafia movements, journalists, mayors and members of the local governments, priests, and ordinary people who allowed me to interview them. Gratitude, admiration, and friendship now inspire my relationship with some of these courageous representatives of the civil society, in particular Pippo Cipriani and Dr. Maria Maniscalco, the former mayors of (respectively) Corleone and San Giuseppe Jato, and Dr. Augusto Cavadi, a Palermitan anti-mafia activist.

This book would be very different if Prof. Bernhard Giesen (University of Constance and Yale) had not been the supervisor of my Ph.D. thesis at the European University Institute. Since 1994, when we first met, his suggestions and criticism have been invaluable in helping me select useful theoretical tools with which to analyze the empirical material gathered in the previous years. I am also grateful to the late Prof. Susan Strange, my cosupervisor, whose occasionally sharp criticism was very helpful in clarifying my arguments and focusing my research.

I would also like to thank the numerous scholars who discussed my research hypotheses and read parts of or the whole text. Prof. Shmuel Eisenstadt (Hebrew University of Jerusalem), Prof. Henner Hess (Universität Frankfurt), Prof. Norval Morris (University of Chicago), and Dr. Umberto Santino (Centro Impastato, Palermo), as well as Profs. Jane and Peter Schneider (City University and Fordham University, New York), read my whole dissertation and offered most useful comments and suggestions. Prof. Thomas Hauschild (Universität Tübingen) and Prof. Fedele Ruggeri (Università di Pisa) commented on my analysis of mafia culture; Prof. Paolo Pezzino (Università di Pisa) competently reviewed my account of nineteenth-century mafia groups and manifestations; Prof. Gianfranco Poggi (Università di Trento), a member of my thesis defense jury, gave me precious hints on the political dimension of mafia associations; Prof. Peter Reuter (University of Maryland and RAND) insightfully commented on the chapters concerning the organization and multifunctional nature of Southern Italian mafia consortia; Prof. Francis Snyder (Université d'Aix–Marseille III), at the time a professor of law at the European University Institute, advised me and encouraged me in my anthropological analysis of mafia legal orders.

I also had most productive discussions with Prof. Claus Eder (Freie Universität Berlin); Prof. Alois Hahn (Universität Trier); Prof. Hans-Jürgen Kerner (Universität Tübingen), who hosted me at his Institute of Criminology in 1997; Prof. Alessandro Pizzorno (European University Institute, Florence); Prof. Vincenzo Ruggiero (Middlesex University, London); Prof. Louise Shelley (American University, Washington, D.C.); Prof. Arpad Szakolczai (University of Ireland); and Prof. Michael Tonry (Cambridge University). Dr. Paola Monzini (United Nations Interregional Crime and Justice Research Institute and Gruppo Abele, Turin), a friend and a former colleague of mine at the European University Institute, intensively discussed with me my research hypotheses. Encouragement and support were also given me by another friend and former colleague, Dr. Anja Hänsch (Universität Göttingen): thanks to her knowledge of both the Italian and German university systems and mentalities she helped me learn how to profit from both cultural traditions.

The drafting of this volume took place mainly at the Max Planck Institute for Foreign and International Criminal Law, in Freiburg, Germany, where I have been working since 1998. It is here, in the Department of Criminology headed by

Hans-Jörg Albrecht, that I believe I have gained the kind of distance and perspective necessary to single out the essential characteristics of the two main Italian mafia associations. Many thanks are thus due to Prof. Albrecht for both the stimulating effect of the new research projects he entrusted me and for granting me the time to distill my analysis of the mafia.

Special gratitude goes to Nicky Owtram, lecturer at the European University Institute, who accurately revised the current manuscript and transformed my English into a correct and easily readable text, and to Brigitte Schwab, the head of the EUI Publications and Alumni Office, which granted me the funds to finance the manuscript revision. I am indebted to my assistant, Irina Mirimovitsch, who helped me create the name and subject indexes, and to Dedi Felman, Christi Stanforth, and Jennifer Rappaport at Oxford University Press for their competent and friendly editorial support. I am also very grateful to Prefect Alessandro Pansa, who provided me with valuable pictures from the archives of the Italian police, and to Letizia Battaglia, who has been fighting the mafia in Palermo with the sole but uncompromising weapons of her camera and civil courage for over the past thirty years and allowed me to publish her beautiful, dramatic photos (Battaglia 1999).

Last but not least, I would like to thank the late Tommaso Buscetta, the first and possibly most important of contemporary mafia defectors, who showed me his trust by meeting me and discussing his life in the Sicilian Cosa Nostra.

In different ways, many of the people to whom I owe my gratitude have devoted their lives to the fight for justice against the mafia. I hope that—by improving our understanding of the Southern Italian mafia phenomenon—my book may contribute to their endeavor.

Contents

Introduction   3
   The Italian and American Mafia: A Comparison   3
   The Italian Mafia: A New Paradigm   13

1. Mafia Associations and Ruling Bodies   24
   Families and Members   26
   Historical Background   33
   The Ruling Bodies of Single Families   40
   The Institutionalization of Superordinate Bodies
      of Coordination   51

2. Status and Fraternization Contracts   65
   Rites of Passage   67
   Ritual Brotherhoods   76
   Mementos   85
   An Idealization of the Mafia Phenomenon?   89

3. Secrecy and Violence   101
   Variations in Secrecy   102
   The Obligation of Silence   108
   The Escalation of Secrecy   114
   Alternative Legal Orders   120
   Mafia Consortia as Illegal States?   130

4. Multiplicity of Goals and Functions   141
   Money versus Power   144
   Neither Enterprises . . .   154
   . . . Nor States   164

5. Mafia, State, and Society   178
   Competition and Complementarity   179
   Mafia and Politics in Republican Italy   191
   A Difficult Liberation   203

Conclusions   220

Notes   229

References   245

Names Index   275

Subject Index   285

A section of photographs follows p. 100.

MAFIA BROTHERHOODS

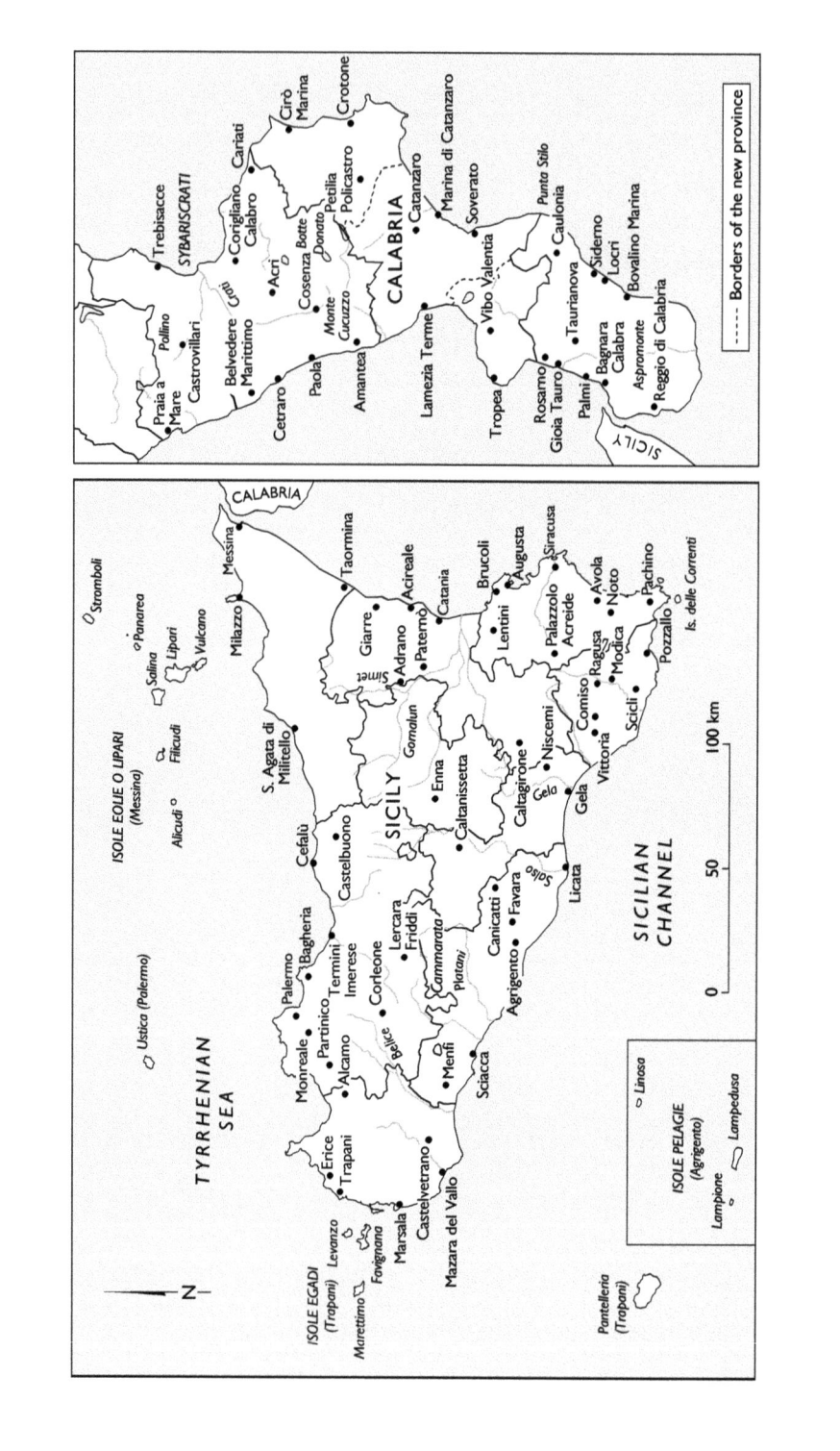

Introduction

THE ITALIAN AND AMERICAN MAFIA: A COMPARISON

Hardly any phenomenon since the Second World War has fascinated the American public more than the Italian mafia. Hundreds of books have been written on this topic, and dozens of movies have been made. Some of these—above all, Mario Puzo's *The Godfather* (1969) and the film adaptation made by Francis Ford Coppola (1972)—have been so successful that they have profoundly shaped a general understanding of the mafia in the United States and elsewhere. For many people the Italian American mafia *is* and *behaves* as it is recounted in these romanticizing novels and films.

Since the 1960s several sociologists, historians, and criminologists (Hawkins 1969; Haller 1970; Albini 1971; Smith 1975, 1976; Nelli 1976) have tried to dispel the mystifying images created by the media and reinforced by the first congressional hearings and public reports (U.S. Senate 1951; 1957; 1963; Kefauver 1951; McClennan 1962). Most academic scholars, however, have overreacted, categorically denying up to the early 1980s the existence of the mafia as a structured and longstanding criminal organization. Due to these contradictory representations, a great deal of confusion dominates the public debate, which oscillates dangerously between self-serving myth and radical skepticism.

Despite this confusion, some facts have now become undeniable in the United

States. Since the late 1970s, a presidential commission, numerous congressional hearings, the legal testimonies and autobiographies of dozens of mafia members, and hundreds of criminal and civil cases have proved the existence of the Italian mafia in America, providing rich and valuable information about its structure and activities (Jacobs and Gouldin 1999).

Knowledge about the Italian mafia in its home country has also increased enormously since the mid-1980s, brought about by the defection of over one thousand members of several mafia and criminal groupings who testified against their former associates. Thanks to their revelations and the determination of a new generation of law enforcement officials, the Sicilian Cosa Nostra and the Calabrian 'Ndrangheta have been singled out as Italy's largest and most powerful mafia associations, and a wealth of information has been disclosed about their inner organization and ideology. The mafiosi's illegal businesses and their infiltration in legitimate industries have also been targeted by criminal investigations. Even mafia groups' shady alliances with politicians and public officials have been prosecuted for the first time, though—as in the case against Giulio Andreotti, who was Italy's prime minister seven times—many high-level defendants have subsequently been freed for lack of evidence.

Similarities . . .

Analysis of the defectors' testimonies, criminal cases, and other sources shows many analogies between the most lasting and successful Italian American mafia association, Cosa Nostra (or La Cosa Nostra, as it was initially and mistakenly labeled by U.S. government agencies, hence the popular acronym *LCN*) and its southern Italian counterparts, particularly the Sicilian Cosa Nostra. This is not surprising: as we have already noted, the American Cosa Nostra originally stemmed from the Sicilian mafia, though it has been a completely independent organization since at least the 1930s.

Just like the Sicilian Cosa Nostra, America's largest and most powerful mafia association is a loose confederation of mafia families that mutually recognize each other but are independent on most issues. The formal hierarchy of the families is also very similar. Both the Sicilian and Italian American mafia groups contain basically the same command positions, which are called by the same (or by very similar) names (Cressey 1969; Anderson 1979: 15–49; U.S. District Court 1994: 4–5). In both contexts, furthermore, superordinate bodies of coordination were set up—in the United States allegedly as early as the 1930s (PCOC 1986a; U.S. Senate 1988; Maas 1969: 33–34), in Sicily first in the late 1950s—to reduce internal competition and violence, resolve disputes, and to plan and implement common actions (see also Jacobs, Panarella, and Worthington 1994: 77–128). Although these so-called commissions have attracted a good deal of popular curiosity, their powers have always been rather limited, particularly in the economic realm, and their institutionalization is still uncertain (Jacobs and Gouldin 1999: 135–37).

Striking similarities can also be detected at the level of culture. As in the Sicilian Cosa Nostra and the Calabrian 'Ndrangheta, members of most Italian American mafia families become so through a ceremony of initiation establishing brotherhood bonds between the novice and other family members (Maas 1969: 96–97; 1997; U.S. Senate 1988: 224; Fresolone and Wagman 1994; see Jacobs and Gouldin 1999: 138). Likewise, the three mafia associations use the codes of honor and *omertà* [silence] to teach their members how to behave and to create a collective identity.

Reinforced by violence and secrecy, in the hands of the members of all three criminal organizations the bonds of brotherhood and organizational reputation become formidable tools to achieve personal and collective goals. But personal goals are subordinated to the goals of the group, as mafia members are obliged to be absolutely obedient to their chiefs, to place the mafia family before all their previous ties (including blood family ones), and even to be ready to sacrifice their own lives if the mafia boss orders it. As Vincent Cafaro was told on the day of his affiliation to one of the five New York Cosa Nostra families: "Once you accept, you belong to us. We come first. Your family and home come second. We come first, no matter what" (U.S. Senate 1988: 224). In the economic sphere, however, the "men of honor" (as they are called in southern Italy) or "made members" or "wiseguys" (as they are known in the United States) enjoy a very high degree of autonomy. Though some profit-making activities—most notably, extortion and business cartels—are centrally managed by the family leaders, even low-ranking "soldiers" are free to set up any lawful or unlawful venture they want. They are in no way obliged to select their partners from within the mafia community. In the United States, for example, mafia members have profited since the 1920s from business alliances with shrewd criminal entrepreneurs belonging to other ethnic groups (see Nelli 1976 and Block 1983). "Made" members are, however, expected to deposit some of the profits drawn from criminal activities into the family's common account and to give a varying percentage of the revenue to their chiefs.

. . . and Differences

Comparative analysis highlights not only the similarities but also the considerable differences existing between the American and Sicilian Cosa Nostras. The most immediate disparity concerns the dimensions and manpower of the two associations, which are inversely proportional to the size of their areas of settlement. The Sicilian Cosa Nostra—like the Calabrian 'Ndrangheta—is composed of about a hundred mafia families and has at least thirty-five hundred full members. The

American Cosa Nostra was traditionally constituted of twenty-four families, but during the 1980s and 1990s several groups were effectively dismantled (U.S. Senate 1988: 103; Jacobs and Gouldin 1999: 135). In 1983, according to data disclosed by the director of the FBI to the President's Commission on Organized Crime, there were approximately seventeen hundred "made members," down from three thousand in the early 1970s (PCOC 1983, 1986a: 35; Reuter 1995: 91). As this downturn has continued, even the 1983 figure is likely to overestimate the current number of American Cosa Nostra members. Thus, considering that Sicily contains about 1.8 percent of the U.S. population and represents less than 0.3 percent of the United States in size, the number of mafia members per inhabitant—and thus the territorial rooting—of the Sicilian Cosa Nostra is much higher than that of its American counterpart, indeed much higher than the mere comparison of membership figures would indicate. Whereas one out of fifteen hundred Sicilian residents is likely to be a Cosa Nostra member (and in the Reggio Calabria province 'Ndrangheta members represent almost 1 percent of residents), in the United States the ratio is over 1:165,000. Even considering that American Cosa Nostra families are traditionally concentrated in the eastern part of the United States and particularly in New York, the gap remains impressive.

The above figures and the different social, political, and economic contexts in which the two associations have operated since their separation are the two most important factors explaining the divergences in their internal organization and activities and their relationship with underworld competitors, civil society, politicians, and law enforcement. As Humbert Nelli put it, "Criminals in Italian-American neighborhoods [tried] to re-create familiar institutions, just as their more law-abiding counterparts. . . . It proved impossible to reproduce homeland institutions exactly; subtly and often unrecognized by the criminal themselves, the patterns and characters of the institutions—in this case, criminal organizations—were altered by conditions, opportunities, and limitations present in the new environment. In the process, the illegal organizations became combinations of the familiar Old World models adapted to New World needs" (1976: 136–37). Despite sharing a formal structure with analogous command positions, the internal organization of a Sicilian and an Italian American mafia family may differ significantly in practice. As the American Cosa Nostra was traditionally composed of twenty-four families, up to the 1980s, most of these had a much larger number of affiliates than Sicilian Cosa Nostra groups, some of which often have fewer than ten "men of honor." According to data released to the Permanent Subcommittee on Investigations of the U.S. Senate in 1988, for example, the five New York mafia families—the most powerful in the whole country—each had more than a hundred "made" members who were known to the police. Indeed, over two hundred members were listed for both the Genovese and Gambino families (U.S. Senate 1988: 776–800). According to a former "soldier" of the Genovese group, the real number was even higher: his family, or "brigade," effectively consisted of over 350 ritually affiliated members and could rely on several hundred associates (ibid.). The sheer size of the American mafia families has long prevented their members from interacting informally with each other, as is instead the case in most Sicilian mafia groups, and has favored internal stratification and segmentation. In the late 1980s, for example, the "soldiers" of the Genovese family were divided into fourteen *regimes* (corresponding to the Sicilian *decine*), each of which was headed by a *caporegime*, who referred to either the *consigliere* [counselor] or the *sottocapo* [underboss]. Only for the most serious questions could the *caporegime* talk directly to the family leader. As a result, many rank-and-file members had never met their chiefs —a very unlikely scenario in Sicilian mafia groups (Maas 1969; 1997).

Considerable differences can also be singled out in the goals pursued by mafia families and their members on either side of the Atlantic Ocean and the concrete activities in which they are engaged. Similarities can be identified only in the activities all three mafia associations forbid (or rather forbade). Among these are the organization of prostitution and the commercialization of pornographic material, which are considered dishonorable (U.S. Senate 1988: 236–37). Virtually unchallenged in Italy, this prohibition has frequently been violated in the United States, in particular by the Chicago family (Landesco [1929] 1968: 25–43; Block 1983: 141–48).[1] Drug dealing also used to be forbidden in all three mafia confederations, but this prohibition has been completely overthrown in southern Italy since the 1960s. Most American Cosa Nostra families, instead, still maintain it at least formally, even though numerous exceptions to this rule have been recounted by defectors and proved by judicial investigations (U.S. Senate 1988: 91–93; 236–37; Bonanno 1983: 149; Peterson 1983: 377–82; Lupsha 1985; Nelli 1976: 232–39; Jacobs and Gouldin: 152–53).

The differences become even more striking once we move from the forbidden activities to those considered legitimate and most frequently practiced by the three mafia associations under examination. The illegal business that has provided Italian American mafia groups with the largest revenues since the repeal of Prohibition —gambling (including horse racing and dog racing, slot machines, casinos, and the numbers racket) (Nelli 1976: 222–33; Anderson 1979: 50–63; PCOC 1985)— has never gained any sort of a foothold in southern Italy. As lotteries are state-run and gambling and betting are by and large lawful activities, no large-scale illegal market open to prey by mafiosi for these services has developed.

Even more significantly, Italian American mafia groups soon had to give up the claim of exercising a political dominion over a specific territory. True, attempts to extort the successful residents of Italian immigrant communities were recorded from the late nineteenth century on, and at the beginning of the following century a wave of blackmail, allegedly orchestrated by the Mano Nera, swept Italian colonies in New York and other American cities (Landesco [1929] 1979:

107–20; Nelli 1976: 69–100). But neither Cosa Nostra families nor other mafia groupings ever succeeded in imposing systematic extortion rackets even within immigrant communities. Italian mafia families, instead, not only "tax" the main productive activities carried out within their communities but also claim a full-fledged political power over their territory, which usually corresponds to a village or town, or to a neighborhood in larger cities.

Except for New York, American cities did not contain sufficiently high concentrations of Italian immigrant populations upon which mafia groups could exert a veritable political dominion. The consolidation of such power was further prevented by the high turnover of residents within local communities, as newcomers from overseas arrived to replace those who had moved out of the ethnic ghettos. Coming from all parts of Italy, many immigrants were not even willing to recognize mafia claims, as they had not encountered the mafia at home. As a result, though mafiosi were occasionally asked to resolve disputes and to mediate conflicts, they never had the prestige and influence in American cities that the original models enjoyed in the Old World villages (Nelli 1976: 37, 137). In America, in other words, mafia political power never attained the degree of legitimacy with which it has long been endowed in the western Sicilian and southern Calabrian countryside and towns.

Whereas the Italian state and the mafia long shared power in large parts of Sicily and Calabria and the power of mafia groups was accepted and even legalized by government representatives, the tolerance and collusion of public authorities have been more limited in the United States. Although the leaders of Cosa Nostra and other criminal syndicates in New York and Chicago did exert great influence over politicians, the political process, and the police up to the Second World War (Nelli 1976: 190–93), their power, which was largely local, declined rapidly in the following decades, as urban machines disappeared and the growth of large federal law enforcement agencies discouraged the development of corrupt long-term relationships between mafiosi and the local police (Reuter 1995). In the postwar period—and most strikingly from the 1970s on—American Cosa Nostra members were unable to rely on the same organic ties with high-ranking politicians and government officials that their southern Italian counterparts have enjoyed to this day.

Too weak and scattered to impose a real political dominion on Italian immigrant communities, American Cosa Nostra families came nonetheless to exercise considerable power through labor racketeering. This activity, virtually unknown to southern Italian mafia groups, is the closest substitute to the political power exerted by Italian mafiosi in their areas of influence. A former member of New York's most powerful mafia family recalls, "We got our money from gambling but our real power, our real strength came from the unions. . . . In some cases we got money from our dealing with the unions, in some cases we got favors such as jobs for friends and relatives, but more importantly, in all cases we got power over every businessman in New York" (U.S. Senate 1988: 225).

The involvement of Cosa Nostra and other crime groups with the unions began in the 1920s when mobsters were recruited by employers to break a strike or, more frequently, by labor leaders to enforce union discipline. From the 1930s on, American Cosa Nostra members and other gangsters infiltrated—and sometimes even created—several labor unions (Nelli 1976: 241–53; Landesco [1929] 1968: 141–67). For several decades Cosa Nostra controlled the International Longshoremen's Association, the Laborers Union, the Hotel Employees and Restaurant Employees Union, and the International Brotherhood of Teamsters. It also controlled dozens of union locals (PCOC 1986b; Jacobs, Panarella, and Worthington 1994: 31–78, 167–210; U.S. District Court 1994; Abadinsky 2000: 311–49). Union power was frequently turned into profit, as Cosa Nostra members embezzled and defrauded the unions and their pension and welfare funds, sold labor peace, took payoffs in exchange for sweetheart contracts, and used their leverage on unions to obtain ownership interests in business and establish and police business cartels. Cosa Nostra's influence in the Laborer's International Union of North America, for example, guaranteed a powerful presence in the construction industry, especially in New York and Chicago (PCOC 1986b; New York State Organized Crime Task Force 1988; see also Reuter 1987 and Kelly 1999).

Translating union control into economic gain fits into the American Cosa Nostra's more general patterns of action. Ever since the 1920s, in fact, violence, brotherhood ties, and organizational reputation have been primarily employed by members of Italian American mafia groups to fulfill a major goal: making money. Mafiosi and other gangsters have thus adjusted to the materialistic nature of American society, which preaches honesty, virtue, and hard work, but places value on the possession of money, no matter how it has been acquired. The mafia adaptation to the American way of life was helped enormously by Prohibition, which lasted from 1920 to 1933 and created moneymaking opportunities undreamed of in previous decades. The bootlegging organization set up by John Torrio and Al Capone in Chicago, for example, showed an annual gross from beer and other alcoholic beverages of at least $60 million and perhaps as much as $240 million—a sum Italian mafiosi could only dream of for half a century (Nelli 1976: 150).

An analogous entrepreneurial transformation took place only much later in southern Italy. There, mafiosi continued to adhere to the value system prevalent in their backward, rural settings and long placed the acquisition of respect above the mere accumulation of wealth. Only in the 1960s did Cosa Nostra and 'Ndrangheta members start to invest an increasing amount of energy in economic accumulation. By doing so, they reacted to wider modernization processes in Italian society, which began to view wealth as the main parameter for assessing social position (Arlacchi 1988: 57–61). Just as bootlegging enabled American mafiosi to build large fortunes rapidly, almost fifty years later it was drug trafficking that provided their southern Italian counterparts with the same opportunity to make money.

From the late 1970s up to the mid-1980s, the production and export of heroin into the United States turned out to be particularly profitable for several Sicilian mafia families. To distribute the narcotics in the United States, the traffickers relied on a network of recently immigrated Sicilian "men of honor" as well as on members of the New York Bonanno mafia group. As many of these used pizzerias as fronts for engaging in heroin distribution, the investigation that exposed this heroin-trafficking conspiracy is known as the Pizza Connection case—to date the largest cooperation scheme between the Sicilian and American Cosa Nostra members ever exposed by law enforcement (Jacobs, Panarella, and Worthington 1994: 129–66).

In the last fifteen years of the twentieth century, however, Sicilian Cosa Nostra families were progressively marginalized from international heroin and cocaine trafficking, and the same fate now seems to be hanging over the Calabrian 'Ndrangheta as well. At least as far as the Sicilian Cosa Nostra is concerned, the manipulation of public contract bids has thus become the major source of revenue since the mid-1980s. Unlike their American counterparts, Sicilian and Calabrian mafia families could not rely on the support of corrupt labor unions to acquire power in legitimate industries. Nonetheless, thanks to the actual use or the mere threat of violence Cosa Nostra and 'Ndrangheta families succeeded not only in extorting money from virtually all the building firms active on their territory, but even in imposing their presence on the preexisting cartels, made up of politicians and legitimate entrepreneurs, that controlled the bidding process (see chapters 4 and 5).

The Common Decline

Whether the result of old-style prohibitions or lack of contacts in drug production areas and entrepreneurial skills, the marginalization from the currently largest and most profitable illegal market—the drug market—is a common trait of these three mafia associations. In both the Old and New Worlds, mafia groups have also suffered major losses incurred by their racketeering activities in legal markets. In Italy the role of the mafia in bid-rigging was exposed in the Clean Hands investigations of the mid-1990s, and southern Italian mafia families were also hit by the sharp reduction of public investment in the following years. Likewise, in the United States Cosa Nostra's labor and business racketeering have been seriously disrupted since the mid-1980s by successful civil RICO suits against Cosa Nostra members, associates, and mob-controlled unions and business enterprises (Jacobs 1999).[2] As the civil RICO litigation prompted a thorough reform of most corrupted unions and businesses, it is unlikely that Cosa Nostra will regain much of its former power again.

These economic difficulties underscore a more general decline, however. In the United States, mafia groups have since the 1960s been increasingly unable to attract able, intelligent, ambitious Italian Americans of the younger generations. Careers in crime offer little to these young men, who seem to prefer careers as lawyers, doctors, army officers, or corporation executives. Even many high-ranking mafiosi have discouraged their sons from entering the mafia, in the hope of providing them with a better life. Very strict recruitment criteria also hinder the internalization of the competencies necessary to compete successfully on international illegal markets and infiltrate legitimate industries. In both Italy and the United States, mafia sodalities insist on recruiting members from a very limited territorial or ethnic background: Sicilian and Calabrian mafia groups admit only men born in their respective regions while the American Cosa Nostra accepts only Italian immigrants and their descendants. And as they both require prospective members to prove their honor by committing violent crimes, mafia associations often end up selecting uneducated, tough felons.

With its traditional emphasis on mutual aid, honor, and *omertà*, mafia ideology is not only increasingly unattractive for prospective recruits but also proves to be less and less effective in securing the compliance of "made members." Due to the growing importance of profit-making activities, the gap between what is described in the initiation rituals and what mafiosi really do in everyday life has widened. More and more mafia members in Italy as well the United States thus realize that the values inspiring mafia ideology are ignored in daily activities, primarily by the family chiefs. Consequently, they feel authorized to deviate from these precepts whenever compliance entails heavy personal sacrifices.

The price of loyalty has also become much higher, as law enforcement repression has increased enormously in both countries since the mid-1980s. As a result, an unprecedented number of mafiosi, including some high-ranking members, have chosen to testify against their former associates. On both sides of the Atlantic Ocean, these testimonies—and, especially in the United States, the conversations intercepted by "bugs" planted in mafiosi's cars, homes, and social clubs—have been used by far-sighted police and justice officials to launch a series of breakthrough investigations and to arrest and convict a high number of mafia members and even numerous family chiefs. Virtually all American Cosa Nostra leading figures of the 1980s and early 1990s are now in prison serving life sentences without parole. Even in southern Italy, mafia associations have been affected by criminal prosecutions as never before.

Mafia decline has been particularly sharp in the United States. There, the local Cosa Nostra seems unable to recover its power over either legitimate or illegitimate markets. Even the Sicilian Cosa Nostra and Calabrian 'Ndrangheta have been seriously hit, though their definitive defeat is far from clear. Traditional mafia and familistic values are still less at odds with the mainstream southern Italian mentality than they are with the weltanschauung and lifestyle of second- or third-generation Italian immigrants, by now fully assimilated into the American "melting pot." Thanks to their territorial rooting and political connections, Italian mafia families still hope to reassert their grip on public contracts, as soon as the funds pledged by the European Union and the Italian state start to pour into the Mezzogiorno—the rural south of Italy—again. In the meanwhile, they are systematically extorting local businesses to pay members' salaries, to assist the families of imprisoned "men of honor," and to pay the mafiosi's legal fees. By keeping a very low profile, Cosa Nostra and 'Ndrangheta hope to exhaust law enforcement pressure and to weaken the popular anti-mafia movement, which came into being after a series of "excellent cadavers" (i.e., murders of high-ranking politicians and government officials) and bomb explosions in the early 1990s (Lodato and Grasso 2001; Stille 1995). They also count on the "ultra-guarantistic" policies of the government elected in May 2001—a government that is curbing the autonomy of prosecutors and judges and sabotaging successful anti-mafia and anti-corruption legal instruments and special units in a misguided attempt to solve the judicial problems of Italy's prime minister, the media tycoon–turned-politician Silvio Berlusconi.

While the definitive defeat of the Sicilian and Calabrian mafia still seems out of reach, there can be no doubt that in both Italy and the United States mafia control over illegal and legal markets has undergone a rapid decline, as have the mafia's political power and legitimacy. Nor have mafia families become a model for organized criminals on either side of the Atlantic Ocean. Though some southern Italian criminal gangs have tried to imitate the mafia's complex canopy of rituals and codes to strengthen their internal cohesion and impress both competitors and victims (Paoli 1996), the mafia subculture has so far not proved to be either exportable or credible beyond the boundaries of its original communities. Nor do the dynamics of illegal markets require or even favor the development of large, mafialike organizations. Indeed, small, flexible enterprises seem to have the advantage, as they can be more easily managed in conditions of uncertainty and lawlessness and are more likely to avoid law enforcement detection.

Despite its literary and film success, the mafia heyday—at least in the United States—seems to be over. Pace the Godfather and his worldwide fans.

THE ITALIAN MAFIA: A NEW PARADIGM

This trial concerns the mafia organization known as Cosa Nostra, an extremely dangerous criminal association that has inflicted, and inflicts, death and terror through violence and intimidation.
—TRIBUNALE DI PALERMO,
Ordinanza-sentenza di rinvio a giudizio nei confronti di Abbate Giovanni + 706 (1985)

Opened by the preceding statement, the indictment against Giovanni Abbate and another 706 mafiosi constituted a major turning point in investigations and knowledge of the mafia phenomenon. These charges were made public for the first time in November 1985 on the instructions of the Palermitan judges forming the first anti-mafia pool, and they described and fully documented for the first time the existence of a formalized and structured mafia association, known by its members as Cosa Nostra.

Totaling 8,607 pages and accompanied by twenty-two volumes of documentary evidence and cross-checks, the charges were the result of a fundamental methodological innovation. The documents described the organization from within, thanks to evidence given by several members of Cosa Nostra, primarily Tommaso Buscetta and Salvatore Contorno. Meticulously checked by Judge Giovanni Falcone and his colleagues, these confessions became the primary source of the indictment, which reconstructed the history of the association over the fifteen years before the trial and led to the charges brought against most of the leaders and members of the Palermitan mafia families associated with Cosa Nostra. Its main theses have been confirmed by the courts in three different instances. The first trial ended in December 1987 with a verdict of 2,665 years of prison sentences, nineteen life sentences, 11 billion *lire* in fees (about $8.5 million at the exchange rate of the time), and 114 acquittals. In January 1992, the Corte di Cassazione (the Italian supreme court of appeal) definitively confirmed both the interpretative scheme presented by the magistrates and most of the previous convictions.

The *Pentiti* and the Old Conceptions of the Mafia Phenomenon

Tommaso Buscetta and Salvatore Contorno were not the only members of the Italian mafia to defect and testify against their former associates. From the mid-1980s on, and especially in the first half of the 1990s, hundreds of mafia members and gangsters began to "cooperate with justice," as this decision is called in Italian legalistic language, deciding to describe their crimes and experiences in the underworld to policemen, prosecutors, and judges. According to data published by the Ministry of the Interior—the official organ responsible for protecting witnesses—the highest peak in this collaboration occurred at the end of 1996, with 1,214 organized crime defectors under the state witness protection program, a number that fell to 1,110 by the end of 2000 (Ministero dell'Interno 1997b, 2001c).

Thanks to their information and the commitment shown by a new generation of law enforcement officers and judges, much more is now known about the mafia and organized crime in Italy than ever before (see Paoli 1998a). This investigative and cognitive achievement has been far from painless: especially in Sicily, several of the magistrates and police officers most involved in anti-mafia investigations were then murdered by the mafia. Among them, the most recent victims are the judges Giovanni Falcone and Paolo Borsellino, the leading figures of the first Palermitan anti-mafia pool. Both were killed in bomb explosions in the summer of 1992, as were Falcone's wife and eight of the judges' police escorts.

While the mafia has been generally treated as a uniquely Sicilian phenomenon, the inside accounts given by these mafia witnesses—or *pentiti* (literally, repentants), as they are usually called—have also provided irrefutable evidence of another secret consortium of mafia families—the 'Ndrangheta, located in southern Calabria.[3] Together with the Sicilian Cosa Nostra, this organization constitutes the empirical object of my research, whose primary source is the statements and confessions of former members of the two mafia associations.

This methodological choice is based on a simple observation. Since the unification of Italy in 1861 the word *mafia* has been at the center of heated debates and has been attributed many different and contrasting meanings, depending on the various points of view and interests involved (Brancato 1986; Tessitore 1997). Interestingly, however, members of the mafia hardly ever took part in these discussions. That is to say, public debate on the mafia was created without any clear understanding of the animus and concrete experiences of its members, even though a few *capimafia* [mafia chiefs] occasionally help spread self-justifying conceptions of the mafia phenomenon.

Before Buscetta's declarations in front of Judge Giovanni Falcone, external observers of the mafia did not have any credible access to the life-world of the mafiosi. Nor did they have tools by which to assess the occasional shreds of information emerging from the mafia microcosm. Until the mid-1980s, confessions made by Buscetta's numerous predecessors were ignored. Contrary to common belief, in fact, Tommaso Buscetta was not the first *pentito* in mafia history. Historical research has recently shown that several trials held in the nineteenth century relied on statements made by mafia witnesses (Lupo 1993, 1994). Even in the twentieth century, in both Sicily and Calabria, several mafiosi broke their commitment—at least partially—to the mafia's code of silence (known as *omertà*) and described their experiences. Melchiorre Allegra (De Mauro 1962a, 1962b, 1962c), Nick Gentile (1993), and Leonardo Vitale in Sicily (TrPA [1985] 1992), and Antonio Musolino (Malafarina 1986) and Serafino Castagna (1967) in Calabria, are just a few of the forerunners of contemporary *pentiti* who have long been forgotten by law enforcement officials and social scientists alike.

Despite the change of perspective fostered by the Palermitan judicial inquiries, the statements made by new and old mafia witnesses have not yet been systematically analyzed by sociologists and criminologists. Indeed, it is probably true to say that most academics from these fields have until very recently viewed them as unreliable and conceptually uninformative. Why is this? In my opinion, the reasons are to be found in the two paradigms that have dominated the postwar scientific debate on the mafia and organized crime, both of which sharply contrast with these defectors' statements.

The first paradigm, prevalent until the early 1980s, presented the mafia as a cultural attitude and form of power, thus excluding any corporate dimension. The many scholars using this framework (including foreign researchers working in the 1960s and 1970s) viewed the mafiosi as individuals who behaved according to specific subcultural codes, but did not consider the mafia a formal organization (Hess 1973; Blok 1988; Schneider and Schneider 1976; Arlacchi 1988; Catanzaro 1992).

Beginning in the mid-1980s, when judicial investigations started to provide clear and solid proof of the existence of well-structured mafia groups, attention shifted toward the entrepreneurial features of mafia actors. Contrasting more or less openly with the "culturalist" view, the mafia was conceptualized as an enterprise and its economic activities became the focus of academic analyses (Arlacchi 1988; Centorrino 1986, 1989, 1993a, 1993b; Santino 1988, 1994a; Pizzorno 1987; Catanzaro 1992; Santino and La Fiura 1990).

These contributions highlighted important aspects of the mafia culture and economy and this book owes much to many of them. However, the analyses produced within these two paradigms miss some other essential aspects of the mafia universe that have been highlighted by contemporary *pentiti*. For instance, studies taking an economic approach to the issue have carefully reconstructed the development conditions and operational mechanisms of mafia businesses, illustrating the threat they have posed to the economic and social growth of wide areas of the country. They have, however, almost totally neglected the cultural symbols and codes, thus preventing any in-depth understanding of the techniques by which mafia groups have legitimized their existence and activity and the reasons underlying their recent state of crisis. At the same time, these analyses have underevaluated the political dimension of mafia action and have thus proved unable to give explanations for the terrorist strategy used by the Sicilian Cosa Nostra in 1992–93.

This research starts from the conviction that it is necessary to remedy the above distortions and to answer some outstanding questions. Its aim is to propose a new conceptualization of the mafia phenomenon, and to thus explain some anomalies that are otherwise insoluble. This will be done by finally taking seriously and meticulously analyzing the statements of former members of Cosa Nostra and the 'Ndrangheta, these two consortia constituting the "hard core" of the wide range of phenomena labeled as typical of the mafia over the past decades.

Four Theses: The Structure of the Book

Four main theses underlie this book, and each of them is explained in a separate chapter. These are followed by a fifth, which briefly reconstructs relationships between the mafia, the state, and society from the mid–nineteenth century to today.

First, contrary to opinions held widely until the early 1980s, judicial inquiries carried out since then have proved that formalized and longstanding mafia groups do exist. Though they are usually called "families" by their members, these groups are completely separate from the blood families of their members. Cosa Nostra and the 'Ndrangheta are the largest and most stable coalitions of mafia groups and are each composed of about a hundred units.[4]

Thanks to the discovery of new documents in various archives and a more objective analysis of those already known to scholars, recent historical research has been able to show that mafia groups have existed in Sicily and in Calabria since the first half of the nineteenth century. In support of this view, the historian Paolo Pezzino states, "While it is true that these sources must be examined with great caution, it is also true that there are so many descriptions of well-structured associations, and this has been confirmed in several judicial proceedings, that it would be difficult to deny their reasonableness" (1987: 954; for a similar opinion see Lupo 1988).

Cosa Nostra and the 'Ndrangheta meet the characterizing criterion of the organization (Weber 1978: 48): each mafia family has its own ruling bodies that are clearly distinct from the authority structure of the members' biological families. Moreover, from the 1950s onward, higher coordinating bodies were set up—first in Cosa Nostra during the early 1950s, and later on in the 'Ndrangheta during the 1990s. These "commissions" are made up of the most important family chiefs.

Although the powers of these collegial bodies are rather limited, the unity of the two confederations cannot be doubted. In fact, their cohesion is guaranteed by the sharing of common cultural codes and a single organizational formula. According to a model prevalent in premodern societies, Cosa Nostra and the 'Ndrangheta are "segmentary societies" (Smith 1974)—that is, they depend on what Emile Durkheim called "mechanical solidarity" (1964), which derives from the replication of homologous corporate and cultural forms.

Second, neither Cosa Nostra nor the 'Ndrangheta can be assimilated to Max Weber's ideal type of legal-rational bureaucracy, as Donald Cressey suggested at the end of the 1960s when describing the American Cosa Nostra (1969). Far from recruiting staff and organizing the latter's work according to the criteria and procedures of modern bureaucracies, mafia groups impose a "status contract" upon their members (Weber 1978: 672). This means that when the novice is initiated into a mafia *cosca* (band), he is required to assume a permanent new identity—to become a "man of honor"—and to subordinate all his previous allegiances to his mafia membership. If necessary, he must be ready to sacrifice even his life for the mafia family.

The ceremony of initiation also creates ritual brotherhood ties among the members of a mafia family. Thus the status contract is at the same time a "contract of fraternization" (ibid.), and new recruits are forced to share what anthropologists call a "regime of generalized reciprocity" (Sahlins 1972: 193–200) with other members. This presupposes a high level of altruism and patterns of behavior with no expectation of short-term rewards. As has been noted since the late nineteenth century, mafia groups constitute brotherhoods whose "essential character" lies in "mutual aid without limits and without measure, and even in crime" (Lestingi 1884: 453). Only thanks to the trust and solidarity created by these fraternization contracts does it become possible to underwrite specific "purposive contracts" and thus satisfy the instrumental needs of single members (see Paoli 1998b).

It is in status and fraternization contracts that both the strength and the weakness of the two mafia confederations lie. On the positive side, Cosa Nostra and the 'Ndrangheta families are guaranteed absolute faithfulness and subordination from their members—members can be counted on to carry out any order they are given, ensuring the organizations an extraordinary elasticity and flexibility. It also means that, in the short term, mafia chiefs can use the members' manpower—and even lives—to fulfill whatever goal suits them.

However, there are also limits and contradictions inherent in relying on this type of contract. In order to be effective, status and fraternization contracts can be forced only on people who are already socialized to certain specific values. This places clear limits on the supply of available candidates from which mafia families can recruit their members. As a result, over the last three decades members have found it increasingly difficult to internalize the competencies necessary to compete successfully in international illegal markets.

Another serious weakness lies in the ever wider gap between the value system endowed through status and fraternization contracts and the concrete actions of most "men of honor," particularly mafia chiefs. Though this tension has always existed, it increased sharply during the last thirty years of the twentieth century as a result of the modernization processes affecting southern Italy, which made the traditional concept of honor and its related lifestyle look obsolete. The changes mafia groups made in order to adapt to the macrosocial transformations have further exacerbated this tension. As a result, the entire apparatus of mafia legitimation has entered into a deep crisis, as shown by the rapid increase of mafia witnesses coming from Cosa Nostra's and to a lesser extent the 'Ndrangheta's ranks from 1992 onward.

Third, secrecy is a defining feature of both mafia consortia. Maintaining secrecy about the group composition, its actions, and its strategies is one of the key duties of "men of honor" in both Sicily and Calabria. In Cosa Nostra, in particular, the obligation on secrecy is absolute, and since the nineteenth century its members have been obliged to keep secret the very existence of the mafia association. Above all, secrecy constitutes a defense strategy. Mafia groups have always used violence to pursue their goals; as a result, since the unification of Italy they have come into conflict with state institutions and have thus needed to resort to secrecy to protect themselves from state repression.

Cosa Nostra and the 'Ndrangheta can, thus, be considered secret societies. Contrary to what is usually assumed, however, secrecy is not an all-or-none condition. Though the pledge to secrecy is mentioned by virtually all known mafia sodalities, there have been considerable discontinuity and difference in the enforcement of secrecy in the history of the two mafia confederations. This is partly because the effective degree of secrecy has always been a reaction to concrete law enforcement action of state bodies. The 'Ndrangheta has traditionally resorted to secrecy much less intensively than its Sicilian counterpart, most likely because national public opinion and the pressure of state apparatuses have been much less focused on Calabria than on Sicily over the years.

Following the increased state repression of the last fifteen years of the twentieth century, both Cosa Nostra and the 'Ndrangheta were forced to raise levels of secrecy. In the Sicilian mafia consortium, this process went so far as to bring into question the institutionalized mechanisms for socializing new members and to drastically reduce social gatherings among its members. This weakened the feeling of belonging created by fraternization contracts, resulting in a sharp increase in the number of *pentiti* who testified during the 1990s.

The adoption of secrecy as a form of existence has also affected the internal organization of the families associated with the two consortia. By defining its external boundaries through secrecy, the mafia group conceives of itself as a living totality, a whole unity, that is, as a closed and self-sufficient world opposing the larger one containing it. This claim manifests itself through the creation of an internal power structure and the development of a system of norms whose respect is ensured, if necessary, by violence. Consequently, Cosa Nostra and the 'Ndrangheta can be considered legal orders alternative to that of the state, as maintained by the Sicilian jurist Santi Romano at the beginning of the twentieth century (1977).

Fourth, in the past hundred years, members of Sicilian and Calabrian mafia families have used the cohesion created by status and fraternization contracts to pursue extremely different ends and carry out greatly varying functions. It is thus extremely difficult to single out a single function or goal that can fully characterize the mafia phenomenon, though this has been attempted by supporters of the enterprise paradigm and, more recently, by Diego Gambetta, who describes the mafia as "an industry of private protection" (1993).

The "official" goal of the two mafia consortia has, actually, been clear ever since the nineteenth century: it is mutual aid, as the quoted statement by the Procuratore del Re Lestingi in 1884 proves. This has now been confirmed by the *pentiti*: Tommaso Buscetta, for example, affirms that "the protection and safeguarding of one's business, the reciprocal support in the defense of economic and power interests was the cement of the whole [Cosa Nostra] building" (Arlacchi 1994: 22). However, although the enhancement of members' interests through mutual aid seems to have been the major "official goal" of mafia associations since their founding, this general aim has been translated into a plurality of "operative goals" (Perrow 1961), depending on the priorities set at different historical moments by the chiefs of each family. This is why it is so difficult to ascribe one single function or goal to the mafia as a whole.

Like all social groups operating on the Durkheimian principle of mechanical solidarity (Durkheim 1964), Cosa Nostra and the 'Ndrangheta constitute functionally diffused associations. As early as 1876, Leopoldo Franchetti highlighted the "extraordinary elasticity" of the Sicilian associations of *malfattori* [evildoers]: "the goals multiply, the field of action widens, without any need to multiply the statutes; the association splits for certain goals, and remains united for others" ([1876] 1993: 100).

Within this wide range of functions one in particular has usually been neglected by the observers of the late twentieth century: the exercising of a political dominion. The ruling bodies of Cosa Nostra and the 'Ndrangheta claim, above all, absolute power over their members, covering every aspect of their lives. They also impose the key principles of their legal order upon nonmembers and, in particular, upon those who collaborate in various ways with mafia members. Through a generalized system of extortion, they tax—as a state would do—the main productive activities carried out within their territory. Mafia associations can thus be regarded as political organizations in a Weberian sense.

These four theses can be summarized in the following way: Cosa Nostra and the 'Ndrangheta are confederations of mafia families, which create ritual brotherhood ties among their members through rites and symbols. They are clearly distinct from the blood families of their members—so much so that they have their own ruling bodies. The two associations resort systematically to violence and secrecy to defend themselves from state repression and to pursue their aims, and they have a plurality of functions within their social environment.

Methodological Notes

It is not easy for either law enforcement officers or social scientists to investigate the mafia. Only rarely, and with great difficulty, can these people observe the activities of a criminal group directly. Due to their recruiting criteria and procedures, however, the obstacles have long proved to be virtually insurmountable in the case of Italian and Italian American mafia groups. Only recently have Italian and, above all, U.S. investigators been able to overcome some of these difficulties thanks to telephone intercepts and hidden microphones in mafiosi's cars, homes, restaurants, and social clubs. To date, however, only an American FBI agent, Joe Pistone, has ever succeeded in infiltrating an Italian (or Italian American) mafia group. Using the name Donnie Brasco, Pistone hung out for about six years (1976–82) with members of the Bonanno mafia family in New York, passing vital information about the mob along to the top echelons of the FBI (see Pistone and Woodley 1987). Although participant observation represents a common research method within social sciences, and even criminology, Pistone's experience has only one academic match in this restricted field of study. In the early 1970s, American anthropologist Francis Ianni (1973) spent two years in close contact with a New York–based Italian American mafia family. Even in this case, however, observation was only partial, since Ianni was forbidden from taking part in the planning and carrying out of any illegal activity. Indeed, the scarcity of information on the family's criminal businesses has been indicated as the main weakness of his study (Reuter 1983: 7).

Although it is clearly possible for a social scientist to carry out a limited participant observation in numerous villages and neighborhoods of the Mezzogiorno (literally, "midday," a nickname for southern Italy), only occasionally will the researcher have the chance to personally witness any external action by mafia groups (such as a robbery, a murder, or the manipulation of public elections). And it is virtually impossible to gain direct access to the internal dynamics of a mafia family. Social scientists are thus forced to rely on accounts given by the police, judicial authorities, and the media and on the reports of key witnesses on these issues.

The mafia is, indeed, a very irksome topic for scientific research. Not only is it virtually impossible to carry out fieldwork, but the many thousands of pages written on the subject are very difficult to assess and to sort out with any clear criterion of reliability. In addition to official documents, such as police investigations, judicial indictments and verdicts, and the occasional reports of government and parliamentary bodies, there is a vast journalistic and fictitious literature fed by popular curiosity. It is therefore difficult to keep separate the social representation of the mafia from what mafiosi themselves actually experience and do (see Tessitore 1997).

In order to deal with these difficulties, the statements of former mafia members who now cooperate with law enforcement agencies have been used extensively and have been given preference over other sources. These confessions have the advantage, as one of the first 'Ndrangheta witnesses put it, to describe the mafia world "from the inside and not only from the outside, as has so far been done through the investigative work of the police and Carabinieri [Italy's military police]" (PrRC 1995: 361) and by academics. In this study in particular, I primarily rely on statements made by the *pentiti* and on other kinds of police and judicial documents to which I had access through the work I did for about three years as a consultant at the Direzione Investigativa Antimafia (DIA) in the Italian Ministry of the Interior, a police agency specialized to fight organized crime.

This reliance on police sources and criminal cases has obviously not been unconditional. First, I have tried to avoid the prejudice that hypothesizes a correspondence between judiciary records and events in the "world out there." In other words, I have always kept in mind that "the legal view necessarily tends to privilege those aspects of real phenomena which assume a greater relevance under the juridical-formal profile, so that the facts reported in the trial papers are not truly such (so as to say) in their factual totality, but are selected and ordered in function of their normative importance" (Fiandaca and Costantino 1990: 87; see also Sbriccoli 1988).

An even greater amount of critical caution has been necessary in dealing with the mafia witnesses' statements, to avoid the risk of accepting and reproducing the worn-out tenets of mafia ideology uncritically or of legitimating lies that may give this or that defendant some kind of advantage. To allay this concern, it is worth remembering that the police officials and prosecutors who gather and first check the witnesses' confessions make an initial screening that is then double-checked by the courts. As far as possible, however, social scientists need to assess autonomously the reliability and coherence of their data.

In particular, it is worth pointing out that even in the case of *pentiti* of proven "judicial trustworthiness," their statements and opinions are greatly influenced by their psychological conditions. No matter what their reasons are, the decision to become a witness always represents a radical change in a mafioso's lifestyle. That is to say, it frequently leads the *pentito* to idealize the group's traditional principles and to contrast them to its current priorities and actions, so as to justify—primarily to himself—his choice first to become a mafia member and then to betray the mafia group (see Di Maria and Lavanco 1995: 70–88).

Caution should not, however, be allowed to turn into a priori skepticism and mistrust. A middle-ground position must be found. Like an anthropologist with his or her informant, I have tried to faithfully interpret the declarations of former mafia members, without fearing the effects of emotions and statements that are to all intents and purposes in open contradiction with the evil and ruthless crimes committed by mafia groups. My attitude is similar to that attributed by Maurice Bloch to Meyer Fortes, one of the fathers of anthropology:

> Fortes's method, which refuses to set aside in any way data from informants whether it be linguistic or otherwise should always be our first guide. If informants stress the morality of kinship then *this* is what we must understand. A method which minimizes such data by dismissing it as "dogma," as "unreal," or a theory like game theory which has no room for it or like the type of functionalism which assumes that form is a direct epiphenomena of use, these methods or theories will mislead since they are not "struggling" with what it is perceived. (Bloch 1973: 86)

This approach has encouraged me to reevaluate the symbolic and moral dimension of mafia relations, the importance of which has been stressed by contemporary *pentiti*. This aspect was virtually expunged from the interpretations of the mafia as an enterprise that were advanced in the late twentieth century in reaction to the previous "culturalist" paradigm. Only by recognizing the strength of cultural codes and moral norms, however, can we understand the mechanisms employed by mafia groups to enhance their internal cohesion and solidarity and the underlying support given to "men of honor" in their communities.

On the whole, though, the use of confessions by *pentiti* for scientific goals presents minor difficulties in comparison to those faced daily by law enforcement bodies. It is not so much the diversity of effects that makes the enterprise of social scientists "easier" (though it is clear that research hypotheses concern general trends and may thus be founded on a less specific and stringent amount of evidence than any judicial provision limiting individual freedom). The difference stems largely from the fact that the information more likely to interest academic students is the least "dangerous" for informants: that is, it is the least likely to entail convictions and retaliation attempts on the part of former mafia brothers. Hence, witnesses have few incentives to lie concerning topics such as the culture and internal organization of mafia groups.[5] Indeed, whereas the investigation of other areas (as, for example, illegal activities) can never be considered fully complete, on these issues the declarations of Sicilian and Calabrian witnesses are highly reliable, consistent, and repetitive.

Theoretically, of course, one cannot rule out the possibility of a collective "conspiracy" by the *pentiti* to give a distorted vision of the mafia or to achieve some other goal. Yet there are, in my view, several reasons justifying a positive—though not unconditional—approach toward this type of source. Foremost, there is the multiplicity and dissimilarity of informants. Then there is the high number of law enforcement officials and independent observers who have gathered their confessions, as well as the diversity of historical points during which similar accounts have been put forward. A third reason is the surprising correlation between today's reports and descriptions of mafia associations dating as far back as the nineteenth century. Instead of assuming, as Raimondo Catanzaro does, that "the formula of the oath reported to us by the *pentiti* almost seems to demonstrate their detailed knowledge of the positivistic literature on criminology" (1992: 200), these analogies can be regarded as proof of the reliability of contemporary *pentiti* statements and of the longevity of southern Italian mafia associations.

Finally, it must be remembered that the information disclosed by mafia defectors has also been confirmed by what is still regarded by some suspicious scholars as the only objective source of information: the wiretappings of conversations among the mafiosi themselves. In addition to the famous conversations taped in Paul Violi's bar in Montreal in the early 1970s (TrPA 1985, V: 845–72), several very interesting and detailed dialogues were wiretapped in 1994 in a Palermitan flat between two mafiosi from Altofonte, a village on the outskirts of the regional capital. After their arrest and imprisonment, and once he understood the importance of the information he had unwillingly disclosed to law enforcement agencies, one of the two committed suicide; the other became a mafia turncoat. As the Palermo prosecutors put it, "in their absolute objectivity, these transcripts give concrete proof—they are after all only 'ordinary' conversations between two middle-ranking men of honor—and confirm all the information on the structure and activity of the criminal organization called Cosa Nostra that has been given to us by the mafia witnesses, and which, nonetheless, some people still occasionally throw doubt on" (PrPA 1993b: 109).

1

Mafia Associations and Ruling Bodies

The word *mafia* is a literary creation, while the true mafiosi are simply called men of honor. Each of them belongs to a *borgata* [neighborhood] (this is the case of the city of Palermo, because in small centers the mafia organization takes its name from the center itself) and he is a member of a family. . . . As a whole this association is called Cosa Nostra.
—TRIBUNALE DI PALERMO,
  Verbali di interrogatorio reso dal collaboratore di giustizia,
  Tommaso Buscetta (1984)

With this statement Tommaso Buscetta began his deposition before the investigating judge (*giudice istruttore*) Giovanni Falcone on July 21, 1984. Following in Buscetta's footsteps, there are now more than five hundred witnesses who have confirmed the existence of both Cosa Nostra and the 'Ndrangheta, because they themselves belonged to one of the two. Since the mid-1980s, furthermore, their statements have been borne out by numerous judicial investigations and several important verdicts have withstood all appeals.

Obscure to the public gaze for many years, Cosa Nostra and the 'Ndrangheta are two nucleii of the vast range of phenomena observers have labeled *mafia*. Given the variety of phenomena involved, however, the meanings attached to the term *mafia* have always been, and remain, very fuzzy (Renda 1985). Indeed, since 1863, when Giuseppe Rizzotto's comedy—*I mafiusi de la Vicaria*—brought it into popular use, the question of its definition has been at the center of heated intellectual debates and political battles attributing the mafia with many sometimes contradictory meanings (see Pezzino 1987; Tessitore 1997). As early as 1886, the author of one of the first books on the topic, police officer Giuseppe Alongi, stressed the variety of and discrepancies between these definitions: "For some the *maffia* does not exist, for others it is a wide and powerful association of evildoers, with a preordered hierarchy, fixed and sociologically evolving; a sort of abnormal state inside the legal state" ([1886] 1977: 3).

A noncorporate conception of the mafia long prevailed in political and scientific discourse. For social scientists carrying out the first field studies between the 1960s and the early 1980s, the mafia was simply a form of behavior and power. Social scientists asserted that while there were single mafiosi, who embodied determined subcultural values and exercised specific functions within their communities, no mafia organization existed as such (Hess 1973; Blok 1988; Schneider and Schneider 1976). In 1983, Pino Arlacchi's successful book *La mafia imprenditrice* [Mafia business] opened with the following statement: "Social research into the question of the mafia has probably now reached the point where we can say that the mafia, as the term is *commonly* understood, does not exist" (1988: 3; see also Catanzaro 1992).

Though these writers by no means openly supported it, it is clear that their interpretations were strongly influenced by a movement known as *sicilianismo* [Sicilianism]. This was a late-nineteenth-century cultural and political movement that opposed what was perceived as an indiscriminate criminalization of all Sicilians by Italian law enforcement and public opinion. Largely promoted by the island's ruling strata, *sicilianismo* also had a second and hidden, but important, objective: consolidating the power of the local upper classes, threatened by the transformations fostered by Italy's unification in 1861 (Dalla Chiesa 1978; Marino 1988; Pezzino 1990b).

In the eyes of the *sicilianisti*, the mafia was merely an attitude, the product of a particularly fierce Sicilian reaction to the foreign powers that had dominated the island for centuries. For example, the Sicilian ethnographer Giuseppe Pitrè, who contributed enormously to the promotion of this ideology, defined the mafia as follows:

> The mafia is neither a sect, nor an association, it has no regulations nor statutes. The mafioso is not a thief, nor a bandit; ... the mafioso is simply a courageous and skillful man, who cannot bear a fly being on his nose; and in this sense, being a mafioso is necessary, indeed, indispensable. The mafia is the awareness of one's own being, an exaggerated concept of individual strength, "the one and only arbiter of any clash in interests and ideas"; from which it derives that he is intolerant of others' superiority, or even worse, *prepotenza* [arrogance]. ([1889] 1993: 292)

This conception of the mafia was, however, contradicted by the results of law enforcement investigations from the mid–nineteenth century on. Though the investigations often disregarded defendants' rights, they targeted numerous associations of evildoers in both Sicily and Calabria. The "judicial" picture is additionally confirmed by other sources, coming from all levels of social class and position, which provided information about "brotherhoods" and "murky societies" of various type and origin. These documents, recently rediscovered by a new generation of historians, prove the existence of stable and formalized mafia groups in both western Sicily and southern Calabria from the late nineteenth century on—the forefathers of contemporary mafia associations.

FAMILIES AND MEMBERS

Despite the judicial successes of the 1990s, the dimensions and boundaries of Cosa Nostra and the 'Ndrangheta, the two associations that constitute the core of the mafia phenomenon, are still uncertain. Even today, we do not know the exact number of groups and individuals forming them.

Cosa Nostra

According to data published by the Direzione Centrale della Polizia Criminale of the Italian Ministry of the Interior (commonly and hereafter referred to as Criminalpol), 181 criminal groups were active in Sicily in late 1994, with almost 5,500 members recognized by the police forces (see table 1.1) (Direzione Centrale della Polizia Criminale 1995; Ministero dell'Interno 1995a). The official categorization is, however, rather approximate and does not specify any internal differences: for example, it does not indicate how many groups are associated with Cosa Nostra nor does it characterize them in any specific way. Further, the official listing does not distinguish the "made" members (that is, those who have undergone a ceremony of initiation) from those called *avvicinati* or *affiliati*, who take part in the group's illicit activities but have not yet been formally initiated.

The only criterion used by the Criminalpol in this listing is the crime of having been a member of a mafia-type delinquent association. This offence was established in September 1982 through the addition of Art. 416*bis* to the Italian

TABLE 1.1. Criminal groups active in Sicily

Provinces	Groups	Affiliates
Trapani	15	524
Palermo	59	1,492
Messina	12	369
Agrigento	47	580
Caltanissetta	18	500
Enna	11	154
Catania	9	1,476
Ragusa	2	110
Siracusa	8	282
Total	181	5,487

Source: Direzione Centrale della Polizia Criminale, 1995

penal code. Police forces and judicial authorities apply this provision whenever the conditions set by Art. 416*bis* are fulfilled, and not even in their intelligence analyzes do they resort to more differentiated criteria to distinguish Cosa Nostra families from other criminal groups.

In order to discover the number of families constituting Cosa Nostra, we thus need to integrate data published by the Criminalpol with empirical information collected at lower territorial levels of analysis. According to numerous *pentiti*, the number of Cosa Nostra families in the Palermo province is close to the Criminalpol estimate. Both Tommaso Buscetta and Francesco Marino Mannoia, a member of the Palermitan mafia family Santa Maria del Gesù, claimed that there were fifty-five mafia families in the city and province (TrPA 1984, 1989). The fifteen families counted by the Criminalpol in the province of Trapani can also be viewed as part of the confederation called Cosa Nostra, since these two administrative districts have been mafia strongholds since the nineteenth century. Instead, according to the estimates made in 1993 by the Direzione Investigativa Antimafia (DIA), only sixteen groups in the province of Agrigento—out of the forty-two registered by Criminalpol—are associated with Cosa Nostra, and the number falls to three in the case of Catania (DIA 1993a; CSM 2001: 18; Ministero dell'Interno 2001a: 118). Furthermore, informants report that nine mafia groups in the province of Caltanissetta and three in the Enna district belong to Cosa Nostra (TrMA 1987: 61–71).

Cosa Nostra did not have any fully developed branches in the provinces of Messina, Siracusa, or Ragusa until at least the mid-1970s. Thus when an interprovincial body of mafia coordination was established in 1975, it was composed of only six provincial representatives (CPM 1992b: 279; TrPA [1985] 1992: 42). With the exception of the Mistretta family, which was considered as forming part of the Palermo group (TrMA 1987: 5), the criminal gangs of the Messina province were, up to the late 1970s, under the influence of the Calabrian 'Ndrangheta and at least the Calabrian *cosca* [band] of Giuseppe Morabito (nicknamed *tiradritto* [the straight shooter]) has exercised considerable power up to the present (CPM 2000: 114–16). After the late 1970s, however, several groups in the province of Messina developed contacts with Cosa Nostra families and some of these, particularly the Catania family, established subgroups in the provinces of Messina and Siracusa (PrCT 1993; PrPA 1994b; Ministero dell'Interno 2001a: 125–26). It is difficult to establish precisely how many of the groups counted by Criminalpol in the three abovementioned provinces (respectively twelve in Messina, two in Ragusa, and eight in Siracusa) actually belong to Cosa Nostra. What is certain, however, is that in eastern and southern Sicily numerous other groups coexist beside the Cosa Nostra *cosche*. Some resemble mafia families, while others are structured as juvenile or urban gangs. Despite their low cohesion and their limited political connections, some of these groups are able to control significant portions of the illegal activities carried out in their territory (Ministero dell'Interno 2001a: 127–30, 2001e: 11–15).[1]

It is no easier to establish how many members, called "men of honor," Cosa Nostra can count. However, according to Leonardo Messina, a former member of the San Cataldo *cosca* in the Caltanissetta province, at least ten people are needed in order to set up a family (CPM 1992d: 534) and, indeed, in many cases the number of "men of honor" affiliated to Cosa Nostra families seems close to this minimum standard according to the findings of a survey carried out by the DIA. In 1993, for example, the nucleus of the Corleone family was formed of only thirty-nine people, including prisoners and fugitives. In another case the *cosca* located in Carini, a village on the outskirts of Palermo, was made up of sixteen "men of honor" and nine *avvicinati*, that is, individuals who help to carry out illicit activities without being ritually initiated (DIA 1993e).

Some *cosche* do, however, have larger ranks—the Palermo family of Corso dei Mille, for example, counted sixty-five "men of honor" and thirty-eight *avvicinati* (DIA 1993c)—but on average *cosche* are quite small. This statistic has been confirmed by a survey carried out by a joint task force of all Italian police bodies on the fifty-six mafia families of the city and province of Palermo in the early 1990s. In this case the average number of members totaled 23.8, including both the ritually initiated "men of honor" and *avvicinati* (Gruppo Interforze 1993a and 1993b). However, if we introduce a distinction between "men of honor" and *avvicinati*— one extremely important in the mafia world—the average number of members of Cosa Nostra families shrinks even further. For example, one of the most important mafia families of the Trapani province, the *cosca* headed by Totò Minore, had only seven "men of honor" (DIA 1993d).

Even the Catania *cosca*, which was the largest family forming part of Cosa Nostra during the 1980s and the early 1990s (before it was decimated by investigations and defectors' testimonies), had a limited number of "men of honor." Only forty-four were recorded by police forces on the basis of accounts by *pentiti* in 1993 (DIA 1993b). Contrary to general practice, however, the Catania family had a large number of *avvicinati* who, according to some mafia witnesses, totaled more than 170 (ibid.). The number of *avvicinati* was actually even larger, because as early as 1984 the Catania mafia family resorted to a highly unconventional and indeed unprecedented measure. Benedetto Santapaola, who then was (and probably still is) the leader of the *cosca*, ritually affiliated Giuseppe Pulvirenti and the highest-ranking members of Pulvirenti's clan, which commanded a large area of the province and was the most dreaded and well organized opponent of the Cosa Nostra family. This automatically led to the inclusion into the Catania family as *avvicinati* of the rest of Pulvirenti's personnel (PrCT 1993: 44–51). In this way, the two groups formed a team of about 400 people.

Such an unusual practice was made necessary by the minority position held by Cosa Nostra in the underworld of Catania, Sicily's second-largest city, and its surrounding province. From the late 1970s onward, this group found itself having to compete with several large and tough urban gangs such as the Cursotis, Laudanis, and Pillera-Cappellos, which had proliferated in the slums of Catania at the beginning of the decade. In spite of their lack of internal cohesion and low economic and political resources, these gangs constantly threatened the supremacy of the Cosa Nostra *cosca* due to the larger number of members and their readiness to use violence (see Rizzo, Savoca, and Sciacca 1994). As a result, the Santapaola family had to recruit a large number of personnel in order to maintain a force capable of deterring these other criminal groups. By increasing the number of the full members—estimated at thirty-five in the early 1980s—only moderately and those of the *avvicinati* abundantly, the Catania family was able to meet this military exigency and, at the same time, it preserved the cohesive and elitist nature of the nucleus constituted by the ritually affiliated "men of honor" (see Ministero dell'Interno 2001c: 12–14).

The 'Ndrangheta

It is no easier to discover which criminal groups belong to the Calabrian 'Ndrangheta. Although some scholars have adopted an extensive definition of the term and therefore use it as a synonym for any criminality of Calabrian origin (Ciconte 1992), I will refer here to a specific confederation of mafia families, located mostly in southern Calabria and specifically in the province of Reggio Calabria.

While Cosa Nostra's stronghold spreads over the provinces of Palermo and Trapani, that of the 'Ndrangheta is much more specific—the village of San Luca on the Aspromonte mountain in the province of Reggio Calabria. Here, according to the former *'ndranghetista* Fonti, "almost all the male inhabitants belong to the 'Ndrangheta, and the Sanctuary of Polsi (located in San Luca district) has long been the meeting place of the affiliates" (PrRC 1995: 4429). The preeminence of the San Luca family is such that every new group—or *locale* [place] as the *'ndranghetisti* often say—must obtain its authorization to operate. Furthermore, according to several witnesses, every group belonging to the 'Ndrangheta "still has to deposit a small percentage of illicit proceeds to the *principale* of San Luca in recognition of the latter's primordial supremacy" (ibid.).

It is fairly probable that all eighty-five criminal groups listed by the Criminalpol in the Reggio Calabria province belong to the 'Ndrangheta (see table 1.2). However, it is very difficult to establish whether they are autonomous *locali* or dependent subunits. A *locale* may have branches, called *'ndrine*, in the districts of the same city, in neighboring towns or villages, or even outside Calabria. In some cases, *sotto-'ndrine* [under-*'ndrine*] may even be established. "In the old times," Francesco Fonti maintains, "there were only a few *'ndrine*, but the enrichment of

TABLE 1.2. Criminal groups active in Calabria

Provinces	Groups	Affiliates
Cosenza	20	1,000
Catanzaro	50	1,000
Reggio Calabria	85	3,000
Total	155	5,000

Source: Ministero dell'Interno, 1994

other families has created an infinite number" (PrRC 1995: 5721). These subunits enjoy a high degree of administrative and operational autonomy. The *'ndrine,* says another mafia witness, Francesco Scriva, "are, to all effects, considered detached sections" (ibid.: 363). They have a leader and independent administrative staff, although their chief may at the same time hold other assignments in the *locale.* In some contexts the *'ndrine* have become more powerful than the *locale* on which they formally depend (ibid.: 5721).

The phenomenology of organized crime in northern Calabria is, instead, much more diversified and fluid. Especially in the areas bordering the province of Reggio Calabria, groups are associated mainly with the 'Ndrangheta. However, most of the seventy criminal groups counted by the Criminalpol in the provinces of Catanzaro and Cosenza do not belong to it.[2] These latter differ substantially from the families belonging to the 'Ndrangheta in their organization, entrepreneurial activities, and political connections. Their cultural background is, however, often similar to those of the Reggio *cosche* due to long-term processes of communication, imitation, and transplant (Paoli 1996). The investigations coordinated by the Direzione Distrettuale Antimafia of the Catanzaro prosecutor's office additionally prove that some of the northern groups are rapidly making up for the gap in political and economic resources that differentiates them from the mafia families of the province of Reggio Calabria (PrCZ 1995; Ministero dell' Interno 1996a: 112–39, 1997a: 167–91, 1998a: 233–64, 2001e: 22–24). A few have already been admitted to the 'Ndrangheta, even if they are in a subordinate position vis-à-vis the Reggio Calabria *cosche* (PrRC 1995: 4449–74). As of today, however, most of the criminal groups of the Catanzaro and Cosenza provinces are still excluded from the mafia consortium (see Ministero dell'Interno 2001a: 94–100, 2000a: 243–66).

As much as in Sicily, in Calabria it is difficult to estimate the number of members of the 'Ndrangheta families and to distinguish the ritual members from those who merely participate in the group's illicit activities. Even more than in the Cosa Nostra, the former as well as the latter are usually sons or relatives of "made" members. "In most cases, one becomes an *'ndranghetista* through family links," the witness Pasquale Barreca points out (PrRC 1995: 233). For outsiders it is therefore in most cases virtually impossible to distinguish the mafia family from the blood family of the most prestigious members.

Contrary to the Sicilian Cosa Nostra, moreover, the *cosche* associated with the 'Ndrangheta make no effort to limit the size of the family nucleus. A common practice among *'ndranghetisti* is the "strategy of maximizing the number of descendants" (Arlacchi 1988: 137), according to which mafia members try to have as many sons as possible. As the witness Antonio Zagari expressed it,

> Many 'Ndrangheta members are obsessed by the idea of having many sons. . . . This is because sons provide the human material necessary to replace the unavoidable losses and to take any revenge necessary. In addition to feuds, this latter is one of the main activities of the Calabrian underworld. A large number of sons or, at any rate, men linked by direct family kinship provides the family chief with more power in the criminal sphere; it is no coincidence that the most powerful *cosche* of the 'Ndrangheta are often made up of men belonging to the same family lineage, who are unlikely to betray each other. (1992: 10–11)

In particular, the frequency with which feuds take place has strongly fostered the practice of "maximizing descendants." Feuds are interfamily conflicts, characterized by a ferocious destructiveness, and can be triggered by very different factors. In Calabria, feuds have long represented a primary channel of social mobility and affirm a newly rising leadership within each community (Piselli and Arrighi 1985). While new hierarchies in Cosa Nostra can be established only through conflicts among "men of honor," and unaffiliated relatives are thus excluded from taking part in these, in the 'Ndrangheta the whole kinship is involved in the fight for supremacy. Moreover, unlike the Sicilian mafia association, until the beginning of the 1990s the 'Ndrangheta did not even attempt to mediate conflicts among associated mafia families. As a result, the duty of vendetta has given rise to a very heavy death toll for many years in Calabria. In Siderno, a small town on the Ionic coast, for example, a feud between two mafia families began with the theft of some guns belonging to one of the *cosca* chiefs and lasted five years, from 1987 to 1991, causing thirty-four deaths (TrRC 1993a).

Even today, the most powerful mafia groups in the province of Reggio Calabria are those with the most members: the smallest *cosche* count from five to ten adult males, the middle-ranking ones from twenty to thirty, while the top positions are held by *cosche* with more than fifty members. Some of the strongest families, like the Piromalli *cosca* of Gioia Tauro, contain more than two hundred adult males (Gruppo Interforze 1991).

International Expansion

Today, members and branches of both Cosa Nostra and the 'Ndrangheta can be found in numerous northern Italian centers as well as in all those foreign countries that have attracted consistent migration flows from southern Italy.[3] For example, representatives or subunits of Cosa Nostra families—called *decine* (a group of about ten people)—have been shown to exist in several northern Italian regions as well as in southern Germany, France, Belgium, the United States, and several Latin American countries. Venezuela, in particular, has become the headquarters of the Cuntrera-Caruana family, and at present constitutes the only case of a Sicilian Cosa Nostra *cosca* that has moved its home seat outside the island permanently (Ministero dell'Interno 1993a: 166–67, 2001a: 112–13; Lodato and Grasso 2001: 65).

The Calabrian 'Ndrangheta has extended its range even further. From the 1960s on, both subunits and entire mafia families have settled in northern Italy and numerous other countries. In several Calabrian immigrant communities in Lombardy and Piedmont, the 'Ndrangheta *cosche* have managed to recreate the same sort of territorial dominion they imposed on their villages and towns of origin. Although no overall statistical estimates are available, there are certainly more than ten Calabrian mafia groups active in northern Italy, and the numbers of those in some way involved in their illicit activities goes into the hundreds (CPM 1994a). In addition to the cells located in Germany, Holland, France, and the United States, the 'Ndrangheta has several very highly developed foreign settlements in Canada and Australia, consisting of several dozens of members grouped into different mafia families (Paoli 1994; BKA 1992; Australian Federal Police 1990; Ministero dell'Interno 2001a: 93–94; CPM 2000a: 102–16). Though enjoying a high degree of operational independence, these units are considered by their own members and their Calabrian correspondents as belonging for all intents and purposes to the 'Ndrangheta.

On the basis of the above data, we can thus state that the Sicilian Cosa Nostra and the Calabrian 'Ndrangheta are each constituted by about one hundred groups. Each consortium consists of at least 3,500 to 4,000 full members (and in the 'Ndrangheta these probably exceed 5,000). However, a much larger circle of people cooperate more or less systematically with mafia members in criminal activities without being ritually initiated into the mafia association.

HISTORICAL BACKGROUND

It is hard to establish with any degree of certainty how Cosa Nostra and the 'Ndrangheta came into being and consolidated. There is no doubt, however, that since the mid–nineteenth century numerous sources have mentioned, and sometimes described in great detail, stable mafia groupings in both Sicily and Calabria. Long ignored by the supporters of a disorganized view of the mafia phenomenon, some of these sources—travelers' diaries, reports by scholars and state officials, and literary *pièces*—were reinterpreted more objectively in the last few decades of the twentieth century. The existence of mafia groupings as early as the late nineteenth century is also proved by several judicial and police documents, mostly dating back to the period before the First World War, which have been retrieved thanks to the patient archival research of a new generation of historians (Pezzino 1987; Lupo 1988; Fiume 1984).

Sicily

The oldest reference to mafia groups in Sicily dates back to 1838. This can be found in a report written by the Procuratore Generale del Re, Pietro Calà Ulloa, to the Minister of Justice of the Bourbonic Kingdom of the two Sicilies, Parisio: "In many villages, there are unions or fraternities—kinds of sects—which are called *partiti*, with no political color or goal, with no meeting places, and with no other bond but that of dependency on a chief, who is a landowner in some cases, and in others a priest. A common fund serves their needs, sometimes to exonerate an official, sometimes to defend him, sometimes to protect a defendant, sometimes to charge an innocent. These form many small governments inside the government" (Ulloa [1838] 1961: 233–35). Four years after Italy's unification in 1861, similar considerations were advanced by the Baron Niccolò Turrisi Colonna, leader of the Sicilian moderates. The mafia was in fact defined as "a sect, which makes new affiliates every day of the brightest young people coming from the rural class, of the guardians of the fields in the Palermitan countryside, and of the large number of smugglers; a sect which gives and receives protection to and from certain men who make a living on traffic and internal commerce. It is a sect with little or no fear of public bodies, because its members believe that they can easily elude these" (1864: 31)

Mafia associations were also mentioned by Leopoldo Franchetti, the liberal Tuscan aristocrat who traveled to Sicily in 1876 with Sidney Sonnino in order to study the island and its inhabitants. In a volume published at the end of the same year, *Condizioni economiche ed amministrative della Sicilia*, Franchetti denied the existence of a single secret sect of *malfattori*, but pointed to the existence of "associations founded regularly with statutes, admission rules, penal sanctions, etc., associations aimed at exercising *prepotenza* [arrogance] and the pursuit of illegal profits" ([1876] 1993: 8).

The clearest references to structured mafia groups can, however, be found in a series of articles and books published in the last two decades of the nineteenth century. They were written by different observers, most of whom were law enforcement officials and followed Cesare Lombroso's School of Criminal Anthropology. Although many of their explicative theories can be criticized, these writers provided detailed empirical evidence about the specific mafia associations discovered and prosecuted at that time.

In the first edition of his book *La maffia* ([1886] 1977), for example, the police official Giuseppe Alongi described in great detail the associations of *malfattori* active along the Sicilian coasts. Developing this theme, in the second edition, published in 1904, he made extensive references to the two main judicial cases of the time. The first case concerned the association of the Fratellanza which, centered in the city of Favara in the province of Agrigento, had established branches in the surrounding centers of Campobello, Canicattì, Comitini, and Palma di Montechiaro. The second case presented by Alongi was about mafia groups that had flourished in the early 1870s in the northern part of the Conca d'Oro (the "golden valley" of fertile citrus groves surrounding Palermo). According to his account, in Bagheria, one of the main centers in Conca d'Oro, a group called the *fratuzzi* [brothers] operated; in Misilmeri, another neighboring town, the *fontana nuova* [new fountain] group was active. In Monreale, two rival *cosche* jostled for supremacy: the *compari* [non-kin united by a ritual kinship], who were called *stoppaghieri* [straw men] by their adversaries, and the *giardinieri* [gardeners]. However, all these groups were allegedly linked to the *cosca* located in the Porta Montalto neighborhood in Palermo, which was ruled by the Amoroso brothers (Alongi 1904).

The association of the Fratellanza was also described in even greater detail by Lestingi, who was public prosecutor in the trial against 168 of its members (1884; see also 1880), and by another investigating judge, Colacino (1885).[4] From their reports, some striking similarities emerge regarding the rituals and organizational structure between this mafia association of the late nineteenth century and those described by contemporary mafia witnesses. These will be carefully analyzed in the following chapters.

In *La mafia e i mafiosi* ([1900] 1988), Antonino Cutrera devoted a great deal of space to the *stoppaghieri* of Monreale. As well as the groups already mentioned, he discussed other mafia associations, such as the Oblonica from Girgenti (contemporary Agrigento), the Scattialora from Sciascia, the Scaglione from Castrogiovanni, and the Zubio from Villabate. Even more interestingly, Cutrera provided a map of the Sicilian mafia that largely corresponds to the descriptions of contemporary *pentiti* (ibid.: 48–80; see also Villari [1885] 1972 and Schneegans 1890).

Furthermore, the police and judicial documents that have come to light through archival work carried out by several historians in the 1980s and 1990s have also shown that several criminal associations were active in western Sicily in the nineteenth century. Enzo D'Alessandro and Giovanna Fiume, for instance, report an organization named Sacra Unione (Holy Union), first mentioned in August 1839, which spread over several villages of inland Sicily (Mazzarino, Aidone, Caltagirone, Mirabella, Delia, etc.) and was headed by a priest. The Sacra Unione ran large-scale cattle-rustling operations and enjoyed protection from the local judicial and economic establishment (D'Alessandro 1959: 60; Fiume 1984: 98–99).

More recently, Salvatore Lupo has discovered a previously unknown source of great interest: a set of thirty-one police documents, covering 485 pages, collectively known as the Sangiorgi Report. This was written between November 1898 and February 1900 by Armando Sangiorgi, who was then *Questore* [police chief] of Palermo, and it attempted to provide a comprehensive picture of mafia criminality in the areas surrounding Palermo through information derived largely from informants. "Like other parts of this and nearby provinces," Sangiorgi stated, "the Palermitan countryside is oppressed by a large association of *malfattori*, organized into branches, divided into groups; every group is regulated by a chief . . . And this union of criminals has a supreme chief" (Lupo 1988: 467). According to the report, the *cosche* had precise, formalized rules and an administrative staff whose positions clearly resemble those described by the *pentiti* a hundred years later. The associates regularly paid a membership fee, assembled in meetings, and took the most important decisions involving group affairs jointly. About 216 men were reported as initiated members of this coalition. According to an estimate attributed to Francesco Siino, allegedly the supreme chief, until 1896 the overall number of people involved was around 670, if the so-called *cagnolazzi* (that is, those that had not undergone a formal ritual of affiliation) were also taken into account (ibid.: 466–67).

Without wanting to support any of those loose definitions presenting the mafia as "an expression of the island's soul" (Titone 1964: 158) or as "a century-old phenomenon" (Cancila 1984), it is, however, possible to discern antecedents to the late-nineteenth-century mafia associations. One of the closest is represented by the *comitive armate* [armed squads], which spread over the whole island in the first half of the nineteenth century. They were particularly evident in the provinces of Palermo, Trapani, and Girgenti, which subsequently proved to be the areas of highest mafia concentration. In the case of the *comitive armate*, the distinction between mafia and banditry, which was emphasized by many scholars until the early 1980s, seems to blur. According to the most adamant supporter of this distinction, the British historian Eric Hobsbawm, banditry represented a primitive form of social protest, whereas the mafia, which initially defended the interests of the rural classes, soon served those of the landowners (1974; but also Hess 1973: 5–12). However, as contemporary historical research has made clear, the *comitive armate*, one of the main forms of banditry in Sicily, were a complex phenomenon and cannot be regarded exclusively as an expression of peasant protests. Notwithstanding their prevalently popular origin, the squads soon set up a close network of collusion, complicity, and mutual exploitation with sectors of the dominant classes and government authorities (D'Alessandro 1959: 132–35; Blok 1972; Fiume 1984; Mangiameli 1990; see also Brögger 1968). Some of them enjoyed the protection and the financial and political support of members of the bourgeoisie and aristocracy and provided them, in exchange, with military services and a share of illegal profits. According to the historian Salvatore Francesco Romano, the groups that were directly sponsored by the land-owning classes (known as *controsquadre*) "probably represent the most meaningful and immediate antecedent and, in any case, the first nucleus and backbone of the mafia" (1963: 96; see also Riall 1998: 53 and Fiume 1991).

The *comitive armate* provided manpower for the rural squads that flocked to Palermo in the 1820, 1848, and 1866 revolts and for the insurrection that accompanied the landing of Garibaldi's troops in Marsala in 1860. According to several contemporary and past observers, rising mafia groups benefited from the organizational skills of the armed squads and, in particular, from those of the *picciotti* ("boys," in Sicilian and, more generally, southern Italian dialect) who took part in the 1860 insurrection (see, among the many, Cutrera [1900] 1988: 165–76; Romano 1963: 92–111; Da Passano 1981; Renda 1984: 208ff.; Recupero 1987a; Pezzino 1995: 7–17; Fentress 2000: 102–5; Santino 2000a).

Calabria

Although the Calabrian mafia phenomenon has historically received much less attention than its Sicilian counterpart, there are several documents proving the existence of well-structured mafia groupings since the late nineteenth century in the region as a whole. There is, however, uncertainty about the names of these entities, which are sometimes referred to with Neapolitan or Sicilian expressions—*camorra, camorristi,* mafia, and mafiosi—and with a plurality of generic or local terms: *picciotti, picciotteria, malfattori,* underworld, Honored Society, "men of honor," Montalbano family, the 'Ndrangheta, *'ndranghita,* and *'ndranghetisti.*

The existence of Calabrian mafia groups is foremost proved by numerous sentences issued by local courts from the 1880s on, which have recently been discovered by contemporary historians (Nicaso 1990; Ciconte 1992). These targeted the members of the *picciotteria* and *camorra,* as the Calabrian mafia groups were then often called. As the judges of the Reggio Calabria court stated in 1897, "the existence of the *camorra* in the Calabrie is not a mere assumption, but an undeniable fact which is clear from the final sentences concerning Nicastro, Palmi, and Reggio" (Nicaso 1990: 69). For instance, in Palmi, a center on the Tyrrhenian coast of the province of Reggio Calabria, 154 men faced trial in 1892 on the charge of belonging to a criminal group located in several surrounding centers. In the same year, the Calabrian court of appeals issued three different sentences against ninety-eight members of a single mafia organization extending from the Aspromonte to the northern boundary of the Reggio Calabria province on its Ionic side: namely, the communities of Africo, Casalnuovo, Roghudi, Roccaforte, Gallicanò, Brancaleone, and Bova. This *picciotteria*, the judges maintained, "had a main chief, Velonà Filippo from Straiti; it had underchiefs in the respective communities . . . and the associates of one village corresponded with those of other villages" (Ciconte 1992: 116).

Accounts of mafia groups were also given in several police reports. In a report dated July 14, 1882, the inspector of public security mentioned "a certain *maffia* or *camorra*, as one might call it" (Crupi 1992: 19). References became increasingly frequent in later documents too. Even the *rapporteur* of the *Inchiesta parlamentare sulle condizioni dei contadini nelle province meridionali e nella Sicilia* [Parliamentary investigation into the conditions of peasants in the southern provinces and Sicily], which was carried out in 1909, recalls the existence of a criminal consortium in the countryside around Reggio Calabria, which he calls *picciotteria* (Lorenzoni 1910: 580–84).

Outlawed groups in the Reggio Calabrian province have been also described in great detail by several Calabrian writers and poets who gained access to information about mafia groups' rituals, slang, and organization due to the groups' low degree of secrecy. At the beginning of the twentieth century, for example, the poet Giovanni De Nava wrote several poems about the *picciotteria*. In a poem entitled *Malavita* [Underworld], for instance, a member of the Honored Society expresses his arrogance and his strength as follows (Crupi 1992: 14–22):

. . . O picciotteddii sgarru, o picciotteddi,	. . . Oh *picciotti di sgarro*, oh *picciotti*,
ch'aviti l'anuranza sta' matina	Who today have the honor
'a scola d' 'i rrasola e d' 'i cutteddi	To learn how to use razors and knives,
v'ambizza cca', sta' manu malandrina.	You like this sly hand, don't you?
Ye' . . . sintiti . . . sugnu camurrista,	Listen to me, I am a *camorrista*,
e sugnu 'u cchiù valenti malandrinu,	And I am the most skillful evildoer;
aundi 'u peri me' faci na' pista,	Wherever I proceed
'a terra trema . . . trem' 'a terra anzinu!	The earth trembles . . . even the earth trembles!

Several Calabrian writers wrote novels and short stories about the 'Ndrangheta up to the 1970s. Corrado Alvaro, for instance, mentioned the 'Ndrangheta in several short stories and, in an article published in 1955 in the *Corriere della Sera* newspaper, described the tangible and legitimate presence of the Honored Society in Africo, his native town, during his youth (Alvaro 1955b; see also 1955a, 1953, 1930). In a partially autobiographical novel, Luca Asprea described the mafia initiation of a young man training to become a priest—hence, the book's title *Il previtocciolo* (1971). Saverio Montalto (1973) devoted a whole volume to the *Famiglia Montalbano* (as he called the local mafia group) and its suffocating presence in San Filipo and Zuccalio, two villages of the Aspromonte. Likewise, Saverio Strati (1957, 1960, 1977, 1979, 1986) wrote about the 'Ndrangheta in several novels and described its initiation rituals and structure in a way that is perfectly compatible with contemporary witnesses' accounts.

A variety of documents of different kinds dating from different periods thus confirms the recent "rediscovery" of mafia organizations made by law enforcement agencies in light of contemporary *pentiti*'s statements. Though it is not possible to reconstruct the initial phases of development of Cosa Nostra and the 'Ndrangheta with any great accuracy, there is no doubt that similar mafia groupings have existed in western Sicily and southern Calabria since at least the late nineteenth century.

Similarities and Analogies

Some surprising similarities exist between mafia organizations of the past and contemporary groupings. They concern the internal organization of the groups and the cultural and symbolic apparatus that are used. These will be discussed, whenever appropriate, in the following sections.

Close similarities, in addition, can be found among the various mafia groups of each region since the late nineteenth century. For example, this is what Antonino Cutrera says about the mafia associations of the provinces of Palermo and Agrigento in 1900:

> When examining the constitution and functioning of all these associations, we can see that while their names may have been different, their criminal aim was identical. Indeed, some of them were connected: they exchanged services and, above all, there was solidarity between them. We can also note many analogies in their casual features, because the organization was analogous in all these associations. If we compare the Stoppaglieri association with the Oblonica from Girgenti, we find out that in both a court was established. . . . Rituals to admit new members, forms of oath-taking, conventional signs of recognition were similar. There was only one aim and the means to obtain it were identical: robberies, extortions, thefts, damage, bloody vendettas, mutual assistance. ([1900] 1988: 121–25)

In addition to Cutrera, several other nineteenth-century sources hypothesize the existence of devices for communicating and coordinating among the various sects of neighboring areas. Questore Sangiorgi, for example, opened his report on the mafia with the following statement: "Powerful and widespread associations have long existed in almost all the communities of the Palermo province. They are connected to one another through relationships of dependency and affiliation, so much so that they almost form a single, large association" (Lupo 1988: 466). According to this document, all the *cosche* on Palermo's outskirts (the so-called Conca d'Oro)—and more specifically those of the villages of Piana dei Colli, Acquasanta, Falde, Malaspina, Uditore, Passo di Rigano, Perpignano, and Olivuzza—were linked to each other by a kind of coordinating body and a supreme chief (ibid.: 466–67; see also Alongi [1886] 1977: 103–4). Likewise, the Calabrian court of appeal in 1890 pointed out that "the several associations established in the above-mentioned villages [that is, Polistena, Iatrinoli (the modern Taurianova), Melicuccà, Molochio, S. Eufemia, Radicena, and Messignadi] were in contact with each other, reciprocally helped each other, and often the members of one village association went to talk with the *picciotti* of another" (Nicaso 1990: 52–54).

Given the bad conditions of the road system in nineteenth-century Sicily and Calabria, which sometimes made communication difficult even between neighboring villages (Schneider and Schneider 1976: 51–55; Bevilacqua 1985: 117–42), these descriptions may seem quite surprising at first glance. Nonetheless, several elements can be mentioned to justify the hypothesis of contacts and even permanent alliances among the mafia associations in each subregional context. We need, first of all, to consider that the status of mafioso has traditionally been associated with professions characterized by a high degree of mobility. According to nineteenth-century sources (and to the scientific inquiries carried out after the 1960s), mafiosi were frequently the *gabellotti* [leaseholders] who managed several distant baronial estates; the *campieri* [herdsmen] who were in charge of single feuds and herds of cattle; the shepherds who periodically moved their sheep from the inland to the sea, in order to find green pastures; the cattle mediators who traveled around buying and selling cows and horses; the *carrettieri* who provided carrier services and, finally, the peddlers who sold their merchandise in different villages (Nicaso 1990: 64, 84; Alongi [1886] 1977: 52–53, 89–91; Schneider and Schneider 1976: 70–71).

Additionally, it must be remembered that in both regions large numbers of people moved seasonally from the inland wheat plantations to the coastal citrus areas. In Sicily, for example, the number of seasonal migrants was estimated at almost 100,000 by the end of the nineteenth century, and there were certainly some mafiosi among them (Barone 1987: 191–200; see also Bevilacqua 1985). Meetings among mafia associates from different villages and provinces also took place during cattle fairs, held periodically in many villages of western Sicily and southern Calabria. For Alongi, these fairs were "true interprovincial congresses of the mafia"

([1886] 1977: 53; see also Cutrera [1900] 1988: 101). Likewise, according to a sentence issued by the Palmi Court in 1901, "the *camorra* was particularly active at cattle fairs" (Nicaso 1990: 29).

Imprisonment also helped foster the development of contacts and ties among members of different groups persecuted by state authorities. In the play by Giuseppe Rizzotto, who first introduced the word *mafia* into the public discourse, the mafiosi were, significantly, convicts in the Palermitan prison, La Vicaria. From the early nineteenth century on, in fact, Bourbon—and then Italian—prisons represented a privileged locus for the creation of friendships and ties among *malfattori* from different towns and villages (Nicaso 1990: 10; Fentress 2000: 149–50, 156; Riall 1998: 212–20), just like today. "In prison," a contemporary mafia witness argues, "friendships are sealed, alliances are bound, and new acquaintances and ritual kinship ties established" (PrRC 1995: 369). Hence, it is quite probable that a process of mutual recognition and cultural harmonization among preexisting associations took place as a result of these moments of interaction and exchange. Even the spread of mafia groups into areas previously unaffected was often carried out through the cooptation of new members in prison. Once these members were released, they founded new mafia groupings. For example, one of the largest mafia networks investigated in the late nineteenth century, the Fratellanza of the province of Girgenti, was founded by some of the inhabitants of Favara (a town of that province) who had been sent into forced residence (*soggiorno obbligato*) on the island of Ustica (Lestingi 1884; Colacino 1885).

THE RULING BODIES OF SINGLE FAMILIES

The *cosche* composing Cosa Nostra and the 'Ndrangheta may be considered fully developed organizations, clearly distinguished from the blood families of their members, because they have ruling bodies to enforce their normative order.

Cosa Nostra and the Myth of Direct Democracy

The official ruling structure of a Cosa Nostra family is similar to that of the Italian American Cosa Nostra, which was first described by Joe Valachi in the 1960s (see U.S. Senate 1963; Maas 1969) and has since been confirmed by most other defectors. Heading each family is a *rappresentante* [representative] or *capofamiglia* [family head], who is elected by the members and constitutes the highest group authority. The family chief avails himself of one or more *consiglieri* [counselors], who are also elected by the associates. They assist him in the most important decisions and, at the same time, check his management of the family (TrPA 1985, V: 810–14,

875–77). In the case of impediments or long-term detention, the family is run by a *vice-rappresentante* [vice representative] chosen by the *capofamiglia* himself. In the larger families, he also selects one or more *capi decina*, who coordinate units of about ten people (ibid.).

The ruling apparatus of Sicilian mafia families has remained very stable over time. Writing at the end of the nineteenth century about the crime situation in the province of Palermo, Questore Armando Sangiorgi described roles and procedures surprisingly analogous to those described by contemporary mafia witnesses: "Each group is regulated by a chief, who is called *capo rione* [district chief] and according to the number of the members and the group territorial extension, an underchief is added to the *capo rione*, who is in charge of replacing him in the case of absence or other impediments" (Lupo 1988: 466; see also the declarations of Melchiorre Allegra dating to 1937, republished in De Mauro 1962a, 1962b, and 1962c; Gentile 1993: 74).

The selection procedures and the competencies of the Cosa Nostra ruling bodies are inspired prescriptively, but not always factually (as we will see in the following section, deviations and violations have always been very frequent), by the principle of direct democracy. Though this may seem strange, there is no real reason to be surprised. Direct democracy is, in fact, the most faithful transposition on a structural level of feelings of equality, solidarity, and fraternity created by fraternization contracts (see chapter 2). Concretely, this form of democracy has been made possible by the typically small size of Sicilian mafia families. In fact, only in small groups—where all members can be assembled in a single place, know each other, and consider themselves equal—can the principle of direct democracy be applied.

This type of administration is characterized by what Max Weber calls the phenomenon of the "minimization of power": the holders of office are obliged to act only according to the will of the group members as a whole, in their interests and by virtue of the authority that the latter have entrusted in them (1978: 289–92). As the *pentito* Tommaso Buscetta states, "the representative was a man of honor who undertook the responsibility of directing a family, while staying very close to the soldiers [men of honor without ruling positions]. The representative had to take charge of the problems of all of these: loads of bother and duties, without any satisfying returns. You got no reward for being a chief, who, more than the manager, was the servant of the family" (Arlacchi 1994: 70). Likewise Leonardo Messina, a former member of the San Cataldo *cosca* in the province of Caltanissetta, a peripheral family that has remained more faithful than others to traditional management principles, points out that "the mafia is a democratic body, one of the most important kinds of democratic bodies that exist. . . . The chief is elected from the base and it is simply not true that he is the most important member: the epicenter is the family itself, and the chief is only its representative. It is always the family which decides; the chief is elected by the base, by the men of honor" (CPM 1992d: 515–16).

In the Cosa Nostra's normative code several measures are in place to guarantee the minimization of power: (1) frequent election of the officeholders and short terms of office; (2) liability to being removed from office at any time; (3) procedures to control the action of rulers through the plenary meetings of the members and the *consigliere*.

First, "The choice of the *capi rione* is made by the affiliates," wrote Questore Sangiorgi in his report in 1898, and this practice is still followed today. Many former Cosa Nostra members now collaborating with the judiciary report that the positions of *rappresentante* and *consigliere* are assigned through yearly elections. In smaller families, the election takes place during an assembly of the family "by show of hands, in front of everyone" (CPM 1992d: 515). The larger ones have enacted more formalized procedures in order to link the democratic principle with the need for security. "When offices are being renewed by elections," recalls Francesco Marino Mannoia, a former member of the large mafia family of the Palermitan Santa Maria del Gesù neighborhood, "the family is dissolved and a trustee chosen, whose duty it is to gather the ballot boxes from the *capi decina*. The latter, who have also resigned from office, meet in a predetermined place and we proceed to open the ballot boxes and to appoint the new *rappresentante* and the new *consiglieri*" (TrPA 1989: 67–68, see also Falcone 1993: 89; TrPA 1985, V: 878–79).

Mafia elections are "a ritual of installation" (Fortes 1962: 86); they confer the right to exercise powers associated with a particular office on the new incumbent and show him his new responsibilities. At the same time, they clarify the distinction between the office and the particular incumbent at any given moment, presenting "the office to the individual as the creation or the possession of society" (ibid.).

Second, not only is the *rappresentante* elected on a yearly basis, but—at least theoretically—he may be removed from office or reprimanded at any time: "The chief who does not foster the interests of the family which has elected him," Leonardo Messina pointed out, "is automatically removed. If he has committed serious misdeeds, he is killed or put *fuori confidenza* [literally, out of confidence, that is, excluded from the life of the family]. If he has only been negligent, he is put to one side and a new chief is elected" (CPM 1992d: 516).

Finally, the performance of the chief is constantly examined by the *consigliere*, who, according to the same mafia witness, "is the man responsible for controlling the head" (ibid.). In other words, it is his duty to supervise the management of the *cosca* activities and particularly of the monetary transactions carried out by the *rappresentante* and his men of trust. In the late 1980s, the San Cataldo family went so far as to establish a ledger, "in order to prevent the chief or the *capi decina* from pocketing more money than is their due" (ibid.: 516).

Violations and Degeneration

The principle of direct democracy has been endlessly violated throughout the history of Cosa Nostra. All democratic organizations tend to turn into oligarchies, as the "iron law" Robert Michels described in the early twentieth century shows ([1912] 1962). Changes of this type are particularly likely in the case of direct democracy, which is a very fragile type of dominion. Within the universe of Cosa Nostra, furthermore, its enforcement has been weakened by a permanent bias: the principle of selection by lot has never been adopted in the mafia consortium, though this is an essential condition for any stable form of direct democracy (see Weber 1978: 948–52).

Instead of this procedure, the *rappresentante* and *consigliere* are—following Cosa Nostra's normative code—chosen from among the most experienced and skillful of the associates. This policy, however, has in practice meant that the most important roles are entrusted to the same people for long periods of time. In other words, officeholders acquire further competencies, increase their social prestige, and consolidate their power position merely by exercising their functions. Moreover, they develop a personal interest in perpetuating their power positions in order to permanently exploit the privileges associated with them. As Max Weber put it, "Every type of immediate democracy has a tendency to shift to a form of government by notables" (ibid.: 291).

As a result of this trend, the ruling positions have in some mafia families been appropriated by the members of specific blood families and transmitted from father to son, to whom a sort of hereditary charisma is recognized. Hence, Stefano Bontade became chief of the important mafia family of Santa Maria del Gesù in Palermo at the age of twenty, replacing his father, don Paolino, who was ill with diabetes (TrPA 1984, I: 131). Likewise, Francesco Madonia inherited the leadership of the mafia family of Vallelunga Pratameno in the Caltanissetta province, when his father was shot in 1978 (TrPA [1985] 1992: 82). Thus, as foreseen by Weber, rule by notables—whom he also called *honorationes*, an expression very well suited to the mafia world—tends to transform itself into patriarchalism and the principle of direct democracy is factually set aside.

The principle of direct democracy is instead openly violated whenever a "man of honor" imposes his leadership through violence. This is by no means unusual: in Cosa Nostra's history there are many examples of *capimafia* replaced through gunfire. Such practice reflects the fact that in the mafia world all power is founded on the capacity to personally employ or command violence. In mafia families, the *honorationes*—mafia members who are most worthy of respect and are most likely to occupy ruling positions—are, in the final analysis, the most violent and shrewd.

Both these trends—the shift toward patriarchalism and the violent appropriation of ruling positions—lead to long periods in office by the same individuals. Likewise, the selective mechanism of yearly elections is de facto emptied of meaning and reduced to a mere ritual of legitimization. "When there is 'harmony' in a family," Francesco Marino Mannoia of the large Santa Maria del Gesù *cosca* stated, "all this is purely formal and elections take place almost always with common agreement" (TrPA 1989: 67; see also TrPA 1985, V: 878; Bonanno 1983: 147; Falcone 1993: 101–2).

While the two types of administration mentioned above both deviate from the principle of direct democracy, they differ substantially from each other in two key aspects: the modalities of legitimation and the relationship between the officeholders and the other group members. When the principles of government by *honorationes* and patriarchalism prevail, the exercise of power by the leader is largely constrained by tradition. Even in areas that are left to his discretion, the leader is supposed to rule in the interest of all members and is largely dependent on their willingness to comply with his orders, since he has no means to enforce them. As long as this philosophy prevails, as in the case of direct democracy, the members are still the chief's fellow members (*Genossen*), not his subjects (*Untertanen*) (Weber 1978: 226–32).

Differently, the violent appropriation of offices entails a departure from previous forms of administration and signals a move toward a patrimonial form of domination (ibid.): the *capofamiglia* no longer heads the family, as if it were *cosa nostra* (our thing)—the common possession of all the affiliates—but as if it were his own personal property. Having imposed his rule through violence, this type of Cosa Nostra boss tends to consider his office a personal right, to increase his own power, and to surround himself with a personal administrative staff, assigning all the other ruling positions to men that he trusts. The domination of the "patrimonial" mafia chief is at least formally still limited by tradition, but it is exercised by virtue of his personal autonomy. The role of the *consigliere*, originally aimed at counterbalancing the chief's power, loses its original importance and associates become subjects of the ruler.[5]

Though the transition is definitively continuous, "patrimonial" domination is typically distinguished from both direct democracy and elementary patriarchalism by the presence of a personal staff. It is a form of domination that gained the upper hand in Cosa Nostra in the last quarter of the twentieth century, even including some families in which the rule of inheritance had so far prevailed. Indeed, as numerous internal sources describe, in those years many family chiefs created a sort of independent and parallel administrative staff superseding the hierarchy of offices molded by Cosa Nostra tradition. The witness Francesco Marino Mannoia affirms that around 1975 he and some other affiliates of the *cosca* of Santa Maria del Gesù were directly dependent on its chief, Stefano Bontade, and responded only to his orders, without forming part of a *decina* (TrPA 1989). Furthermore, since the end of the 1970s the chiefs of the *mandamenti* (districts incorporating an average of three mafia families) have set up specialized military units, called *gruppi di fuoco* [hit squads], whose action is not supervised by the single family assemblies.

The trend toward the establishment of an administrative staff directly dependent on the chiefs was greatly furthered by the rise of the Corleonesi in the late 1970s. This was a coalition of mafia families headed by the chief of the Corleone *cosca*, Salvatore "Totò" Riina. In the early 1980s, the chiefs of the coalition revolving around this *cosca* started to gather around themselves "men of honor" whose ritual affiliation was accomplished in great secrecy and whose status was kept hidden from other members of the *cosca*, as well as from those belonging to other mafia families (see chapter 3).

With time, the mafia chiefs who directly command their own personnel can rid themselves of the constraints set by this tradition and operate following their own personal judgments and interests. Patrimonialism thus turns into a detraditionalized variant called "sultanism" by Max Weber and, subsequently, "personal rulership" by Günther Roth: this type of detraditionalized patrimonialism is personal rulership on the basis of loyalties that do not require any belief in the ruler's unique personal qualification, but are instead inextricably linked to material incentives and rewards (Weber 1978: 231–35; Roth [1968] 1971; see also Eisenstadt 1971). As was long the case with Totò Riina, the "sultanic" leader may have great power, but his legitimacy is precarious.

The very fact that all power rests on violence has, however, so far hindered the full institutionalization (and legitimation) of patrimonial forms of domination in Cosa Nostra. Violence, in fact, is a powerful factor against the consolidation of peaceful mechanisms for the transfer of power, such as the rule of inheritance or the right of the chief to choose his successor. Thus a chief may occupy all the administrative positions of a *cosca*, but his supremacy can be challenged at any moment, and whoever is stronger, shrewder, or in any way more able to form a powerful coalition of mafia adherents, can come to power.

At least in principle, violence is a resource open to everybody, which supports and perpetuates the presupposition of equality among the members of a mafia *cosca*. Even those with more powerful connections or greater economic power can be ousted by more violent members. In 1958, when Luciano Liggio murdered Michele Navarra, the undisputed chief of the Corleone mafia in the late 1940s and 1950s, he had no resource other than his physical strength and the support of a group of violent men. Liggio came from a family of humble peasants and had for several years been a simple "soldier" of the Corleone *cosca* and one of Navarrra's protégés. Navarra was instead a doctor, occupied several key positions within the Corleone establishment, had powerful political connections, and enjoyed a remarkably high level of prestige (CPMS 1971: 65–130). Likewise, less than twenty years later, Liggio's successor, Salvatore Riina, and his rural allies—the *viddani* [peasants], as they were contemptuously called by their Palermitan rivals—succeeded in ousting the city leadership, although the latter initially had a formidable advantage in terms of economic, social, and political resources (see Bolzoni and D'Avanzo 1993).

Violence is thus linked in a contradictory relationship to the principle of direct democracy. On the one hand, by favoring the rise of shrewd military chiefs, it fosters the most glaring violations of its prescriptions. On the other, by blocking the consolidation of peaceful mechanisms of power transfer, it prevents its definitive abandonment and reinforces the feeling of equality among associates.[6]

The 'Ndrangheta Families: Ranks and Power Positions

Contrary to the beliefs held until the end of the 1980s, the importance of blood ties in 'Ndrangheta mafia families does not mean that the mafia families correspond merely to the kin of their most powerful associates. In reality, the 'Ndrangheta *locali* (as mafia families are often called in Calabria) have developed a complex system of ranks and power positions that clearly differentiates them from the biological families of their members.[7]

This system of ranks and power positions was developed in response to the fundamental need to protect the center of the association from repressive state action. In this respect, it is the horizontal structure of Cosa Nostra families that should be considered an anomaly. In other words, the traditional organization of Sicilian mafia families, with no internal stratification and (formal) subscription to direct democracy, has survived for as long as it has thanks only to the limited number of affiliates and strength of the boundaries created by fraternization contracts (see chapter 2). These boundaries categorically separate the society of "men of honor" from the world of noninitiates.

On the contrary, in the 'Ndrangheta, which has historically enforced a much lower degree of secrecy than its Sicilian counterpart, the lowest ranking affiliates form a sort of buffer region between the core of the higher ranking members and the external world. Their "formal separation" (Simmel 1950) has already been effected, since the novices swear a solemn promise of faithfulness and secrecy. However, their access to important information, that is, their "material separation" (ibid.), takes place only gradually: new members are trained into the practice of secrecy and, in case of any leaks, there is not much they can reveal. The *pentiti* are very much aware that the function of a hierarchy of ranks is to protect the center. "The 'Ndrangheta," says Calogero Marcenò, a former high-ranking member of the Milan Mazzaferro clan, "is a very segmented criminal organization and the affiliates with an inferior *dote* [rank] do not know anything, if not very vaguely,

> **SOCIETÀ MAGGIORE**
>
> associazione o società
> trequartino o quintino
> vangelista
> santista
> camorrista di sgarro
> camorrista

> **SOCIETÀ MINORE**
>
> picciotto sgarrista
> picciotto liscio

FIGURE 1.1. The ranks of a family belonging to the 'Ndrangheta. *Source*: Mafia witnesses' statements in several proceedings issued by the Reggio Calabria and Milan courts throughout the 1990s (TrMI 1993, 1994a, 1994e; PrRC 1995; TrRC 1999).

about the level superior to the one they belong to" (TrMI 1994e: 159; see also TrRC 1993b).

The weakening of group cohesion produced by these strong levels of stratification is counterbalanced by the grouping of the members coming from the lower and higher ranks respectively. Within these two subunits, the *'ndranghetisti* experience community life with their peers. As Gaetano Costa puts it, "the 'Ndrangheta is organized into societies, one above the other, starting from the *società minori* [minor societies] of the *picciotti* and *camorristi* up to the *società maggiori* [major societies] of *sgarro, santa, vangelo*, and *trequartino*" (PrRC 1995: 4986).

The two lowest ranks in a family belonging to the 'Ndrangheta are those of *picciotto liscio* and *picciotto di sgarro*. The first is the name given to new members when they are initiated; members are allowed into the second rank through another ritual ceremony only after at least six months of mafia membership. According to most sources, members from these two ranks constitute what are known as *società minori* (PrRC 1995: 5720–21; but see, contra, TrMI 1994e: 150–52) (see figure 1.1).

The *picciotti* called *sgarristi* can be appointed to various ruling positions in the *società minore*, which include the *capo giovane* [young chief], *picciotto di giornata* [day boy] and *puntaiolo* [knife expert]. The "young chief" rules over the lower section of the *locale* and maintains contact with members of the *società maggiore*, enforcing its orders. The *picciotto di giornata* distributes duties among the *picciotti* and coordinates

FIGURE 1.2. The ruling offices of a family belonging to the 'Ndrangheta. *Source*: Mafia witnesses' statements in several proceedings issued by the Reggio Calabria and Milan courts throughout the 1990s (TrMI 1993, 1994a, 1994e; PrRC 1995; TrRC 1999).

their actions. Lastly, the *puntaiolo* is in charge of the *bacinella*, the fund to which all members of the *società minore* contribute (see figure 1.2).

Originally, the 'Ndrangheta's hierarchy comprised only two other ranks: those of *camorrista* and *sgarrista*. Since the 1970s, however, the new ranks of *santista*, *vangelo*, *trequartino* or *quintino*, and *associazione* have been added. All members with at least the rank of *camorrista* form the *società maggiore*. Like its lower counterpart, the *società maggiore* has its own ruling positions, voted on through yearly elections (TrMI 1994e: 155ff). These offices are those of *mastro di giornata* [day master], *contabile* [accountant], *mastro di buon ordine* [good order master], *capo società* [chief of the society] and/or *capo locale* [family chief].

The task of the first office, otherwise known as *crimine* (PrRC 1995: 5739), is to transmit the orders of the *società maggiore* to the chief of the *minore*, and more generally the *mastro di giornata* carries out functions similar to those of the *picciotto di giornata* in the lower group. In a code found by police forces in the 1960s, his duties are listed in the following way: "To observe what happens in the area of influence, to welcome the affiliates of other villages, to understand the reasons for their visit, to follow the movements of police forces, to warn the chief when crimes are carried out, to protect, if ordered to do so, whosoever carries out crimes authorized by the organization and to ensure him a refuge" (Malafarina 1986: 81).

The position of *contabile* corresponds to that of *puntaiolo* in the *società minore*, since the *camorrista* holding this office manages the common fund (*cassa comune*, or *bacinella* in the 'Ndrangheta slang). The *mastro di buon ordine* instead has no corresponding position in the *società minore*: the *'ndranghetista* fulfilling this role is a kind of "peace judge," settling any disputes that break out among the affiliates. Lastly, the *capo locale* is the group leader; he is aided by the *capo di società*, who replaces him when necessary, and he is entrusted with the custody of the arms belonging to the group. According to other sources, however, these two ruling positions often overlap and the chief of the family is also called *capo di società* (PrRC 1995: 5739; TrMI 1994e: 153–57, 163).

As in Cosa Nostra, the 'Ndrangheta's internal organization has remained relatively stable over time. Contemporary *pentiti*'s accounts are surprisingly similar to the descriptions found in several police and judicial documents dating back to the late nineteenth century. In a report written on September 4, 1896, for example, the *brigadiere* Antonio Boarzi, chief of the Carabinieri station in Seminara, states as follows: "The society is composed of a *capobastone* [chief], a *contabile* [accountant], the *camorristi*, and a *camorrista di giornata*, a *capo giovane* [young chief], the *picciotti di sgarro*, and a *picciotto di giornata*. The first, the *camorristi*, are called *Compagnia della Maggiore* [major community], the others, the *picciotti*, *Compagnia della Minore* [minor community]" (Malafarina 1983: 218).[8]

From Patriarchalism to Patrimonialism

The 'Ndrangheta's ruling offices are not set up as part of the chief's personal administrative staff, nor is the chief supposed to distribute these offices among his most trusted aides. Although the principle of direct democracy does not have the same predominance in Calabria as in Sicily, even in this case we are prescriptively—if not always factually—dealing with the most elementary forms of traditional domination, in which the officeholders are supposed to act only according to the will of the group members as a whole, in their interest and by virtue of the authority that the latter have entrusted them.

Significantly, chiefs of Calabrian mafia families come to power either through their membership in a traditionally ruling blood family, a typical characteristic of patriarchalism, or as a result of their own military or political merits: this is typical of what Weber called administration by notables or *honorationes* (1978: 290–92). Since the 1970s, for example, Domenico Libri, the oldest of the brothers heading the blood family of the same name, has led the Libri *cosca*. Contemporaneously, Giuseppe Piromalli, the eldest of his blood kin, has ruled the most powerful mafia group in the Gioia Tauro plain over the last thirty years. He inherited this position from his eldest brother Girolamo "Mommo," who died of natural causes in 1979 (Silvestri 1999). Ruling positions are not assigned only according to seniority, however—the candidate has to demonstrate his military and political worth. Hence, for instance, it was the shrewd and violent Pietro Labate who took over leadership of the homonymous *locale* ruling the Gebbione district of Reggio Calabria from his father, rather than his older but less skillful brother Paolo (TrRC 1994a).

No matter what the selection procedures are, the leader of a family belonging to the 'Ndrangheta is supposed to rule in the name and the interests of the whole mafia community. "Every chief [has] . . . decision of life and death over his men" (PrRC 1995: 4427), and has the right to expect absolute obedience. However, his power is constrained by tradition and his authority derives from the respect of tradition. Thus, lacking a personal staff of patrimonial type, he is still largely dependant upon the willingness of the *cosca* members to comply with his orders. On this point, the Calabrian *pentiti* are unanimous: within both the *società minore* and the *maggiore* the offices are assigned through annual elections and, according to some, any affiliate may ask for the renewal of all the ruling positions inside the group at any moment of the year. In this case, both the *capo giovane* and the *capo locale* are obliged to "declare that from then on everybody is on the same level and we proceed to the election of the new offices" (TrMI 1994e: 153). The only obligation on the proponent at this point is providing a lunch for all the family members. Theoretically then, as in the Sicilian Cosa Nostra, members of the Calabrian mafia are viewed as fellow members of the family chief, and not as subjects. However, even in Calabria, there is a constant drift toward a patrimonial type of administration of these groups. Single individuals or blood families often succeed in indefinitely appropriating power over the group and tend to assign offices either to kinsmen or to trusted aides. Hence, elections are more of a ritual to legitimate choices that have already been made autonomously by the ruler and the mafiosi holding ruling offices end up serving as the latter's personal staff.

As in Sicily, furthermore, changes in leadership frequently take place through violence, as in the succession of mafia leaders in the city of Reggio Calabria. Domenico Tripodo ousted the old Reggio *capobastone*, Domenico Strati, following a conflict lasting for two years (1958–59) (Gambino 1977). His dominion over the Reggio Calabria 'Ndrangheta lasted until the early 1970s, when the De Stefano brothers challenged him. The De Stefanos were members of Tripodo's *cosca* who had acquired considerable financial resources through tobacco smuggling and had secured the support of the other major 'Ndrangheta chiefs in the province. Within two years (1974–76) they moved from being simple mafia members to being the new "lords" of Reggio Calabria. Their rise is described in great detail by the *pentito* Giacomo Lauro, who held several important positions in the Reggio Calabria mafia:

> In 1970 . . . the De Stefanos . . . were nobody, they were nobody. The De Stefano brothers became the owners of Reggio Calabria after the war, the first mafia war. In the city center of Reggio Calabria, Cicco Canale *"u gnuri"*

ruled—I do not want to swear, but who the fuck were the De Stefanos in the 1970s? They had killed a certain Sergi for four oxen, for a fraud of four oxen in Modena. . . . These were the De Stefanos. They committed petty fraud for four cows, . . . then with cigarettes and . . . the other clans' friendship and money in their hands, they armed themselves for war. (PrRC 1995: 4832–35; see also Barone 1989–90)

As in the Sicilian mafia association, however, the frequent resort to violence to acheive power in a family has prevented the institutionalization of a patrimonial type of administration and the development of a consistent ideology of legitimation.

THE INSTITUTIONALIZATION OF SUPERORDINATE BODIES OF COORDINATION

In both Cosa Nostra and the 'Ndrangheta, the ruling bodies have been most institutionalized at the level of single families. Their competencies are well defined, their powers are recognized as legitimate by members, and the "men of honor" occupying these positions usually have sufficient means to make their orders respected.

Indeed, for many years the power apparatuses of the single families were the sole ruling bodies within the two associations. Only in the late 1950s, in fact, did Cosa Nostra families in the Palermo province create a superordinate body of coordination: the so-called provincial commission. A regional commission covering all of Sicily (made up of representatives of the six Sicilian provinces where Cosa Nostra had settlements) was also set up in the mid-1970s, whereas in the 'Ndrangheta an analogous process of centralization started only in the early 1990s.

Unity and Segmentation

Despite the recent creation of coordinating bodies, there has long been a sense of unity between the single families, a feeling that they formed part of a larger group. All the former mafia members now collaborating with the judiciary have unanimously underlined this. Although they recall the greater autonomy enjoyed by single mafia families before the establishment of superior bodies of coordination, they emphasize the idea that each family belongs to a larger whole; indeed, they take it virtually for granted. "Substantially," Francesco Marino Mannoia states, "Cosa Nostra, as the phrase itself states, is a single and unitary organization. . . . I am therefore staggered by reading in newspapers that there is somebody who still doubts this elementary truth that each of us learns the moment he enters the organization" (TrPA 1989: 63).

What is it that has enabled the roughly one hundred mafia families belonging respectively to Cosa Nostra and the 'Ndrangheta to perceive themselves as small parts of larger groups? Why were their members certain of this unity, even before unitary ruling bodies were created? To answer these questions, it is useful to borrow a concept from anthropology. This is because, since the times of Sir Henry Maine, anthropologists have also had to deal with a large number of primitive societies lacking centralized ruling bodies. Initially defined as "stateless" or "acephalous societies" (Fortes and Evans-Pritchard 1940), they were subsequently fully recognized as unitary social, cultural, and political entities, despite their lack of central political organs. The unifying feature here is the overt recognition by all the groups of other similar and associated groups; in this sense societal boundaries coincide with the maximum range of structurally homologous units recognized by the others (Smith 1974: 98). These federations are called "segmentary societies," clearly an appropriate term for describing the two mafia associations examined here.

As in numerous traditional societies, even in Cosa Nostra and the 'Ndrangheta the extensive replication of corporate forms provides systemic unity to what may seem a mere aggregation of distinct entities. Even before the creation of the superordinate bodies of coordination, the boundaries of the two associations were defined by institutional similarities, including parallel features in the organizational model, culture, and normative rules. Cosa Nostra and the 'Ndrangheta are hence united by what Emile Durkheim called "mechanic solidarity": typical of the premodern world, it is a solidarity deriving "from likeness, since the society is formed of similar segments and these in their turn enclose only homogenous elements" (1964: 176–77).

The Commission for the Palermo Province

Until the end of the 1950s coordination inside the Sicilian Cosa Nostra was ensured by informal meetings among the most influential members of the most powerful families. The *pentiti* recall that in each administrative district (*provincia*) a member was given the largely honorific title of "provincial representative" and was placed in charge of defending local interests in the larger gatherings. On this matter, in 1937 Melchiorre Allegra, a physician in Castelvetrano (in the province of Trapani) who was also a member of the local mafia family, claimed: "The different provinces were usually reciprocally independent in the sense that relations between them were maintained by the various *capi provincia*. These established a substantial, but informal, link that—through their meetings—bound the various groups together in all the provinces" (De Mauro 1962a). The power asserted by these assemblies of mafia chiefs can thus be described as "sporadic" (Popitz 1990: 44–46). In fact, they met rarely, were allowed to take decisions exclusively as delegates of the single *cosche*, and were completely dependent upon the latter to enforce their decisions, because they did not have an independent administrative staff.

In 1957, however, according to Tommaso Buscetta, the American mafia boss Joe Bonanno suggested that the families of the Palermo province establish a commission based on the analogous body set up by the American Cosa Nostra at the beginning of the 1930s. According to Buscetta, who was actively involved in this phase, and to several other mafia witnesses who refer to these events from hearsay, the chiefs of the Palermo province thus formalized these occasional meetings into a permanent, collegial body—the provincial commission—to which specific competencies were entrusted.

Several important innovations were put forward to revise the American model.[9] First of all, in order to limit the number of the commission members and to speed up its decision making, intermediate-level districts were created, called *mandamenti* (literally, districts), each of which represented the territory of three or four neighboring families having the right to elect its own representative (called the *capo mandamento*). According to the *pentiti*, the families of the Palermo province were grouped into about fifteen *mandamenti* throughout the 1980s and early 1990s.[10]

Furthermore, in compliance with the principle of direct democracy, Gaetano Badalamenti, Salvatore Greco, and Buscetta himself proposed a specific rule to avoid the excessive concentration of power in the hands of few individuals. It was therefore decided that only the "men of honor" holding no ruling office inside their own family—that is, the simple "soldiers"—could be elected as members of the provincial commission. Along similar lines, it was agreed that the provincial commission would have not a chief but only a secretary, whose "duty," Buscetta recalls, "was to send out invitations for the meetings" (TrPA 1984, II: 90; see also more generally Arlacchi 1994: 60–74; TrPA 1985, V: 813ff.). Neither of these two clauses of democracy, which were aimed at preventing the rise of an oligarchic or monocratic leadership, was respected for long. The first proposal was immediately dropped due to the opposition of some *capifamiglia* who threatened to veto the establishment of the new body. The second measure, though strenuously defended by some "men of honor," was abandoned with the rise of the Corleonesi, an alliance of mafia families grouped around the Corleone *cosca* headed by Totò Riina, which from the early 1980s on progressively occupied all the most important power positions within Cosa Nostra.

The provincial commission originally had two main competencies. The first belonged to the judicial sphere: as we will see in chapter 3, the provincial body was called to settle conflicts among the families and single members and to prosecute the most serious violations of the mafia normative code. Second, the commission was entrusted with the regulation of the use of violence.

From its inception, the commission was given exclusive authority to order the murder of police officials, prosecutors and judges, politicians, journalists, and lawyers, because these killings could provoke retaliation by law enforcement and thus damage the whole mafia community. To limit internal conflicts, furthermore, it was agreed that each family chief had to ask the commission's authorization before killing any members belonging to another *cosca*, while they were initially left with the power to decide independently on the elimination of their own group members. In 1977, however, the compulsory preventive deliberation of the commission on all the murders of "men of honor" became the rule (PrPA 1993a: 45–46, 1993c: 66–69; TrPA 1985, V: 902–6).

Until the early 1980s the commission's competencies were often disregarded. Due to its collegial constitution and to the wide autonomy left to the family chiefs, the new institution was unable to prevent or regulate conflicts at the societal level. "Collegiality," as Weber pointed out, "almost inevitably involves obstacles to precise, clear, and above all, rapid decisions" (1978: 277). Before the early 1980s, moreover, the commission had no autonomous administrative staff and had to rely on the *capi mandamento* and, below them, on the single *capifamiglia* to enforce its rulings.

Beginning in the late 1970s, however, the assembly was increasingly occupied by the Corleonesi coalition during what has been inappropriately called the second mafia war. Thanks to a shrewd manipulation of Cosa Nostra's rules and the elimination of its most powerful rivals, the coalition led by Totò Riina was able to appropriate virtually all the positions of commissioner (*capo mandamento*). The wing headed by Gaetano Badalamenti and Stefano Bontade, which defended the existing balance of power between the single mafia families and the commission, was overwhelmed, losing any power to strike back. Between 1981 and 1982 more than two hundred mafiosi were killed in the Palermo province. To these a considerable number of "disappearances" must be added, as many "men of honor" were eliminated without leaving any trace, victims of the *lupara bianca* method (PrPA 1993a: 141–228).[11] During the same period, similar murders also took place in the other Cosa Nostra districts, where Corleonesi's allies ruthlessly killed all the most prestigious leaders of the losing wing.

Besides using violence, Totò Riina also imposed his supremacy by shrewdly exploiting a competence specific to the commission, foreseen to solve only the most serious intrafamily conflicts and up to that point used only very rarely: the power to suspend the leaders of a family and to name a *reggente*, a temporary chief (TrPA 1985, V: 811, 876). As Leonardo Messina recalls, the Corleonesi "subverted the democratic criteria of the nomination of chiefs, by putting their men in all the key positions and at all levels" (PrPA 1992: 257, 50). With behavior typical of a "sultanic" leader, Riina went as far as to change the traditional territorial divisions among Palermitan mafia families and to create a new and large *mandamento* in order to give one of his protégés, Raffaele Ganci, chief of the Noce family, a position inside the commission (PrPA 1993a: 65–66). As a result, from the mid-1980s on all

TABLE 1.3. Rate of mafia murders reported in the Palermo province out of the regional total, 1983–1997

	Palermo 1	Sicily 2	Palermo's rate %
1983	36	61	59.0
1984	17	34	50.0
1985	14	28	50.0
1986	12	59	20.3
1987	14	63	22.2
1988	34	93	36.6
1989	45	160	28.1
1990	13	150	8.7
1991	32	253	12.6
1992	28	200	14.0
1993	5	85	5.9
1994	17	90	18.9
1995	22	88	25.0
1996	10	66	15.2
1997	5	32	15.6

Source: Elaboration on ISTAT data

the commissioners and their substitutes were direct representatives of the Corleonesi coalition.

Representing a single coalition, the commission became more efficient in controlling internal conflicts, as is clearly shown by the statistics concerning mafia murders (see table 1.3). In the early 1980s, the province of Palermo, which accounts for about 25 percent of the island's population, had a murder rate almost two times higher than the rest of Sicily, registering more than half of all the murders committed in Sicily. From 1986 on, however, the trend inverted sharply and, except for 1988 and 1989, the murder rate for Palermo has constantly been lower than the population rate. In 1993 it was as low as 5.9 percent out of the regional total.

At the same time, however, the provincial assembly lost its decisional autonomy and became a mere enforcement body for decisions made in the meetings held by Totò Riina and his closest group of allies. "With the power gained by the Corleonesi and their allies," Buscetta states, "the traditional organizational structures had a purely formal value . . . the decisions were taken before . . . and the commission was nothing but the faithful executor of orders" (TrPA 1984, I: 98–99, 31; II: 12). Another witness, himself a member of the superordinate body as chief of the Porta Nuova *mandamento*, revealed that "usually Riina . . . did not call the whole commission in the same place, but in separate groups, in different places" (PrPA 1995b, III: 47). According to several recent disclosures, indeed, even the decision to kill Judge Giovanni Falcone, the "supreme" enemy of the Cosa Nostra, was taken autonomously by Salvatore Riina and his adviser Bernardo Provenzano and only later communicated to all the other commissioners (TrCL 1994a: 74–75; see Bianconi and Savatteri 1998).

Coordination Mechanisms in Other Sicilian Provinces and at the Regional Level

The creation of the commission for the province of Palermo entailed a strengthening of the superordinate coordinating mechanisms in the island as a whole. Though some Palermitan *pentiti* mention the existence of analogous collegial bodies in all the Sicilian provinces where Cosa Nostra is active (TrPA 1985, V: 813), according to local sources coordination among the single mafia families is still ensured by "provincial representatives," who are chosen from the most influential chiefs of the area and helped by one or several *consiglieri* (CPM 1992c: 517; PrPA 1993c: 63; Ministero dell'Interno 2001e: 11–14).

Even in the province of Trapani, one of the traditional strongholds of the Cosa Nostra, a body comparable to the Palermitan commission was not set up. Until 1986 this province was represented in the regional arena by a *rappresentante* elected by the leaders of the five *mandamenti* (Trapani, Castelvetrano, Alcamo, Marsala, and Mazara del Vallo) formed by the seventeen families active in the district. This position was held successively by the chiefs of the most powerful and prestigious district units in this area, first the Minore from Trapani and then the Rimi from Alcamo. Until his death in 1975, the office was later entrusted to Vincenzo Rimi, famous throughout Sicily for his charisma and wisdom, and he held it until his death in 1975. His successor, Totò Minore, was *rappresentante provinciale* until 1983, when he was killed, presumably by the Corleonesi. Only after the death of Girolamo Marino, chief of the Paceco family and provincial *rappresentante* for about three years, was a collegial body of coordination established. This was not a commission, however, but a triumvirate composed of Vincenzo Virga, the chief of the Trapani family who was arrested in March 2001, Francesco Messina Denaro from Castelvetrano (later replaced by his son) and, until 1992, the year of his elimination, Vincenzo Milazzo, *capomafia* in Alcamo (TrPA 1994a; see also CSM 2001: 16–17 and Ministero dell'Interno 2001e: 11).

The model provided by the Palermitan provincial commission was instead followed in a more consistent way at the regional level. Proposed by Pippo Calderone, who was then head of the Catania family, a regional commission, also called *regione* or interprovincial commission, was created in the mid-1970s. The *regione* gathered the representatives of the six Cosa Nostra provinces (thus excluding Messina, Siracusa, and Ragusa, where the Cosa Nostra has no branches). Calderone's goal was to set up a forum in which to discuss and peacefully settle disputes among the families from different provinces and to plan the most important economic and military activities (CPM 1992a: 279–80; TrMA 1987: 4–8; PrPA 1992: 253–55).

The regional body followed the same destiny as its provincial predecessor, however. The precautionary measures taken to hinder the emergence of a single individual or territorial center were progressively circumvented or openly ignored. For example, the chief of the commission was originally supposed to be only a primus inter pares and was hence named "secretary." Nonetheless, Michele Greco, the first secretary of the commission and a pawn of Riina's, soon managed to take on a leading role in it. Thanks to Riina's support, he used his position to set up an independent administrative staff by selecting a group of affiliates who were directly dependent on him from different Palermo families. "In this way," as Antonino Calderone, a mafia defector and the brother of the proponent of the regional commission, recalls, "he more or less built an army for his own use" (TrMA 1987: 44; Arlacchi 1993: 130).

Even the measures aimed at removing the new body from the suffocating influence of the Palermo commission remained moot: it was originally established that the interprovincial commission would meet once a month in different provinces. However, after only a short time a permanent seat was established in the Favarella, Greco's estate on the outskirts of Palermo, and the commission continued to meet there until Greco's arrest in 1986.

The Corleonesi managed to fill all the positions on the regional commission beginning in the early 1980s. From then on, in fact, its members were no longer freely selected by the *capimafia* of the single provinces, but were chosen on the basis of their alliances with the ruling elite.[12] Furthermore, as had happened at the provincial level, the collegial principle was gradually emptied of any meaning. Over the years, the *regione* was exclusively called to legitimize decisions that had already been taken in more restricted and informal circles (PrPA 1992: 217; TrPA 1984, II: 12).

This weakening of collegiality and the progressive rise of a monocratic leadership did not hamper the (limited) efficiency of the two commissions. On the contrary, during Riina's quasi-dictatorship both assemblies progressively acquired further competencies in addition to the judicial functions and regulation of the use of violence originally entrusted to them. An increase in the scope of power is, in fact, a typical side effect of the process of institutionalization and integration of power positions (Popitz 1990). Over the years, Cosa Nostra's two superordinate bodies became increasingly involved in the management of the economic and political resources of the whole association, consistently contributing to the maximization of their exploitation. As Buscetta put it, "the commission was originally established in order to settle the contrasts among the members of various families and their respective chiefs; later on, its function was extended so that it regulated and coordinated the activities of the families of a province" (TrPA 1984, I: 22).

Even though the members' entrepreneurial autonomy remained extensive, the existence of the two coordinating bodies facilitated the pooling of capital and the joint exploitation of channels and contacts in order to make investments in both licit and illicit markets (see chapter 4). This turned out to be particularly advantageous throughout the 1970s and early 1980s, when the economic resources of the Cosa Nostra affiliates were limited and the Palermo provincial commission allowed several families and "men of honor" to become financially involved in wholesale drug trafficking. Into the early 1990s the two coordination bodies occasionally pooled money from different mafia families to finance the largest business deals (PrPA 1992: 212).

Moreover, halfway through the 1970s the provincial commission was entrusted with the regulation of tobacco smuggling, in which all the main Palermitan mafia families were then involved. The action of the commission was twofold. First, it forced the biggest smugglers—such as Palermitans Tommaso Spadaro and Nunzio La Mattina and Neapolitan Michele Zaza—to enter the Cosa Nostra "in order to make them more compliant with its wishes." Second, it imposed shifts for the landing of cigarette boxes from the ships stopping in Tyrrhenian waters: "A ship was unloaded for the Commission [which then was distributed among different families of the island], one for Calò and his associates, one for La Mattina and associates, and a fourth for the Neapolitans (Zaza and associates)" (TrPA [1985] 1992: 91; see also 1989: 71).

The centralization process initiated by the creation of the two commissions was also exploited by Riina to gain direct control over the economic and political resources of the single families and to maximize their exploitation. In particular, during the Corleonesi dictatorship, Cosa Nostra succeeded in influencing the adjudicating of public work contracts over a large area of Sicily, reaching high-level agreements with politicians and national building companies. This contrasted with past behavior, when the single mafia families had been content to request a "protection tax" from the companies winning a public contract on their territory (TrPA 1991, 1993b, 1998; see chapter 4). Most probably, not even the terrorist attacks carried out by Cosa Nostra in 1992 and 1993 would have possible had there not been a central body of coordination capable of exploiting the human and military resources of the whole organization and the web of connections held by Cosa Nostra in mainland Italy.

From the *Crimine* to Cosa Nuova

Unlike Cosa Nostra, the 'Ndrangheta managed to maintain a horizontal organizational structure up to the early 1990s, avoiding the establishment of a formal superordinate body. Information recently disclosed by several mafia witnesses has, however, undermined the myth of the absolute autonomy and self-sufficiency of Calabrian mafia families, which was believed by social scientists for many years.

Despite the lack of a permanent superordinate body, in reality the 'Ndrangheta *cosche* created stable mechanisms for coordination and dispute settlement as early as the end of the nineteenth century, as criminal cases of the time show (Ciconte 1992: 9–33, 118–27; Nicaso 1990). Contacts and meetings among the chiefs of single mafia units were frequent. At least since the 1950s, but probably even earlier, the chiefs of the 'Ndrangheta *locali* have met regularly near the Sanctuary of Our Lady of Polsi in the Aspromonte region during the September Feast. In 1969 the police raided a meeting near the sanctuary, in the Montalto locality, and captured more than seventy *'ndranghetisti*, while some others managed to escape. However, the importance of this meeting was underestimated for a long time by many observers given their view of the mafia as a disorganized phenomenon (PrRC 1995: 276–80; Malafarina 1986: 37; Ciconte 1992: 318–20).

These annual meetings, known as *crimine*, have traditionally served as a forum to discuss future strategies and settle disputes among the *locali*. "On these occasions," according to Calogero Marcenò, one of the many *pentiti* who have described them, "the strategies of the organizations are decided, we plan possible kidnappings, and we discuss trade and eventual conflicts among groups" (PrRC 1995: 4447). Moreover, the assembly exercises weak supervisory powers over the activities of all mafia groups. As another witness, Cesare Polifroni, explained, "all the villages are called one after the other before the *crimine* and every *capo società* must give account of all the activities carried out during the year and of all the most important facts taking place in his territory such as kidnappings, homicides, etc. He must also communicate the number of new affiliates and the eventual punishment given to transgressors" (ibid.: 5024–25).

These meetings can be seen as a typical case of "merger collegiality" of independent units (Weber 1978: 276), where mechanisms are envisaged in order to prevent the development of permanent power imbalances. In the case of the 'Ndrangheta, a strong emphasis was placed on the temporary nature of the position of *crimine* chief, where a new representative was to be elected at each meeting. "The *capo crimine*," Zagari remarks, "does not hold office permanently, but is elected only when several *cosche* and *capi di società* meet; . . . once the meeting of the *crimine* is ended, the *capo crimine* loses his absolute power and goes back to the role and rank that he had before being nominated" (TrMI 1994a: 122–24).

However, as in Cosa Nostra and the single Calabrian mafia families, the principles of equality and collegiality have over time been progressively weakened by the emergence of forms of personal or group rulership, while the selective mechanism of elections has been largely reduced to a mere operation of legitimation. Though "every *santista* may be elected chief," the defector Albanese points out, "the stronger group usually holds this office" (PrRC 1995: 5741). For example, from the beginning of the 1960s until the outbreak of the first mafia war in 1974, the position of *capo crimine* was held by Antonio Macrì from Siderno. Domenico Tripodo, *dominus* of the city of Reggio Calabria and the surrounding areas, Girolamo "Mommo" Piromalli, chief of the most powerful *cosca* on the Tyrrhenian coast, and Macrì formed a sort of triumvirate, whose senior position was recognized by all the other family chiefs and whose advice was in most cases followed without protest (ibid.: 276–94). Since the mid-1970s, according to several *pentiti*, members of the Nirta family from San Luca and the Piromalli from Gioia Tauro have rotated among themselves the position of *capo crimine* (PrRC 1995: 5024).

In contrast to the Sicilian case, however, neither the collegial bodies nor their chiefs managed to preserve any precise spheres of competencies for themselves or to develop an administrative staff of their own with which to implement their decisions and punish any disobedience. Hence, up to the early 1990s both the *crimine* and its charismatic leaders depended on the consensus and cooperation of the most influential mafia members and relied on the good will of single *capifamiglia* to have their orders obeyed. For example, though Antonio Macrì opposed kidnappings and drug trafficking, these activities were carried out by several *cosche* of Platì, San Luca, and the Gioia Tauro plain, and Macrì had no means by which to prevent or punish these violations of the traditional mafia code. Indeed, he may have paid for his opposition with his life, as his murder in 1974 was presumably organized by the supporters of economic modernization.

The *crimine*'s most serious weakness, however, consisted in its incapacity to pacify conflicts between mafia families and to control the level of mafia violence. The assembly of the chiefs had no authority to intervene either in family feuds or in other armed conflicts, which were considered the exclusive competence of the single mafia units. As a result, the Reggio Calabria province has traditionally been characterized by an extremely high rate of violence and murder, much higher than any other Italian area.

The peak of this was reached during the so-called second mafia war, which lasted from November 1985 until 1991 and involved the struggle between two coalitions of Reggio Calabria mafia families, headed respectively by the De Stefanos and the Imerti-Condellos. In that period, 1,038 murders were reported in the province of Reggio Calabria, more than half of which (564) were certainly attributable to mafia conflicts. During those six years, even though accounting for only 3.6 percent of the Italian population, the Calabria region had a share of 16.4 percent of the murders that occurred in the whole of Italy. This gap is even more striking if the province of Reggio Calabria is considered alone. Although this province hosts roughly 1 percent of the total Italian population, the murders reported in Reggio Calabria represented 11 percent of the national total (table 1.4).

The necessity to regulate the use of violence seems to have been the main rea-

TABLE 1.4. Murders and mafia murders reported in the Reggio Calabria province, 1985–1991

	1985	1986	1987	1988	1989	1990	1991
Murders	82	107	126	161	158	213	191
Rate per 100,000 inhabitants	13.9	18.1	21.3	27.2	26.7	36	33.9
Mafia murders	15	48	50	88	111	110	142
Rate per 100,000 inhabitants	2.5	8.1	8.5	14.9	18.8	18.6	25.2

Source: ISTAT and CED, Ministero dell'Interno, various years

son for establishing a permanent higher commission in 1991 during the long negotiations to end the second mafia war. It was to be endowed with well-defined powers in the settlement of disputes and empowered to make peace agreements between two or more contending units. The powerful 'Ndrangheta chiefs in the Gioia Tauro plain and on the Aspromonte mountain played the role of arbiters during these negotiations, together with representatives of the Australian and Canadian settlements (PrRC 1995: 4461–74; TrRC 1993b). The Sicilian Cosa Nostra also contributed substantially to ending the infighting and to the subsequent setting-up of a superordinate body. In all likelihood the Cosa Nostra suggested the creation of a body similar to the Palermo provincial commission. Indeed, according to Pasquale Barreca, a former member of the De Stefano wing, "the role of Cosa Nostra was decisive for the conclusion of the war" (PrRC 1995: 5067).[13]

The idea of a centralized planning and decision-making locus was also fostered by the previous, more limited experiences of coordination, which had involved groups of Calabrian mafia families and had been necessary for either military or economic reasons. During the first and, to an even greater extent, second mafia war between the Reggio Calabria mafia families, groups had to learn to take coordinated action and entrust some of their autonomy to a supreme military chief (TrRC 1993b: 44–50). Increased involvement in economic activities also contributed to undermining the autonomy of the single families. As several investigations have proved, coordination came to be a necessary condition for the management of kidnappings and the purchase of large quantities of drugs (PrRC 1993b; see chapter 4).

Despite these prior experiences, the creation of a collegial body modeled on the Cosa Nostra provincial commission constituted a considerable innovation in the history of the Calabrian mafia association. The new institution, as Pasquale Barreca points out, had "the authority of a true hierarchical superordinate power" (PrRC 1995: 4476) with exclusive competence over some specific issues. According to Gaetano Costa, the change was also marked by the adoption of a new name for the whole association. Following the Sicilian example, the 'Ndrangheta is now called the Cosa Nuova, the new thing (ibid.: 4452–53; but this piece of information has not been confirmed by other sources). Called *camera di controllo* [control chamber], *camera di canalizzazione* [canalization chamber], or more simply "province" in mafia slang, the new collegial body is composed of three lower collegial bodies, significantly known (as in Sicily) as *mandamenti*. The Ionic and Tyrrhenian bodies respectively gather the most important chiefs of the mafia families on the Ionic and the Tyrrhenian sides of Calabria. In a third "central" *mandamento* the families of the city of Reggio Calabria are included (ibid.: 4469; see also CPM 2000a: 97–101; Ministero dell'Interno 2001e: 21, 2001a: 101–2).

The collegial body's primary function is the settlement of family disputes. According to the new dispositions, in fact, any controversy between the *cosche* must be submitted to the attention of the collegial body before violence can be used, whereas smaller conflicts arising within the same group are still left to the jurisdiction of each family chief. If the decisions of the commission are ignored by one of the parties involved, all the *locali* belonging to the 'Ndrangheta are expected to line up against whoever has violated the collective decision (PrRC 1993b: 26–27; PrRC 1995: 4468). According to law enforcement agencies, this has been rather successful since, thanks to the commission's intervention, feuds between the Asciutto-Grimaldis and Zagari-Violas in Taurianova and between the Commissos and Costas in Siderno have been settled. In addition, conflict between two traditionally rival families in San Luca has been kept in check (TrRC 1999; interviews 18 and 19). The "province" has, however, not succeeded in halting the feud between the Cordì and Cataldo families in Locri nor that between the Belcastro and D'Agostino in Sant'Ilario dello Ionio (Ministero dell'Interno 2001a: 103). Despite these weaknesses, the sharp decrease of murders in the Reggio Calabria province during the 1990s seems to owe much to the peacekeeping role played by the 'Ndrangheta's provincial commission. While more than one hundred mafia murders were perpetrated yearly at the beginning of the 1990s, in 1998, 1999, and 2000 the number of mafia homicides recorded in the Reggio Calabria province dwindled from fifteen to thirteen to one (CPM 2000a: 97–101).

Finally, the commission is also held responsible for representing the whole association before other crime consortia and for maintaining contacts with Masonic lodges, colluding politicians, and deviating institutions, in order to maximize 'Ndrangheta gains in the economic and political sphere (PrRC 1995: 4469–80).

Centralization and Resistance

During the last thirty years, both Cosa Nostra and the 'Ndrangheta have undergone a process of centralization that has weakened their traditional segmentary organization. In the case of Cosa Nostra, this centralization began with the constitution of the commission for the province of Palermo in the late 1950s and its regional counterpart in the mid-1970s. In the Calabrian association, from the early

1990s on, the "sporadic" powers of the *crimine*—annual meetings of all the family chiefs—have been widened and entrusted to a permanent higher body specifically endowed with the power to intervene in the affairs of single *locali*.

This process of centralization is well suited to the relationship that has evolved between mafia groups and surrounding society over the last thirty years. By ensuring a more economic and rational use of violence, it represents an attempt to comply with the lower levels of tolerance shown by state institutions and civil society toward any private, unauthorized resort to violence.[14] The creation of superordinate bodies of coordination is also consistent with the growing emphasis placed by mafia associations on economic activities in order to keep pace with wider economic and social transformation processes.

In the Sicilian mafia consortium, centralization moved into a new phase during the late 1980s and early 1990s, characterized by the de facto relinquishment of the principle of collegiality and the rise of a monocratic leadership. At least until his arrest in January 1993, this position was held by Salvatore Riina of the Corleone family. In both confederations, moreover, the interfamily centralization process has been paralleled by an intensified drift toward patrimonialism, which has granted wider and more indiscriminate powers to the chiefs. As the prosecutors of the Reggio Calabria Procura put it, "new rules have replaced the traditional ones, which remained valid only for the lower ranks and the naive, but certainly did not constrain characters like Antonio Nirta or Giorgio De Stefano [the leaders of two powerful 'Ndrangheta clans], who . . . moved with easiness among state apparatuses, secret services, and subversive groups" (PrRC 1995: 6520).

Whether these innovations are being institutionalized is, however, still uncertain. Any form of "merger collegiality" is by its nature rather unstable and tends to evolve (Weber 1978: 276) toward monocratic or oligarchic forms of power management—as was the case of the Cosa Nostra—or to return to the original segmentary structure. However, the transformation of the two assemblies into monocratic bodies has not been successful even in Cosa Nostra: "centralized dominion" has not yet transformed itself into "daily practice" (Popitz 1990: 60–62). Riina's attempt to install himself as dictator over the whole of Cosa Nostra was thwarted by his arrest in January 1993 and, though information is scarce, his successor Bernardo Provenzano seems to have more modest ambitions and has even had to deal with challenges to his authority since the mid-1990s (Lodato and Grasso 2001: 72–74; Ministero dell'Interno 2001a: 114–15, 2001d: 8, 2001e: 11).

In reality, however, even Riina did not manage to fully legitimize his role as dictator during the twenty years he spent in hiding. Despite his merciless elimination of dozens of adversaries, he had to cope with the more or less open resistance of a large number of mafia members up to the early 1990s. And even though men he trusted were placed at the head of the most important mafia families, they also tried to maintain autonomous spheres of power.

Beyond personal interests, it is the segmentary system itself that tends to maintain its configuration, blocking any other forms of differentiation. As Niklas Luhmann puts it, "every tendency toward asymmetrization [that is, away from the symmetrical equality of segmentary societies] is treated and suppressed as a deviation from the valid order and the typology of correct behavior. Precisely because segmentation, reciprocity and inclusive hierarchies are already evolutionary achievements every effort is made to preserve them. The system does not look for development; instead, it stabilizes its forms of differentiation" (1990: 429; see also Giesen 1989).

In the case of the mafia families, though the higher bodies of coordination guarantee a more rational and efficient exploitation of military and economic resources, a return to the status quo ante is favored by the lack of an effective internal circulation of information. This inefficiency is typical of segmentary differentiation but in mafia families is particularly enhanced by the need to prevent information from being leaked to state law enforcement agencies. Nobody—not even Riina at his most powerful—is able to know and control everything that happens inside Cosa Nostra (see, for example, Arlacchi 1994: 87–88). This, of course, weakens any form of centralized dominion.

Finally, the need for secrecy and security—which initially favored the rise of institutions with the power to limit interfamily conflicts—today hinders any attempt at abandoning the traditional segmentary structure (see chapter 3). Lacking any stratification mechanisms to separate them from the "soldiers," contemporary Cosa Nostra chiefs seem to support an inversion of the centralization process in order to protect themselves from betrayals and vendettas. For example, they avoid large collegial meetings where they could be surprised by law enforcement agencies or adversaries. According to several sources, even the Palermitan provincial commission (undoubtedly Cosa Nostra's most consolidated collegial body) has not held full meetings since 1994 (interviews 8 and 21). According to some investigators, Cosa Nostra's strategic decisions are currently made by a sort of directory, composed of Provenzano and three other high-ranking "men of honor," who, however, meet rarely.[15] As a result, the range and discretion of each family chief's power has grown considerably, probably reaching levels similar to those prior to 1957 (see CSM 2001; Ministero dell'Interno 2001a: 108–9; Lodato and Grasso 2001: 53–55, 70–72).

Thus it can be claimed with some confidence that despite the experiments carried out in the last four decades of the twentieth century, the ruling bodies of single families remain the real centers of mafia power, and segmentation is the prevalent form of differentiation.

2

Status and Fraternization Contracts

At the end of the meeting, I felt as if I had grown in stature; I was no longer a nobody, but a *camorrista*, somebody who had to respect the law of honor and to ensure that it was respected by others.
——S. CASTAGNA,
Tu devi uccidere (1967)

Serafino Castagna, a long-forgotten forerunner of contemporary *pentiti*, described his formal initiation into the 'Ndrangheta in this way in his memoirs, published in the late 1960s. Twenty years later, the Sicilian witness Gaspare Mutolo echoed these comments, making surprisingly similar observations: "When I became a member, it was for me a new life, with new rules. For me only Cosa Nostra existed" (CPM 1993b: 1225).

Sicilian and Calabrian mafia associations do not recruit their members following the procedures typical of modern bureaucracies. Only with a systematic distortion of empirical data can they be identified with the Weberian ideal type of legal-rational bureaucracy—which Donald Cressey suggested in the late 1960s when discussing Cosa Nostra's analogous American organization (1969). It is not only the formal structure and daily management of power, described in the previous chapter, that render an analogy of this kind untenable. The weakness of this thesis can be identified even more clearly in the pact that every family makes with its adherents during the ceremony of initiation.

Far from recruiting their staff and organizing their work according to the criteria and procedures of modern bureaucracies, Cosa Nostra and the 'Ndrangheta gain much of their strength through reliance on a premodern contractual form. On entering a mafia family, the new member does not bind himself—as utilitarian analyzes maintain—to respecting a contract aimed at exchanging goods or economic performances. Instead, he underwrites what Max Weber called a "status contract."

As opposed to "purposive contracts," which are typical of market societies, the status contract "involves a change in what may be called the total legal situation (the universal position) and the social status of the persons involved." A status contract does not entail the mere promise of specific tasks in exchange for a monetary or material reward, but commits the party to "make a new 'soul' enter his body" and to become "something different in quality (or status) from the quality he possessed before" (1978: 672). The status contract is also a "fraternization contract," as the members of a mafia *cosca* are obliged to consider themselves brothers (ibid.).

As in a religious conversion, the new member undergoes a process of "alternation," a resocialization implying a near-total transformation of identity and a redefinition of all previous allegiances (Berger and Luckmann 1967: 156–63). This transformation must be imposed through symbolic action—an action very important in the life of the families associated with Cosa Nostra and the 'Ndrangheta, as mafia witnesses frequently point out. Their statements on these topics, however, have so far been largely neglected—if not laughed at—by social scientists, who still largely support a utilitarian and economic vision of the mafia phenomenon. More generally, this vision has induced an underassessment of the strength of cultural codes, and this deficiency is increasingly being recognized even by those scholars who previously stressed the entrepreneurial and acquisitive dimension of mafia action (Pezzino 1997; see also Li Causi and Cassano 1993; Santoro 1998). The relevance of cultural codes was, however, very clear to Judge Giovanni Falcone. "Today," he stated in an interview, "the application of these codes is certainly more unscrupulous, but assuming that they no longer work makes of the mafia a purely criminal organization whose only goal is the pursuit of profit. This is an enormous mistake of perspective which leads us to plan even repressive strategies incorrectly" (1989: 204; see also 1993).

While the relevance of culture was, instead, clear to the foreign researchers who carried out the first fieldwork studies in Sicily during the 1960s (Hess 1973; Blok 1988; Schneider and Schneider 1976), their analyzes remain unfocused, because they were linked to a noncorporate vision of the mafia.[1] As a result, neither this first generation of scholars nor their successors, largely constrained by utilitarian schemes, have been able to appreciate the importance of the cultural dimension of mafia associations or to fully understand the meanings that individuals attach to their mafia membership.[2]

In reality, it is in the interest of mafia families to use symbols and rites extensively. This is because it is only by employing these instruments that they are able to exercise unconditional claims upon their associates and to create brotherhood ties among them. Symbols and rituals, in fact, act not only at the normative level, but also involve the deeper spheres of the cognitive and the emotional. They are able to "convert the obligatory into the desirable," by inducing subjects "to want to do what they must do" (Turner 1967: 30). Symbolic action provides mafiosi with a specific definition of social reality: it creates what Berger and Luckmann call a "subuniverse of meaning" (1967: 61–72) that defines the group collective identity and forces novices to modify their identities to make them compatible with the collective one. Members of the mafia are thus made to conform through the constraining force of rules and their related apparatus of sanctions, as well as through the internalization of a life vision filtering the perception of the outside world and the choice of adequate behavior (see Cohen 1974; Kertzer 1988; Eisenstadt and Giesen 1995).

The key value of the mafia subuniverse of meaning—that set of cultural codes, rituals, and norms through which mafia associations justify their existence and impose a new status on their associates—is honor. Through the manipulation of this code, once widespread over the Mezzogiorno, the *cosche* belonging to Cosa Nostra and the 'Ndrangheta teach their members essential tasks and, at the same time, legitimize their power within their communities of settlement.

RITES OF PASSAGE

The initiation ceremony during which a status contract is imposed upon each new adherent constitutes—to use the expression made famous in the early twentieth century by the Belgian ethnographer Arnold van Gennep (1960)—a veritable *rite de passage*. It is a symbolic representation of death and resurrection, thanks to which the initiated person is reborn as "a new man, with a new outlook and a personality reshaped by the values of his new environment" (Mackenzie 1967: 18).

The ritual of mafia affiliation usually leaves a deep and lasting impact upon those who undergo it. According to Calogero Marcenò, a former affiliate of a Calabrian mafia family in Lombardy, "the ceremony is an intense emotion for the person to be initiated, so much so that many sweat and tremble" (TrMI 1994e: 151). Serafino Castagna, the once famous "monster of Prestinaci," describes his feelings during the ceremony of affiliation to the 'Ndrangheta in the following way: "I remember it as if it were yesterday, the Holy Monday of 1941, April 7, when the chief of the *'ndrina* called me *picciotto*.... I was intensely moved, when I understood that I had become a member of the society.... In a clear voice, I swore the oath which I have never forgotten" (1967: 31, 35).

The Initiation Ceremony

Despite local variants, the initiation ceremony consists of three main stages in both the Cosa Nostra and the 'Ndrangheta: (1) the presentation of the candidate by a member to the whole group; (2) the description of the association and its basic rules; and (3) the swearing of the oath by the novice.

Various features of great symbolic relevance are also used by both Cosa Nostra and the 'Ndrangheta during the ceremony, most notably the iconography and terminology of the Catholic religion and blood. In the 'Ndrangheta the ceremony is known as "baptism" (TrMI 1994e: 147–49; Ciconte 1992: 32–35) and in both associations the candidate swears the oath—the most important moment of the ritual —with the burning image of a saint in his hands. In both contexts, furthermore, before being burnt the image is stained with some drops of the neophyte's blood.

The symbolic meaning of these elements is evident: religious references aim to give sacral value to the ritual and thus reinforce its imperativeness, while blood presents a strong "multivocality" (Turner 1967, 1995), transmitting several meanings at the same time. In other words, blood calls on the candidate to undergo a process of rebirth, implies a sort of natural kinship to which all the members belong, and illustrates the ultimate punishment to be inflicted in the case of betrayal. "One goes in and comes out of Cosa Nostra with blood," the Catanese informant Antonino Calderone was told at the moment of his affiliation. "You will see for yourselves, in a little while, how one enters with blood. And if you leave, you'll leave with blood because you'll be killed" (Arlacchi 1993: 68).

Many Sicilian *pentiti* have described the ceremony of initiation in Cosa Nostra since Tommaso Buscetta's initial disclosure of its existence in 1984. Though there seem to be several differences in the ritual among the families, its main steps follow a general pattern. The candidate or, more usually, the candidates are presented to the entire family by the "men of honor" responsible for their education and assessing their criminal reliability. After the family chief has explained the main rules of Cosa Nostra to them, each novice is asked to choose a godfather. This member then makes a small cut on the index finger of the candidate's right hand so that some blood drops on the image of a saint, usually Santissima Annunziata [Our Lady of the Annunciation] (Falcone 1993: 85–87). With this picture burning in his hands, the new member then swears an oath of faithfulness to the organization, usually as follows: "I burn you as paper, I adore you as a saint; as this paper burns, so my flesh must burn if I betray the Cosa Nostra" (PrPA 1992: 3). This oath seems to have remained much the same over the decades; in 1885 Tommaso Colacino reported that the novices of the Fratellanza from Agrigento repeated the following formula: "I swear on my honor to be faithful to the Fratellanza, as the Fratellanza is faithful to me. As this saint and these few drops of my blood burn, in the same way I will pour all my blood for the Fratellanza; and as this ash cannot go back to its former state and this blood to its former state, in the same way I cannot leave the Fratellanza" (180; see also De Mauro 1962a).

The ceremony of initiation as a whole has in fact undergone few changes over the last hundred years. In *L'uomo delinquente* [The delinquent], published in 1875, Cesare Lombroso described a procedure surprisingly similar to the accounts given by contemporary mafia witnesses: "The *initiand* proceeds into the room and stops in front of a table, on which the effigy of a saint is spread. He offers his right hand to the two *compari* and these, pricking his forefinger, make as much blood drip as suffices to wet the effigy. The *initiand* swears his oath on this image, then burns it with a candle; from then on he is greeted as a *compare* and must carry out the next execution agreed on by the assembly" (Lombroso 1878: 343; see also Cutrera [1900] 1988: 119–20).³

In contrast, the ceremony of affiliation in the 'Ndrangheta is considerably more elaborate than that staged by its Sicilian counterpart. In the Calabrian association, the ritual starts with the presentation of the novice—called *contrasto onorato* or *cardone*—before the so-called *società minore*, the lower level of each mafia family. As in the Sicilian case, the presentation is made by a member who acts as the novice's sponsor and has previously taught him some ritual formulas to be repeated during the initiation. The rite itself begins with an exchange of cues between the chief of the *società minore* and the novice, which go as follows: "What are you looking for?" the first asks. "Blood and honor," the aspiring member answers. "Why, don't you have it?" the chief again asks and the candidate replies, "I have it to give and take."

The candidate is then submitted to one or several trials of courage. In one of these, according to witness Calogero Marcenò, the novice is asked to put the palm of his hand on the top of a knife, which is held by the chief. While some of the others present prepare a basin to show the new candidate that blood is going to pour, another member pretends to hit his hand, in order to test his courage (TrMI 1994e: 147–49; Strati 1977: 90–92).

Once the trial is over, the *società* holds three votes marking the candidate's gradual admission to the organization. The first vote is called by the chief: "On this pleasant afternoon, with the permission of the *camorrista* whom we have as head, *capo giovane*, and *puntaioli*, I proceed to the first vote on the novice's account, starting from the *picciotti* on my right. If before I knew him just as a young man, from now on I recognize him as a *giovane d'onore*, belonging and not belonging to this honored society." The second vote is then introduced: "On this pleasant afternoon, with the permission of the *camorrista* whom we have as head, *capo giovane*, and *puntaioli*, I proceed to the second vote, starting from the *picciotti* on my right. If before I knew him as a *giovane d'onore*, from now on I recognize him as an orally nominated *picciotto*, belonging and not belonging to this honored society." Finally, the third vote celebrates the entrance of the new member into the *cosca*: "On this pleasant afternoon, with the permission of the *camorrista* whom we have as head, *capo giovane*, and *puntaioli*, I proceed to the third vote, starting from the *picciotti* on my right. If before I knew him as a fully made and orally nominated *picciotto*, from now on I recognize him as my faithful companion. I will eat with him, divide right and wrong with him, I will defend his flesh, skin, blood, and bones to the last drop of blood. If he fails and fails again, swindles and stains honor, these crimes are on his own charge and to the discredit of the society" (Malafarina 1986: 92).

When these votes are concluded, the new member is asked to swear an oath of loyalty and obedience toward the group, with the bloodied and burning image of a saint in his hands. Several versions of this formula, given by different internal and external sources, have been given. Serafino Castagna recalls that he pronounced the following words: "I swear in front of the organized and loyal society, represented by our honored and wise chief and by all the associates, to accomplish all the duties which are imposed on me and to which I am bound, if necessary with my own blood" (1967: 35; see also PrRC 1995: 5721–22; TrMI 1994e: 147–49; Asprea 1971: 170–72; Malafarina 1986: 84ff.).

In both associations, simpler and shorter rites are enacted in prisons with affiliates belonging to different families. A simplified variant of the ceremony is also used in the Calabrian confederation to affiliate 'ndranghetisti's sons. The boys are submitted to a sort of preinitiation in their early years, leading to the qualification of *giovani d'onore* (boys of honor), and are thus regarded as *mezzo dentro* and *mezzo fuori*— half in and half out of—the criminal group. This status not only implies a shorter procedure of affiliation, but also guarantees a faster career path within the 'Ndrangheta (TrMI 1994a: 120, 1994e: 151; PrRC 1995: 362ff; Asprea 1971: 170–74).

While Cosa Nostra does not allow the sons of mafia members to move along a quicker career track, it does grant a special type of affiliation to men of high political and social standing. This is termed "reserved," because it is revealed to only a restricted circle of "men of honor." The procedure entails a shortened rite that sometimes does not even involve a formal oath. Originally this alternative rite had two main aims: to keep secret the mafia membership of these subjects, who are usually well known in the wider society, and, at the same time, to prevent them from being continuously asked for favors by other associates. For example, the initiation of Nino and Ignazio Salvo, who were two of the most important figures on the Sicilian economic and political scene for about thirty years, was kept secret for a long time (TrPA 1984, I: 19; TrMA 1987: 123; TrPA 1989: 53).

Under the aegis of the Corleonesi, this kind of reserved affiliation has been extensively granted, going well beyond its traditional application, precisely because of the high degree of secrecy. For example, Giuseppe Marchese, a witness from the ranks of the Corleonesi coalition, was affiliated in 1980, "upon a personal decision of Riina, who deemed that his membership to Cosa Nostra was to be kept confidential. In this way Marchese could work exclusively for Riina and his uncle, who at the time was the chief of the Corso dei Mille family" (PrPA 1993a).

Finally, in the Calabrian 'Ndrangheta rites are also observed for each passage of rank in the mafia hierarchy. Each of these ceremonies has specific formulas and gestures, with details varying from group to group, but all include some basic steps: a further trial of courage, the swearing of an oath, three votes of admission, the making of a mark on the initiate's body, and a final rite of communion (TrMI 1994e: 147–54; PrRC 1995: 365–68). Figure 2.1 shows three pages of a code of the 'Ndrangheta describing in faulty Italian the rite granting the rank of *santista*.

1

COME-SI-FORMA-LA-SANTA-
D.-SANTA-SERA-ALISANTISTA-!-
R.-SANTA-SERA-
D.-SIETE-PRONTI-PER-FORMARE-LA-SANTA.
R.-SIAMO-PRONTISSIMI.-(GRAZIE)
D.-GIUSTO-APPUNTO-QUESTA-SANTA-SERA-
NON-FACCIO-ALTRO-CHE-NELLA-SOLITUDINE
E-NEL-SILENZIO-DI-QUESTA-SANTA-NOTTE-
ILLUMINATA-DELLA-LUCE-DELLE-STELLE-E-
DELLO-SPLENDORE-DELLA-LUNA-A-FORMARE-
QUESTA-SANTA-CORONA-DAL-CAPO-
SANTISSIMO-SOTTO-CAPO-SANTISTA-MASTRO-
DI-CONTROLLO-E-SCORTA-DISTACCATA-GUAR-
VATAZUVI-PER-FEDERIZZARE-E-GIURAMENTO-
GIURO-SU-QUESTA-ARMA-E-DI-FRONTE-A-
QUESTI-NUOVI-FRATELLI-DI-SANTA-DI-
RINNEGARE-LA-SOCIETÀ-DI-SGARRO-E-F-
QUALSIASI-ORGANIZZAZIONE-E-DIVIDERE-
PARTE-ALLA-SANTA-CORONA-E-DIVIDIRE-
SORTE-E-VITA-CON-QUESTI-NUOVI-FRATELLI
1-NUOVO-ELETTO-DEVI-RISPONDERE-LO-GIURO
D.-SAGGI-FRATELLI-SIAMO-PRONTI-PER-

2

LA-FEDERIZZAZIONE?-
R.-SIAMO-PRONTISSIMI-
D.-A-NOME-DELLA-SACRA-CORONA-PASSO-
LA-PRIMA-VOTAZIONE-SU?-SE-PRIMA-LO-
RICONOSCEVO-PER-UN ████████████████
UOMO-APPARTENENTE-ALLA-SOCIETÀ-DI-SGARR.
ADESSO-LO-RICONOSCO-PER-UN-FRATELLO-DI-
SANTA.-NON-ANCORA-APPARTENENTE-
D.-A-NOME-DELLA-SACRA-CORONA-PASSO-LA-
SECONDA-VOTAZIONE-SU?.-SE-FINO-ADESSO-
RICO-NOSCIUTO-UN-FRATELLO-DI-SANTA-
FRA-RICONOSCIUTO-UN-FRATELLO-E-DI-SANTA-
NON-ANCORA-APPARTENENTE-ADESSO-LO-
RICONOSCO-APPARTENENTE-NON-FEDERIZZATO-
A-QUESTO-PUNTO-SI-FA-LA-CROCE-SULLA-
SPALLA-DESTRA-E-CON-UN-BACIO-SULLA-
CROCE-E-IL-GIURAMENTO-DEL-VELENO-
(GIURAMENTO-DEL-VELENO)
D.-A-NOME-DELLA-SANTA-CORONA-E-DI-FRONTE-
A-QUESTI-FRATELLI-DI-SANTA-GIURO-DI-PORTAR
SEMPRE-CON-MÉ-QUESTA-BOCCETTA-
DI-VELENO.-E-SE-PER-DISGRAZIA-DOVREI-
TRADIRE-QUESTI-NUOVI-FRATELLI

3

DI-SANTA-DI-AVVELENARMI-CON-
LE-MIE-STESSE-MANI-
D.-A-NOME-DELLA-SACRA-CORONA-E-DI-
NOI-TUTTI-SAGGI-FRATELLI-PRESENTI-
E-ASSENTI-PASSO-LA-3ª-E-ULTIMA-VOTAZION.
AL-NUOVO-FRATELLO-A-NATO-ABBRACCIATE-
FEDERIZZATO-E-BACIATO-CON-GIURAMENTO
GIÀ-FATTO-E-CON-LA-CROCE-SULLA-
SPALLA-DESTRA-GIURANDO-CON-LUI-DI-
ESSERE-FEDELE-CON-GIOIA-E-SANGUE-
(SFORNARE-LA-SANTA)
D.-SANTA-SERA-ALISANTISTA-
R.-SANTA-SERA-
D.-SIETE-PRONTI-PER-SFORMARE-LA-SANTA-?
R.-SIAMO-PRONTISSIMI-
D.-IN-QUESTA-SANTA-NOTTE-SOTTO-
LA-LUCE-DELLE-STELLE-E-LO-SPLENDOR
DELLA-LUNA-E-SFORMATA-LA-SANTA
CORONA
CI-3-CALALERI-DONORE-
1º GIUSEPPE-MAZZINI-
2º GIUSEPPE-GARIBALDI-
3º GIUSEPPE-LA-MARMORA-

FIGURE 2.1. Ritual formulas from a code of the 'Ndrangheta. Courtesy Col. Angiolo Pellegrini.

Separation, Transition, and Incorporation

The ceremony of mafia initiation is comprised of the three phases making up a rite of passage. The first foresees a rite of "separation," by which the individual is separated from his initial state and starts the "transition": this second stage was called "liminal" by Arnold van Gennep, from the Latin *limen*, meaning "threshold." A further ritual, termed "incorporation," ends this phase and emphasizes the individual's integration into his new state (Gennep 1960).

In both Cosa Nostra and the 'Ndrangheta's ceremonies of affiliation, the phase of separation begins when the initiate is asked to detach himself from all his previous allegiances or at least to subordinate them to mafia membership. The Catania witness Antonino Calderone, for instance, recalls that during his own affiliation he was told that "Cosa Nostra . . . comes before everything. It comes before your father and your mother. And before your wife and your children" (Arlacchi 1993: 68).

The transitional phase is particularly marked in the Calabrian association: the three votes reported above perfectly exemplify the progressive admission of the novice into the society. Even the threshold finds physical expression in the circle formed by the members of the *locale*, into which the new member is fully admitted only at the end of the ceremony of initiation.[4]

Finally, in both associations the phase of incorporation starts when the new affiliate is embraced by his new comrades (PrRC 1995: 4435; Arlacchi 1993: 67–69). In the 'Ndrangheta initiation ceremony the acceptance of the new affiliate is frequently symbolized in yet another way: all the members present suck the blood that pours out of a small cut made on the novice's hand (Strati 1977: 92; see also Castagna 1967: 40–41; TrMI 1994e: 148). In Cosa Nostra, adherents often show their benevolence toward the new member by giving him substantial financial premiums. According to Leonardo Messina, these may amount to "a hundred or two hundred million *lire* or fifty, ten, or five, [respectively, about $80,000; 160,000; 40,000; 8,000; or 4,000 at the exchange rate of the time][5] depending on the possibilities and wealth of the family" (CPM 1992d: 515).

The Status of "Man of Honor"

Mafia initiation rites are not only rites of passage. By solemnly staging the stepping over of a line establishing a fundamental division in the social order, the ceremonies of mafia affiliation are also "rites of institution" (Bourdieu 1991). These not only accompany a transition symbolically, but also consecrate and legitimate an arbitrary boundary and remind whoever goes beyond its threshold of the new attitude and behavior he is required to assume. "The act of institution," Pierre Bourdieu notes, "signifies to someone what his new identity is, but in a way that both communicates it to him and imposes it on him by stating it in front of everyone and thus informing him in an authoritative manner what he is and what he must be" (ibid.: 120–21; see also La Fontaine 1985). It is significant that both mafia organizations use the following slang expression to indicate the recent affiliation of a novice: "He has been made into a man."[6]

Through the rite of institution, the new affiliate is called on to become a "man of honor," and to behave as such in both his private and public life, fully assuming all the rights and duties associated with his new status. It is precisely because of the breadth of this change, involving all facets of the individual's personality, that the mafia cannot be defined as a profession, as Marco Santoro proposed (1995), if by this one means the modern understanding of doctors, lawyers, or engineers. That is to say, membership in a mafia association cannot be considered merely an occupation characterizing one's position in the economic sphere. Like the professional roles shaped in premodern times, such as those of priest or military official, being a mafioso represents a permanent status, calling into play one's total psychic and social life. As Judge Giovanni Falcone point out, admission to a mafia group "commits that individual for the rest of his life. Becoming part of the mafia is equivalent to a religious conversion. One cannot retire from the priesthood . . . or from the mafia" (Falcone 1993: 85). The same point is also made by Calogero Marcenò, the former chief of 'Ndrangheta's Varese subdivision in northern Italy. "It is absolutely impossible for the affiliates," he notes, "to be released from the association's oath and bond. It is a bond that can be undone only with the death of the affiliate, with betrayal, or by the chiefs themselves, in the case the affiliate is no longer worthy or deserving enough to be considered a man of honor" (TrMI 1994e: 124).

The status imposed by both Cosa Nostra and the 'Ndrangheta upon their new members is primarily defined by the cultural code of honor. Members of families belonging to Cosa Nostra call themselves "men of honor" and, though less frequently, 'Ndrangheta affiliates use the same expression to talk about themselves. 'Ndrangetisti also frequently describe their association as an Onorata Società [honored society], as did Cosa Nostra members in the past (Gentile 1993). Indeed, the word 'Ndrangheta means "society of the men of honor," deriving from the Greek ανδραγαθοσ, indicating "a noble, courageous man, worthy of respect as a result of his capacities." In the dialect of Greek origin that is still widespread on the Aspromonte mountain, this word still has a decidedly positive connotation and 'ndranghetisti are thought of as valorous men (Martino 1988: 16, 1983).[7]

In the last two decades of the twentieth century the notion of honor has been the focus of many studies, and numerous anthropologists have underlined its multivocality and plurality. Research carried out in the 1960s and 1970s tended to emphasize its spread over all traditional Mediterranean societies (Peristiany 1974; Pitt-Rivers 1968; Davis 1977; Blok 1984), elaborating a cumulative concept of honor.

More recent studies, however, have stressed the plurality of honor definitions both among different communities and, within these communities, among different social strata (Wikan 1984; Di Bella 1980).[8] Nonetheless, since the mid–nineteenth century the mafia—viewed either as an attitude and behavior of single individuals or as an organization—has been traditionally associated with a specific concept of honor widespread in western Sicily and southern Calabria and confirmed today by mafia witnesses.

As Leopoldo Franchetti pointed out in the 1870s, a mafioso is a "man who knows how to make others respect his rights, leaving aside the means that he uses to achieve this aim" ([1876] 1993: 97; see also Lorenzoni 1910: 676–79). Honor, here identified with mafia behavior, lies in virility and strength, in the ability of every male to defend his person and his property rights: the virginity and chastity of the women of his family, the integrity of his livestock, and the fruits of his agricultural labor. In particular, the woman is considered the repository of the family's honor, because she is the most important element of the family patrimony, ensuring its continuity and growth. Her honor thus defines the honor of all the male family members and enhances the group's cohesion (Schneider 1971).

Ultimately, the gaining of an honorable reputation can be made and maintained only through force and physical violence (Hess 1973: 46–48; Blok 1984; Schneider and Schneider 1976: 86–102; Schneider 1969). Indeed, in nineteenth-century southern Italy, where state institutions were unable to provide protection, give security to their subjects, or govern conflicts, there was no better way to prove one's honor than committing a murder or some other arrogant act. "In many parts of Sicily," Franchetti again notes, "the most effective way to make oneself respected is to have the reputation of having accomplished some murders" ([1876] 1993: 36).

It is no coincidence that in both associations all members—other than those affiliated because of their high political or social rank—must prove their honor by carrying out a murder or some sort of violent action that demonstrates their physical strength and courage. The ability to use violence is the primary criterion for assessing the value of a "man of honor." "Murder in particular," argues the witness Vincenzo Marsala, son of the *capomafia* from the village of Vicari in the Palermo province, "leads to prestige in a mafia family. This is the test by which the value of a man of honor is demonstrated. In this case, he is said to be a man of value. And the more important the murder, the greater the mafioso's prestige" (TrPA [1985] 1992: 71–72; see also Lodato 1999: 180).[9]

Members of mafia associations must also follow conservative norms concerning sexual and family morality, deriving from this concept of honor. Though women are excluded from the mafia group, which is a society of men, "the mafia ideology often makes reference to female purity" (Di Bella 1983: 235). Every "man of honor" has, first of all, to safeguard the chastity of his female relatives—his sisters, his wife, and his daughters—in order to enter and remain a member of the group. Neither of the two southern Italian mafia associations accept illegitimate sons or men who have failed to avenge an attack on their honor, especially the betrayal of their wives, as members.

Sound and proper behavior is also expected of the "men of honor" themselves: divorce is still prohibited and even extramarital relationships are condemned. During the 1970s, for example, Tommaso Buscetta was suspended for six months from Cosa Nostra because of his affairs (Falcone 1993: 62–63), and at the beginning of the following decade, Franco Adelfio, underboss of the Villagrazia family on the Palermo's outskirts, was removed from office because at the moment of his arrest he was with a woman who was not his wife (TrPA 1989: 28). Likewise, the Calabrian defector Serafino Castagna (1967: 61–62) recalls that in the late 1960s an adherent to his 'ndrina was expelled because he was unwilling to murder the man who had seduced his sister.

The punishment of such behavior has meanwhile become much less common and greatly depends on the rank and power of the affiliate accused. However, these rules are still considered part of the mafia normative code and can be enforced by mafia chiefs whenever they feel it right to do so. Despite repeated violations, in fact, the code of honor constitutes the pillar of mafia associations' collective identity: "Like all synthetic and absolute idioms," Marcella Marmo remarks, the code of honor "cannot be analyzed by looking at the deviation in values and behavior with respect to reality, but as a model-function of the group cohesion" (1989: 191).

Claiming to embody honor in its highest form, members of mafia associations have in the past had no difficulty in affirming their superiority and legitimating their power in communities that also believed in the key principle of the code of honor: namely, as Lorenzoni puts it, that "it is a debt of honor to revenge offences personally" without resorting to the help of the state (1910: 677). Manipulating and exploiting widespread values for their own purposes, the mafia *cosche* were long regarded as legitimate entities by large sections of the local population. It would be, however, an oversimplification to assume that adhesion to the code of honor by mafia members has been merely utilitarian, in order to guarantee their dominion over local communities.

As a key element of mafia collective identity, honor defines the status of the member within a mafia association and its prescription is still internalized by many mafia members, despite its loss of significance in the wider society. Adhesion to the code of honor is at times so strong that even today some *capimafia* severely punish its violation, even when they are carried out by members of the bosses' own blood families. Hence, for example, in 1980 the Calabrian mafia boss Antonino Labate ordered his daughter to be killed, when she—married and the mother of five children—had an extramarital affair, thus dishonoring the whole family (TrRC 1994a: 48–50).

RITUAL BROTHERHOODS

Like most status contracts, the pact sanctioned by the ceremony of mafia affiliation is at the same time a "contract of fraternization" (Weber 1978: 673). The rite of mafia initiation establishes a ritual kinship between the novice and the rest of the group: the members of a mafia family must consider themselves brothers, part of a single collective entity (see Paoli 1998b). Upon affiliation with a mafia family, the new member enters into an almost religious communion with the other members of the mafia community, with whom he becomes "the same thing." That is, as the Palermitan prosecutors note, he becomes part of a common body, losing the identity of "his own thing," of belonging to himself and his own blood family, and subjugating himself to the norms and interests of the association (PrPA 1993c: 189–94).

It is indeed significant that the expression "è la stessa cosa" (this is the same thing) is used in the Sicilian consortium in order to introduce a "man of honor" to a third affiliate (TrPA 1985, V: 822, 879). In the 'Ndrangheta the analogous, though weaker, expression "this is a friend of ours" is heard on similar occasions (TrMI 1994e: 159).[10] This sense of common belonging is also clear in the name adopted by the Sicilian association for at least the last fifty years: Cosa Nostra, our thing. Furthermore, the basic units of both consortia are called "families." Although mafia groups, especially in Sicily, are clearly distinguished from the blood families of their members, the term evokes and at the same time prescribes the cohesion and solidarity of blood ties.

Analogies and Differences

Contracts of fraternization are not peculiar to mafia associations. Indeed, although this concept has so far been rather neglected by sociologists in general, fraternalism has been one of the most widespread forms of social organization from the times of antiquity until now (Clawson 1989; Ownby 1996; Tegnaeus 1952). Henry Maine, one of the fathers of modern anthropology, regarded the legal invention allowing the creation of artificial family relations as "the earliest and most extensively employed" and added that "there is none to which I conceive mankind to be more deeply indebted" (1887: 130–31).

It is by no means particular to so-called primitive societies, either. Even in the Middle Ages, the act of associating a stranger to a group was, according to Marc Bloch, likely to take the form of a fictitious fraternization, "as if the only really solid contract was one which, if not based on actual blood-relationship, at least imitated its ties" (1975: 131). As Clawson points out, "in societies where kinship remained the primary basis of solidary relations, fraternal association was effective because it used quasi-kin relations to extend bonds of loyalty and obligation beyond the family, to incorporate people into kin networks, or to create new relations having some of the force of kinship" (1989: 15). Guilds, journeymen's societies, religious confraternities, and village youth brotherhoods were founded on the social metaphor of brotherhood.

The widespread use of fraternization contracts was also illustrated by Max Weber. His studies on the city (1978, chap. 16) show that not only were both ancient and medieval cities constituted as—or at least felt by their members to be—a brotherhood, but that all their smaller associations—no matter whether they were religious, professional, or military—were also founded on rituals of fraternization. The importance of status and fraternization contracts also emerges from the colossal work *Das deutsche Genossenschaftsrecht*, which Otto von Gierke dedicated to German fellowships. Examining the unions that developed at the end of the Middle Ages, Gierke makes some observations that can easily be applied to mafia associations: "The bond was an extremely close one.... Hence, they were called brotherhoods, for brothers were the first and closest fellows. This most significant name was the only one which remained common to all forms of voluntary unions. It takes us one step further toward a recognition of their nature. Brothers are not bound together for one specific purpose: their relationship contains the whole person and extends to *all* aspects of life" ([1868] 1990: 47).

In particular, the bond established by mafia contracts of fraternization has strong links with the institution of coparenthood known as *comparaggio* in Italian. Until only a few years ago it was widespread in the Mezzogiorno as well as in those areas of Europe, such as Spain and the Balkans, where the development of industrial capitalism, the rise of a middle class, and the disintegration of a feudal order have been slower. Through baptism, this cultural mechanism establishes a ritual relationship among the child, his parents, and his ceremonial sponsors, who become coparents—in Italian, *compare* or *commare*. Similar, strong ritual links can also be created through other religious events—betrothal and marriage—between the betrothed/groom and his witness (Mintz and Wolf 1950; Foster 1953; Ishino 1953; Guderman 1973; Pitt-Rivers 1973; Bloch and Guggenheim 1981).

As in mafia relationships, the bond between *compari* is frequently stronger than those between blood relatives and is thought of as indissoluble: *Cumpari semu, cumpari rimarremu. Veni la morti e nni spartemu*, a Sicilian coparenthood formula states [We are *compari* and *compari* we will remain. Only when death comes will we part] (Cutrera [1900] 1988: 58). It is significant that mafiosi, especially the Calabrian ones, routinely call themselves *compare*, whereas they reserve the term *'Zi* [uncle] for older and more authoritative chiefs (PrRC 1995: 4422).

Mafia bonds can thus be considered part of the broad category of "ritualized personal relations" defined by Shmuel Eisenstadt (1956; together with Roniger 1980, 1984) and including, besides coparenthood, a variety of phenomena such as blood brotherhood, blood friendship, "best friendship," and the relationships of contractual servantship existing in several regions of Asia. Mafia relationships meet the four basic characteristics described by Eisenstadt (1956: 90): (1) they are as particularistic as kinship relations; but (2) in contrast with blood relations, they are voluntary; (3) they are personal as opposed to anonymous relations, directed toward universalistic categories of people; and (4) they are institutionalized in ritual terms. Unlike most cases of blood brotherhood and ritual kinship, however, mafia relations are not dyadic but polyadic and, far from manifesting themselves in vague clientelistic networks, they are institutionalized in permanent organizations.

Subordination and Self-Denial

For the affiliates, the mafia association represents a sort of "great mother," to which absolute respect and subordination is due (Di Forti 1982; Di Lorenzo 1996). Indeed, the mafia group is often called Mummy, and the transfer of mother images into mafia slang is frequent. The most powerful 'Ndrangheta chiefs are called, for example, *mamma santissima* [most sainted mother]. Through this analogical procedure, every affiliate is taught that from the moment of his initiation all aspects of his life—even the most intimate ones—are automatically subordinated to his mafia membership: "Cosa Nostra is the mother who belongs to the sons and to whom they belong forever, in the indissolubility of a symbiotic relationship" (Di Lorenzo 1996: 54).[11]

Through fraternization contracts, each of the families belonging to Cosa Nostra and the 'Ndrangheta aims to become what Emile Durkheim defines as a "clan": that is, an organization that has "a mixed nature, at once familial and political. It is a family in the sense that all the members who compose it are considered as kin of one another." However, although many bonds are consanguine, the group also includes non-kin. The clan is, at the same time, "the fundamental political unity: the heads of clan are the only social authorities" (1964: 175). As in simple societies, mafia groups claim to be the only world for their members and their chiefs demand to exercise absolute authority over affiliates. The absoluteness of such a claim was clear to the prosecutors of the Procura della Repubblica di Palermo: "From the moment of his *combinazione* [the ritual affiliation], the man of honor progressively becomes aware of having lost a meaningful part of his autonomy and individuality. He no longer 'belongs to himself,' because he now belongs to the Cosa Nostra, he is an integral part of a system that organizes his life. In any moment, he must be 'available,' he must behave in full conformity to the Cosa Nostra's behavioral code not only within the mafia community, but also outside in the society" (PrPA 1993c: 189–90).

Even the most intimate aspects of a mafioso's life are subordinated to his mafia membership. A "man of honor" wishing to marry a woman who does not form part of the traditional mafia environment must inform the chief of his family beforehand. The chief, after carrying out due inquiries, will give either his authorization or his negative, binding opinion based on the woman's credentials and family background. Only in the first case is the mafioso allowed to marry, while in the second, if he does not comply, he will be cast out and, in the most extreme cases, even permanently expelled.[12]

Blood kinship bonds must also be put aside when necessary. If a *cosca* or a higher body of coordination of either of the two confederations decides to kill the relative of a "man of honor," he has to accept the decision without showing any resentment or sorrow—indeed, he must accept it as a right and necessary measure. As the *consigliere* of the Castelvetrano family explained to his protégé, the orders of the superiors must never be questioned, even when they seem to be contrary to the evidence. "Once, when we were talking," a former "soldier," who has now become a witness, recalls,

> He showed me the palm of his hand and asked me: "How many are these? How many fingers are there in this hand?"
> "*Vossia*, what kind of question are you asking me, how many fingers are there?"
> "Yes, how many fingers, you must tell me how many fingers there are."
> "Well, five."
> "Five? Look at them well."
> "What do I have to look at? Five fingers are five fingers."
> "Look at them well."
> "I can look at them all day long, there are always five."
> "I don't believe it. There are four of them."
> "*Vossia*, are you joking?"
> "I say the truth, I don't joke. I never joke about serious things."
> "Vabbè, *vossia* says four fingers, but I see five."
> "No, look, there are four. And do you want to know why there are four?"
> "Yes, yes, why?"
> "Because I tell you so. You see five fingers, but I tell you, there are four. Now how many fingers do you see?"
> "*Vossia*, four."
> "Good." (Bettini 1994: 90)

Mafia "soldiers" must face and accept the reality constructed and transmitted to them by their chiefs. Subordination to the group is such that the affiliate of a Sicilian or Calabrian mafia group may even be entrusted with the task of facilitating or actually carrying out the murder of one of his relatives. In the mid-1990s, for example, the *pentito* Calogero Ganci, son of the mafia boss Raffaele, confessed that he had killed his wife's father, Vincenzo Anselmo, because the two blood families had found themselves in opposing coalitions during the Sicilian mafia war of the early 1980s (*La Repubblica*, June 20, 1996; see also Nicotri 1996).[13]

According to the status contract underwritten during the ceremony of affiliation, mafia affiliates must be prepared to risk or even sacrifice their own life, in order to protect or enhance the superior interest of the whole association. If a "man of honor" is ordered to carry out a murder or to accomplish any other risky action, he is expected to obey without any thought for considerations relating to either his physical security or his penal term. In May 1989, for example, on Riina's orders the brothers Giuseppe and Antonino Marchese killed their *capomandamento*, Vincenzo Puccio, in one of the cells of the Palermitan prison Ucciardone by repeatedly hitting him with a pan. As a result, they considerably worsened their own judicial situation (PrPA 1993a: 340–61).

The grip of symbolic codes is such that, at least up to the end of the 1980s, most Sicilian adherents of Cosa Nostra considered it a great privilege to become a member of the specialized hit squads responsible for carrying out the most important or dangerous actions. In mafia jargon, the killer in these cases is called a "valorous man of honor" or "somebody who runs" (PrPA 1993c: 193).

"Communitas" and Reciprocity

Though real life is often very different, relationships among Cosa Nostra and 'Ndrangheta associates are prescriptively a form of *communitas*, which the British anthropologist Victor Turner describes as full, unstructured, and unmediated communication, even communion, between equal individuals, deriving from a common experience of liminality, such sharing a rite of passage (1995, 1992). In both consortia, the mafia membership gives rise to a sort of brotherly equality[14] among the affiliates that cancels all differences in status, wealth, and power existing in the external world: "Belonging to the Cosa Nostra," Buscetta maintained, "implied being men of honor: this was the heart of everything. One could then invent hierarchies, positions, commissions, but within each family you breathed an air of equality because we all felt that we belonged to a very special elite" (Arlacchi 1994: 69–70).[15]

In particular, to use Turner's terminology, mafia associations can be regarded as a type of "normative *communitas*," which attempts to capture and institutionalize the spontaneous *communitas*, arising from the experience of liminality, in a system of ethic precepts and legal rules. This operation can be compared to Weber's "routinization of charisma," although in this case the charisma is pentecostal, since it descends on a group and is evanescent rather than a stable personal attribute. Through this process, the existential *communitas* loses spontaneity and immediacy, is organized into a viable social system, and incorporates some of the elements of what Turner considers its antithesis—"structure" (1995: 131–32, 1992: 58–61).

In both the Cosa Nostra and the 'Ndrangheta, the experience of *communitas* reaches its apex in relations among the members of the single mafia family. That is to say, relationships between family associates are constructed prescriptively, if not concretely, on the principle of "generalized reciprocity," which presupposes altruistic attitudes and behavior with no prospects of short-term rewards (Sahlins 1972: 193–200; see also Gouldner 1960). The members of a mafia family are duty-bound to help each other materially and financially when requested or in case of need, and to unfailingly maintain principles of honesty and correctness in their mutual interaction. As shown in the introduction, mutual aid has been singled out as the "official goal" of mafia associations since their founding. And though this goal has been systematically neglected by contemporary social scholars, it was already clear to observers in the nineteenth century. For example, it is striking that back in 1885, Tommaso Colacino defined the Fratellanza of Favara as "a monstrous degeneration of the fruitful principle of *reciprocanza*": "By turning upside down all moral meaning, mutual aid was a very important law in that association, because its statute affirmed that all the affiliates were to help and protect each other in case of damage or injury, without hesitation, without dislike for anyone, *sicut cadaver*" (1885; see also Lorenzoni 1910: 680).

The obligation on mafiosi to correctness and solidarity does not concern only affiliates to the family to which the member belongs, but extends—at least in principle—to all mafia brothers. "Men of honor" are duty-bound, in particular, to help fugitives, regardless of whether they are part of the family or not. "There is an irrefutable obligation on members," a Calabrian mafia witness maintains, "to give hospitality to those in hiding and, if they do not, they incur the so-called sanction of *infamità*" (PrRC 1995: 361). Additionally, all affiliates must be ready to help each other in dangerous situations. "One precise obligation of the members of the honored society," Serafino Castagna notes, "is to intervene to help the threatened associate, passing him the *sferro* or *arma infame* [a knife or firearm], if he by chance lacks it, and to defend him, if he is losing" (1967: 63).

The duty of solidarity is particularly strong in prisons, where imprisoned "men of honor" should put aside all the disagreements that might have seen them opposed in the outside world. Although many exceptions to this rule have been recorded (to the point that mafia members have been murdered in prison by other "men of honor"), prisons are prescriptively considered neutral ground (TrPA 1989: 54, 1984, I: 120). Tommaso Buscetta remembers that during his imprisonment in the Palermo prison of Ucciardone, he had to show friendship and respect even to Giuseppe Sirchia, the killer of one of his closest friends, Bernardo Diana, whose death was avenged only after Sirchia's release (TrPA [1985] 1992: 47; Biagi 1990: 99–101).

In order to avoid a worsening in the conditions of the prison regime, mafiosi are not even supposed to escape from prison, although in recent times there have been several violations of this rule. In the past, however, this norm was so deeply internalized that several mafia affiliates avoided escaping, considering it dishonorable. The most famous example is that of Vincenzo Rimi, one of Cosa Nostra's charismatic figures of the 1950s and 1960s. Though imprisoned for a murder he had not committed, Rimi repeatedly refused to escape, according to several mafia witnesses (TrPA 1985, V: 825).

Generalized reciprocity also entails a moral dimension. As the anthropologist Meyer Fortes showed, all kinship relations, being founded on generalized reciprocity, are moral: that is, they predicate the axiom of amity, the prescriptive altruism exhibited in the ethic of generosity (1970: 219–49). In traditional societies, this rule imposes a clear juxtaposition between the kinship and nonkinship spheres of social action. Although Sicilians and, more generally, southern Italians have often been accused of "amoral familism" (Banfield 1958), family morality has been strongly defended by the Sicilian political scientist Gaetano Mosca, who considered it a typical trait of the ethos of his people in contrast to northerners' universalistic orientation: "Whatever you may believe to the contrary, the Sicilian has a very wide moral sense, but this moral sense differs considerably from that of northern Italians. His morality, for example, preferably explicates itself in the relationships with private persons instead of carrying out scrupulously the citizen's public duties" (1949: 229).

Anthropologists agree unanimously that this moral obligation is particularly strongly rooted in relationships that are deliberately created by mutual agreement between parties, and not imposed by the random outcome of birth (Evans-Pritchard [1933] 1963: 160–61; see also Hocart 1935). All types of ritual brotherhoods bind their members to unquestioning amity, mutual protection, and goodwill, but they do so more rigorously than true kinship. In fact, they prohibit the jealousy and competitiveness that seem to be inherent to true consanguinity (Fortes 1970; Tegnaeus 1952; Pitt-Rivers 1973).

The existence of a mafia morality and its juxtaposition to the official morality and to state laws have been highlighted by the journalist Felice Chilanti, who helped the Italian American mafia boss, Nick Gentile, write his memoirs in the 1960s: "Nick Gentile is an old mafioso and gangster who reasons with a very special mentality. I believe he is seventy-five years old: but even now, when he talks about 'law' and 'morality,' he refers only to the mafia. The codes, the states, etc., are matters which do not concern him and of which one must be as wary of as mysterious businesses" (1993).

This moral dimension to the mafia phenomenon should not, of course, give rise to an idyllic representation of the two crime consortia examined here. As we will see in the following pages, the mafiosi not only frequently commit evil actions against nonmembers, but also routinely violate the above-mentioned moral prescriptions while interacting with their comrades. Nonetheless, the moral foundations of the mafia order are underlined by most *pentiti* coming from both Cosa Nostra's and the 'Ndrangheta's ranks and, following the methodological principles described in the introduction, their statements are here taken seriously and not a priori discarded, as has been the case in most economically oriented studies. To fully understand the mafia witnesses' words and accept the morality of mafia groups, it is necessary to abandon the traditional assumption of functionalist arguments that finds the cause of social facts in the uses to which they are put. As Maurice Bloch argues, "If motive and effect are not identical, there is no problem in seeing 'morality' as an essential aspect of the actor's motive while the effect is entirely other, an observation of the scientist whose value depends on his methods of observation and his categories of measurement which when dealing with such facts as the distribution of goods and services are not likely to include 'morality'" (1973: 75). In the case of mafia consortia, the split between motive and effect is helped by their reliance on fraternization contracts, which are nonspecific and long-term. This produces a high degree of flexibility to long-term social change and allows the use of mafia bonds for the fulfillment of different short-term needs, without reducing them in either nature or time to a single type (ibid.: 86–87; Mintz and Wolf 1950: 347).

Whatever their original goal, the solidarity ties created by mafia fraternization contracts also end in fostering the exploitation of mafia affiliates by family leaders, cloaking the inherently exploitative nature of their relationship. In other words, while the principle of generalized reciprocity obliges mafia chiefs to behave altruistically toward their lower ranks, it also enables them to exploit their subordinates in order to achieve their own, short-term goals. Bound by mafia fraternization contracts, the "soldiers" of both Cosa Nostra and the 'Ndrangheta have no choice other than to comply with the orders of their superiors, no matter how "evil" these may be.

Elitism and Ethical Dualism

Like the adherents of a religious sect, the members of Cosa Nostra and the 'Ndrangheta families feel "morally qualified" (Weber 1946: 310) and, in the certainty of belonging to an elite association, they develop a strong feeling of superiority toward the external world. For the *'ndranghetisti*, the witness Antonio Zagari recalls, "there are only three categories of men in this world: men of honor, *stivaglia* (which covers all state servants), and 'infamous individuals' (who range from police informers to any honest citizen who dares to report any injustice done by the mafiosi to state authorities)" (1992: 21).[16]

In Cosa Nostra this "aristocratizing motive" (Simmel 1950: 365) is historically connected with its need to differentiate itself from the wide phenomenology of behavior labeled as mafioso by external observers. This is, for example, what Antonino Calderone pointed out in his talk with the sociologist Pino Arlacchi: "It's important to distinguish between the true mafiosi—those of the Cosa Nostra—and others.... This matters to all mafiosi. It's important: men like us are mafiosi, the others are whatever. We are men of honor. And not so much because we have taken an oath, but because we are the elite of the criminal world.... Every man of honor feels this way. He knows it, he repeats it to himself continually. He feels superior to all other criminals" (Arlacchi 1993: 20).

As in all communities founded on the principles of segregation and exclusiveness (Weber 1978: 493–99; see also Giesen 1995), the mafia collective is self-perceived as the only reality within which the dignity of person is recognized. Conversely, the external world is usually pictured as an enemy reality, inhabited by "dehumanized" individuals, reduced to things and inanimate objects. It is thus the phenomenon of the "double morality" brought to its extreme consequences. The moral principles valid for in-group members, whether blood family components or religious or ideological comrades, differ substantially from their moral obligations toward out-group individuals. While the rules of brotherhood and piety dominate community life, every outsider is considered an enemy in relation to whom no ethical restriction applies.

The spread of double morality in Sicily was singled out by Henner Hess in the early 1970s. It prescribes an altruistic attitude toward blood relatives, *compari*, friends, clients, and patrons, but also fosters the disregard of the state legal order (1973: 23–52). There is no doubt that this attitude was—and to a certain extent still is—widespread in southern Italy, and not only there (see Trigilia 1999). However, it is in mafia consortia that the principle of ethical dualism finds its fullest application, so much so that outsiders are not even considered to be human beings.

In the 'Ndrangheta, the different attitudes to be shown toward mafia brothers and nonmembers are taught to new initiates through codes of "politics" and "false politics." These two codes are explained in the following way to the main character in Luca Asprea's novel *Il previticciolo:* "Politics ... is the beautiful art, which teaches us to live in kind, loving, and sincere harmony with all worthy and deserving men, and especially with *mastri* and faithful comrades.... False politics ... is the art that teaches us to deal with people who are arrogant and unworthy, the infamous and *sbirri* [i.e., law enforcement officers]" (1971: 175; see also PrRC 1995: 4444; Malafarina 1986: 85).

This ethical dualism is promoted to such an extent that "men of honor" do not usually feel any sense of guilt or sorrow when they kill somebody who is not a mafia member or who has been expelled by the ruling bodies, since they do not consider the victim to be a human being and therefore do not view him as worthy of emotional involvement (PrPA 1993c). For example, the *pentito* Antonio Patti, a "man of honor" belonging to the Marsala family in the province of Trapani, pleaded guilty to almost fifty murders and admitted that he had always considered his actions "normal" services. Though he frequently did not even know the identity of the victims, he felt no moral guilt at all about his actions, as he just obeyed his chief's orders (PrPA 1996a).

As in Patti's case, the emotional detachment shown by many mafia killers in murdering unknown persons, adversaries, or even their former colleagues is frequently enhanced by the above-mentioned process of submission by individuals to the group. The kind of obedience low-ranking members have to show removes their sense of responsibility for these crimes, which is further negated by some other ad hoc measures. These include the fact that the most serious crimes—and specifically, murders—are usually carried out by a group and the identity of the killers is kept hidden even within the mafia association itself. Such arrangements are obviously made for practical reasons. Yet, at the same time, they prove to be highly effective in suppressing individual personalities, and in freeing single "men of honor" from the moral responsibilities of their actions—in making them feel extraneous, different, and superior to the world of noninitiates.

MEMENTOS

Several institutions, norms, and rituals have been developed by both mafia consortia to strengthen and renew daily the brotherhood ties created by the affiliation ritual and to remind the "men of honor" of the duties deriving from them.

Redistribution and Common Account

In both Cosa Nostra and the 'Ndrangheta, the feeling of common belonging among the members of each family is strengthened principally by sharing the proceeds of some illegal activities. In most *locali* of the 'Ndrangheta and even in the larger Sicilian mafia groups—such as the Santapaola family in Catania—this practice is today fully institutionalized, as family chiefs pay monthly salaries to all members of the *cosca*. According to the former chief of a settlement of the 'Ndrangheta in Lombardy, for example, these salaries "consist of at least three million *lira* [about $2,400], which is considered the minimum required to support one's own family" (TrMI 1994e: 153–57).

Such practice represents a clear example of what anthropologists call "redistribution" or "pooling." This foresees the collection of goods from members of a group and its subsequent division within the group by a chief. In this respect, it is worth highlighting that while redistribution and reciprocity are often seen as alternative models of satisfying material needs in simpler societies, according to Marshall Sahlins the former may be regarded as a subtype of the latter, given that "pooling is an organization of reciprocities, a system of reciprocities within a social group" (1972: 188–89).

Another application of the same principle is also represented by the *bacinella* (literally, basin), an institution spread throughout the Calabrian context and in the Catania family of the Cosa Nostra. This is a common fund [*cassa comune*] used to deal with the exceptional financial needs of affiliates, to meet their legal expenses in the case of trial, to support the families of the imprisoned or dead members, and, occasionally, to integrate monthly salaries. In Calabria, the *bacinella* used to be filled with a sort of entry tax—called the *dritta*—which was paid by new members, with occasional contributions from individuals (Nicaso 1990; Ciconte 1992). According to several nineteenth-century documents, an entry tax was also imposed upon the new members of Sicilian mafia associations (Alongi [1886] 1977; Cutrera [1900] 1988; Pezzino 1990a: 210). No admission tokens of this kind have been mentioned by any contemporary *pentiti*. In both Calabria and Catania, the *bacinella* is funded exclusively by the periodical deposits of affiliates, which usually correspond to about 15 percent of illicit profits (Castagna 1967: 36; TrMI 1994e: 153–57; PrRC 1995: 4439).

Whether or not it is symbolized by the existence of a common fund, in both associations the duty of solidarity among affiliates is supreme, especially toward members who are on the run or are in prison (TrPA 1985, V: 877). This kind of duty constitutes a basic feature of the mafia community, as numerous sources have pointed out since the late nineteenth century. The first three rules of the statute developed by the Setta degli Stoppaglieri, a group active in Monreale and the surrounding area in the 1870s, were—according to Antonino Cutrera—the following:

> 1. To help each other (and for this reason it was originally called a mutual aid society) and to revenge the offences to the associates with blood.
> 2. To provide and foster, by all means possible, the defense and liberation of the member who was unfortunate enough to fall into the hands of justice.
> 3. To distribute among associates (following a criterion set out by the chiefs) money deriving from blackmail, extortion, and thefts carried out together, giving more to needy members when distributing the booty.
> (Cutrera [1900] 1988: 119; see also Alongi [1886] 1977: 101–2; Nicaso 1990: 21)

Today, as in the past, the prestige and authority of a mafia chief are measured by his ability to give assistance to fugitives, to support the expenses of imprisoned members and their families, and to guarantee these prisoners short sentences through intimidating or corrupting the judges and jury.[17]

Rituals of Communion

Several rituals created by mafia fraternization contracts reinforce the sense of belonging to a community. For instance, until the late 1970s, Sicilian "men of honor" kissed each other on the mouth when they met—a practice later abolished for security reasons (TrPA [1985] 1992: 7; CPM 1992b: 319).

In the Calabrian mafia consortium, meetings following precise rituals take place every week between members of the two segments—*società minore* and *società maggiore*—constituting each group (PrRC 1995: 365–66).[18] The unity of the whole 'Ndrangheta is further established by the meetings, called *crimini*, that the mafia chiefs used to hold—and still hold—every year near the Sanctuary of Our Lady of Polsi during the September Feast in the Aspromonte region.

In Cosa Nostra, instead, meetings between "men of honor" do not take place following any detailed or rigid ritual schemes.[19] Although they have often been compared to business meetings by the media, Sicilian mafia family gatherings are usually very informal and the most important decisions are often made during common meals, called *schiticchio*, which take place either in a restaurant or in the open air on a country estate (Schneider 1969; Colaprico and Fazzo 1995: 88–90).

In both associations, moreover, the feeling of common belonging is reinforced by the frequent and informal interaction among single mafiosi and their blood relatives. As Tommaso Buscetta points out, "the mafiosi do nothing but stay together, even with their relatives, from morning to night. Their social life is almost all within the 'small antique world' of Cosa Nostra" (Arlacchi 1994: 19; see also Colaprico and Fazzo 1995: 88–91).

Furthermore, the *comparaggio* is often practiced by mafiosi of both syndicates in order to reinforce solidarity ties. "Coparenthood is the safe way to have sure and trusted accomplices, because one never fears betrayal by a *compare*," Antonino Cutrera noted at the end of the nineteenth century ([1900] 1988: 58; see also TrAG [1986] 1988: 270ff.). Even today, the bond of *comparaggio* is felt to be so strong and incorruptible that a "man of honor" is expected to intervene in support or defense of his *compare* and even to avenge his death.

Within the 'Ndrangheta, fictive dyadic kinship bonds can also be created through an ad hoc rite. During a family meeting, the chief officially recognizes the friendship between two affiliates by imposing so-called blood bonds [*vincoli di sangue*]. In the words of the *pentito* Francesco Fonti, "this rite takes place in the presence of the *capobastone*, who pricks the right finger of the two affiliates and then unites them in such a way that there is a 'blood contact.' Mixing these up, the blood of the two members falls on a holy image, which is later burnt. The *capobastone* seals this bond with his presence and with these words: 'From now on you are brothers, the blood of one is in the other, only more blood or an infamous action may untie this bond'" (PrRC 1995: 5726).

Sisters and Wives

Bound by the fraternization contracts, members of both mafia associations are also obliged to consider the women belonging to another affiliate's family as sisters. "One of the inviolate rules of our tradition was that no family member should fool around with another family member's wife or female relative" (Bonanno 1983: 154; see also U.S. Senate 1988: 224). The violation of this rule, which constitutes a pillar of the mafia system of reciprocity, still authorizes the offended member to avenge the wrong by killing the guilty woman and her seducer.

Women are also used as a commodity to strengthen the mafia brotherhood. Though there are an increasing number of exceptions, marriages are usually a means to establish ritual kinship bonds among mafia adherents, and specifically to seal alliances with prestigious and powerful mafiosi and their families. The force of these ritual ties is extremely important. If a "man of honor" has marriage links with an important mafia chief, his own prestige is considerably boosted. Throughout the 1970s, for example, the importance of the Rimi family from Alcamo and the Minores from Trapani was powerfully enhanced by their relations of ritual kinship with the most influential Palermitan families, such as the Bontades, Badalamentis, and Inzerillos. Indeed, it was the close connection with these same families that determined their persecution by the opposing Corleonesi coalition in the early 1980s, when the latter group imposed its supremacy on the entire Cosa Nostra (TrPA 1994a).

In the Calabrian mafia consortium, where kinship relations are even more important than in Sicily, the symbolic strength of the marriage bond is such that by creating an alliance between two blood families, a wedding may dangerously weaken the cohesion of the overall mafia association. In other words, a marriage between the members of two blood families belonging to the 'Ndrangheta establishes such close ties of generalized reciprocity that they may well overturn the mafia equilibrium of a local territorial context and cause an armed conflict. The second mafia war, for example, was triggered by the marriage between Giuseppina Condello—sister of the Condello brothers, underbosses of the Reggio Calabrian mafia chief Paolo De Stefano—and Antonino Imerti, the leader of the neighboring mafia group in Villa San Giovanni. The conflict exploded in 1985, two years after the marriage, and saw practically all the mafia families in the city of Reggio Calabria grouped into either one of two opposing factions. As Giacomo Lauro, former associate of the Imerti wing, recalls, the marriage

> gave rise to the birth of an alliance between these two families, one of which, the Imerti, usually operated outside the Reggio territory, exercising its power exclusively in the Villa San Giovanni area. Very quickly, Paolo De Stefano became envious and fearful that this marriage, which produced mafia alliances and a subsequent increase in the power of the Condello group, would result

in the group's greater autonomy in the *locali* of Mercatello and Archi Carmine. For these reasons, fearing Antonino Imerti's arbitrary insertion in these areas and fearing that his own group would be threatened by the Condellos, De Stefano decided to end the alliance. He thus decreed that Antonino Imerti should be killed, although he avoided taking responsibility for this and made it seem that others had done so. (PrRC 1995: 514)

Another example of mafia alliances being established through marriage can be seen in the events taking place after those described above. To avenge the failed attempt on Antonino Imerti that Lauro described, Paolo De Stefano was murdered on October 10, 1985. The way in which the De Stefano clan prepared itself for the coming fight was through another marriage, between Orazio De Stefano, Paolo's younger brother, and Antonietta Benestare, niece of the old mafia boss Giovanni Tegano. Celebrated on December 2 of that same year, the wedding sealed the alliance between the De Stefanos and the powerful Tegano mafia family (ibid.: 3344).[20]

AN IDEALIZATION OF THE MAFIA PHENOMENON?

The emphasis placed on mafia status and fraternization contracts could be perceived as an idealization of the mafia phenomenon. This would, however, be unjustified. These contracts, with their ceremonial and sophisticated symbolic-ritual apparatus, enable mafia groups to instruct their members to consider the role of "men of honor" as their destiny and to build a communal social relationship. In mafia families, however, there are elements not only of the gemeinschaft pole, but also its opposite, gesellschaft. As Weber pointed out when reelaborating Ferdinand Tönnies's celebrated dichotomy, the two poles do not represent two historically sequential and disjunctive types of society, but are simultaneously present—though in different and variable measure—in the great majority of social relationships (1978: 40). In mafia families, the strength of community bonds creates those conditions of trust and solidarity, on the basis of which it becomes possible to underwrite specific purposive contracts.

As is true of other ritualized relationships, mafia groups represent a combination of specific exchange with what is termed in anthropological literature as "generalized exchange." This expression, coined by Marcel Mauss in his *Essai sur le don* (1990) and later developed by Claude Lévi-Strauss, is nowadays employed to distinguish the nonutilitarian and unconditional relationships necessary to establish conditions of basic trust and solidarity in society and to uphold what Emile Durkheim called the "pre-contractual elements of social life" (see Eisenstadt and Roniger 1980, 1984). The creation of community bonds thus simply constitutes a precondition for promoting the personal interests of the affiliates through mutual support.

Like other personal ritualized relationships in traditional societies, the mafia appears to be characterized by "a peculiar and distinct type of combination of instrumental and solidary relationship, in which the solidarity provides the basic framework, yet within this framework various instrumental considerations, albeit very diffusely defined, are of paramount importance" (Eisenstadt 1956: 91). Membership in a mafia group is, hence, typified by a crisscrossing of instrumentality and solidarity, of personal selfishness and unconditional involvement. Anyone giving weight to only one side of this opposition fails to understand the deeper meaning, as well as the strength and resilience, of this relationship.

The Bonds of Brotherhood

In the scientific debate that has involved the mafia in the 1980s and 1990s, the acquisitive and instrumental dimension of mafia action has been strongly emphasized. Contemporary mafiosi have usually been pictured as modern entrepreneurs who aim to maximize profits and rationally assess the potential costs and benefits of each of their actions. Indeed, some scholars have applied this conception to the mafiosi of the past as well (see chapter 4). Those who do so, however, do not only renounce any understanding of the reasons for the mafia brotherhoods' long existence; even worse, they are also unable to perceive the consortia's limits and weaknesses, which have in fact fostered their current crisis.

The most striking limit derives from the fact that status and fraternization contracts can be imposed only on individuals who already know and at least vaguely subscribe to the values associated with the contracts themselves. This represents a heavy constraint on the recruitment of new affiliates. Those who know nothing about mafia honor and have not grown up within a specific subculture may eventually undergo a ceremony of mafia initiation, but will accomplish only with great difficulty the process of alternation that the ceremony symbolizes, that is, assuming a new identity and subordinating all their previous ties to the mafia group. Aware of this constraint, the families belonging to Cosa Nostra and the 'Ndrangheta accept almost exclusively the sons and relatives of "men of honor" or individuals who have grown up in their own towns or neighborhoods. "My family," Leonardo Messina recalls, "traditionally belongs to Cosa Nostra and I represent the seventh generation belonging to Cosa Nostra; I was affiliated not because I was a robber or because I was able to kill, but because I was bound to become a member by family tradition" (CPM 1992d: 513). Likewise, according to Pino Scriva, one of the first *pentiti* coming from the Calabrian mafia consortium, "It is very unusual for a *'ndranghetista*'s son not to follow in his father's footsteps" (PrRC 1995: 363–64).

Due to the increased geographical mobility and the wider extension of illicit trades of "men of honor," some exceptions were made to this rule during the last thirty years of the twentieth century. In the late 1970s, for example, in order to gain control of the cigarette smuggling trade, the Palermitan families of Cosa Nostra affiliated several Campanian gangsters and *camorristi*, going so far as to set up a mafia family in the province of Naples (TrPA [1985] 1992: 90–96). Likewise, in the following two decades some Calabrian mafia groups located in Lombardy recruited several members from the northern Calabrian provinces and other Mezzogiorno regions. For example, the Calabrian Mazzaferro clan, which was one of the strongest in the Milan area for more than a decade, admitted Calogero Marcenò, who was born in Sicily in the province of Caltanissetta, as one of its members (TrMI 1994e). A strong geographical bias still exists, however. No Sicilian or Calabrian mafia family has ever admitted individuals born outside southern Italy or in families that did not originate there. Indeed, most mafia groups seem to have remained faithful to the tradition and still accept only candidates originating from their own villages or neighborhoods. "The Platì group," explains Saverio Morabito, a former leader of the group's drug trafficking unit in Milan, "which has settled here in northern Italy, has always had contacts with everybody, but has never allowed anybody to join its permanent staff if they don't come from Platì" (Colaprico and Fazzo 1995: 88).

This geographical specificity is consistent with the other widespread custom adopted by both Cosa Nostra and the 'Ndrangheta in tracking and "educating" candidates for several years before formally admitting them into the group: "The initiation starts . . . much earlier than the rite itself" (Siebert 1994: 30). Leonardo Messina recalls, Cosa Nostra members "follow you from childhood—they raise you, they teach you to shoot, to kill, to place bombs, you are a robot: you are chosen. . . . After a period of 'approach,' which can last one, five, or twenty years—it depends on the person—somebody comes and tells you that it is high time for you to enter Cosa Nostra" (CPM 1992c: 514–15; see also PrRC 1995: 233, 363–64).[21] This long period of preparation strengthens the effectiveness of the affiliation ceremony and creates the best conditions to make sure that the new adepts adhere to the "subuniverse of meaning" associated with mafia status and fraternization contracts not only formally but also substantially.

Due to the strictly "local" recruitment criteria and procedures, mafia groups find it very difficult to internalize the competencies and international contacts that are necessary to acquire and maintain a relevant position on today's world illegal markets. A good example of this can be seen in the fact that neither the Sicilian nor Calabrian mafia association has ever succeeded in playing a significant role in the wholesale sector of the illegal arms market. They are certainly present as buyers in this marketplace, as they need to satisfy their own military needs. It is striking, however, that they have never managed to enter the more profitable field of wholesale illicit transactions in arms as mediators. The illegal sector constitutes, in fact, only a small section of the much wider legal arms market (see Naylor 1995) and Cosa Nostra and 'Ndrangheta *cosche*—given their lack of contacts abroad and inability to recruit members with the necessary contacts and skills to trade in arms—have always remained on the periphery of both.

Likewise, they have for a long time now found it difficult to launder the proceeds of their illicit trading. Both associations have recently dealt with this problem by sending the children of the most powerful families to educational institutions that will equip them with the necessary economic and financial know-how and, more recently, by trying to recruit better educated felons (Ministero dell'Interno 2001d: 11). In the past, however, Cosa Nostra and 'Ndrangheta bosses were often forced to entrust their money to nonmafia members and in more than one case they lost several hundred million *lire* [hundreds of thousands of U.S. dollars] in mistaken investments that ended in bankruptcies. Exemplary in this respect is the case of the Banco Ambrosiano, which laundered and reinvested the illicit capital of several clans belonging to Cosa Nostra for many years before collapsing in 1981 and leaving debts of more than 1 billion U.S. dollars (TrMI 1989; TrRO 1992; see also Calabrò 1991; Cornwell 1983; Paoli 1993).[22]

A Precarious Balance

The rigid restrictions surrounding the recruitment of new affiliates are not the only constraint deriving from the contracts governing the mafia families. There is also a potential for fragility and disorder in the combination between the abovementioned features of specific and generalized exchange. This is to be found in the need to establish a balance between these two different registers and to prevent the predominance of self-interest over the set of values that status contracts imply. As Shmuel Eisenstadt and Luis Roniger point out (1984), a tension between relationships of solidarity and concrete obligations characterizes all ritualized personal and patron-client relationships. Mafia families are no exception. In the daily life of Cosa Nostra and 'Ndrangheta *cosche*, the prescription of group fraternity and solidarity can be weakened, if not completely undermined, by conflicts of interest, rivalries, and the personal ambitions of members attempting to exploit the strength of mafia ties for the achievement of specific personal or factional goals.

Indeed, the noble principles of brotherhood and solidarity are frequently recalled publicly by the very adherents willing to betray them, in order to promote their own *particulare* [interests]. In Sicily, as early as the late nineteenth century "mafiosi used to stress relations of friendships in order to accomplish a killing effectively without giving rise the suspicion of either victim, public opinion or the law" (Blok 1988: 173). Numerous examples of this practice can also be found in the statements made by contemporary *pentiti*. Accordingly, Rosario Riccobono, chief of the Partanna Mondello family on the outskirts of Palermo, was killed in 1982 at the end of a sumptuous Christmas lunch attended by all the most important mafia bosses of that period. After the meal, Riccobono and other eight fellows of his *cosca* were separated off from each other and strangled one by one by their table companions (PrPA 1993a: 205–28).

Understandably, "men of honor" soon learn to be skeptical about the noble principles prescribed by status and fraternization contracts and adopt a cautious —if not openly distrustful—attitude toward most of their mafia brothers. This precarious balance between generalized and specific exchange is also threatened by the process of institutionalization. The consolidation of instrumental and power relations necessarily weakens the fraternity and equality prescriptively at the core of mafia relationships. In becoming institutionalized, the *communitas* incorporates elements of its antithesis, the "structure," and is polluted by the latter (Turner 1995: 131–32, 1992: 58–61).

To reduce the pollution of community feelings by power relations, Cosa Nostra families—and to a lesser extent the 'Ndrangheta ones—apply the principle of direct democracy for the internal regulation of power. As we saw in chapter 1, this principle attempts to minimize the distance between the chief and his simple affiliates. At least theoretically, the affiliates are fellow members and not subjects of the boss, and thus have the right and duty to control his actions and to prosecute any abuse of power that he might commit. In practice, however, deviations from this model are very common, and though no alternative principle of legitimation has arisen, some members manage to stay in power for a long time, forcing other members to work for their own exclusive personal interests.

Sometimes it is the chiefs themselves who instruct affiliates to be cautious and to distrust their colleagues, in order to gain their absolute trust. The most widespread strategy for achieving such a goal is for members to narrate "tragedies" [*fare il tragediatori*], to make things up with the precise aim of sowing discord within the association or of denying their responsibility for some event. This betrays a key norm of the mafia normative system that—according to *pentiti*—should be unfailingly observed by "men of honor": to tell one's fellow members the truth. In the Castelvetrano mafia family, for example, the two most important figures, Francesco Messina Denaro and Antonio Capogreco, encouraged feelings of suspicion and mistrust among their subordinates by resorting to a number of tactics. As Vincenzo Calcara reports, every now and then Capogreco, his godfather, told him that another "man of honor" had complained about him, asked him to follow the movements of another associate, or made him suspect that others were checking on him, too: "He stirred up trouble and invented 'tragedies,' so that no positive feeling would come into being between us soldiers. The family and the rules had to come first. . . . I always had to be on the alert, to distrust everybody and answer only to Capogreco . . . and since he knew that the most widespread sensation among men of honor is mistrust, having taught me to doubt others he then wanted to convince me to trust him blindly" (Bettini 1994: 114).

Until the end of the 1970s, the implementation of these manipulative practices was left to the discretion of the chiefs of single families. Each of them was free to choose the combination of force, suspicion, and appeal to traditions through which to enforce and legitimize his own power and to secure his subordinates' obedience. In Sicily, however, the above-mentioned techniques have been more and more frequently resorted to following the rise of the Corleonesi in the early 1980s. That is to say, their rise to power in Cosa Nostra was achieved by setting members of other families at odds with each other, by creating "tragedies" and stirring up other families' "soldiers" against their chiefs. Distrust and suspicion became the norm, leading mafiosi to doubt the good faith of their fellow members, subordinates, and chiefs.

Though profitable in the short term, this strategy shook the fragile balance between generalized and specific exchange on which both mafia associations are based. It is important to remember, however, that not even in the Sicilian Cosa Nostra have the Corleonesi's policies been the only disrupting factor at work. Other long-term processes also contributed to the erosion of the precontractual foundations of the mafia order. Far from being the only cause of this, the innovations introduced by the Corleonesi are in reality a consequence of these processes —they were a reaction to the progressive loss of trust within the mafia consortium due to other reasons.

Modernization and Conflicts

During the last thirty years some of the fundamental features of the mafia "subuniverse of meaning" have been undermined by the process of modernization that Italy has undergone since the Second World War.

It is, above all, the code of honor, through which mafiosi have legitimized the use of private violence and the exercise of political functions in their own communities, that has undergone the most striking changes. Even the lifestyle associated with this image—an aristocratic vision, whereby the "man of honor" is freed of having to dirty his hands through manual labor—has been progressively substituted by the more "trivial" pursuit of money. In the surrounding society, income is now the main parameter by which the value of an individual and the basis of his reputation are established. To avoid marginalization and to maintain their social status, the members of mafia *cosche* have largely embraced this new set of values, identifying honor with money, and they have increasingly devoted time and energy to economic enterprises in order to maximize their profits (Arlacchi 1988).

As we will see in chapter 4, this change has been quite successful. During the 1970s and 1980s most mafiosi accumulated wealth on an unprecedented scale.

However, this very success has given rise to growing tensions in the precarious balance between generalized and specific exchange. As early as the early 1980s Tommaso Buscetta complained that mafia community bonds were being corrupted by the spread of economic relationships among mafia members. In his view, business relations among the members should be inspired by the same principle of correctness and loyalty regulating other spheres of mafia interaction. "If you do business with other men of honor, you have a duty to behave correctly and always to tell the truth," the old mafioso recalled. In reality, however, swindles and frauds became increasingly frequent among the Cosa Nostra affiliates (TrPA [1985] 1992: 91; see also 1989: 79). Buscetta also pointed out that the number of alliances with nonaffiliates had multiplied since the early 1970s. In the sectors of tobacco and drug smuggling, "the cleavages among different families were no longer respected, in the sense that everybody could associate with whoever they wanted." Indeed, this kind of activity had necessarily fostered "resort to nonmafiosi and this is one of the main causes of the confusion which has arisen . . . in relationships among the various families and men of honor" (ibid.).

In stimulating partnerships with nonmembers and increasing the number of economic deals among "mafia brothers," the entrepreneurial transformation of mafia associations has led to a weakening of the in-group morality. In general terms, this kind of development follows a process described by Weber: "The course of development involves . . . the bringing in of calculation into the traditional brotherhood, displacing the old religious relationship. As soon as accountability is established within the family community, and economic relations are no longer strictly communistic, there is an end to naive piety and its repression of the economic impulse" (1981: 356). As far as Cosa Nostra and the 'Ndrangheta are concerned, the same process was later underlined by mafia witnesses, who reported many other cases showing that an in-group morality was no longer applied to business deals among "men of honor" (see Bettini 1994: 112ff.).

Furthermore, mafiosi's growing involvement in economic activities has put the mafia subuniverse of meaning, on which the associates' identity and mafia groups' legitimation to rule have long been founded, under a heavy strain. This increasing predominance of economic activities has thus produced a "cultural lag" between mafia institutions and the traditional legitimation machinery of their members. The latter has not kept the same pace of development as the former, and thus there is a growing discrepancy between the effective behavior of mafia members—what they aspire to and the ways in which they actually pass their time—and the ways in which they explain and justify their actions.

Just like the two underlying institutions that gave rise to it, the mafia subuniverse of meaning is the product of a social construction process that has been going on for over a hundred years. As time has passed, it has also been institutionalized, achieving a certain degree of autonomy vis-à-vis the two mafia consortia that originally underpinned its creation and development (Berger and Luckmann 1967). Given the multivocality and flexibility of its symbolic features, this set of codes can be modified or adapted in the short run, but it cannot be rewritten easily or completely. Like their members' individual and collective identities, the legitimation of Cosa Nostra and 'Ndrangheta *cosche* has also been constructed over several generations following specific cultural codes that cannot be changed overnight (see Giesen 1993 and 1995; Eisenstadt and Giesen 1995).

Furthermore, in their traditional formulation these codes transmit fundamental messages for the preservation of mafia groups. With its emphasis on physical strength and the use of violence, for example, the traditional concept of honor cannot easily be discarded. In fact, its maintenance is made necessary by the illegal status of the two consortia and their consequent exclusion from state protection. Even nowadays, with few exceptions, every member of Cosa Nostra or the 'Ndrangheta *must* be able to use or command violence in order to protect his person and his property and reaffirm the mafia dominion through the intimidation or physical elimination of anyone who challenges it.

The growing gap between the mafia apparatus of legitimation and the two underlying mafia consortia has clearly produced tension and conflicts among "men of honor." These have, above all, developed over the generations. In the Calabrian 'Ndrangheta, for example, some illicit activities that were previously prohibited by the traditional mafia code were authorized in 1974, after the murder of don Antonio Macrì from Siderno, the most charismatic *capomafia* of the old guard, who fiercely opposed any changes (PrRC 1995).

In the Sicilian province of Agrigento, the generation conflict was solved—during the same period—in a less violent way by ousting the old *capomafia* Paolo Campo and by the subsequent rise to power of Carmelo Colletti. The two bosses' diverging styles clearly emerge from the proceedings of the Villaseta trial, which took place in Agrigento in the mid-1980s. In the investigating judge's indictment, Carmelo Colletti was described as "the prototype of the new mafioso who has emerged and consolidated in the years following the postwar period, when the mafia, though not abandoning the countryside . . . discovered the new sectors of activities: supplies to the public administration, public contracts and subcontracts, laundering money of illicit origin, and the flourishing drug trade, which all offered large and otherwise impossible profits" (TrAG [1986] 1988: 140).

Campo fiercely opposed this lifestyle. In a judicial deposition, the old *capomafia* said that "Colletti . . . did not have my respect, because he was excessively avid; he had the mentality of the businessman, a mentality that is foreign to me. I have always tried to keep away people like Colletti" (ibid.: 280). And he proceeded to defend his view of *mafiosità*, clearly distancing himself from innovators such as Colletti:

> I declare myself innocent of the crime of delinquent and mafia association, meaning that I have never committed crimes, nor have I associated with others to this end. I must say, however, that I was born and I will die a mafioso, if by *mafia* one means, as I do, to do good to one's neighbor, to give something to those in need, to find work for the unemployed, to bring help to those who are in a difficult situation. In this sense, I have been, I am considered, and I consider myself a mafioso. In my opinion, those harming others and especially those trafficking drugs are not mafiosi; they are just simple delinquents. These substances are ruining the new generations. When I meet somebody who trades drugs, I immediately push him away from me because I have a loathing of him. (Ibid.: 279–80)

The trial provided clear evidence that even Campo was not as innocent as he made himself out to be. However, this speech shows the strength of traditional cultural codes, on the basis of which he had built his identity as a mafioso and legitimized his power. Unlike Colletti, these codes prevented him from considering some illicit activities as suitable, while allowing and even encouraging him to commit others.

In addition to intergenerational conflicts concerning the kinds of activities to be carried out, the cultural lag mentioned above has given rise to conflicts along a vertical line within each mafia unit, between low- and middle-ranking "men of honor" and their chiefs. Whereas many of the chiefs invest much of their time and energy in accumulating wealth, lower-ranking members are still socialized to understand "honor" in a traditional way, that is, as the capacity to use violence. Such a lag—that is, the gap between the "updated" conception of honor which is adopted by the higher-ranking members and the official one, which is transmitted to the younger members—is, first of all, the result of the backwardness of the mafia body of knowledge and legitimation theories that are transmitted to mafia neophytes. However, the emphasis on physical strength and courage in the education of new *picciotti* is also in the interests of the mafia chiefs, who need a private army to defend themselves and their properties from the attacks of rivals and from law enforcement action.

Perceiving a discrepancy in values, low-ranking members increasingly feel exploited by their chiefs. A former member of the Castelvetrano *cosca*, for example, stated that after working for several years as courier in the drug-trafficking business he and some of his associates were "fed up eating only the crumbs while the chiefs were pocketing billions" (Bettini 1994: 10). In several cases, the full realization of the extent of exploitation makes the structure of mafia legitimation crumble, suddenly revealing its inconsistencies. It opens the way to rebellion against the chiefs or—as in the above-mentioned case—to defection from the group and a painful distancing from the members' own past: "Distrust in my chiefs grew as blind obedience withered inside me. In my opinion, they simply used their power, discipline, and our duty to execute orders, their shrewdness and power to sow discord to pursue their own affairs, interests, and wealth. They cared nothing about Cosa Nostra, the family, truth, or respect. They used men as puppets for their own goals and then got rid of them" (ibid.: 187–88).

Thus the growing involvement of Cosa Nostra and 'Ndrangheta families in entrepreneurial activities, itself a reaction to the changes in the cultural orientations prevalent in society at large, has shaken the apparatus of legitimation developed by the mafia consortia through their more than century-old history. It thus has undermined the pact of solidarity among group members, unveiling conflicts of interest between mafia soldiers and chiefs.

The Crumbling of Moral Ties

Pressured by the intensification of law enforcement action and the subsequent internal transformations (see chapter 3), many older mafiosi have since the mid-1980s drastically reduced the time they previously spent instructing novices and strengthening the feeling of common belonging. As a result, a growing portion of the new affiliates, having grown up in a society that regards economic success as the basis of social reputation, subscribes only superficially to the prescriptions deriving from mafia status and fraternization contracts. For this group, acceptance into a mafia family represents a convenient means of advancing economically and socially. Rituals and symbols have increasingly come to be seen as a cumbersome superstructure, the legacy of a remote past that now has only a limited influence. In other words, entrance into a mafia family no longer involves a complete transformation of the novice's identity or the subscription of a fraternization pact with fellow members. To a much larger extent than in the past, adhesion to a mafia group is almost exclusively instrumental, based on a utilitarian assessment of costs and rewards. "From what I understand," recalls Gaspare Mutolo, a Palermitan mafioso of the old generation, "the way that a Palermitan citizen perceives this situation today is different from the way that he would have perceived the mafia twenty years ago. Today, many young men enter the mafia out of need, not because they particularly desire to become mafiosi or delinquents. In the mafia, they see enrichment, success, a world that offers everything a young man demands from life" (CPM 1993b: 1222). Hence, nowadays if this new generation of "men of honor" see that the balance between costs and rewards is likely to tilt to their disadvantage for any reason, they can rapidly revise their decision about forming part of Cosa Nostra or the 'Ndrangheta without implying any radical redefinition of their personal identity or any severing of deep emotional ties.

As Durkheim pointed out at the end of the nineteenth century ([1899–1900]

1984), no community can exist without a system of moral values but, once the values are codified into a set of rules, respect for them can be imposed with severe sanctions. This was the strategy Totò Riina adopted in the late 1980s and early 1990s, when he attempted to combat the loosening of moral ties by resorting increasingly to violence and imposing a climate of terror. Action of this kind, however, cannot go beyond a certain limit, because in the long run no social system can exist only by relying on the threat of sanctions.

It is the weakening of the feature of communal solidarity that has caused the recent growth of *pentiti* in the two mafia associations and, above all, in Cosa Nostra. In the second half of the 1980s, Buscetta's choice to cooperate with the judiciary was followed by a few mafia members: Salvatore Contorno, Antonino Calderone, Francesco Marino Mannoia, and a couple of others. In the early 1990s, however, there was a sharp rise in this number. Illustrative of this trend is the fact that as of December 31, 1996, 1,273 witnesses were under the state protection program—a figure that has remained relatively stable in the following years. More than 1,200 of these were former members of criminal groups. About 35 percent of them formed part of Sicilian crime coalitions, whereas the percentage of *pentiti* coming from the ranks of Calabrian mafia and pseudomafia groups was more modest (13 percent) (Ministero dell'Interno 1997b; see also 2001c).

As in a chain reaction, the multiplication of *pentiti* has further undermined the feeling of common belonging within the mafia. Above all in Cosa Nostra, suspicion and mistrust now pollute all relationships indiscriminately since no "man of honor" can be sure that in the near or far future he will not be betrayed by his own mafia brother. Thus, the "logic of appropriateness" is no longer able to constrain the "logic of instrumentalism" (March 1981). Once arrested, many mafiosi distance themselves from their former roles as "men of honor" and reject its prescribed behavior. When they face the choice of spending the rest of their life in prison or gaining a shorter conviction and access to alternative sanctions by cooperating with the judiciary, they drop their previously shared common values and sense of belonging to a moral community. Instead, following a merely instrumental reasoning, they opt rationally for the solution that presents the best cost-benefit ratio.

Thus, in these moments of crisis, a significant number of mafiosi abandoning the role of "men of honor" assess the pros and cons of group loyalty according to procedures that follow rational choice assumptions (see Gambetta 1993). Far from being the norm, however, this attitude appears to be the result of the crumbling of the mafia legitimization system and the disruption of the precarious balance between specific and generalized exchange.

To cope with the growing number of *pentiti*, Bernardo Provenzano, the new Cosa Nostra leader, is said to have drastically restricted the number of new initiations and fostered a return to old mafia principles and rules. According to Piero

Grasso, chief prosecutor in Palermo, the Cosa Nostra leadership is also favoring candidates coming from traditional mafia families whose blood relatives are already "men of honor" (Ministero dell'Interno 2001a: 109, 2001e: 11; Lodato and Grasso 2001: 8, 70–71). It is far from clear whether these measures will be sufficient to re-create the precontractual bases of trust on which the whole mafia edifice rests. There are no doubts, however, that Cosa Nostra's long-term survival depends on the reconstruction of those bases.

Tommaso Buscetta testifying at the first Palermo maxitrial, as shown by a closed-circuit TV.
Photo © Letizia Battaglia, reprinted by permission.

Salvatore Contorno, one of the first contemporary mafia witnesses. Photo courtesy Italian Police.

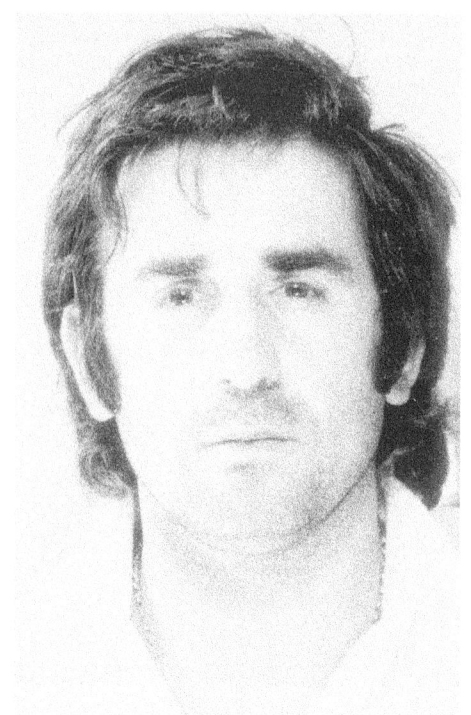

Murder of Stefano Bontade, head of the Palermitan Santa Maria del Gesù mafia family and leader of the Cosa Nostra "losing wing," which was defeated by the Corleonesi in the second Sicilian "mafia war." Photo from Palermo, April 24, 1981, courtesy Italian Police.

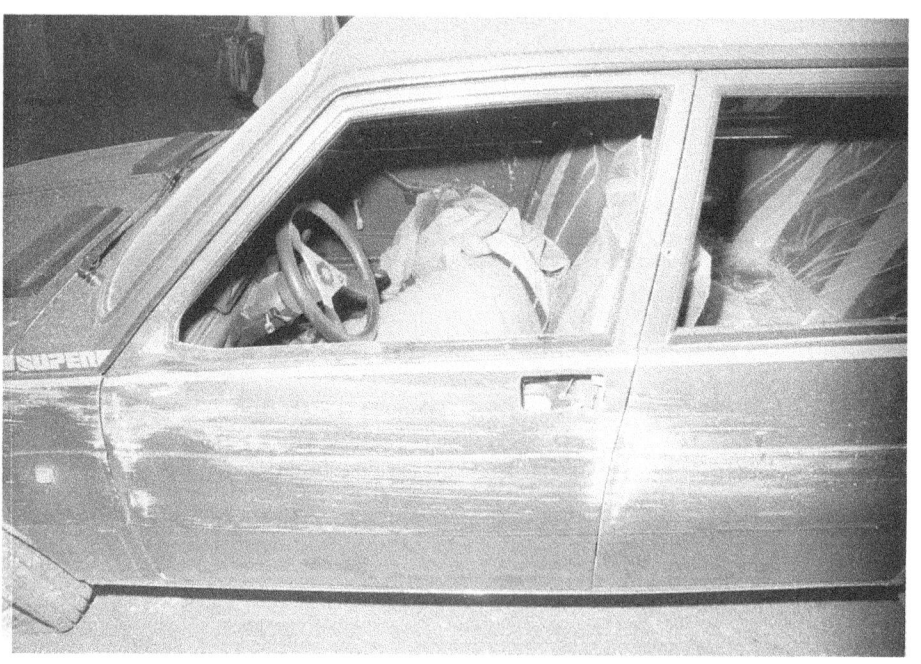

The effects of the bomb explosion that killed Judge Giovanni Falcone; his wife, Judge Francesca Morvillo; and three policemen of their escort on the highway between Palermo's airport and city center on May 23, 1992. Regarded by Cosa Nostra as its most dangerous enemy, Falcone had coordinated the most successful anti-mafia investigations in the 1980s, including the first Palermo maxitrial. Falcone was killed four months after the maxitrial's first-degree convictions were confirmed by the Italian Supreme Court of Appeals. Photo courtesy Italian Police.

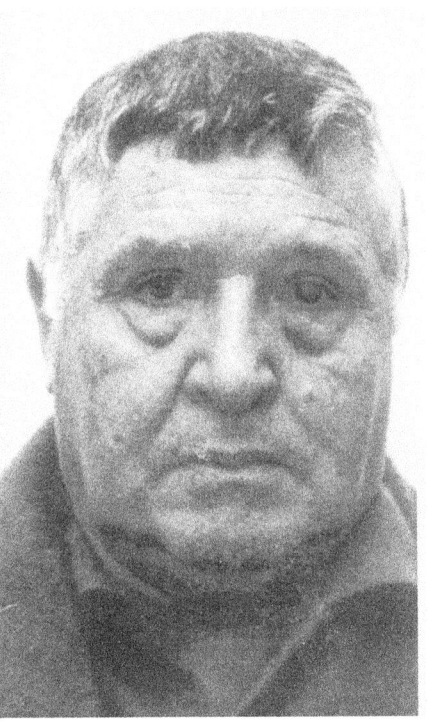

Salvatore "Totò" Riina, Cosa Nostra's leader in the 1980s and early 1990s. Photo courtesy Italian Police.

Judge Paolo Borsellino with the widows of two state officials (policeman Vito Schifani and chief prosecutor Gaetano Costa) murdered by the mafia. In May 1992, a month before this photo was taken, a bomb explosion had killed Judge Giovanni Falcone, his wife, and three men of his escort (including Schifani). In July 1992, about a month after the photo, Borsellino, Falcone's closest collaborator and designated successor, was also murdered by Cosa Nostra. Photo © Franco Zecchin, reprinted by permission.

Giulio Andreotti, a leading figure of Italy's postwar politics and a seven-time prime minister, and Salvo Lima, his political lieutenant in Sicily. Andreotti was prosecuted but acquitted for the crime of participating in a mafia association; Lima was killed by Cosa Nostra in March 1992. Photo © Casasoli/Team/Agenzia Grazia Neri, reprinted by permission.

Paolo Romeo, leading figure of Reggio Calabria's De Stefano mafia group and member of parliament in the Partito Socialdemocratico Italiano for several sessions. In October 2000, Romeo was sentenced to five years in prison for being a member of a mafia-type criminal association. Photo © Casasoli/Team/Agenzia Grazia Neri, reprinted by permission.

Giusi Di Salvo and the women of the anti-mafia association on the spot where Rosario Di Salvo and Pio La Torre were murdered. La Torre was a Communist member of parliament; he had denounced mafia infiltration in the Sicilian economy and proposed the 1982 anti-mafia bill a few months before his death. Photo © Letizia Battaglia, reprinted by permission.

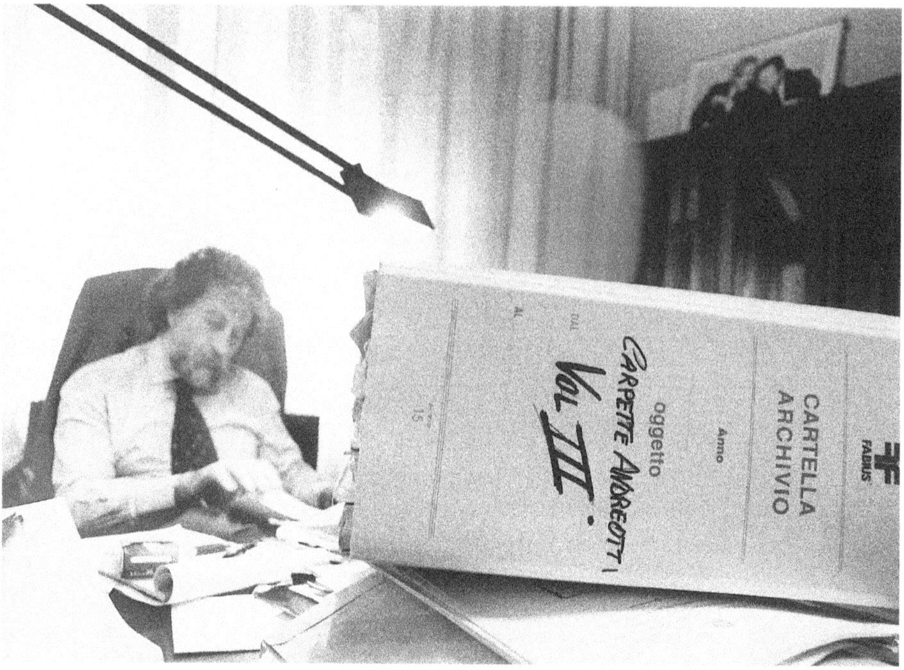
CARTELLA
ARCHIVIO
Anno
oggetto
CARPETTE ANDREOTTI
VOL. III

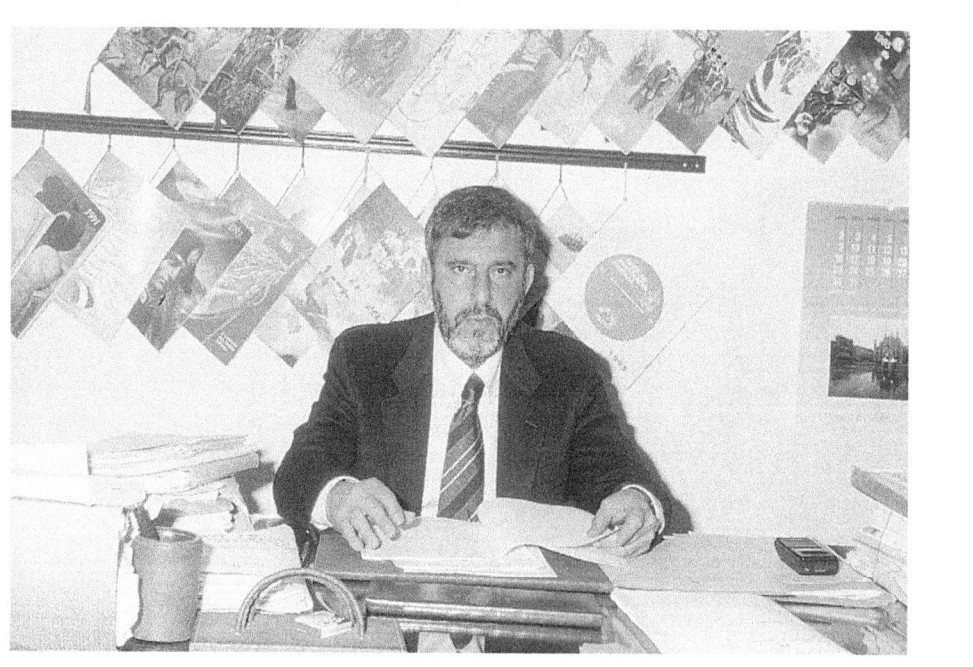

Maria Maniscalco, up to May 2002 the anti-mafia mayor of San Giuseppe Jato, a high-mafia-density town in the Palermitan inland.
Photo © Letizia Battaglia, reprinted by permission.

Facing page, top: Robert Scarpinato, one of the prosecutors in the trial against Giulio Andreotti. Photo © Letizia Battaglia, reprinted by permission.

Facing page, bottom: Salvatore Boemi, adjunct chief prosecutor and head of the Direzione Distrettuale Antimafia in the Reggio Calabria court. Photo © La Rosa Reintzsch/Agenzia Grazia Neri, reprinted by permission.

Anti-mafia education in a primary school in Palermo. Photo © Letizia Battaglia, reprinted by permission.

3

Secrecy and Violence

The interests and honor of the association come before those of your family, parents, sisters, and brothers. The association is your family from now on and, if you commit *infamità* [that is, betraying or endangering the group], you will be punished with death. As you are faithful to the society, in the same way the society will be faithful to you and will help you in times of need. This oath can be broken only with death. Do you accept all this? Will you swear to it?
—PROCURA DELLA REPUBBLICA DI REGGIO CALABRIA,
  Richiesta di ordini di custodia cautelare in carcere e di contestuale rinvio a giudizio nel procedimento contro Condello Pasquale + 477 (1995)

These were conditions for entry into the 'Ndrangheta as they were explained to Francesco Fonti during his initiation ceremony. They leave no room for doubt that one of the most important duties prescribed by mafia status and fraternization contracts is allegiance to the association, and that this allegiance must not be broken through either speech or action, on pain of death.

For no less than a hundred years now this duty of allegiance has implied keeping at least some aspects of mafia group life secret. It is interesting to note that as early as the nineteenth century the code of the Stoppaglieri sect from Monreale added an oath of secrecy to the three prescribing mutual help between members. This rule, which followed three recorded in the 1870s, went as follows: "To maintain the oath taken and to conserve secrecy, on pain of death within twenty-four hours for transgressors" (Cutrera [1900] 1988: 119).

In the first mafia consortia, which developed in the mid–nineteenth century, the emphasis on secrecy was probably induced by the emulation of bourgeois secret societies—such as the Carboneria and the Freemasonry—which were then widespread over all southern Italy (Pezzino 1990a, 1990b, 1992a; Recupero 1987b; Hobsbawm 1974). When the legal status of the forerunners of contemporary mafia *cosche* was still uncertain, secrecy was probably more a strategy to enhance group cohesion than a necessity imposed by state repression. As the years went by, however, it became an indispensable instrument for mafia consortia in their attempt to avoid the criminalization procedures to which they were exposed—at least formally—by Italian state authorities. In fact, though with huge discrepancies between *Sollen* and *Sein* (that is, between what was officially stated and what was effectively done), state officials have since the late nineteenth century denied any legitimacy to and have—at least in principle—fought all those collective subjects that refuse to recognize the state's monopoly of violence or to subject themselves to its legal order.

In mafia consortia, the link between secrecy and violence is indissoluble: violence leads to secrecy and this, in its turn, compels the use of violence. Given that they claim the right of violence, mafia associations are forced to resort to secrecy to avoid state repressive action. Though state institutions have made pacts with representatives of mafia power over the years, they have—at least in principle—always opposed mafia groupings. Formally recognizing mafia legitimacy was, in fact, untenable for state institutions, since this would have entailed a weakening in their own right to exercise power. Once secrecy is adopted, violence becomes an indispensable resource for mafia associations. Self-excluding from state jurisdiction through secrecy, mafia groups cannot do without violence to solve internal conflicts, defend common interests, or guarantee the effectiveness of their legal order.

VARIATIONS IN SECRECY

Contrary to common belief, secrecy is not binary—in the sense that it exists or does not exist—but is rather a gradual property that can be adopted in varying degrees. Although it has been persistently ignored by sociology, secrecy represents a generalized phenomenon. Indeed, for an individual the possibility to maintain a secret, to choose between secrecy and openness, seems to be a necessary condition for the process of individuation itself. Summarizing the psychological literature on the theme, Sissela Bok notes that "control over secrecy provides a safety valve for individuals in the mists of communal life, some influence over transactions between the world of personal experience and the world shared with others. With no control over such exchanges, human beings would be unable to exercise choice about their lives" (1984: 20; see also Hahn 1997).

Likewise, all organizations need to resort to some degree of secrecy in order to survive. That is, information control defines not only individual, but also collective boundaries (Tefft 1980). According to Norman Mackenzie, groups can be classified on the basis of their attitude toward secrecy into four different types—"open," "limited," "private," and "secret." In his view, an "open group" is one that poses no restrictions on admission and has no secrets for its members or outsiders—nor does it have any specific aims or rules. A good example of an open group is a group of vacationers. A "limited" group, for instance, a voluntary association, selects its members according to particular rules or objectives, but does not restrict the discussion of its affairs to the public. A "private" group, instead, has a restricted membership, its affairs are not usually rendered public, and some of its activities may be kept secret: examples range from a private business company to a government. Finally, there is the "secret" organization, for which secrecy is a defining condition of its existence (1967: 13–14; see also Warren and Laslett 1980; Giannini 1988).

Can Cosa Nostra and 'Ndrangheta mafia families be included in the latter category? Absolutely, but only if secrecy is not considered to be a fixed and unchanging phenomenon that has molded the two consortia throughout their existence without introducing any temporal or spatial variations.

Emulation and Decay

According to a hypothesis that has gained increasing credit among historians, the first Sicilian mafia associations found inspiration for their symbolic and organizational apparatus in the secret political movements flourishing in the first half of the nineteenth century, particularly in the Carboneria, a bourgeois political association fighting for political reform that was widespread throughout the Kingdom of the Two Sicilies.[1] This process of emulation on the part of mafia associations was probably unwillingly fostered by the repressive action carried out by the Bourbon police, which ruthlessly opposed all liberal political initiatives. As a result, on several occasions during the Restoration—and particularly after the repression of the 1820 *moti* [revolts]—the Sicilian representatives of the Carboneria and Freemasonry were arrested by the Bourbon police and detained in the Vicaria Palermo prison, where they mixed with other convicts. Several patriots wrote in their memoirs that during their imprisonment they were treated with great respect by the common prisoners, even those belonging to the camorra (the underworld leadership). As several reports of Bourbon police officials show, there is little doubt that secret society rituals spread rapidly inside prisons and on the islands where defendants were sent into forced residence (Labate 1909, I: 267ff.; Brancaccio di Carpino 1901; Nicastro 1961; see also Falcionelli 1937: 10–56; Falzone 1987: 71–72).

A minimal hypothesis, about which there is a growing consensus, asserts that the diffusion of the Carboneria, Freemasonry, and, to a lesser extent, Giuseppe Mazzini's revolutionary movement contributed to the spread of an actual culture of sects and secret associations, which favored the rise of mafia organizations (Recupero 1987a; Giarrizzo 1989: 700). According to Paolo Pezzino (1990a, 1992b), however, there are grounds for going even further and hypothesizing that the former actually influenced the latter. In his view, there are clear links between the spread of secret societies, the popular squads that were active in the numerous protests that shook Sicily during the nineteenth century, and the early presence of mafia associations. The latter, in fact, first developed in those areas of Sicily where liberal secret societies, such as the Freemasonry and the Carboneria, were most rooted and most actively cooperated with popular squads in insurrections.

Several elements back this thesis. For example, it is highly significant that the Fratellanza of Favara, one of the largest nineteenth-century mafia associations with branches in several towns and villages of the Agrigento province, practiced rites and initiation procedures of Masonic derivation, explicitly referring to the "universal republic." Likewise, the Stoppaglieri of Monreale allegedly used rites of a Masonic type, while its founder, Giuseppe Palmeri from Nicaso, was a member of Mazzini's revolutionary movement for the independence and unification of Italy, which was also heavily influenced by the Freemasonry (Pezzino 1990a: 153–54; Lupo 1993: 59). The influence of liberal secret societies upon the formation stages of contemporary mafia associations is also echoed in the legends recounted by today's mafia members. According to Tommaso Buscetta, for example, the current Cosa Nostra was once known as Carboneria—a clear reference to the liberal secret society bearing the same name (Biagi 1990: 200).

It is, of course, up to historiography to find out the extent to which Sicilian and Calabrian mafia groups stem from secret liberal political movements. Whatever the strength of these ties, however, in the second half of the nineteenth century secret societies undeniably underwent a process of degeneration and decay, with tangible changes in the high level of moral integrity and reputation that they had held over the previous 150 years. Up to the mid–nineteenth century, secret sects represented important vehicles of modernization and enlightenment. According to Frances Yates (1975), as early as the sixteenth century the propagation of alchemy and the definition of the first rules of modern scientific thought were fostered and protected by the secrecy of small groups of adepts. The relationship between Masonic lodges and the Enlightenment has proved to be even closer and more stringent. Reinhart Koselleck argues that through Masonic lodges the bourgeoisie acquired a social form of its own, and the lodges became "the strongest political institution of the eighteenth-century moral world" (1988: 79). According to Margaret Jacob (1991), the hundreds of Masonic lodges founded in eighteenth-century Europe were crucial to the development of modern civil society (see also Halevi 1984). Likewise, for Jürgen Habermas the Freemason lodges secretly anticipated the assembly of private citizens into a public "as a public sphere still existing behind closed doors" (1989: 35; see also Giarrizzo 1994). Finally, secret revolutionary movements promoted the liberal revolutions that took place in nineteenth-century Europe and contributed to the rise of more democratic regimes (Billington 1980).

From the mid–nineteenth century onward, however, this model of association increasingly spread among the lower strata, who used it for the pursuit of private, mostly illegal aims. Even bourgeois sects of liberal origin rapidly underwent a progressive degeneration, and most of them disappeared within a few decades. The only association to survive this period, the Freemasonry, has also since then lost touch with its initial ideals (Jones 1967; Knight 1985).

Defense Strategy

In Sicilian and Calabrian mafia groups, the adoption of secrecy has never been a matter of principle only, promoted by ideals or by the desire to copy liberal secret sects. Secrecy has always been an important defense strategy used to avoid state repressive action. This can be seen in the fact that throughout their history the families of both groups have regulated the degree of secrecy they enforce at any one time according to the amount of attention they are given by national public opinion and the state law enforcement apparatus.

For example, since Unification, the Sicilian mafia has been the object of heated public debates and parliamentary inquiries, and western Sicily has been swept by violent and repressive central government campaigns more than once (Pezzino 1987; Renda 1985). Thus it is no simple coincidence that the prescription of secrecy has always been observed much more strictly and effectively in Cosa Nostra than in the 'Ndrangheta. In the latter case, instead, the *cosche* have never needed to be quite so secret, because they have never attracted the same amount of attention at the national level.

Empowered by such neglect, the units constituting the 'Ndrangheta were until recently fully recognized and legitimate collective subjects in their local communities. The only precautions they needed to take were to exclude outsiders from participating directly in their association life and to protect their rituals and symbols as well as the identity of some of their affiliates (see Castagna 1967). Cosa Nostra's "men of honor" were fully aware of this lower level of secrecy and tended to treat members of the 'Ndrangheta with a sense of both contempt and superiority as a result. The 'Ndrangheta, Tommaso Buscetta remembers, "represented a sui generis entity, from our point of view, as a consequence of its lack of seriousness in recruitment and of its very low—almost nonexistent—secrecy" (Arlacchi 1994: 53).

In late-nineteenth- and early-twentieth-century Sicily too, however, the single *capimafia* had a high degree of visibility and legitimacy within their local society. Important functions of social and political integration that the new Italian state was unable to carry out on account of its lack of status were—sometimes officially but more often unofficially—delegated to mafia leaders and their groups. Regarded as members of the local ruling classes, mafia chiefs exercised not only power but its legitimated version: authority. It is difficult to assess exactly to what degree people were aware that the power of some individuals was founded on their membership in a mafia association. It is certain, however, that everybody knew who the mafiosi were and turned to them to ask for favors and recommendations. As Gaspare Mutolo, a former member of the Partanna-Mondello family (on the outskirts of Palermo), recalls,

> the mafiosi of the past were people characterized, in my opinion, by wisdom and to whom people went to ask for advice.... I will give you a simple example: if a young man quarreled with his fiancée, neither he nor his mother went to talk about it with the head of the *carabinieri*, but turned to the person who was likely to be the mafioso of that area ... the mafiosi were those that commanded, the wise men.... If you looked for a job, you did not go to the Employment Office, but you looked for it through the mafioso, who, if it was felt to be appropriate, talked with the head of the Employment Office. (CPM 1993b: 1222)

Though interruptions and inversions have occurred, a long-term trend can be identified: in both Sicily and Calabria there has been a progressive decrease in the visibility of mafia sodalities and their members. With time, secrecy has become a crucial factor on which the survival of the whole mafia group, and above all its chiefs, depends. This trend has been particularly noticeable since the 1970s, as the mafia consortia have lost the popular legitimacy they previously enjoyed in their local communities and anti-mafia action by government agencies has intensified (see chapter 5). Since then, secrecy has prevailed over any other organizational need.

Concentric Circles

Variations and discontinuity in the enforcement of secrecy can also be seen in other dimensions than that of time. This is because, far from being an unchanging property, secrecy is relational. As the history of families belonging to Cosa Nostra and 'Ndrangheta demonstrates, the degree to which it is used varies depending on the external referents with whom the individual or the organization has to deal.

Even though members are instructed to regard *omertà* as an absolute duty, each mafia family is surrounded by concentric circles of adherents, accomplices, and sympathizers, and secrecy objectively increases as we move from internal to external circles. The innermost circle with the lowest requirements of secrecy is formed of those who, though not yet ritually initiated, cooperate with the *cosche* on a continuous basis, in most cases hoping to join in the future. "Around every man of honor of a certain rank," Calderone argues, "there is always a circle of twenty, thirty, youths who are nobodies wanting to become somebodies" (Arlacchi 1993:

149). In the Sicilian tradition these are known as the *avvicinati* [approached]. In the 'Ndrangheta, instead, a distinction is made between the *giovani d'onore*, the sons of mafia members who will be fully initiated when they grow up, and the *contrasti onorati*, that is, the men who do not belong to a family of mafia traditions, but who participate in some of the *locale*'s illicit activities, showing courage and reliability (CPM 1993b; PrPA 1992: 44; TrMI 1994e).

The second circle consists of people linked by bonds of biological or ritual kinship to members of the mafia group. These individuals belong to different social classes and maintain a nonsystematic, but fully trustworthy, relationship with mafia members, providing them with information, favors, hiding places, and protection.

Then there are those who have no formal or blood links with the members of a mafia family, but who gravitate to it for a variety of reasons, often sporadically, either for interest or gain, with no more involvement than this. These are usually individuals forming part of the underworld, such as robbers, thieves, moneylenders, and swindlers, as well as representatives of economic and financial crime and "approachable" politicians and public administrators. These people certainly know they are dealing with mafiosi, but are kept in the dark about the mafia group, its internal organization, rituals, and codes.

Like the lowest ranks of the 'Ndrangheta initiates, the concentric circles have a dual function of linking and dividing. They protect the center from external observation and, at the same time, irradiate its sphere of power into a much wider social context than the restricted one of the members (see Simmel 1950).

In many centers of southern Calabria and also, though less strongly, in western Sicily, the local population has also long constituted a further protective circle. Within local communities mafia families exercise their power and, at the same time, hide themselves, thus becoming invisible to external observers. Not everybody, of course, colludes. However, many people, as the judge Antonino Filastò noted in an article published in 1906 in the *Gazzetta di Messina e delle Calabrie*, "though feeling nauseated by and tired of foul mafia actions, are silent and endure them . . . for the sake of caution. They are not shrewd or wicked enough to become members; neither do they have enough courage to rebel and they are, thus, suspended between two opposing forces, waiting for providential help to come to take them away from the fray."

Active protection and support are instead guaranteed to mafia groups by members of the more internal circles, which Filastò described in detail at the beginning of the twentieth century:

> The circle of sympathizers is a totally different thing. Sympathizers do not form part, that is, of the mafia ranks, with whom they simply have a psychological affinity, but they play the part of the gentlemen and, as such,

they are the indispensable witnesses who guarantee the honesty of their friends before official justice. As a reward, they receive special attention and special favors from the honored society. What a rabble of honest people, Zola would say! If one adds to all this the very entangled network of kinship bonds and electoral interests operating around the underworld, one understands why it lives, grows, and prospers undisturbed. The sympathy of friends, the fears of shy people, interest and kinship relationships create a sort of protective barrier around it against the possible assault of official justice. (Malafarina 1986: 119)

THE OBLIGATION OF SILENCE

Clearly, the obligation of secrecy is one of the most important duties associated with the status of "man of honor," involving the symbolic and ritual apparatus of the group, its illicit activities, its members and, in Cosa Nostra, the existence itself of the mafia group. Indeed, the link between status and fraternization contracts, on the one hand, and the obligation of secrecy, on the other, is very close. The feeling of common belonging created by the former is a necessary condition for the maintenance of the latter—mistrust is the breeding ground of suspicion, the antithesis of secrecy, and may rapidly undermine the obligation of secrecy that each member has taken vis-à-vis the others. At the same time, the actual commitment to secrecy strengthens the bond created by status contracts: as Koselleck puts it, mystery has "the twin function of uniting and protecting the society" (1988: 80).

Given the different histories of the two associations, even today it is above all Cosa Nostra that emphasizes the above prescriptions. The bond of secrecy shapes every moment of the life of the Sicilian "man of honor," who must not—for one moment or as the result of a banal distraction—forget that he has sworn himself to silence before his mafia brothers. "In Cosa Nostra," Francesco Marino Mannoia states, "it is a given and accepted fact that in betraying the oath of faithfulness made to the organization, there can be no other outcome than death, and this hounds the traitor for the rest of his days" (TrPA 1989: 88). In the 'Ndrangheta, the obligation of secrecy is included in the status contract imposed on each new member at the moment of his initiation, but it is supposed to be strictly respected only when *'ndranghetisti* deal with law enforcement officials and judges. In other social relationships, the modulation of secrecy is left to the discretion of the single *'ndranghetista*.

Omertà

The cultural code that symbolizes, despite its multivocality, the obligation of secrecy is *omertà*. The core of this code consists in the categorical prohibition of cooperation with state authorities or reliance on their services, even when one has been victim of a crime. Such is the force of this prohibition that even if somebody is condemned for a crime he has not committed, he is supposed to serve the sentence without giving the police any information about the real criminal. More generally, *omertà* prescribes silence, as many Sicilian proverbs state (Pitrè [1889] 1993: 295; Alongi [1886] 1977: 56–57):

Lu parrari picca è 'na bedd' arti.	To talk only a little is a beautiful art.
La vucca è traditura di lu cori.	The mouth is the betrayer of the heart.
Passu lungu e vucca curta.	Long steps and short tongue.
Zoccu nun ti apparteni nè mali, nè beni.	Say neither good nor bad about what does not belong to you.
La tistimunianza è bona sinu a quannu nnu fa mali a lu prossimu.	It is all right to witness things as long as they do not harm your neighbor.

It is clear that such normative prescriptions, which originated in the longstanding diffidence that Sicilian and, more generally, southern people have felt toward state authorities, have always been functional to the needs of all those who routinely break state laws, and in particular to members of mafia associations. As early as the last few decades of the nineteenth century, several police officials and independent observers pointed out the practical advantages offered by the code of *omertà* to the *facinorosi* [evildoers]. On this issue, Franchetti's observations are the most enlightening:

> In Palermo . . . the single common interest that constantly unites criminals is the preservation of their class as such—in other words, impunity in the exercise of violence, whatever its purpose might be, against the forces meant in general to suppress it. The rules of conduct which prevail in this group and are imposed materially or morally on the rest of the population are rules that, by the nature of things, are effective in protecting the use of violence. Like other social rules, they set aside the momentary and immediate interests of individuals—indeed, they are often in conflict with these. Hence, the code of *omertà* in Palermo does not allow exceptions and effectively puts up with very few ([1876] 1993: 129–30; see also Alongi [1886] 1977: 55–58)

This interpretation was, however, fiercely opposed by several members of the Sicilian aristocracy and bourgeoisie during the 1880s. Outraged by accusations of complicity with the mafia by northern public opinion, they supported the so-called Sicilianist movement (see chapter 1) and attempted to reevaluate the concept of *omertà*, as they had done for the mafia itself. In both cases, the main cultural "entrepreneur" of this political-cultural operation was the Sicilian ethnographer Giuseppe Pitrè. In contrast to those who claimed that the etymological origin of the term *omertà* came from *umiltà* [humility] (Alongi [1886] 1977: 55; see also Pezzino 1995: 24), Pitrè traced it back to *omineità* and, allegedly relying on preceding oral sources, considered the latter word as an equivalent of the Latin *virtus*. In his interpretation, *omertà* came to be identified with honor itself and was hence defined as "a feeling in its own right, which consists in making oneself independent from social laws, . . . in resolving all controversies through force or, at most, with the arbitrage of the most powerful representatives of *omertà* in the area" ([1889] 1993: 294).

In a frame of this kind, silence was no longer an obligation functional to the interests of evildoers, but a necessary condition for achieving honor: "The basis and support of *omertà* is silence. Without it, the *omu* could not be *omu*, nor could he maintain his unchallenged superiority" (ibid.). Conversely, anyone who "grassed on" his colleagues to a judge or, even worse, who became a police informant, was defined as an *infame*. He was, Pitrè says, not only "materially lost," given the implacability of mafia revenge, but also "morally lost" (ibid.: 300).

Mafia associations drew two considerable, lasting advantages from this act of mystification that identified honor with *omertà* to provide a positive picture of Sicilian values. First, they were able to mask their own need for secrecy with an ideological cover-up and to propose their members as champions of *omertà*, understood as the "quality of being *omu*" (ibid.). Second, they benefited from the diffidence promoted toward state authorities by the Sicilianist movement and for many years exploited to their own advantage the powerful moral sanction that it brought to bear on those who appealed to the state for the protection of their rights (Dalla Chiesa 1978; Marino 1988, 1986).

Prescriptions and Prohibitions

In mafia families, the induction of novices to the art of silence does not take place in the ritualized and structured way common to many primitive secret societies (Webster 1932; Eliade 1959; Mendelson 1967), nor does it impose difficult or painful tests. Nonetheless, the new mafia member undergoes a long and thorough path of training that, as mentioned by numerous mafia witnesses, frequently starts long before his formal affiliation to the mafia group. This starts with the observation of a potential candidate by older "men of honor" from his own area or town from when he is about fifteen, to see if he is "suitable material"; if the result is positive, he is progressively trained to internalize mafia values, most of all honor and *omertà*.

Cosa Nostra requires that the mentality and behavior of a mafioso be inspired by silence, reserve, and reticence, even with regard to the smallest details of everyday life. According to Buscetta, for example, "in the Cosa Nostra of my youth, even the fact that a man of honor went to buy the newspaper and began to read a report of the crime news was censored. Why give an outsider, maybe a policeman, the opportunity to see that you were interested in certain events? The shrewd man of honor certainly reads the newspaper, but asks somebody else to buy it and opens it in a corner, or in his house, in private, without showing anyone what he is doing" (Arlacchi 1994: 86–87). To maintain the secrecy surrounding the association, the families forming part of Cosa Nostra oblige their members to behave with stringent self-control and self-discipline, as well as prohibiting them from getting drunk or using drugs. "A man of honor who gets drunk," a *pentito* from the province of Trapani has declared, "may say too much and unwillingly betray his friends" (Bettini 1994: 108, 122).

This commitment to secrecy is so radical that Sicilian "men of honor" are taught to conceal their own importance, and to minimize any signs of their power. The following episode exemplifies this very well. When a photographer tried to take a picture of don Calò Vizzini, one of the most important chiefs of the Cosa Nostra in the 1950s, he exclaimed, surprised and indignant: "Me in a photograph! Why? I'm nobody. I am just an ordinary citizen." And to the journalist Indro Montanelli, who wanted to interview him, Vizzini protested: "It is funny! People believe that I say little from caution. No. I say little, because I know little. I live in a village, I seldom come to Palermo, I know only a few people" (Montanelli 1973: 112). Contrary to what might be expected, but in line with the above statement, different sources have shown that, from the late nineteenth century on, true mafiosi adopted a style of speaking and behavior that reflected brotherly bonhomie, dressing rather drably and anonymously, living an unassuming and conservative lifestyle; indeed, they even paid formal homage to state authorities (Alongi [1886] 1977: 54–55; Pitrè [1889] 1993: 299–300).

The obligation to secrecy also shapes interaction among mafia members. In the Cosa Nostra, the emphasis placed on a reserved and reticent style of behavior has favored the development of a clear and synthetic code of communication recognizable to fellow members. This was noted as early as 1886 by Giuseppe Alongi: "It is strange that in these hot and imaginative countries, where the ordinary way of speaking is so mellifluous, hyperbolic, and figurative, that of the *maffiosi* is brief, down to earth, and resolute" ([1886] 1977: 54). As it is today, a hundred years ago a few words, a metaphor, or even a glance sufficed to convey information among members.

The slang used by the 'Ndrangheta does not share any of the stylistic characteristics of brevity and precision typical of its Sicilian counterpart. Indeed, more generally, the Calabrian mafia families are much less rigorous than the Cosa

Nostra in enforcing secrecy. Some rules aimed at protecting the inner core of the association are, however, applied punctiliously even in the Calabrian mafia confederation. For example, as in Cosa Nostra, 'Ndrangheta members are not allowed to ask their mafia brothers any questions. "You only listen to what the *compare* spontaneously declares," Gaetano Costa claimed, "but you are never allowed to ask questions" (PrRC 1995: 4990; see also TrPA 1984, I: 49; PrPA 1992: 139; and U.S. Senate 1998: 225). In particular, Calabrian "men of honor" are prohibited from inquiring about the ranks of their superiors. "The rule," Antonio Zagari maintains, "states that persons of a superior rank are not obliged to reveal their rank to inferiors. Conversely, it is absolutely forbidden for lower-ranking affiliates to ask anybody questions about the hierarchical position of elders and superiors" (TrMI 1994a: 122).

In both associations, it is forbidden to write down any information concerning the mafia group. In Cosa Nostra this prohibition is categorically respected, so much so that no exception has yet been recorded.[2] In the 'Ndrangheta, instead, exceptions are the rule. Ever since the late nineteenth century, in fact, written documents listing rites and esoteric formulas have been periodically discovered in southern Calabria and in Canada and Australia (Gambino 1975: 7–28; Ciconte 1992: 21–45; Malafarina 1986: 48–55).

Rituals of Separation and Signs of Recognition

In the Cosa Nostra, the boundary between the initiates and the outsiders created by the rite of mafia initiation is strengthened by the rigid obligation to silence on members. Thus, secrecy draws a line around each mafia family, sealing it into a perfect unit and separating it from the outside world (Simmel 1950: 362–63). In the Calabrian association, instead, the boundary between the mafia group and the external world is much less clear due to lower levels of secrecy. In contrast to Cosa Nostra, however, the Calabrian *locali* use symbols and rituals of separation extensively as tools to maintain these boundaries. These, incidentally, have been largely abandoned by Cosa Nostra, which regards them superfluous and even dangerous for its own invisibility.

One of these, for example, is the particular brand of slang called *bacchiaggiu*, used by the 'Ndrangheta *cosche* as a way of marking its boundaries and strengthening its collective identity. The use of this in-language characterizes and protects communication among the *'ndranghetisti*, making it obscure and unintelligible to anyone outside the group (Falcone 1983). *Bacchiaggiu* distorts and even coins *de novo* expressions and words borrowed from the Calabrian dialect and standard Italian. According to Antonio Zagari, for instance, members of the police forces are described as *migni* or *sbirrami*; the Carabinieri, in particular, are labeled as *strisci russi*, referring to the red stripes on the trousers of their uniform (Zagari 1993: 20–23).

Initiation into the 'Ndrangheta is thus also "a linguistic initiation" (Crupi 1992: 115).³

Separation of the mafia group from the outside world is also emphasized by rituals of purification, which are performed at the beginning of each mafia assembly in order to clean the location of any prior presence of state officers (PrRC 1995: 363, 4441). According to a code found by the police in the 1960s, the formula pronounced by the family chief goes as follows: "In the name of the organized and faithful society, I proceed to the first vote on the account of this *locale* and I baptize it . . . with my faith and my long speech. If up to this moment, I recognized it as a dark place of transit, from now on I recognize it as a sacred, saintly, and inviolable place, where any body of society can meet and disband" (Malafarina 1986: 89).

Both associations have developed various measures to regulate the trespassing of the ritual boundary and also to prevent the casual infiltration of noninitiates into the mafia community. For example, in the past, both Cosa Nostra and the 'Ndrangheta used particular signs to recognize each other, and thus to establish the membership of individuals.⁴ One of these, used extensively through southern Italy, was a tattoo of five dots, forming a star on either the hand or other parts of the body (Ciconte 1992: 40–42). In societies with a low rate of literacy, as was the case of the rural Mezzogiorno in the nineteenth century, tattoos represented the most direct and reliable means to demonstrate one's status and, particularly, one's membership in a group. Being easily recognizable, the star tattoo is no longer employed by Cosa Nostra. It has, however, been recently adopted as a defining mark by groups belonging to a rival Sicilian confederation called Stidda [star].

Even in the 'Ndrangheta, the practice of tattooing is now slowly dying out. As Antonio Zagari points out, "it is now considered a drawback to let oneself be recognized through obvious signs whose meaning is not secret" (TrMI 1994a: 119). Other signs of recognition are, however, still widespread. In particular, the Calabrian mafiosi routinely employ ritual sentences and gestures to declare their mafia membership and to recognize other mafia members. Indeed, a ritual formula, called *copiata* [copy], and some ritual movements are associated to each rank of the 'Ndrangheta.⁵

In Cosa Nostra all these procedures for recognition have long since been abandoned,⁶ given the low degree of security and the high and unavoidable risks of copying associated with them. The very logic of secrecy has fostered their abandonment, since, though they are easy to apply and are psychologically powerful, they can easily be exploited by members of rival groups and law enforcement officials to infiltrate or throw the whole association into disorder. As a result, all signs of recognition in the Sicilian mafia organization have been replaced by the strict rule that two "men of honor" who do not know each other can be introduced only by a third affiliate who is fully aware of the status of both (TrPA 1984, I: 92, 1985, V: 821–22).⁷

THE ESCALATION OF SECRECY

In the last thirty years of the twentieth century, both mafia confederations were forced to increase their levels of secrecy in order to counterbalance the weakening of their popular legitimacy and the intensification of law enforcement action. Also part of this long-term trend is the above-mentioned creation of higher bodies of coordination. In both cases, the main purpose of these collegial bodies has been to regulate the internal and external use of violence to reduce the visibility of the association.[8]

Beyond the establishment of superordinate bodies of coordination, the increase in secrecy has been particularly noticeable in the Calabrian consortium, whose degree of secrecy was quite low until then. In this association, but to a more limited extent in Cosa Nostra as well, significant innovations have been introduced to protect the center of the organization. These hinder the internal circulation of information and widen the distance between the chiefs and lower-ranking affiliates. In other words, secrecy has become more "reflexive" (Luhmann 1990: 450–55; see also 1972). The mechanisms and strategies initially developed to protect the association from external threats have been increasingly employed within the mafia group itself. In both Cosa Nostra and the 'Ndrangheta, new levels of internal secrecy have been established, so much so that in the latter consortium a secret society within the secret society has been set up: the Santa. This is composed of an elite of *'ndranghetisti*, and lower-ranking affiliates were originally unaware of its existence.

The Santa

Unlike the lower ranks, the *dote* [rank] of *santista* and higher levels do not belong to the traditional stratification system of the Calabrian 'Ndrangheta, nor are they the product of a hundred-year-old process. They are, instead, innovations introduced in the early 1970s to maximize the power and invisibility of the most important mafia chiefs. According to the *pentito* Giovanni Gullà, the Santa, the name of which derives from the shortening of *mamma santissima*,[9] represents "an occult stage inside the 'Ndrangheta, since its rank is known only to other *santisti*. To give an example, if a *'ndranghetista* presents himself to other *'ndranghetisti* of another group, he must reveal his rank of *picciotto, camorrista, sgarrista,* etc., but not his eventual rank of *santista*, which he should reveal only and exclusively to other *santisti*. . . . The Santa can be explained as forming a 'secret sect': the intention was to create a power structure, unknown to the others, in order to gain larger benefits" (PrRC 1995: 5737).

The Santa was originally envisaged as a very exclusive body: "The rank of *santista* could be conferred on no more than thirty-three people and attributed to new subjects only in the case of the death of another *santista*" (ibid.: 4987). However, as the years went by, "a sort of inflation took place in assigning the status of *santista*," and, therefore, around 1978, a new higher rank, *vangelo* [gospel], was established. Later, this was followed by the institution of the position of *trequartino* [three-quarters] or *quintino* [fifth] and, finally, by the highest rank of *associazione* [society], reserved for the supreme chiefs (ibid.: 323; TrMI 1994a: 119).

The institution of the rank of *santista* was fostered at the end of the 1960s by Girolamo "Mommo" Piromalli, leader of the Piromalli mafia family in Gioia Tauro, and by the chiefs of several other families. They were eager to modify the traditional rules of the association in order to enter the public work market and start illegal activities such as drug trafficking, which were prohibited by the 'Ndrangheta's traditional code but promised to be very profitable. According to Gaetano Costa, "It was Mommo Piromalli who—given the enormous interests which then existed in the Reggio Calabria area (the railroad stump, the steelwork center, and the port in Gioia Tauro, etc.)—entrusted himself with the rank of *santista*, in order to assert his higher authority and hence directly control the public works. He said that this rank had been given him directly in Toronto, where there was a very important *'ndrina*" (PrRC 1995: 4987).

The rules adopted by the Santa marked a considerable departure from the 'Ndrangheta's traditional code in terms of permissible activities, relations with state authorities, and criteria of affiliation. "In the past, the organization opposed the state and members were forced to live on so-called *sgarro* [extortions and thefts] or on the proceeds of other illicit activities" (ibid.: 6599). Instead, in the opinion of the *pentito* Giuseppe Albanese,

> the Santa aimed at any form of illicit earnings, the commission of crimes which the 'Ndrangheta had not previously allowed (kidnappings and drug trafficking). Unlike in the past, the *santista* was authorized to have contact with the representatives of [state] institutions. Furthermore, the *santista* could be chosen from among persons of any social background. This is also a major difference because in the past, access to the 'Ndrangheta was granted only to the offspring of "honored" families: i.e., families which had no connection with state institutions and were not dishonored by infamous facts. (Ibid.: 6601)

It was precisely on account of these innovations that the new institution was opposed by the more traditionalist chiefs. Among these were Antonio Macrì from the Ionic town of Siderno, the 'Ndrangheta's charismatic leader of the 1960s, and Domenico Tripodo, who was then *dominus* of the Reggio Calabria mafia. Only at the end of the so-called first mafia war, which took place in 1974–76 and led to their deaths and the consequent rise of the De Stefano brothers as the new leaders of the Reggio Calabria mafia, was the new institution fully recognized.

As soon as the Santa was accepted, the profitable practices of kidnapping and drug trafficking also gained full legitimation. Several 'Ndrangheta families had already started carrying out these activities in the early 1970s, though they had been condemned by the traditional wing. Moreover, the Santa allowed the *capimafia* to establish close connections with state representatives and officials, so much so that some of them were affiliated with the Santa. These connections were often established through the Freemasonry, which the *santisti*—breaking another rule of the traditional code—were allowed to join (see also chapter 5).

The very creation of the Santa was greatly influenced by the Freemasonry, with which the 'Ndrangheta chiefs developed ties during the Reggio Calabria revolt of 1970 (triggered by the central government's decision to make Catanzaro—instead of Reggio Calabria—the new official seat of regional administration; see Lombardi Satriani 1971). According to the former chief of the Messina *'ndrina*, Gaetano Costa, Mommo Piromalli "who was famous for being a Mason, or—at any rate—extremely close to the Mason circles . . . introduced the rule . . . according to which any member of the Santa could join the Masonry" (PrRC 1995: 5730). And indeed, according to another mafia witness, Albanese, "all the *santisti* were part of the Masonic brotherhood or, at least, the chiefs of the Santa were full members" (ibid.: 6602).

Further proof of the close ties between the Santa and the Freemasonry is given by the analogies between the rituals, symbols, and organizational rules of the two secret societies. Meetings among *santisti*, for example, are opened "in the name of Giuseppe Mazzini, Giuseppe Garibaldi, and Giuseppe La Marmora," three major figures of the Italian Freemasonry, who are personified during the same meetings by three *santisti* (ibid.: 4985).[10] Even the ceremony of initiation, called *fedelizzazione* in the slang of the 'Ndrangheta, uses terms that clearly originate in Masonic rites. For example, during the ceremony the officiant asks: "Do you know the family of the Masons?" The novice must answer: "No, but if necessary I embrace it with my skin, flesh and bones, swearing the loyalty asked of me to the family of the holy order of the Masons" (ibid.: 4983). Furthermore, as in Masonic practice, while the new member's name is communicated to all the existing members, theirs are initially not disclosed to him.

The founding of the Santa parallels an analogous process in the Freemasonry, also involving the creation of secret or "covered" lodges beside or within official ones. As the *pentito* Giovanni Gullà points out, "the Santa, as a secret sect, is the exact correspondent of the covered Freemasonry vis-à-vis the official one" (ibid.: 5737). In the same way as the secret lodges were formed in the Freemasonry, the Santa and the higher ranks were created to reinforce protection around the inner core of the association through secrecy. In this way, the Santa and the higher ranks functioned to remedy the 'Ndrangheta's traditional low degree of secrecy. As Giuseppe Albanese noted in a memorial submitted to the investigating judges in

1984, the 'Ndrangheta was originally set up as "a secret organization, but nothing secret has remained [because] many had discovered it, revealing the modalities of the organization and its laws" (ibid.: 5738).

Lower-ranking members function as a large protective ring around the nucleus of the Santa. "It is clear," witness Michele Ierardo states, "that the Santa has overturned the rules of the traditional mafia. This carried on, however, since it was the fundamental presupposition for both the existence and the profitable activities of the Santa" (ibid.: 5736). To ensure the protection of the Santa, its members are even authorized "to betray a hundred *camorristi* or *sgarristi*" by giving "tip-offs" to police forces (ibid.: 6601).[11]

Obstructions and Deviations

Nothing comparable to the Santa has been created in Cosa Nostra. Nonetheless, over the last two decades of the twentieth century it too registered a greater move toward secrecy, even though—as described above—this was already much more pervasive than in the 'Ndrangheta. In both associations, the increase in secrecy has fostered a sharp weakening of community life, in order to reduce the risks of being arrested or intercepted by law enforcement agencies. With regard to this, Antonio Zagari states, "We of the 'Ndrangheta working in the Varese province [in northern Italy] met only when there was a specific reason to do so, although once upon a time the rule was for members of a *cosca* to meet regularly, once or twice a week, even when there was nothing to discuss or to decide on" (TrMI 1994a: 131–32).

Internal barriers through which information must pass in order to circulate have also been strengthened, though in reality this process was never either fast or easy, due to the segmented nature of the two associations. "Not all men of honor," Salvatore Cancemi, who was chief of the Porta Nuova *mandamento* [district] in Palermo for many years, stated, "know everything about what happens in Cosa Nostra. Indeed, the rule is compartmentalization" (PrPA 1995a, III: 75). Likewise, according to Leonardo Messina, "the circulation of information within the organization is very limited" (PrPA 1992: 45). In Cosa Nostra the preexisting obstructions were considerably strengthened by the Corleonesi. "'Compartmentalization,' which restrains the circulation of knowledge within Cosa Nostra," the Palermitan prosecutors noted, "became increasingly marked in the Corleonesi period following the strategy of power concentration pursued by Salvatore Riina" (PrPA 1995a, III: 75).

In reality, Riina and his close allies exploited these barriers to internal information flows to foster conflicts among the members of different *cosche* and to impose their power on a large section of the association. In the mafia world, in fact, it is rather easy to delegitimize a "man of honor" through the spread of slanderous rumors. Given the existing barriers to the circulation of information, the member is left powerless to defend himself before the association as a whole. Totò Riina was very skillful in exploiting this feature to his own advantage: the murders of most of his rivals were preceded or, more rarely, followed by maneuvers of delegitimation, to weaken their prestige and their allies' and subjects' loyalty.[12]

Since the early 1980s, the families belonging to the Corleonesi coalition have also resorted extensively to so-called reserved affiliations to hide the identity of their members from rival *cosche* and protect themselves from the *pentiti*'s revelations. According to Leonardo Messina, a former member of a rival group, the Corleonesi "are setting up another structure based on secrecy that will replace Cosa Nostra. . . . All the traditional men of honor belonging to Cosa Nostra are a problem for the Corleonesi. They have already been identified by the various *pentiti*. . . . There are already men both in the Palermo area—I know some of them—and in Nisseno [Caltanissetta province] who have not been introduced to anybody, although they carry on doing business. It is a sort of parallel Cosa Nostra" (CPM 1992d: 520; see also TrMA 1987: 3). The inquiries carried out after the capture of Totò Riina—which took place in January 1993—did indeed reveal that the closest circle around "the chief of all chiefs" consisted of "men of honor" affiliated through a reserved procedure. These men were unknown to most other Cosa Nostra members and guaranteed the fugitive a secret and parallel net of communication and hiding places (TrPA 1994b).[13]

Mistrust and Suspicion

After Riina's arrest, the need for secrecy became so strong that it led to the overturning of one of the main legitimizing tenets of the association: the admission of novices with a ritual of affiliation. According to several *pentiti*, the *capimafia* belonging to the Corleonesi coalition perform initiation rituals more and more rarely, relying instead on men who are not formally affiliated to Cosa Nostra (the *avvicinati*). The *pentito* Mario Santo Di Matteo says of this, "It is now a very widespread practice within the Cosa Nostra . . . to surround oneself with trusted men who are not affiliated and therefore remain outside the circle of acquaintances of Cosa Nostra men. They are usually 'clean' people who have to play cover-up roles for their respective referents in the Cosa Nostra" (qtd. in Lo Forte 1996; see also PrPA 1996b: 13).

Through changing their recruitment criteria in this way, Corleonesi chiefs hoped to achieve a series of specific goals. First, they aimed to increase their own invisibility, and thus security, by hiding themselves within a group of nonritually affiliated people. Second, they wanted to create a set of mutually independent networks of logistical contacts and support, among which they could easily shift in case of need. Third, not being bound by the mafia rules of solidarity and fraternity, they thought that they could drastically limit the amount of shared information, thus minimizing the negative consequences in case of betrayal.

The protection provided by this circle of uninitiated subjects has, however, proved to be totally illusionary. Such a strategy can work as long as the *avvicinati* remain unknown to the chiefs of rival families and law enforcement institutions. However, on arrest, they become a major threat to the Corleonesi chiefs. For example, the most significant backlash has been that most of them have soon begun to cooperate with the judiciary, providing valuable and updated information to police officials and setting them on the track of important fugitives. Thanks to the statements of some *avvicinati*, two of the most authoritative of Riina's successors—Leoluca Bagarella, Riina's brother-in-law, and Giovanni Brusca, head of the San Giuseppe Jato family, since the 1970s one of the closest allies of the Corleone *cosca*—were arrested in June 1995 and May 1996 respectively.

The behavior of these unaffiliated supporters can be seen as confirmation of the importance of secondary socialization processes within mafia groups. These people have not learned about the mafia "subuniverse of meaning" (Berger and Luckmann 1967; see chapter 2); they have not been indoctrinated with the values of solidarity, honor, and *omertà*; they have no feeling of belonging to the association, nor do they feel that they must obey it at all costs. Faced with the possibility of spending the rest of their life in prison, no internalized cultural orientation or emotional bond constrains them from opting for the most advantageous solution: betraying a society to which they were never admitted formally (Buscetta 1999: 64–65).

Thus, taken to its extreme consequences, the logic of secrecy ends up undermining the social bases of mafia order. "Secrecy, which used to be a means to pursue one's goals more effectively, became the most important feature of the organization and gave rise to complexity and disorder" (Maniscalco 1994: 105). Raised to the status of a norm regulating the whole of community life, it led to misunderstandings, resentment, fears, rivalries, and even longstanding, violent clashes among "men of honor."

Two contradictory messages are thus given to Cosa Nostra members today. On the one hand, they are still taught to regard other members as their own brothers and to interiorize the principles of solidarity and generalized reciprocity, even though the emphasis on these messages is no longer as strong as it used to be. On the other, they are ordered to be diffident and reserved, to control and conceal their emotions, and to trust nobody. Once mistrust and dissimulation of one's feelings predominate and become habitual, it is difficult to avoid treating one's own associates in the same way. This point is vividly made by a former affiliate of the Castelvetrano family: "For Cosa Nostra it is very important to recruit soldiers who are able to disguise their feelings, cheat the enemy and, at the same time, to be loyal with friends. These are qualities difficult to find in a man. When lying becomes a second nature, one ends up lying all the time, for shrewdness or personal profit, with enemies, friends, and relatives. Lies and loyalty struggle to find a place within the same person" (Bettini 1994: 73).

The spread of suspicion and mistrust was strongly accelerated by Riina's power strategies. Riina not only ruthlessly killed dozens of his enemies but also fostered and exploited rivalries among the leaders of the Corleonesi wing. By undermining their reciprocal trust and pitting them one against the other, Riina was able to prevent all of them from gaining too much personal power. The way he manipulated situations around him can be seen, for example, in the string of events triggered by the murder of Pino Greco. This was carried out by Vincenzo Puccio and Giuseppe Lucchese, two of Greco's closest collaborators. As a reward, Puccio was granted the prestigious position of chief of the family and *mandamento* in Ciaculli, previously held by Greco. However, four years later, after Puccio began to let it be known that in his opinion Riina had too much power and he started to organize a group to counter this, he too was murdered in the Palermitan Ucciardone prison by two members of his own *mandamento* (ibid.: 340–62).

The Corleonesi ruled Cosa Nostra through simulation and dissimulation. The victim of a murder was often approached by another "man of honor" enjoying his trust, leading him to feel relaxed enough to reduce his usual precautions. In this way he became much more vulnerable and was therefore easier to murder. When Giovanni Prestifilippo's murder was being planned, a member of his own family, Giovanni Drago, was charged with both assisting and murdering him. Thus, Drago passed information about his movements to the hit squad that would actually kill him, as well as taking part in the murder himself (PrPA 1993c: 195–98).

In the long run, this kind of behavior can have devastating effects, as the defections affecting Cosa Nostra in the 1990s show. The trust and solidarity that were drastically weakened by Riina's power strategies and the feeling of common belonging among the *cosche* members that was squandered constituted essential and irreplaceable elements for the survival of mafia families.

ALTERNATIVE LEGAL ORDERS

Founded on systematic resort to secrecy and violence, the normative systems developed by Cosa Nostra and the 'Ndrangheta constitute a legal order alternative to that of the state. Through secrecy, mafia associations present themselves as self-sufficient entities, independent of the state that has criminalized them and aims—at least in principle—to suppress them. Thanks to violence, they guarantee the effectiveness of their own legal order and prosecute any violations of it. The two mafia confederations thus constitute independent law communities. As Pino Scriva, one of the first *pentiti* of the Calabrian 'Ndrangheta, has described, "the organization lives and works almost as an alternative to state organization. The norms governing it are perfectly well known to members and are in antithesis to state laws" (PrRC 1995: 361).

The normative codes of the two consortia are not written; nonetheless, their basic substantial and procedural rules emerge with great clarity and force from the accounts of former insiders who today cooperate with the judiciary and from a set of external sources dating from different historical moments. As early as 1905, for example, in a sentence concerning the Honored Society, the Corte d'Appello delle Calabrie argued: "It is true that it did not have a written statute, but this fact reveals the sophisticated shrewdness of the Society. This, fearing that the Statute could fall at some point into the hands of Justice, cunningly abstained from compiling it. But although it lacked a written Statute, the refined and special obligations to which all the affiliates had to be sacrally submitted, were nonetheless sanctioned by norms" (Nicaso 1990: 70).

Santi Romano's Theory of Law

The thesis that Cosa Nostra and the 'Ndrangheta are law communities independent of the state is not new. At the beginning of the twentieth century, the Sicilian lawyer Santi Romano maintained that criminal organizations constitute an "alternative legal order" [*ordinamento giuridico alternativo*] (1977). Published for the first time in 1918, Romano's statements were subsequently used to justify the introduction of the "crime of delinquent association" into the Rocco penal code as well as the indiscriminate anti-mafia campaigns of the Fascist regime.[14] It is probably for this reason that Romano's theory has been ignored or rejected by virtually all the scholars who have studied the mafia phenomenon since the Second World War:[15] all the more so since his views were incompatible with the "disorganized" view of the mafia, which prevailed for so many years.

Now, however, that the existence of mafia groups in Sicily and Calabria can no longer be doubted, it is possible—and even necessary—to reassess the theses of this important Sicilian jurist in a more detached way. To do so, it is indispensable to distinguish between Romano's propositions and the political uses to which his theory has been put. Too often, in fact, the two levels remain indistinct. In Diego Gambetta's *Sicilian Mafia*, for example, Romano's theory is presented as the theoretical justification of Italian corporatism and, as such, drastically rejected:

> Romano's position has been very influential in Italy, although not so much in mainstream legal thinking, which is firmly statist, as in politics. It has enjoyed popularity with all kinds of anti-liberal circles right, left, and center. It was used to support corporatism, and the state as mediator between organic inde-

pendent bodies.... And it provided legal grounds for the claims to independence of the Catholic church and its institutions.... Since the last war this relativist view has survived *mutatis mutandis* in the peculiar mixture of cynicism and Catholicism which represents the quintessence of Italy's political structure. (1993: 5–6)

In reality, nothing of this kind can be found in Romano's main *oeuvre*, *L'ordinamento giuridico*. Unlike legal positivism, which was then dominant, Romano proposed a theory of law as institution, an idea that was also supported by other European intellectuals (Maurice Hauriou in France, for example). The nucleus of his theory can be synthesized in the following: whenever there is a "society ordered through an organization"—which Romano defined as an institution—there is law (*ius*) (1977). From this proposition, he inferred the corollary that even a criminal association, insofar as it expresses an internal organization, has a legal order. In his words, "A revolutionary society or a crime association do not constitute law for the state that they want to demolish or whose laws they violate in the same way that a schismatic sect is declared illegal by the church. This, however, does not exclude the possibility that in these cases there are institutions, organizations, and orders which, taken by themselves and intrinsically considered, are legal" (1977: 44, 122–23).

No defense of the mafia phenomenon can be found in Romano's thinking. He never mentions the word *mafia*, but only refers generically to criminal associations. Nor does he ever question the legitimacy of state action against these unrecognized legal orders: "Not only do the actions carried out in conformity with the order of the organization itself constitute crimes, but the simple fact of establishing and then ordering such an organization may also be considered a crime. ... In these cases, the state order fights the orders that menace either its own existence or, at least, the most important goods that the state aims to protect with as much strength as possible. Far from granting them the status of 'legal orders,' it strikes out against them, regarding them as the most serious illegal facts, that is, as crimes" (ibid.: 197–98).

In reality, notwithstanding the biased interpretations that developed in the years following publication of his work, the Sicilian jurist never intended to make antistate or illiberal claims. Indeed, as Norberto Bobbio argues,

> Romano is a moderate pluralist; that is, he believes in the beneficial effects that the emergence of social groups, such as the unions, may have toward a better articulation of the relationship between single individuals and the state. Nonetheless, he still considers the state the final and necessary moment of any organized society. Even more so, he is theoretically a pluralist, but ideologically a monist. In conclusion, he states that whatever the ongoing social transformations, the principle of a superior organization cannot be given up.

... This superior organization cannot but be the "modern state." (1977: 183–84; see also Fiandaca 1994)

The "institutionalist" theory can instead be criticized for its simplistic identification between legal order and institution and his superimposition of the two corresponding levels of analysis. According to Romano, in fact, "every legal order is an institution and, vice versa, every institution is a legal order" (1977: 27). Going beyond a positivist and state-centered conception of law, Romano's work had the merit of stating clearly for the first time in Italy that law is the product of social life and exists only when there is a set of rules composing a system. His assertion that any organized social group constitutes a legal order is, instead, too radical, because the normative systems of any collectivity are thus raised to the rank of a legal order (Bobbio 1958: 5–23).

Between Positivistic and Anthropological Conceptions of Law

Not all normative systems can be regarded as independent legal orders, unless we want to share the claims of some contemporary legal anthropologists that every society has a multiplicity of "legal levels," which range from family to the state, and that "law"—as a social phenomenon—exists in all of them. The path pursued here is an intermediate one between the traditional positivistic conception of law and the most extreme claims of legal pluralism.

On the one hand, it is clear that mafia associations cannot be recognized as independent juridical communities within a positivistic framework of law. In the classical formulation of this approach, which was proposed by the British legal reformer John Austin in the nineteenth century, laws are the commands of the sovereign, the supreme legal authority of an independent political society, and are typically expressed through legislation and supported by state sanctions.[16] By conceiving law as a property of the society as a whole, all subgroups—associations as well as residential and kinship groups—are a priori excluded from the possibility of creating and enforcing an autonomous system of legal rules on their adherents.

On the other hand, we do not want to identify law with the customs of a society as, for example, Bronislaw Malinowsky did in the 1920s in the small, very influential booklet *Crime and Custom in Savage Society* (1961), now seen as the first paving stone to the establishing of legal anthropology as a discipline in its own right. According to the British scholar, law is "a body of binding obligations regarded as right by one party and acknowledged as duty by the other, kept in force by the specific mechanism of reciprocity and publicity inherent in the structure of ... the society" (1961: 58). Nor should law be defined as virtually every form of rule pertaining to an organized group in any society: that is, to maintain—referring to Karl Llewellyn and E. Adamson Hoebel's famous definition—that "the total picture of law-stuff in any society included, along with the Great Law-stuff of the Whole, the sublaw-stuff or bylaw-stuff of the lesser working units" (1941: 28; see also Pospísil 1974).

If we adopted this position, the specificity of mafia legal orders would be lost, as all the normative systems of any collective group would be considered legal orders. But there are not only contingent reasons to discard the most radical versions of legal pluralism. Anthropological research has had the undeniable cultural merit of fostering the awareness that law is not a merely a Western concept. It has also pointed out the inadequacy, in a cross-cultural framework, of those European axioms that identify law with a centralized administration and its apparatus of tribunals, registries, legislatures, and police. The universalist zeal of anthropological scholars, however, leads some of them to obscure the specificity of the legal phenomenon, by blurring it into one of social control.[17] In this respect, the thesis advanced by Sally Falk Moore seems to be more balanced. Recognizing that law is a category of Western culture, the American scholar suggests the less Western-bound term of "reglementation" to name rules that "are made within organizations other than the State, both in societies without government and in societies having an overarching state organization" (1978: 17–18).

The legal orders of Cosa Nostra and the 'Ndrangheta are something more and different than the normative system of other secondary formations. It should not be forgotten that in modern societies all centers of normative production are subordinated to the state and that their rules are valid insofar as they do not oppose state laws. Whenever the rules of a corporate group fail to be effective or are changed and/or manipulated to the disadvantage of single members, these can always turn to the state to have their rights protected and sue the group itself. Likewise, each secondary formation has the right to turn to the state whenever it clashes with another group.

In contemporary societies, it is hard to find any legal systems that are completely independent of the state. According to Lauren Benton (1994), even the participants in informal economies rarely perceive their actions as belonging to an unregulated area, independent and opposed to state law, and, indeed, they are influenced in their interaction more by the law than by the norms of the informal sector.

Contrary to most other groups of modern societies, mafia consortia do not recognize the primacy of state law; rather, they claim the autonomy and self-sufficiency of their own legal order. As Donald Cressey remarks, "organized criminals, like prisoners, live outside the law and in response to this outlaw status they, like prisoners, develop a set of norms and procedures for controlling conducts within their organization" (1969: 175). Following a practice widespread in premodern societies,[18] mafia groups set themselves apart as a separate "law community," establishing and enforcing their own "special law." They reject the state monopoly of violence and routinely resort to violence in order to impose the respect of their own legal order and to prosecute its violations (Weber 1978: 694–96).

On entering a mafia family, members are required to interiorize the mafia normative system and to commit themselves to respecting it throughout their life, no matter whether they continue to actively participate in the group life itself. This obligation derives from the fact that mafia associations bind their adherents, as mentioned above, to the respect of a status and fraternization contract that can be rescinded only with their death (see chapter 2). Hence, even members who have been temporarily suspended, and even the lucky and rare ones who have been definitively expelled without being killed, must still continue to observe the rules of the association (TrPA 1985, V: 816).

Sicilian and Calabrian "men of honor" are also bound to the principle of exclusiveness: that is, they must pay respect exclusively to the mafia legal order, though they are authorized to take state laws into account when it is to their advantage to do so, in order to avoid state sanctions. Given its illegal status, however, neither the association nor its members can turn to state authority to solve eventual conflicts or to see their rights respected without admitting the inadequacy of the mafia normative order. For example, only in the mid-1970s were Cosa Nostra affiliates allowed to report the theft of their cars. This decision was taken at the end of a fierce debate, and was approved only in order for the owner to avoid being linked to any illegal activities that might be carried out by someone else using the stolen car (ibid.: 828–29; TrPA 1984, II: 137–38).

Unlike groups recognized by state law, Cosa Nostra and the 'Ndrangheta claim to be in a position of mutual exclusiveness and therefore of equality with the legal order backed by state authority. A former member of the Castelvetrano mafia family was, for instance, often told that "Cosa Nostra [does] . . . not recognize the authority of state, to which it was and it will always be opposed. . . . Our homeland is the family, and it must be defended to the last" (Bettini 1994: 86–88).

The otherness of the mafia legal order vis-à-vis the state is also strengthened by numerous subordinate rules. In both consortia, law enforcement officials and their sons are absolutely prohibited from becoming members and, in Calabria, at one time any contact with the representatives of state institutions was also forbidden. Although the latter rule has been relaxed in recent times, exceptions to the former are still extremely rare.[19] In addition, in the Calabrian association a strong emphasis has traditionally been placed on carrying out illegal activities to reinforce its contrast with the state order. Pino Scriva elaborates:

> It is fundamental to earn one's income not through work, but through the *sgarro* [above all, extortions and thefts], that is, illegally. This traditional rule

has been slowly modified because there are some members who have accumulated enormous wealth and, hence, plan formally licit activities besides the illicit ones. It is certain, however, that illicit activities are never abandoned, both because crimes offer an easy means of self-financing and also because, in a delinquent context, the mafiosi essentially draw their prestige from the criminal activities that they accomplish. (Ibid.: 361–62)

Another rule prescribes that imprisoned "men of honor" must reject the "food of the government." Although the exceptions to this rule have been numerous, its aim is clear: to underline the distance separating mafiosi from state institutions and to emphasize the scorn of the former toward the latter (TrPA 1985, V: 823; Arlacchi 1994: 186–87). In the 'Ndrangheta, otherness from the state legal order is also conveyed by its vocabulary. Not only are the meetings among the chiefs called *crimine*, but the adjective "criminal" is usually used in a positive way to indicate members who are brave. According to Antonio Zagari, for example, a 'ndranghetista who wants to praise an associate would express himself as follows: "That guy comes from a good criminal root" (TrMI 1994a: 120–21).

Rules of Primary and Secondary Type

Like all fully fledged legal orders, the statutes of Cosa Nostra and the 'Ndrangheta consist of "rules of primary type" and "rules of secondary type." Such a distinction was put forward at the beginning of the 1960s by H. L. A. Hart in his influential book *The Concept of Law* (1994) and echoes—or rather, specifies—the differentiation, more familiar to jurists, between norms of behavior and norms of structure or competence (Bobbio 1960: 21).

Rules of primary type establish obligations and require individuals to do or to abstain from certain actions. In Cosa Nostra and the 'Ndrangheta, in particular, they prescribe the duties associated to the status of "man of honor" and, though unsystematically, most of them have been reviewed in this and the preceding chapters. Rules of secondary type establish the ways in which the rules of behavior can be conclusively ascertained, introduced, eliminated, and varied, and their violation conclusively determined. It is the introduction of this second type of rule that allows the passage "from the pre-legal into the legal world," by converting "the regime of primary rules of obligation into what is indisputably a legal system" (Hart 1994: 94).

According to Hart, there are three different types of secondary rules in fully developed legal systems: "rules of recognition," allowing the conclusive identification of primary rules of obligation; "rules of change," setting the way in which new rules can be enacted and old rules eliminated; and "rules of adjudication," empowering members of the society to make authoritative decisions as to whether, on any particular occasion, a rule has been broken. The latter also establish the individuals or bodies authorized to adjudicate and lay down the procedures to be followed. In most cases, rules of this type also confer the exclusive power to grant penalties and direct their application upon judges (ibid.: 91–99).

Neither of the normative codes of the mafia associations includes specific rules of recognition and change. That is to say, no clear device is provided to identify and change the primary rules of obligation. Unlike state laws, the rules composing Cosa Nostra's and the 'Ndrangheta's legal orders are not authoritatively listed in any written document: no Magna Carta or penal or civil code exists. Likewise, the rules of change are not as clearly defined as those of a fully developed legal system: there is no permanent collegial body with the exclusive function of introducing new primary rules for the behavior of the life of the group or of some of its segments and eliminating old rules. Nor is the procedure to be followed in legislation defined in rigid terms.

Nonetheless, at least since the late nineteenth century both mafia societies have clear rules of adjudication. These give different bodies judicial power and confer a special status to their decisions on breaches of obligations. These rules mark the passage from custom to law and separate legal rules from social norms. In fact, the violation of legal rules is, unlike moral norms, sanctioned externally but, as opposed to social norms, is institutionalized: that is, their sanctioning is regulated by fixed, precise norms and is entrusted to some members of the group (Bohannan 1967; Bobbio 1958: 191–201). A system that has rules of adjudication is necessarily also committed to rules of recognition, though of an elementary and imperfect sort. "This is so," as Hart points out, "because if the courts are allowed to make authoritative determinations of the fact that a rule has been broken, these cannot avoid an authoritative determination of what the rules are" (1994: 97). If only embryonically, rules of adjudication also contain rules of recognition, pointing to primary rules through judicial bodies, which thus become a source of law.

In both mafia associations, the punishment for some rule violations is, according to the code of honor, directly entrusted to the aggrieved individuals. Still today, if victimized by nonmembers, Cosa Nostra and 'Ndrangheta members are required to do justice by themselves. The failure to do so may imply suspension or expulsion from the family. Thus, as in many simple societies, mafia affiliates are expected to act as "private prosecutors" of a private injury. By doing so, they become public officials *pro eo solo delicto*, representing not only their own or their blood family's interest, but also the general social interest of the mafia group. Though the group may not intervene overtly, the injury is considered to be against the society as a whole, insofar as each mafia member has the precise duty to support any associate seeking revenge (Hoebel 1954: 27–28).

Cosa Nostra and the 'Ndrangheta have, instead, different and longstanding rules concerning the reaction to wrongs inflicted upon "men of honor" by other mafia members. Since the institution of the provincial commission, Cosa Nostra prohibits its members from taking revenge for offences committed by other mafia members on their own. The provincial and regional commissions claim the right to examine all cases of conflicts among mafia brothers and, eventually, to impose the most appropriate sanctions. Since 1957, violence against another member of Cosa Nostra has been authorized only under conditions of immediate threat.

In the 'Ndrangheta, instead, up to the early 1990s both the single mafia families and members were entitled—and to a certain extent obliged if they did not want to lose their honor—to react directly against all the violations which affected them directly, even if they were committed by associated individuals or units. The mafia consortium as a whole was not entitled to intervene and had no means of stopping the lasting conflicts deriving from this procedure of adjudication. "Feuds," a Calabrian witness notes, "were regarded as exclusively personal [sic] matters among the families" (PrRC 1995: 287) and even the most charismatic mafia members had no authority to intervene to settle them. Only with the establishment of the *camera di canalizzazione* in the early 1990s has the adjudication of *'ndranghetisti*'s wrongs vis-à-vis other members been removed from the sphere of single families and centralized in a higher body of coordination. Since then—as mentioned in chapter 1—feuds have drastically declined.

In both legal orders, then, there are specific rules to punish rule violations that do not directly impinge on the honor of a member or his blood family. In the Sicilian confederation as in the Calabrian one, their adjudication was originally assigned to the general assembly of each mafia family. Antonino Cutrera refers, for example, to two nineteenth-century Sicilian associations, the Stoppaglieri of Monreale and the Oblonica of Girgenti, with courts composed of the members, which "judged about other people's life and goods" ([1900] 1988: 121). This formally democratic adjudication system even took the rights of the defendants into some account. The Palermitan groups, described by Questore Sangiorgi at the turn of the twentieth century, granted the accused members the right to defend themselves before the group (Lupo 1993). In the Oblonica, a first-degree sentence could be appealed in front of a court called *turno* (Cutrera [1900] 1988: 121). A veritable hierarchy of adjudication bodies also existed even in the 'Ndrangheta. Above the assembly of each family, there was "a sort of court . . . composed of the most deserving *capibastone* of the district. After the '*crimine* of first instance' there was the provincial or veracious *crimine*, which was, in its turn, a kind of supreme court. This was composed by the three chiefs who held command in the three administrative districts of the province and, eventually, other chiefs of equal merit, even if the latter did not hold command positions" (Montalto 1973: 330).

The Calabrian *locali* still resort to this collegial procedure of adjudication for all members' violations that do not directly affect the prestige of a single *'ndranghetista*. "For the crimes committed by *picciotti, camorristi,* and *sgarristi,*" Pino Scriva states, "the 'Ndrangheta court is competent, and is formed by those participating in the various assemblies of *picciotti, camorristi,* and *sgarristi*" (PrRC 1995: 366). The collegiality of the judicial process is, however, more apparent than real. Decisions are usually taken either by the chief of the family assembly or, in the case of interfamily meetings, by the most authoritative members. According to the Calabrian writer Saverio Montalto, the lower-ranking affiliates are often not even granted the right to vote (1973: 330). In his turn, the *pentito* Francesco Fonti recalls that only the chiefs and the *contabile* are empowered to determine a violation and thus to assign an appropriate punishment, whereas the *'ndranghetista* holding the role of *mastro di giornata* acts as prosecutor (PrRC 1995: 4439–40; see also Sergi 1991: 67–70).[20]

The 'Ndrangheta's legal order entails a relatively differentiated set of sanctions. The lightest type of punishment, to be applied when offences do not endanger the existence of the society, consists of a fee. Then, there is a *zaccagnata*, that is, a stab with a knife, carried out by the *puntaiolo* of each group either on the belly or in the back of the guilty *'ndranghetista*. More serious types of punishments consist in the temporary suspension of the offender and retrocession to lower ranks. In the case of more serious misdeeds, a sanction "capable of humiliating any pride" (Castagna 1967: 43) used to be imposed by the traditional code of the 'Ndrangheta, but contemporary *pentiti* no longer mention it. According to Serafino Castagna, this consisted in a ritual ceremony in which the condemned was undressed and, using a brush, other affiliates covered him with excrement. The next sanction is definitive expulsion, by which the sanctioned member acquires the status of *tralasciato* [neglected] and his former associates are obliged to break off all relationships with him. However, since "it is a very remote possibility that a man expelled from the 'Ndrangheta keeps on living" (TrMI 1994a: 124), this last punishment is usually transformed into a death sentence (see also Ciconte 1992: 42–43, 66–67; PrRC 1995: 4439–40).

In Cosa Nostra, the collegial system of adjudication at the family level has long been relinquished, even from a formal point of view. In all likelihood, though it is impossible to establish with any great precision exactly when, judicial functions have been entrusted to the chief of each *cosca* since the early decades of the twentieth century. The chief thus has the power to inflict sanctions of all kinds, including death, on his family members.[21] The family assembly can take over its original power of adjudication only when the chief himself comes under scrutiny.

With the creation of the Palermo provincial commission, however, the collegial system of adjudication has reproduced itself at the interfamily level. The new superordinate body was initially entrusted with the solution of conflicts among members of different families. From the late 1970s, however, even the solution of the most serious intrafamily disputes has been removed from the discretion of family chiefs and given to the exclusive competence of the commission.

According to Tommaso Buscetta, one of the reasons leading to the establishment of this new committee was the desire to prevent hurried decisions from being taken and to entrust a collegial body with the exclusive power of sentencing a "man of honor" to death (Arlacchi 1994: 66). As long as the Palermo provincial commission maintained a pluralistic and democratic character, such aim was largely achieved. Up to the late 1970s, the commission imposed relatively mild sanctions on mafia members who violated Cosa Nostra's rules, since it acted as a compensation board for the interests and opinions of all its members, none of whom had enough power to overwhelm the others. "The deliberation to kill a man of honor," the Palermitan prosecutors note, "was an *extrema ratio*, which had to be approved after the critical assessment of all the *capi mandamento* representing different factions" (PrPA 1993c: 211). Instead of resolving things in such a dramatic way, the committee members often preferred to suspend the guilty offender or to expel him from the organization by "putting him out of the family" [*messa fuori famiglia*] (PrPA 1992: 7). Periodically, at Christmas and Easter, the committee granted amnesties to all the "men of honor" who had been suspended and they were once again admitted to their respective families (TrPA 1985 V: 826–27).

Since the early 1980s, however, Cosa Nostra's punitive system has become considerably stricter. Death penalties have become more frequent, and any grading in the selection of sanctions has been abandoned (PrPA 1993c: 210–11, 57–58). Since Riina's coalition gained supremacy inside Cosa Nostra, the murder of "men of honor" no longer constitutes the penalty justified by a serious breaking of Cosa Nostra rules. Losing any rooting in the normative *corpus*, it has become "the privileged instrument to guarantee the stability and supremacy of the monolithic ruling group and to block any attempt by this or that man of honor to set up or consolidate autonomous power positions, which may upturn the power relations" (PrPA 1993c: 212). Such a drastic shift was largely produced by the de facto abandonment of the collegiality principle and the rise of a monocratic leadership inside Cosa Nostra. As foreseen by Durkheim, the intensity of punishment becomes "greater . . . the more the central power assumes an absolute character" ([1899–1900] 1984: 102), whereas collegiality favors greater thoroughness in the weighing of administrative and judicial decisions.

MAFIA CONSORTIA AS ILLEGAL STATES?

To what extent can mafia legal orders be considered not only alternative to the state ones, but also as equivalent to the latter? How far can the analogy between mafia and state be pushed? As will be made clear below, it cannot be extended beyond a certain limit if we want to factor in the specificities peculiar to the normative systems of Cosa Nostra and the 'Ndrangheta. This is essentially because although the bodies and rules they have set up emulate the constitutive principle of the modern state, the two systems are fundamentally different; consequently, Cosa Nostra and 'Ndrangheta can rather be equated to institutions and codes developed by preindustrial societies to resolve conflicts and punish nonconformist behavior.

The Limits of an Analogy

Contrary to modern state systems, custom constitutes the main source of law in the legal orders of Cosa Nostra and 'Ndrangheta. Many of their rules of behavior are the product of a slow process of sedimentation and reflect customs and collective expectations. These are legal rules because "their respect is guaranteed by an external and institutionalized sanction" (Bobbio 1958: 198; see also Hoebel 1954; Bohannan 1967). Nonetheless, they remain largely superimposed upon habits and regularities of behavior. And although their violation is usually sanctioned by adjudicative bodies, their repeated disrespect may allow them to fall rapidly into disuse. As Roberto Mangabeira Unger notes, "there is a point at which deviations from the rule remake the rule itself" (1986: 49). Far from being the result of any rational planning, many normative changes in the two mafia normative systems have been fostered either by the repeated violations of a specific norm or by the progressive consolidation of a new custom through the repetition of a certain act.

In the two mafia consortia, this slow development—which remains largely elusive even to group members—is further eased by the lack of written rules. In neither Cosa Nostra or the 'Ndrangheta are the primary or secondary rules fixed in writing, and this fact makes their gradual transformation easier, as Marc Bloch noted with reference to feudal customary law: "The very authority that was ascribed to tradition favored the change. For every act, especially if it was repeated three or four times, was likely to be transformed into a precedent—even if in the first instance it had been exceptional or even frankly unlawful. . . . Conversely, a rent which ceased to be paid for a certain number of years, or a ceremony of submission once omitted, almost invariably fell into desuetude by prescription" (1975: 114–15).

Important changes have been introduced into the customary law of the two mafia syndicates in this kind of largely unconscious and unplanned way. Some activities that used to be strictly prohibited—such as drug trafficking and, in the 'Ndrangheta, having ongoing contact with state officials—have now become legitimate. Specific obligations, like the payment of an entry tax, have been abandoned, while others—such as those concerning sexual morality—are progressively falling into disuse following the cultural evolution of society at large. Saverio

Morabito, whose declarations helped the first in-depth judicial investigation about the northern Italian branches of the 'Ndrangheta, described the latter's slow but inexorable decline:

> The mafia world is the same everywhere. Buscetta was considered unreliable because he had a lover, the man of honor is assessed as such also because he does not do certain things. The Calabrian, both down South and here [that is, both in their home region and in northern Italy], have the same type of principles. But they are all false.... I came to the conclusion that maybe Totò Riina is the only one in Italy who respects this bullshit of a commandment, since he keeps on preaching that you should not betray your wife. Apparently, he is the exception that confirms the rule. (Colaprico and Fazzo 1995: 86–96)

Despite the clear importance of customs in the legal orders of both Cosa Nostra and the 'Ndrangheta, these should not be perceived as exemplifying pure forms of the customary law. Although their rules are not written, the normative systems of both mafia associations can more appropriately be described as forming part of a mixture of the two wider and—from an evolutionary point of view—simpler types of the tripartite classification of law developed by Roberto Mangabeira Unger (1976): "customary law" and "bureaucratic" or "regulatory law." The rules belonging to "regulatory law" are public and positive, deliberately imposed by centralized rulers rather than spontaneously produced by society. Indeed, to stress their source of production Unger has also called this kind of rule "bureaucratic."

In both Cosa Nostra and the 'Ndrangheta, bureaucratic law consists largely of the commands given by the family chiefs and the superordinate commissions. Ever since the late nineteenth century, in fact, the ruling bodies of both consortia have not only claimed and progressively obtained adjudication functions, appropriating them from the assemblies of members, but have also set rules that are supposed to be respected by all their subordinates. They have thus developed a new source of law, which entails more explicit rules of change and recognition. As the American anthropologist Hoebel said, "the legal significance of the chief is, of course, that his personal law can with tribal backing become public law" (1954: 323).

The norms explicitly formulated by the rulers in both mafia segmentary societies primarily concern secrecy. Though the code of *omertà* was once widespread in southern Italian society at large, prescriptions concerning secrecy have always been explicitly asserted by the family chiefs, who have adapted them—either reinforcing or weakening them—to the changing needs of the group. Moreover, precisely in order to increase the invisibility of the association, the ruling apparatuses of the two confederations strictly regulated the use of violence by members over the last forty years of the twentieth century (see chapter 1). Likewise, the rules constituting "the mafia constitutional law" (Fiandaca 1994: 31)—that is, the norms disciplining the composition and competence of the ruling offices and regulating affiliation ceremonies—did not rise spontaneously, but have deliberately been fixed by the mafia ruling bodies.

The fact that some parts of mafia normative systems can be described as bureaucratic law does not, however, entail any close analogy with the modern democratic state, at least in its ideal-typical traits. Despite the existence of primary and secondary rules, it would be a serious analytical mistake to assimilate the legal orders of the Cosa Nostra and the 'Ndrangheta to the rule of law of contemporary states. The substantial gap existing between the mafia legal orders and the rule of law emerges particularly clearly if one uses a third type of law classified by Unger, the "full legal order," as a term of comparison. This category, which may more appropriately and specifically be defined as "rule of law," lists the ideal-typical traits of the legal orders developed by Western liberal states. According to Unger, a full legal order exists when law is public and positive, as well as autonomous and general (1976: 52). Like bureaucratic law, its rules are explicitly stated and enforced by an identifiable government that is clearly separate from the larger society.

Unlike bureaucratic law, however, the full legal order is autonomous in a methodological, institutional, and occupational sense. First, its rules are envisaged according to its own logic, which is different from that of scientific explanation and moral, political, and economic discourses. It is also institutionally autonomous, since its rules are applied by specialized institutions whose main task is to adjudicate. Moreover, occupational autonomy stems from the fact that a special group, the legal profession, defined by its activities, prerogatives, and training, staffs the legal institutions and engages in the practice of legal argument. Lastly, the legal order of modern states aims toward generality and uniformity of application among subjects: its precepts are expected to address broadly defined categories of individuals and acts and to be applied without personal or class favoritism. Hence not only is adjudication carried out by specialized bodies, but legislation is also separated from administration and each function is fulfilled by independent agencies (ibid.).

Neither Cosa Nostra's nor the 'Ndrangheta's legal order presents any trait of Unger's third type of law. For example, there is no separation between administration, adjudication, and legislation. In both mafia societies, the family chiefs embody all these functions contemporaneously. Even in Cosa Nostra, which is more sophisticated than its Calabrian counterpart, the process of functional differentiation is only partially complete, since its two main superordinate bodies—the commission for the province of Palermo and the regional commission—simultaneously fulfill legislative, administrative, and judicial functions. As Donald

Cressey put it with reference to the commission of the American La Cosa Nostra: "This body serves as a combination board of business directors, legislature, supreme court, and arbitration board" (1969: 111).

Likewise, even the distinction between specific commands and general rules is blurred because they are issued by the same offices. Furthermore, no matter whether they concern legislation or adjudication, the decisions made by the family chiefs or the collegial bodies are far from being shaped by independent legal reasoning or from being subordinated to an established legal code. Unconstrained by the lack of any written codification, they frequently reflect the interests of the individual or group holding power at any particular moment. The point is well made by the Calabrian *pentito* Giuseppe Albanese: "In the case of disputes the *capo crimine* exercises the function of judge of *omertà* and must be impartial, although this never happens, since he always sides with the stronger group" (PrRC 1995: 5741; see also Colaprico and Fazzo 1995: 86–87).

Custom and Commands

The 'Ndrangheta—throughout its existence—and Cosa Nostra—until the consolidation of a monocratic leadership—have largely succeeded in maintaining a precarious balance between customary and bureaucratic law and in keeping the shortcomings and aberrations of the latter under control. The segmentary structure of both mafia consortia has long forbidden the complete subordination of decision making to the power interests of those holding ruling positions. Thus, as long as the segmentary organization is not shaken by the centralization process and every family enjoys a high degree of autonomy, no single mafia chief can modify the core rules of the collective normative system.

It is true that those holding real power within the two organizations have been able to secure a high degree of impunity for themselves by conditioning the judicial process within the mafia in their favor. Additionally, they have often been able to transform "old antipathies" in "crimes to be punished with death," to rid themselves of old competitors and enemies (Gentile 1993: 85). However, until the rise of the Corleonesi coalition, none of the *capifamiglia* ever had enough power to impose normative innovations upon the whole association. Indeed, the single leaders found it difficult to impose profound normative changes even at the family level. In the Calabrian mafia segmentary society as well as, up to the beginning of the 1980s, in its Sicilian counterpart, the freedom of chiefs has always found an insurmountable limit in customary law. The boundaries of the whole segmentary association are defined by these rules, and subscribing to them is a necessary premise for mafia associates and families to be recognized as legitimate by the chiefs of other corporate units. Antonio Zagari describes the strength of such a constraint in the Calabrian 'Ndrangheta: "Every group is independent of the others and is ruled by a *capo società* who has the faculty and power to act autonomously from the chiefs of other *cosche*, even if these are higher in rank. The only restraint is constituted by the rule to reciprocally respect territorial boundaries and to be at the disposal of each other for the more general interest of the association. Though divided into many cells, *this refers in all cases to one single set of rules*" (PrRC 1995: 374, emphasis added).

Nor has the establishment of higher bodies of coordination substantially increased the autonomy of mafia chiefs or allowed them to introduce substantial changes into the normative codes of the two consortia. The evolution of Cosa Nostra's provincial commission since its founding in the 1950s is a good case in point. As long as Cosa Nostra maintained a horizontal structure, formed by a plurality of families that were sovereign over their own territory, the function of the commission was to mediate the positions and interests of the various *capi mandamento* (district chiefs and commissioners), as none of them had enough power to overthrow all the others. Moreover, the commission's competencies were originally quite limited, exclusively concerning the regulation of violence and the determination of violations of primary rules by the single mafia families and members whose alleged breaches impinged the interests of other groups.

The most meaningful change sparked off by the institution of the provincial commission was the formalization of the rules of both change and recognition, although the normative code remained unwritten as a consequence of the pledge to secrecy. Since the late 1950s the commission has become the main seat for introducing new primary rules and correcting or eliminating old ones. An illustration of this primordial legislative activity has been provided by Gaspare Mutolo, former member of the Partanna-Mondello *cosca*:

> When we took, for example, the decision, . . . there was a time when there was a problem: whether it was acceptable or not to go the Carabinieri and to report the theft of a car belonging to a man of honor. It is probably the only time that the commission gathered for a minor issue, but it could become a very important matter because, if my car is stolen and somebody else uses it for a robbery, I would pay for the robbery. The commission met to say: "If you realize that your car has been stolen, you can report it to the police, at the police station." (PrPA 1995b: 103–4)

As long as the commission remained not only formally but also substantially collegial, its powers to legislate and adjudicate were heavily constrained by its commitment to the rule of unanimity. As already mentioned, this commitment prevented heavy, indiscriminate sanctions from being imposed upon the guilty "men of honor." But it also meant that the violations perpetrated by the most powerful mafiosi who either sat in the collegial body or had close connections with its components went largely unpunished. Even in the late 1970s, for example, the commission was unable to sanction repeated breaches of its exclusive competence on a matter that could have disastrous consequences for the whole association: the decision to eliminate politicians and public officials.

The commission's weakness is clearly proved by the results of judicial investigations concerning a series of "excellent murders," murders of high-ranking public figures. Law enforcement agencies have, in fact, demonstrated that Carabinieri colonel Giuseppe Russo, the secretary of the Palermitan Christian Democracy, Michele Reina, Judge Cesare Terranova, and Carabinieri captain Emanuele Basile were all killed autonomously in the late 1970s by Corleonesi affiliates who neither consulted nor warned the provincial or the regional commission (TrPA 1987b: 1244–54). Soon after, to demonstrate his independence from the collegial body, one of the chiefs of the rival coalition, Salvatore Inzerillo, ordered the execution of the chief prosecutor Gaetano Costa, who had issued arrest warrants for several members of Inzerillo's group (TrPA 1984, I: 31–35). Torn by internal divisions, the commission was able neither to start investigations in order to collect independent proof on these cases, which constituted a glaring violation of the mafia legal order, nor to sanction any of the offenders.

The impunity of mafia bosses was also reinforced by the fact that the commission lacked any autonomous administrative apparatus to enforce its own sentences. Hence, even when it succeeded in issuing a formal note of condemnation, the collegial body had to rely on the willingness of the single family chiefs to enforce its decisions.

Riina's Dictatorship and Its Consequences on the Legal Order

The rise of Riina's monocratic leadership notably increased the legislative and adjudicative powers of the provincial commission and its counterpart at the regional level. Far from bringing the Cosa Nostra's normative system closer to Unger's third type of law (the full legal order), however, this development broke the fragile balance between customary and bureaucratic law (the first two types of law Unger singles out, which are both present in mafia legal orders) and enhanced the contradictions typical of the bureaucratic type.

Bureaucratic law is, in fact, plagued by internal conflict, constantly affected by the opposing demands of instrumentalism and legitimacy. Due to its lack of autonomous checks and balances, this type of law can be easily exploited by the rulers to satisfy the most unrestrained ambitions of power, but in the long run this may easily undermine the legitimacy of the whole legal order. According to Unger, "if the normative order is constructed as a set of tools with which to satisfy the power interests of the rulers, it will lack any claim to allegiance, save the terror by which it is imposed. Moreover, it will fail to satisfy the need of rulers and governed alike to justify the structure of society by relating it to an image of cosmic and social order" (1976: 65). From the early 1980s on, Cosa Nostra's normative system became a tool to foster the power interests of Riina and his closest allies. By placing his most trusted associates in positions on the provincial and regional commissions, Totò Riina succeeded in freeing himself from the controls and balancing policy resulting from Cosa Nostra's original segmentary organization. In other words, he entirely subjugated the two superordinate institutions in order to extend his personal power over the entire mafia consortium.

The mixture of legislative and judicial functions within the same collegial bodies gave Riina and the closest of his allies a tremendous power of intervention, allowing them to introduce significant normative changes and then to either enforce or deny these same provisions merely according to the interests of the moment. During the 1980s, in particular, several normative innovations were introduced to undermine the autonomy of the single corporate units and to allow the Corleonesi to intervene in the internal matters of all the families. The commissions' competencies were widened and endowed with an independent staff and a permanent hit squad with which they could execute death sentences directly. The new role of "ambassador" was also established: starting in the late 1980s Riina named personal representatives—known as his "ambassadors"—to whom he entrusted single provinces or specific markets, thus going over the heads of the competent family chiefs (CPM 1992d).

The Corleonesi also modified some key precepts of mafia customary law, impinging on values around which the collective identity of the whole association and the status of the "men of honor" had long been constructed. For example, they repeatedly broke a seemingly inviolable rule, according to which women and, in general, unaffiliated relatives should be kept out of Cosa Nostra's internal dynamics (PrPA 1993a: 363–74). From 1982, the Corleonesi murdered more than twenty of Buscetta's relatives, the majority of whom were totally extraneous to Cosa Nostra, first to prevent Buscetta from leading the coalition adversary to Riina's and then to avenge his betrayal. Again, to punish Francesco Marino Mannoia's decision to collaborate with the judiciary, even the taboo on involving women was broken. On November 23, 1989, his sister, mother, and aunt were all murdered (PrPA 1993a: 363–74).

In addition, the rule obliging Cosa Nostra members to tell the truth also became a series of empty words, with which only subordinates were expected to comply. To assert their supremacy, the Corleonesi encouraged soldiers to betray their *capifamiglia* by weaving a web of infiltrates into all the main *cosche*, in order to receive immediate reports of possible criticism against their leadership. They created rivalries within families to weaken their unity and used the ambitions of those aspiring to higher-ranking positions to let them kill their own hierarchical superiors. They organized disinformation campaigns to put other affiliates and the police on the wrong track. By making others appear responsible for their own murders, they aimed to avoid retaliation and gain precious time to kill whoever wanted to avenge the victim.

Even the Corleonesi's own legislative innovations were denied or neglected when they no longer suited the rulers' effective interests. In the early 1980s, for example, the provincial commission, already dominated by the Corleonesi, established a new rule according to which, once arrested, "men of honor" would automatically lose their offices on the grounds that the imprisonment would impede them from having access to a steady and detailed flow of information. In reality, the intent of the new norm was to get rid of the "old guard" of mafia chiefs, and Riina succeeded in placing his own trusted men at the head of many families and in the superordinate collegial bodies. Nonetheless, once leading exponents of the Corleonesi coalition started to be arrested from the mid-1980s onward, this norm soon fell into disuse (PrPA 1992: 252).

The Corleonesi's legislative decisions often took the form of rules applicable to very general categories of persons and acts, but, as with the commands of the sovereign in states at the dawn of modernity, this was mostly only an expedience, a way to get things done more effectively. In other words, referring once more to Unger, in the mafia world "there is no commitment to generality in lawmaking and to uniformity of adjudication, that must be kept regardless of their consequences for the political interests of the rulers" (1976: 67). That is to say, as long as he detains power, the sovereign may issue whatever commands he likes.

No longer restrained by the reciprocal supervision of independent segmentary units, even the adjudication process was increasingly manipulated in order to enhance the Corleonesi's power interests. The bosses belonging to the traditionalist wing during the mafia war, and, later on, even many of Riina's former allies, were ruthlessly murdered after resorting to pretexts designed to "put them in the wrong light." This is, for example, how Mariano Agate, chief of the Mazara del Vallo family and one of Riina's trusted men, justified the murder of Francesco Caprarotta and Vincenzo D'Amico, respectively representative and *consigliere* of the neighboring Marsala family in the Trapani province, according to the reconstruction provided by Antonio Patti, a former affiliate of the latter *cosca*:

> Before Christmas 1991 . . . Agate Mariano told me: "If you tell me, we will call all the members of the Marsala family and kill them all, one by one, or at least Vincenzo [D'Amico] and Ciccio Caprarotta. We must add Tano and Ciccio." This was how he referred to Francesco D'Amico. Francesco Messina, called U' Muraturi [the Mason] was also present. Hearing these words, I was upset, but not shocked. I already had the feeling that the *rappresentante* and the *consigliere* of my family were no longer well viewed by the Mazara people and Agate Mariano. They were forbidden to leave Marsala and any movement of theirs had to be referred to Agate Mariano and Ciccio U' Muraturi.

The reason for such a break—as explained to me by Agate Mariano—was that Vincenzo D'Amico had made the serious mistake of beginning an extramarital affair with the wife of Evola Giuseppe, a man of honor from Castellammare. Furthermore, Ciccio U' Muraturi was particularly angry with Vincenzo D'Amico because in 1988, when we were all in prison, the Mazara family had given thirteen hundred million *lire* [about one million dollars] to the Marsala one, but, according to Messina, D'Amico had appropriated this money and bought fields and houses for his own blood family. I must say, however, that I learnt from my brother-in-law, Titone Antonino, that the true reason why D'Amico and Caprarotta were eliminated was totally different. It lies in their refusal to comply with Agate Mariano's proposal to kill Dr. Paolo Borsellino, then chief prosecutor at the Marsala court. My brother-in-law told me that he had learnt the matter directly from Vincenzo D'Amico and said nothing else on the matter. (PrPA 1996a: 543–44)

Long ignored violations of traditional rules of behavior—in this case, the duty of marital fidelity and solidarity toward the family—were suddenly punished with great severity, when the chiefs wanted to rid themselves of this or that "man of honor." An extramarital relationship was, likewise, the pretext used to remove Balduccio Di Maggio from his fairly high position within the San Giuseppe Jato *mandamento*, as a result of a quarrel with the Bruscas, the undisputed *domini* of the local mafia group.[22] Di Maggio's affair was, in fact, a long-standing relationship begun several years earlier and which, up to that point, had not given any cause for complaint or been an obstacle to his promotion within Cosa Nostra.

Thanks to this policy, during the 1980s Totò Riina and his closest allies strengthened and extended their power over the whole of Cosa Nostra. In the long run, however, they undermined their own basis of legitimation. In fact, the incessant distortion of rules and the loss of traditional values are the two reasons most frequently presented by the *pentiti* to justify their decision to break the Cosa Nostra oath of *omertà*. They lament the precarious and illusory nature of the mafia legal order, asserting that the rules are changed, distorted, disregarded, and then reapplied according to the contingent interests of those in power. The motivations of a recent mafia witness are described by the Palermitan prosecutors with these words: "He originally had an unconditional and complete trust in Riina and in the rules of solidarity, which he thought were the fundament of their association. After a while, however, he began to understand that, for Riina himself and for the others closest to him, these rules were merely a pretense and could be betrayed in order to seize personal advantage and absolute power, which was supported by an irreversible death strategy" (PrPA 1992: 32–33).

Likewise, in a hearing before the Parliamentary Anti-mafia Commission Gaspare Mutolo justified his choice to become a mafia witness in the following way:

The change, my change of mind is due, first of all, to all those persons killed without reason of whom I was very fond. One becomes fond even of animals, hence, with better reason, of friends. But the most terrible thing for me was when they started to kill women and children. I remember that in the past, for example, if a murder was ordered, the killers, if they found the victim accompanied by his wife or his daughters, watched him, went back, and postponed the execution. Today, instead, this rule does not hold. . . . Virtually all the mentality of the Cosa Nostra has changed and I no longer saw myself reflected in it. Truly, I no longer saw the Cosa Nostra as following the ideal for which I had entered it.

I want to repeat: when I became a member . . . there were very precise behavioral rules: at least what was stated were very wonderful things, because there was respect for each other, readiness to help for whatever goal if another needed you, respect for the others' women as if they were your sisters. It was a new world that fascinated me a lot. (CPM 1993b: 1224)

It would be a gross oversimplification to impute the contemporary crisis of Cosa Nostra exclusively to Riina's sultanic leadership. Far from being a mere intervening variable, the dictatorship of the head of the Corleone family was, above all, a reaction against the progressive decadence of the mafia moral tenets. In its turn, this breakdown was largely produced by the mafia attempts to keep the pace with the social, economic, and cultural modernization processes that affected the Mezzogiorno in the last three decades of the twentieth century. Notwithstanding the claims of totality and self-sufficiency deriving from secrecy, Cosa Nostra and the 'Ndrangheta are secondary formations heavily dependent on the outside world to continue their existence and to pursue their goals.

Multiplicity of Goals and Functions

You must remember that the families have their own businesses and that these involve everything going on in the families' territory. For example, a family in Rome would be interested in all the activities there, whether they had to do with politics, public works, extortions, drug deals, etc. . . . In practice, the family is sovereign, it controls everything happening on its territory.
—COMMISSIONE PARLAMENTARE D'INCHIESTA SUL FENOMENO DELLA MAFIA E SULLE ALTRE ASSOCIAZIONI SIMILARI, *Audizione del collaboratore di giustizia Leonardo Messina* (1992)

In this way witness Leonardo Messina tried to explain the political dimension of mafia activity to members of the Parliamentary Anti-mafia Commission in 1992. Messina is not the only former member of mafia associations to have focused on this. Several other *pentiti* have also done so, providing very similar descriptions, and the concrete activities of the families associated with Cosa Nostra and the 'Ndrangheta also confirm it.

The statements given by mafia witnesses and the results of law enforcement investigations are, however, inconsistent with all the interpretations of the mafia phenomenon that have dominated since the early 1980s, which consider the mafia an economic enterprise. As Umberto Santino noted at the beginning of the 1990s, "in the last few years the idea of analyzing the mafia phenomenon as an enterprise has become increasingly popular. It is not a very original approach, since Franchetti and Sonnino have already talked about an 'industry of crime,' but it has marked a step forward to overcome the stereotypes of traditional and modernized 'mafiology' and to structure scientific analysis" (Santino 1990: 17–18).

It is worthwhile briefly reviewing these "economic" interpretations before considering the conceptual changes brought about by *pentiti*'s declarations. In his successful book first published at the beginning of the 1980s, Pino Arlacchi was the first scholar to talk about the "entrepreneurial mafia" [*mafia imprenditrice*], highlighting mafiosi's growing involvement in licit and illicit economic activities

(1988). Arlacchi, however, was also fully aware that there would be an unavoidable clash between market logic and the mafiosi's adherence to traditional values and models. This has not been the case of most subsequent analyses, which, with very few exceptions (Centorrino 1986, 1989), have tended to reject any notion of an "entrepreneurial transformation" of mafia *cosche*, usually ascribing a primarily economic-oriented behavior even to traditional mafiosi and neglecting the impact of traditional imprinting on the behavior of contemporary mafia entrepreneurs. Thus, in the reflections of several scholars, mafiosi of the past have been identified *tout court* with the few figures who showed a clearly modern acquisitive attitude in the traditional economic and social system of western Sicily and southern Calabria and have been presented as the true expression of the local bourgeoisie. In their turn, contemporary mafia groups have been assimilated into the model of legal business firms.

According to Raimondo Catanzaro, for instance, "the only commonly agreed upon identifying characteristic is that the Mafia exists to make profits illegally" (1992: 3) and what links the mafia to common organized crime is their shared "organizational stability, their being shaped in the form of a 'firm' within the field of normal economic activities" (1991: 4). Catanzaro thus identifies the mafiosi with the *gabellotti* [leaseholders] and the *campieri* [herdsmen] working on the large estates in internal Sicily and he concludes that all the traditional ways of exploiting peasants in the system of great estates were forms of mafia accumulation (1991: 46–49, 1992: 31–34). Likewise, several historians have presented the mafia as the "violent middle class." According to them, the typical traits of the "mafia bourgeoisie" are the systematic use of violence and "the aspects of social mobility of the participants, their vocation to maximize profits and to penetrate into new market dimensions" (Pezzino 1993: 68; see also 1987, 1988; Recupero 1987b; Lupo 1988, 1993; Pizzorno 1987).

Contemporary mafia enterprises are, instead, identified with those which "perform legal . . . [and] illegal production activities and employ violent methods to discourage competition" (Catanzaro 1992: 203; see also Catanzaro 1986 and Santino 1988; Santino and La Fiura 1990). The continuity between these forms of mafia entrepreneurship is stated but not proved, while the mafia can no longer be distinguished from large sectors of the Sicilian bourgeoisie and, at the same time, loses any peculiarity vis-à-vis other types of organized crime.

A variant of the long-dominant enterprise approach has recently been proposed by Diego Gambetta, according to whom the mafia must be seen as "a specific economic enterprise, an industry which produces, promotes, and sells private protection" (1993: 1). By shifting attention away from traditional licit and illicit entrepreneurial activities, Gambetta's work points to one of the most important functions historically played by Sicilian and Calabrian mafia groups and paves the way for a reassessment of the political dimension of mafia associations. His interpretation can, however, be criticized for his one-sided emphasis on protection, which can be justified only by a very selective reading of past and present sources. As David Nelken states, "Gambetta's insistence that the Mafia is and has always been in the protection business is somewhat essentialist. The wide range of activities in which the Mafia plays a part makes generalization difficult" (1995).

Like the former analyzes, moreover, Gambetta's assessment is linked to a functionalistic approach, according to which the evolution and organization of a social phenomenon can be deduced from the functions it plays. This approach was somehow necessary, as long as no precise empirical reference had yet been provided for the mafia phenomenon and a "disorganized" view of the mafia prevailed. That is to say, if mafiosi were viewed as individuals with no connection to each other (and this was certainly the approach initially taken by most scholars), the only way of unifying the amorphous mass they formed and of distinguishing it from the rest of society was to hypothesize that they shared one or more functions and values. Functionalist "cages," however, can and must be abandoned as soon as we acknowledge the existence of stable mafia groups in western Sicily and southern Calabria from the late nineteenth century on.

This path is, moreover, consistent with the most recent findings of organization studies, although for many years these represented organizations as rational machines, designed to fulfill precise and stable goals (see Morgan 1986). According to the position dominant today, however, it is unrealistic to define an organization with reference to a single function or goal. Both functions and goals change with time and are subject to continuous negotiations among the members of a group, even though the group structure and culture are not necessarily modified (Georgiou 1973; Scott 1987). Mafia groups, indeed, represent a perfect demonstration of this thesis. Mutual aid, which has been the "official goal" of mafia associations ever since their founding, has been translated into a plurality of "operative goals" (Perrow 1961), which have been selected through negotiations among changing coalitions of "soldiers" and chiefs.

There is, additionally, a specific reason that makes the "functionalist" approach particularly unsuitable to study mafia groups. Given the historical period during which the groups rose and the criminalization process they have since undergone, they could take only a marginal part in the process of functional differentiation that has invested European societies, and Italian society in particular, over the last hundred and fifty years. Far from being economic enterprises aiming at the maximization of profits, then, mafia associations are functionally diffused entities, which claim to exercise a political dominion over their areas of settlement.[1]

MONEY VERSUS POWER

Though it became increasingly important in the last thirty years of the twentieth century, enrichment was never the exclusive—or even the main—goal of "men of honor." Granted, the most prominent mafiosi have always tried to officialize the honor obtained with violence, by improving their life standards and by buying mobile and immobile properties, and the most violent or shrewd ones have usually succeeded in doing so. Ever since the nineteenth century, reports have abounded that mafiosi bought fields and stakes in mining, gained the control over large estates belonging to noble families, and mediated profitable transactions in wheat, land, and other commodities (Fed. PCI-CL [1964] 1976; see also Pezzino 1990a: 205–18; Barone 1987).

Since the 1960s, then, members of mafia families have invested an increasing amount of energy in economic accumulation, adapting themselves to the wider ongoing modernization processes in Italian society, which began to view wealth as the main parameter for assessing social position (Arlacchi 1988: 57–61). For mafiosi, however, wealth has never been a goal in itself nor, despite its growing importance, is it so today. More than becoming wealthy, members of mafia associations have always aimed to gain power over their communities, occupying the central points of the local social, economic, and political systems. And this general aim, which was translated into a plurality of specific goals, was not only pursued by individuals—as most social researchers hypothesized up to the mid-1980s; it was most frequently attempted and accomplished by the mafia group as a collective subject.

Manifold Forms of Economic Action

A multiplicity of licit and illicit economic activities have been carried out by mafia families and their members ever since the late nineteenth century. Profit-making activities are, however, not systematically planned or coordinated by each *cosca* or by the mafia consortium as a whole. Indeed, there is a high degree of variability and flexibility in the development and management of business activities, so much so that no one model dominates. Granted, illicit activities are sometimes run by the heads of the single families and the profits divided more or less equally between the affiliates. In the 'Ndrangheta this practice has become institutionalized to such a degree that nowadays members receive a monthly salary of at least three million *lire* (about $2,400 in the early 1990s; see chapter 2).

Some businesses even encompass the involvement of more than one family. Investigations carried out during the 1990s revealed numerous joint ventures created by several coalitions of Calabrian *locali* to import huge quantities of drugs. An inquiry by the Direzione Distrettuale Antimafia in Reggio Calabria, for instance, revealed that in 1989 a "cartel" of *cosche* of the province had been set up to finance and organize the import of several lots of heroin, each of which weighed about five hundred kilograms, and cargoes of cocaine of up to three hundred kilograms at a time (PrRC 1993b). Investigations carried out by the Turin prosecutor's office showed that the 5,490 kilograms of cocaine seized at the outskirts of the city in March 1994—up until 1999, the largest seizure ever made outside production areas—had been purchased by a coalition of seven Calabrian mafia families originating from villages on the Ionic coast of the province of Reggio Calabria: the Mazzaferros, Pesces, Ierinòs, Cataldos, Barbaros, Morabitos, and Romolas. In the two years preceding the seizure these groups had financed another seven shipments of drugs, totaling at least eleven tons (TrTO 1994; see also CPM 2000: 103–4).

Even extortive kidnappings have sometimes been organized jointly. According to the reconstruction made by the Reggio Calabria prosecutor's office, the main mafia families of San Luca, Platì, and Natile di Careri on the Aspromonte mountain ran at least nineteen kidnappings together during the 1980s and then reinvested the proceeds of this activity in drug trafficking (PrRC 1992b, 1992c, 1992d, 1993a; CPM 1998).

On some occasions the superordinate bodies of coordination have themselves collected money from several mafia families to invest it in large-scale business activities. This happened most frequently in the 1970s, when the Cosa Nostra members entered the international heroin wholesale trade and were for some years able to refine and export large quantities of heroin into the United States, allegedly satisfying up to 30 percent of the local demand (Arlacchi 1988: 196). During those ten years, the commission for the Palermo province even set up a loose—and largely ineffective—regulation of tobacco smuggling in the southern Tyrrhenian Sea, which involved Neapolitan and Palermitan professional smugglers together with "men of honor" (see chapter 1).

In many other cases, however, single "men of honor" run illegal businesses on their own, entering into partnerships with members of their own or other mafia families and even with nonaffiliates. In the 'Ndrangheta, higher-ranking members usually take on the status of *libero e vincolato* [free and tied], which enables them to carry out illegal activities individually, freeing them from the obligation to share any profits with their fellow members (TrMI 1994a: 123). In Cosa Nostra, this duty of solidarity still formally exists today, especially when the business is large scale. After a successful robbery or illicit transaction, it is considered appropriate to provide the chief of one's own family with a portion of the booty as a sign of respect and subordination. Nonetheless, even in Cosa Nostra there has been since at least the 1970s a clear trend toward the expansion of individual entrepreneurial autonomy.

Emblematic in this respect is the large transcontinental heroin trafficking, which was described in the first Palermitan *maxiprocesso* [maxi-trial]. In the descriptions provided by the media, it is often stated that this business was dominated by Cosa Nostra as a single organization. A careful reading of judicial papers, however, reveals that the different stages in the production and distribution system were run by members of various families who, far from considering themselves part of a single economic unit, were very jealous of their own networks of clients and/or suppliers and of their particular specialization. On the matter, the investigating judges of the first anti-mafia pool state the following: "De facto autonomous, but functionally linked, structures have been created inside Cosa Nostra, running the different phases making up the complex drug trade, while the 'men of honor' who do not have operational responsibilities in the trade may financially contribute to it, sharing profits and risks to different degrees" (TrPA 1985: 1887).

By creating a climate of trust, common membership in Cosa Nostra enhanced the development and consolidation of business exchanges. These, however, can hardly be likened to the relationships among the departments of a single business company. They were, instead, transactions among enterprises so distinct that, despite the mafia brotherhood ties, the respect of contracts was guaranteed by all the means open to them, including the threat and the use of violence.

The import of large lots of morphine was begun by Nunzio La Mattina, a former smuggler from the proletarian Kalsa neighborhood in Palermo, who had been affiliated to the Porta Nuova family by Pippo Calò because of his connections in international illegal markets. Antonino Rotolo, Tommaso Spadaro, and Giuseppe Savoca soon joined La Mattina, but "each worked on his own and kept the secret of his own organization jealously to himself." Palermitan investigating judges estimated that Nunzio La Mattina and Antonino Rotolo bought about two tons of morphine for an overall price of 55 million dollars in less than two years (ibid.: 1879–80).

Some other mafia members were responsible for the processing of drugs in clandestine laboratories, working for themselves as well as for other enterprises. According to the *pentito* Salvatore Contorno, there were at least seven drug laboratories in western Sicily in the early 1980s, each of which was run by a Cosa Nostra *cosca* or a group of "men of honor" (TrPA 1985, IX). Francesco Marino Mannoia, who was then very much sought after because of his chemical competencies, recalls that he worked in several laboratories, processing morphine belonging to different members (TrPA 1989).

Finally, other "men of honor" were in charge of the transportation of the heroin, and its wholesale distribution, in the United States. Among them, a preeminent role was played by the Bontades, Inzerillos, and Badalamentis, whose blood and mafia families had extensive branches in North America. The heroin was wrapped in cellophane packages labeled with special marks to distinguish the different owners. This was mainly because each of them was responsible for the quality of his lots. The freedom wielded by participants was such that, according to Buscetta, whoever wanted to do so could pick up his share of the processed product in Sicily and arrange distribution independently (TrPA 1985, IX).

Far from being stable and centralized entities, many of the enterprises founded by "men of honor" resemble what anthropologists call "action sets": temporary coalitions that are formed to pursue specific goals and, once these are achieved, are disbanded (Schneider and Schneider 1976; Blok 1988: 136ff.; see Boissevain 1974). Sometimes the *cosca* runs an illicit business directly. More often, however, its members set up illegal enterprises, which—due to their heterogeneous composition, average short-term life, and financial and managerial independence—usually remain sharply distinct from the mafia group(s) to which these "men of honor" belong. This form of cooperation was already widespread in the late nineteenth century, when it was used to organize raids, extortive kidnappings, and cattle rustling. The organization of the poaching was exemplary, and, according to Alongi, constituted "the traditional crime industry of the *maffia* in feudal properties and large estates" ([1886] 1977: 82). As several sources state, cattle thefts were carried out by bands of five to ten people, some of which were exclusively composed of mafia members, some only of bandits. More often, members came from both groups, with leadership varying between the two. With some external support, these bands often also ran the subsequent phases—which included clandestine butchering, the acquisition of false documents (called *bolletta*), and transport to urban markets—to disband and meet again, whenever the next good opportunity presented itself (Alongi [1886] 1977: 82–96; Lorenzoni 1910: 696–97).

In the licit economic sphere, moreover, each "man of honor" enjoys full autonomy and is free to make business deals with whomever he wants. He does not even have to cede a quota of his profits to his mafia family. "Legitimate businesses," Antonino Calderone was told straight after his initiation, "were something entirely personal and unrestricted. The family couldn't interfere in such questions. Private property was recognized, and everybody was free to do what he wanted with it" (Arlacchi 1993: 71).

Though illegal trades today constitute a frequent and usually permanent activity for most mafiosi and a substantial source of revenue for almost all the *cosche* of the two mafia consortia, there are no grounds for describing the latter as enterprises. There is even less justification for equating Cosa Nostra and the 'Ndrangheta with multinational corporations, as has been proposed by various observers in the recent international debate (Sterling 1990, 1994; Williams and Florez 1994). Even in the Cosa Nostra, the superordinate bodies of coordination, which have existed since the 1950s, have been only sporadically involved in the direct planning and management of entrepreneurial activities. There is only one major exception to this: from the mid-1980s on Cosa Nostra has taken part in the manipulation of the bidding processes through which the province of Palermo and, at a later stage, the Sicilian region assigned their public work contracts. Thanks to the mediation of a nonmember, Angelo Siino, Totò Riina managed to insert Cosa Nostra, functioning as a single collective subject, into the *comitati d'affari* [business committees]. Formed of politicians, public officials, and large national firms, these were informal and usually illegal coalitions that largely controlled the market for public contracts in Sicily and the rest of the country (TrPA 1991, 1993b, 1998).

The illegal acquisition of public work contracts in the short time frame between the mid-1980s and 1992 constitutes, however, the only time Cosa Nostra has ever tried to manage an entrepreneurial activity in a unitary way. It is no coincidence that it occurred at the same time as the push toward power centralization pursued by Riina—an operation which came to an end with his arrest in January 1993. Except for this case, no other example is known of unitary management of an economic venture by a Cosa Nostra provincial or regional commission. Only by systematically distorting the empirical data can, therefore, the commissions be represented as the management board of a single, large-scale "firm" called Cosa Nostra—a sort of Mafia Inc. that does not actually exist, but is often described as such by the media and some scholars as well. As a matter of fact, the single mafia families—and, as mentioned above, increasingly, even the single "men of honor"—enjoy full entrepreneurial autonomy, and at the interfamily level, there is no obligation to share illicit proceeds either. Such a moral duty was not even felt by the Sicilian *cosche* that in the early 1980s controlled the final and most lucrative phase of the transcontinental heroin business and rapidly accumulated previously unimaginable profits (Lodato 1999: 48). It was also to control this traffic that the Corleonesi initiated the war against the coalition headed by Stefano Bontade, and despite the larger economic means and the wider network of international branches, the Bontade-Spatola-Inzerillo-Badalamenti coalition was defeated.

Profits and Wealth

It was only through tobacco smuggling, and subsequently heroin trafficking, that many "men of honor" began to obtain large amounts of money rapidly and to emerge from a long period of difficulty during the 1960s and 1970s, when Cosa Nostra families had been particularly hard hit by a tough repressive campaign. This had been precipitated by the explosion of a car in 1963 in Ciaculli, on the outskirts of Palermo, which cost the life of seven law enforcement officials. "At the end of the trial in Catanzaro," which concerned this explosion and a series of murders in the early 1960s known as the first Sicilian "mafia war," Antonino Calderone remembers, "after the mafia had been brought to her knees in 1963, [the mafiosi] were starving to death after five years in hiding or prison. They were literally starving to death. Stefano Bontade used to say that luckily Masino Spadaro did a little bit of cigarette smuggling and gave him part [of the profits], because they were starving to death" (CPM 1992c: 299). Cosa Nostra men managed to get into the market of international cigarette trafficking by imposing first their protection, and later their involvement, upon the Neapolitan and Palermitan smugglers who had run this activity ever since the 1950s. "At the beginning of the 1970s," the same witness goes on, "Naples was a little Eldorado for Sicilians, because cigarette smuggling was already going on" (CPM 1992b: 316; see also TrPA [1973] 1980).

Though some members of Cosa Nostra had organized drug deals since the 1940s (Comitato Provinciale Stupefacenti di Roma [1971] 1980; Guardia di Finanza [1971] 1980a, [1971] 1980b; CPMS [1972] 1976, 1976b; Paoli 1997: 296–98), it was only thirty years later that drug trafficking become an ongoing and economically significant activity for a large number of mafia families and single members. It was through the importing and processing of morphine and the export of heroin between the late 1970s and the mid-1980s that, in Calderone's words, "richness came, we all became rich. With cigarettes we had earned well, but it was not a strong source [of income]; what changed Cosa Nostra's life has been drugs, which drove them crazy and allowed them to earn a huge amount of money" (CPM 1992b: 319). Calderone's words have been confirmed by another "historical" witness, Tommaso Buscetta, who expressed himself as follows before the Palermitan investigating judges: "Coming back to Palermo in June 1980, I realized that more or less all Cosa Nostra members were now wealthy. Stefano Bontade explained to me that this was all because of drug trafficking" (TrPA [1985] 1992: 96; see also Anonimo 1990: 163).

Before entering the large-scale illicit trade in cigarettes and drugs, few members of the Sicilian and Calabrian mafia *cosche* were rich. Broadly speaking, it was only the chiefs who managed to improve their financial positions, often from a modest starting point. Some evidence of this is given by the examples of the most famous Sicilian mafiosi during the 1950s—Calogero Vizzini, Giuseppe Genco Russo, and Vito Cascio Ferro, who started out as poor farmers and managed to accumulate both properties and prestige during their mafia careers (Hess 1973: 44–46). Sometimes, however, even simple "soldiers" were successful in their licit entrepreneurial activities. For example, one of these, Antonino Sorci, became significantly better off in the postwar period, so much so as to be known by the nickname of *Ninu 'u Riccu* [Nino the Rich Man] in mafia circles (TrPA [1973] 1980: 1430–37).

Before the 1970s, however, only a few mafiosi were substantially wealthy. Most of them earned their living by their own legal means and professions, which they had usually started before entering the mafia group (TrPA 1984; TrMA 1987). Out of the 218 mafiosi registered by Questore Sangiorgi in his report at the beginning of the twentieth century, the largest group was represented by *salariati fissi* [employees] responsible for running and safeguarding agricultural enterprises. In the list, we find forty-five gardeners, field guards, stewards, and administrators, plus another six mechanics charged with running the irrigation system. Then there were twenty-six landowners who possessed gardens, buildings, and land, many of whom—according to the Questura—had achieved such status only recently. Another twenty-five people can be grouped under the category of mediators—traffickers, brokers, and merchants—while twenty-seven were farmers, farmhands, and farm laborers. Some typical figures moving between the city and the countryside were also included: seven carters and eleven goatherds. Finally, there was a small number of retailers: shopkeepers, bakers, shoemakers, peddlers, errand boys, stonecutters, and so on (Lupo 1993: 83–85; see also Hess 1973: 54).

These data confirm the analyzes made by Sicilian political scientists Pasquale Villari and Gaetano Mosca in the late nineteenth and early twentieth centuries. For Villari, writing in 1875, "the wealthy peasant and the *borgese*, as they say here, from Monreale, Partinico [small centers in the plain surrounding Palermo, the so-called Conca d'Oro], etc., the *gabellotti* or the lease-holders, and the rural guards of these same places constitute the principal nucleus of the mafia" (1972: 85). Likewise, according to Mosca, the mafiosi "are almost always small landowners and tenant farmers, field guards or land agents, mediators or small merchants specializing in citrus fruits, livestock, and other agricultural products" ([1900] 1949: 229–30; see also Lorenzoni 1910: 680–81).

Though most traditional mafiosi did not accumulate fabulous wealth thanks to their mafia membership, and indeed earned much of their living with a licit profession, it is nonetheless true that in their occupations they profited from their reputation as "men of honor," from the network of contacts held by their mafia brothers and, whenever necessary, from the military potential of the mafia group. More than financial gain, the main advantage drawn from mafia membership was often safety and protection. In this respect it is significant that many of the occupations related to mafiosi by nineteenth-century sources share a common characteristic: whoever undertook them had to be able to defend himself and his property, as the law enforcement apparatuses were unable to ensure public order in either the citrus fields of the Palermitan Conca d'Oro, the large estates of the inland, or on most of the island roads.

Mafia brotherhood ties also favored trades and economic initiatives, as they promoted trust among members of different biological families. "It was wonderful," noted Buscetta, "feeling that you were a friend of people whom you had never met before: you went into a city, into any place and, with a letter of presentation, you were welcomed like a brother" (Biagi [1986] 1990: 94). This was particularly important in the nineteenth century, when all the Mezzogiorno was characterized by a low degree of "systemic trust" (Luhmann 1979), because the state was unable to enforce contracts and prosecute contract breaches. Like the Protestant sects Weber considered essential for the birth of capitalism, mafia *cosche* acted as guarantors for the reliability and seriousness of their members. However, unlike the Protestant sects, they were willing to resort to violence—mainly against nonmembers but, if necessary, against members of other mafia families as well—whenever agreements were not respected.

Status and Power

Despite the advantages granted by mafia membership, most mafiosi could not or did not want to pay much importance to the idea of becoming rich until the late 1950s. Antonino Calderone recalls that up to the beginning of the 1960s "in some villages there were men of honor doing manual jobs and this was a shame. We then let them work as guardians or something else.... My brother said: 'What a pity that a man of honor goes hoeing!'" (CPM 1992b: 334). In reality, for many members mafia initiation involved only an improvement of their status. This already represented a considerable step forward, especially when the initiand belonged to a low social stratum, as the writer Saverio Strati described: "He was isolated, he did not see anyone, he did not have anywhere to go, there was neither a party section, nor a cinema, nor a bar. At the most, he spent his time in the square where the herdsmen met among themselves; and also the sons of the craftsmen met among themselves. We were divided even among the poor people! Therefore, in order not to be cut off, in order not to be scorned and treated as an animal, a poor devil joined the 'ndrina. In order to be protected and to feel a man, since they said to him: 'you are *omo*'" (1977: 9–10).

Actually, the accumulation of wealth did not even constitute the primary aim of the mafia leaders. As late as the 1950s, Buscetta points out, "money was not the basis of everything. It was not compulsory to get rich in order to maintain one's position as a man of respect. A man could be a revered and respected *capomafia* without having lands and palaces" (Arlacchi 1994: 110). In the 1950s, for example, the head of Buscetta's mafia family, Gaetano Filippone, was far from wealthy (Buscetta 1999: 19). More than money, the chief aimed to accumulate power, which he expected to be able to exercise mainly within his neighborhood or village. This was indeed another reason for his not being able to afford to move to a large city, or to enter the property-owning bourgeoisie, since a change of this kind would have weakened his legitimacy in the eyes of the lower strata.

The mafiosi's hierarchy of goals reflected a value system that was widespread throughout the traditional Mezzogiorno: as Denis Mack Smith points out, "the accumulation of wealth was less admired than the acquisition of respect in this society" (1968: 395). Until the 1950s, in fact, wealth was only one of the parameters —but certainly not the main one—by which a man's capacity to make himself respected was assessed. Physical strength and the ability to use or command violence usually ranked higher. The owning of land by a mafioso could reflect a good position in the hierarchy of honor and in itself be a source of honor. In the low and middle social strata most mafiosi came from, however, this position could be maintained only if it was accompanied and backed by violence (Hess 1973: 43–48; Davis 1977).

Notwithstanding its growing importance, profit is today still not the only credo of "men of honor." According to the Palermitan Prosecutor, Roberto Scarpinato,

> the true goal is power. The obscure evil of the organization chiefs is not a thirst for money, but a thirst for power. The most important fugitives could enjoy a luxurious life abroad until the end of their days. Instead they remain in Palermo, hunted, in danger of being caught or being killed by internal dissidents, to avoid the loss of their territorial control and the risk of being deposed. Marino Mannoia once told me: "Many believe that you enter Cosa Nostra for money. This is only part of the truth. Do you know why I entered Cosa Nostra? Because before in Palermo I was Mr. Nobody. Afterward, wherever I went, heads lowered. And this for me was worth any price." (1992: 94)[2]

Even mafia investment strategies are dictated more by the search for power than by the maximization of profitability: "The mafia is ready to sustain high costs to avoid losing power on the territory and, to pursue this objective, it can even sacrifice, if necessary, the strategies of business development" (Becchi and Rey 1994: 75). It is no coincidence, in fact, that since the 1980s the families and members of both confederations have employed a significant portion of the money accumulated with tobacco and drug trafficking to buy—either directly or through fronts—a large number of small and medium-sized companies in their area of dominion. According to data collected by the Confcommercio in 1992, about four thousand Sicilian retail shops—about 10 percent of all those active on the island—are either run or directly controlled by members of crime groups. It is an estimate that is hard to verify. What did emerge very clearly in a survey commissioned by the association of the Youth Branch of the Confindustria (Italian Industrialists' Association) in 1993 was that 55 percent of the owners of Calabrian, Sicilian, and Campanian firms claimed that in their particular sphere of activity it is current practice for businesses to yield a quota of their ownership to a variety of people who are tied to illegal or suspect businesses (Ministero dell'Interno 1994a).

In some contexts, Cosa Nostra and the 'Ndrangheta *cosche* have even succeeded in establishing monopolies that are not imposed through violence, but are built on the effective ownership of all the local firms in a certain area. For more than a decade, for example, the Frascati brothers virtually controlled the market for new and old vehicles in Reggio Calabria, functioning as front men for the Libri *cosca*. They owned the agencies of Peugeot-Talbot, Alfa Romeo, BMW, Volvo, Honda, Suzuki, and Nissan. Having no need to make any immediate profits and being able to rely on cash from illegal sources, the Frascatis' firms managed to put other agencies out of business in a very short amount of time since others could not afford to give the discounts that the Frascatis offered (PrRC 1995: 6318–405). This strategy was described in very cloaked terms by Ramiro Ramirez, the former owner of one of the car agencies forced to close, in a judicial testimony:

> The progressive decrease of the Ramirez agency's sales must be attributed to the fact that the new agency Autoelite [owned by the Frascatis] offered very low prices that we could not match because, by calculating the company's costs, we would have sold under cost. In order to face competition, the Ramirez agency necessarily had to offer further discounts to clients, but this sale policy subsequently led to the failure of my firm. A bankruptcy that could not touch the Frascatis, because they had, in my opinion, a greater economic power. (PrRC 1995: 6339)

In other cases, both money and violence are employed—in variable combinations—to monopolize licit activities in a local context. This was, for example, the strategy of the De Stefano brothers, who during the 1980s controlled virtually the entire Reggio Calabria wholesale meat market. Using intimidation and threats, they forced butchers and supermarkets to buy meat from their companies. Their monopoly extended over all the city, with the exception of the Gebbione quarter, where the powerful Labate family had maintained its dominion and suppliers. In the late 1980s, when the De Stefano clan became involved in the mafia war and could no longer operate in the neighborhoods dominated by rival clans, the Labates, who had remained neutral, managed to extend their power to other areas of the city. Seven years later, the official turnover of the butchering companies controlled by the Labates had grown by three times, escalating from 2 billion *lire* in 1987 (over 1.5 million dollars at the exchange rate of the time) to more than 6 billion in 1992 (almost 5 million dollars; see TrRC 1994a: 124–26). The same combination of money and violence was employed by Francesco Serraino (known as the "mountain's king"), Rocco Musolino, and Francesco Antonio Gioffrè to gain control of the wood industry in the Aspromonte mountain as well as by other *'ndranghetisti* to acquire many of the shops located in Reggio Calabria's principal avenue, Corso Garibaldi (CPM 2000a: 72–73, 40–42).

Lastly, largely neglecting profit maximization strategies, the leaders of mafia families—especially in Calabria—have bought large pieces of land in their communities of residence. From the early 1970s on, for example, the *cosca* headed by

Saverio Mammoliti from Castellace in the Reggio Calabria province acquired the property or the direct or indirect enjoyment of wide extensions of land in the councils of Castellace, Oppido, Cosoleto, and Santa Cristina in the Gioia Tauro plain. By imposing heavy extortion taxes on them or by damaging their trees and products, the Mammolitis forced most landowners to sell their properties at a price much lower than the market one. In addition, even when they did not succeed in obtaining legal ownership of the lands, they frequently gained de facto control of the farms, selling the products and even collecting the relative farming subsidies. The estates belonging to the Cordopatri family, for example, were exploited from 1964 up to the late 1980s by the Mammolitis through a front man, who paid only a symbolic rent. When Barone Francesco Cordopatri finally succeeded in recovering control of the property in 1990, he was unable to pick the olives because his offers of employment were systematically turned down by local laborers, afraid of offending the Mammolitis. After his murder in July 1991, his sister attempted to continue, but she too faced insurmountable problems (PrRC 1992a). Only after her courageous denunciation of this situation to the police in summer 1994—once the Finance Ministry had threatened to confiscate her property for not paying taxes on the land (whose products her family had not enjoyed since the 1960s)—was the attention of national and international public opinion finally brought to the case (CPM 1994b). Baronessa Cordopatri was granted an extension to pay her taxes and the decade-long territorial expansion of the Mammolitis finally began to be halted (see CPM 1995).

NEITHER ENTERPRISES . . .

Despite the popularity of analogies between mafia groups and modern enterprises, the mafiosi's growing involvement in entrepreneurial activities does not mean that they subscribe to the rules of modern capitalism. Like the seafarers of antiquity and the Middle Ages, mafia entrepreneurs are pleased to take whatever they can get by force and fraud and have recourse to peaceful bickering only where they are confronted with a power equal to their own or where they regard it as shrewd to do so for the sake of future exchange opportunities (Weber 1978: 640). Fearing no retaliation, for example, Franco Coco and Giuseppe Flachi, two high-ranking members of the 'Ndrangheta in Lombardy, killed several Turkish traffickers in the late 1980s, in order to avoid paying for the huge stocks of heroin that the Turks had bought them. According to Salvatore Annacondia, an Apulian gangster who had a longstanding friendship with the two *'ndranghetisti*, Coco and Flachi "made [the Turks] deliver lots of heroin, paying them only partially and postponing full settlement to the next delivery and letting their debts grow enormously. Finally, on taking delivery of yet another load, they killed the Turkish couriers and squashed them down to the size of a can with a car-wrecking press. Coco told me about this, when he explained their methods to me" (TrMI 1994c: 682).

Violence constitutes one of the routine resources employed by "men of honor" and mafia families to gain or maintain their market positions and to increase the competitiveness of their commercial enterprises. It is also for this reason that Cosa Nostra and 'Ndrangheta groups cannot be understood through exclusive reference to the concept of economic enterprise. This is because, typically, an economic enterprise does not resort to violent means to achieve its ends, structuring exchanges through peaceful methods. Weber shows that this kind of activity contrasts that of the political sphere: "The appropriation of goods, through free, purely economically rational exchange . . . is the conceptual opposite of appropriation of goods by coercion of any kind, but especially physical coercion, the regulated exercise of which is the very constitutive element of the political community" (1978: 640).

The Political Dimension of Mafia Associations

Violence is not used by the mafiosi only to promote their economic interests; nor is it employed exclusively within the mafia consortia to guarantee the validity of their legal orders. Through the threat or actual use of violence, mafia associations attempt to force some of their rules on nonaffiliates, claiming the right to threaten, render inoffensive, or even to physically eliminate whoever endangers their power positions and economic activities. To use Weberian terminology again, we can say that mafia associations come into being as "voluntary associations" (*Vereine*), that is, as social groups that claim authority only over voluntary members, but they frequently end up acting as "compulsory organizations" (*Anstalte*), social groups whose legal order is forced with relative success onto the surrounding population (ibid.: 52).

As this claim is exercised over a specific territorial context, mafia consortia can be regarded as "political organizations" (ibid.: 54).[3] Any *cosca* associated with either Cosa Nostra or the 'Ndrangheta claims sovereignty over a well-defined territory, usually corresponding to a town or a village. Only in large urban agglomerations, such as Palermo, Reggio Calabria, and a few other Calabrian towns, does the territory of each mafia family correspond to one district. This bond with the territory is so close that, although the families are occasionally referred to by the name of their chief or the blood family constituting its core, Sicilian and Calabrian mafia groups are usually named according to the city or district in which they are located. In conversations among "men of honor," hence, reference is made to the Trapani family, to the *locale* of Pellaro in the province of Reggio Calabria, to the Corleonesi coalition. As Pino Scriva, one of the first Calabrian *pentiti*, states,

"Thus we have different and numerous families and, more precisely, one 'Ndrangheta overseeing Rosarno, one looking after Cittanova, another looking after Gioia Tauro, one for Melicucco and many others too" (PrRC 1995: 363; TrPA [1985] 1992: 41).[4]

The principle of territorial sovereignty has shaped relationships among the corporate units of the two mafia segmentary associations since the nineteenth century. "One of the mafia rules," noted Questore Sangiorgi in the report he wrote at the turn of the century, "is the respect of others' jurisdiction, the violation of which constitutes a personal insult" (Lupo 1993: 82). In neither confederation are members authorized to commit crimes on the territory of another family without asking for prior permission from the local mafia chief. As a Calabrian witness puts it, "One of the fundamental operating rules of the 'Ndrangheta concerns municipal territoriality, and it concerns competence to operate.... The activities of all the members must be carried out within the family territory (known as *locale*) and, above all, no trespassing on the territory of other families is allowed" (PrRC 1995: 362; see also TrMI 1994e: 161–65). In particular, as many different *pentiti* have pointed out, no murder may be committed within the area of influence of a given *cosca* without the consensus of its chief. Even when, in the Sicilian mafia association, the murder is decided autonomously by the provincial or regional commission, the representative of the family on whose territory the event has to take place must be warned in advance.

The violation of such a norm is considered a serious offence to the honor of the family head, who is supposed to react with determination in order to preserve his reputation and to discourage any further attacks on his authority. It is not only a matter of principle, there are also serious practical consequences. When a serious crime, such as a murder, is carried out on the territory of a *cosca* without the prior authorization of its chief, the members of that *cosca*, especially those on the run, and the illicit activities of the whole group are seriously endangered. Clearly, at least initially, police investigations will concentrate on the area where the crime took place (PrPA 1993c; TrPA 1985, V: 896–901).[5]

The Claim to Govern

In the areas dominated by the 'Ndrangheta, nobody, not even the unaffiliated, is allowed to carry out any illicit activity without the authorization of the local mafia family. Each Calabrian *locale*, in fact, aims to monopolize the totality of illegal enterprises and does not allow any, even minor, crime in its jurisdiction—and this seems to confirm Thomas Schelling's thesis that the tendency toward monopolization is a defining characteristic of organized crime (1971). An indirect proof of the 'Ndrangheta's monopolizing claim is given by the official crime statistics published by the Italian Statistical Office (ISTAT). These show that the province of

TABLE 4.1. Thefts reported in the provinces of Reggio Calabria, Palermo, and Catania and in Italy, 1990–1994

	1990	1991	1992	1993	1994
Reggio Calabria	6,689	6,274	8,451	8,972	9,052
Palermo	42,964	46,917	37,497	34,668	36,418
Catania	45,384	53,369	35,980	27,626	28,556
Italy	1,605,329	1,702,074	1,477,955	1,369,623	1,338,555

Source: ISTAT and Ministero dell'Interno, 1991–95

Reggio Calabria, though holding a record number of violent offences, has very low absolute and percentage values as far as thefts are concerned. Between 1990 and 1994, for example, a minimum of 6,274 and a maximum of 9,052 thefts were reported in the province of Reggio Calabria, whereas in the province of Palermo the range was between 34,668 and 46,917 (see table 4.1). On average, in the five years under examination, 1,398 thefts per 100,000 inhabitants were reported in Reggio Calabria. This is less than half the national average (2,603) and almost two thirds lower than the rates recorded in the provinces of Palermo (3,257) and Catania (3,709 per 100,000 inhabitants) (see figure 4.1). Many factors affect official theft rates, ranging from the level of urbanization to the age structure and policing. Nonetheless, the gap between the Reggio Calabria province and the rest of the country is so huge that it may well be hypothesized that the 'Ndrangheta's control represents an important contributing factor.

Sicilian mafia families also used to try to control all the illicit enterprises taking place in their communities, sanctioning crimes committed by nonaffiliates. This is still carried out in some villages and small towns of the province of Tra-

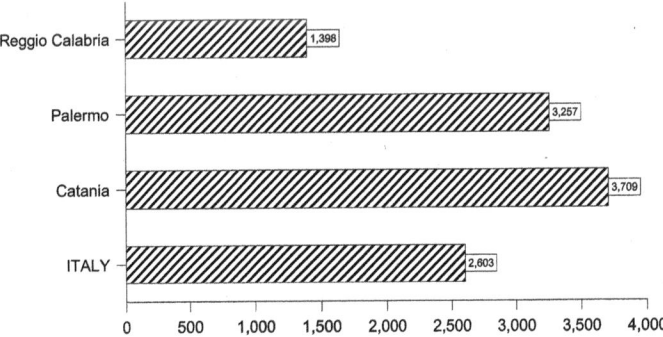

FIGURE 4.1. Average rate of reported thefts per 100,000 inhabitants in the provinces of Reggio Calabria, Palermo, and Catania and in the whole country, 1990–1994. *Source*: ISTAT, several years.

MULTIPLICITY OF GOALS AND FUNCTIONS

157

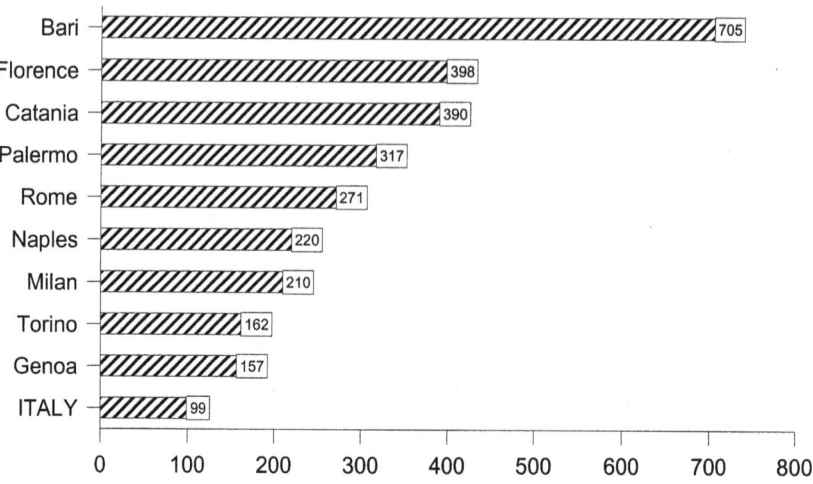

FIGURE 4.2. List of the first nine Italian cities ranked according to the rate of reported bag-snatchings per 100,000 inhabitants, 1985–1994. *Source:* ISTAT, several years.

pani and, to a lesser extent, in some centers of the neighboring province of Palermo, where the presence of Cosa Nostra is traditionally more extensive. In most of the island, however, the *cosche* have long given up any claim to controlling all the criminal acts occurring in their territory.

Cosa Nostra families tend instead to allow thieves and robbers a certain degree of freedom, and have adopted a different strategy of trying to make them request prior authorization before carrying out their crimes and to cede a percentage of their criminal profits after. As a result, even those provinces where Cosa Nostra is more firmly rooted have one of the highest rates of property crimes (thefts, robberies, extortions, etc.) in Italy. On average, between 1987 and 1996, 11 percent of all the robberies reported in Italy took place in the province of Palermo alone. This implies a rate of 268.1 robberies per 100,000 inhabitants, five times higher than the national average of 55.5.

The record number of reported bag-snatchings also shows Cosa Nostra's lack of willingness to regulate minor criminal activities. Thus we see that the city of Palermo ranks fourth among Italian cities listed according to the rate of reported bag-snatchings per 100,000 inhabitants between 1985 and 1994, coming well above other areas that are famous for their high levels of petty crime, such as Naples (see figure 4.2).

What are the reasons for this change and the different policy adopted by Cosa Nostra families and those of the 'Ndrangheta? The main explanation lies in numbers. According to cautious and probably underestimated evaluations, the members of all Calabrian crime groups constitute 2.7 per 1,000 inhabitants of the regional population, while in Sicily the corresponding rate is 1.0 per 1,000 (including not only Cosa Nostra members, but also the participants in other criminal groups). In the province of Reggio Calabria, 'Ndrangheta members represent about 1 percent of residents (more precisely 9.1 per 1,000 inhabitants) (Ministero dell'Interno 1994a: 154). If the surrounding entourage is also taken into account—and this may include a number of people ten times larger than the ritual members of the *cosca*—it is easy to understand why the Calabrian *locali* have fewer problems than their Sicilian counterparts in controlling petty crime. Thanks to their numerical consistency, the Calabrians have managed to build a true mafia class, endowed with long-term stability and capable of influencing the social, economic, and political life of entire communities.

Given the extreme rigidity of their recruitment policies, Cosa Nostra families instead often find themselves in a minority position with their competitors and are hence unable to control the whole underworld. This difficulty was admitted even by Giovanni Brusca, the man who was supposed to become Totò Riina's heir, but who in fact became a mafia witness after his arrest in 1994: "Many believe that Cosa Nostra heads all criminal activities. That in Palermo or in Sicily every illegal activity is controlled by the mafiosi. People believe that prostitution and burglaries, bank robberies, and car thefts are all entries in the budget of the Mafia Inc. Those that I have just listed are external activities, known about, tolerated, and controlled by men of honor. But they are separate worlds, which only rarely come into contact with each other. In some cases, there might be some collaboration, but this is only in very special cases" (Lodato 1999: 67).

By giving free rein to common criminals, Cosa Nostra families can at least console themselves with the idea of having a large reservoir of criminal manpower from which they can select the "best" talents to be incorporated into the *cosche*. It is a way of making virtue of necessity, as it appears from the recollections of another defector, Francesco Marino Mannoia: "In the past petty crime was not tolerated and as a result robbers and thieves were often killed by Cosa Nostra; nowadays, instead, the exact contrary takes place . . . and the most effective common criminals are carefully observed in order to assess whether or not to enroll them in Cosa Nostra" (TrPA 1989: 19).

By showing a conciliatory attitude toward urban criminals, Cosa Nostra members also expect to obtain a direct monetary return. Whenever it is possible, in fact, Cosa Nostra associates try to expropriate through extortion some of the proceeds deriving from the illicit activities carried out by nonaffiliates (TrPA 1984, II: 138). This kind of behavior, in which nonaffiliated members of the underworld are forced to "pay dues," constitutes, according to Thomas Schelling, a typifying element of organized crime (1967, 1971). Contrary to the assumptions made recently by Diego Gambetta (1993), however, who adopted and widened the American economist's theses, the mafiosi do not provide "real" protection services to gangsters, but merely sell protection against themselves. Only rarely do their services include an even vague promise that Cosa Nostra will defend underworld members against any action taken by law enforcement agencies or rival groups. For underworld members, then, the mafiosi are simply extortionists, as Schelling himself had recognized: "[Organized crime] 'protection' is primarily against the one who offers it, but it has to include protection against rival taxing authorities" (1971: 649; see also Monzini 1997).

In southern and eastern Sicily, where a plurality of mafialike and gangster groups have long undermined the sovereignty of Cosa Nostra, the families associated with this consortium are no longer even able to provide the latter type of protection and, thus, to impose a regular and exclusive "tax" on underworld activities. In Palermo, however—at least up until the early 1990s—Cosa Nostra *cosche* still "taxed" a considerable amount of local illicit activities regularly, severely sanctioning all attempts by small criminals to avoid paying. As an important investigation of the Palermo Prosecutor's Office demonstrates, in these cases there is no gradation of sanctions, and the criminals who are considered guilty are punished with death. Sebastiano Briolotta, for instance, was shot in 1986 because he "carried out thefts and robberies without the prior permission of the family" (PrPA 1993c: 349). Another gangster, Salvatore Faia, was killed in 1989, because he murdered his wife's lover on the territory of the Brancaccio family without asking for its authorization (ibid.: 348–57).

In dealing with urban gangsters, the Palermitan Cosa Nostra also tries to assert the rules of its legal order, especially when the reputation or the properties of "men of honor" are at stake. Hence, for example, Francesco Bertolini was murdered in the late 1980s because he had courted the wife of a Cosa Nostra member who was in prison. The Masucci brothers, skilled robbers, were killed after they had "disturbed" the relatives of some important "men of honor," the Tinnirellos. Antonio Traina was eliminated after burgling the house of a Cosa Nostra member; Giuseppe Sichera, because he had not paid his debts to the Graviano brothers, influential members of the Brancaccio family (ibid.: 358–79). Along the same lines, several car and jewel fencers were murdered because they did not follow a new rule made by Cosa Nostra: namely, to keep any stolen goods for at least twenty-four hours before transforming them for resale, in order that the owners who went to Cosa Nostra, rather than the police, in an attempt to recover their valuables could be satisfied (Grasso 1998).

This norm was an attempt by Cosa Nostra families to reestablish their longstanding and widely recognized function as the protectors of property rights. According to several observers, it was common, especially in inland Sicily, to go to *capimafia* to recover stolen property of any kind from the late nineteenth century on. Above all, this kind of mediation by the mafia was frequent when cattle or sheep were stolen. Livestock represented the most valuable and common booty at that time, so much so that, according to Jane and Peter Schneider, large-scale rustling was "one of the most important indigenous commercial activities" (1976: 70). Then, like today, mafiosi acted as mediators between the owner and the thieves, who often returned most of the animals in exchange for a generous tip and the nonreporting of the theft to the police (Alongi [1886] 1977: 82–96; Lorenzoni 1910: 696–97; De Francisci 1996).

Mafia mediation was usually more effective than any intervention of the police; this was recognized even by Cesare Mori, known as the "Iron Prefect," who conducted ruthless anti-mafia campaigns in Sicily during the first ten years of the Fascist regime. According to his data, in 75 percent of the cattle-rustling cases police authorities failed to achieve any results; in 15 percent they managed to find the criminals; in only 10 percent of the cases, however, did they also manage to recover the stolen animals. On the contrary, in 95 percent of all the cases, mafia mediation meant that the owner recovered 70 percent of his stolen cattle (1993: 72–73). Despite the much-discussed transformation of the mafia to entrepreneurial activities, contemporary "men of honor" still take this duty seriously. Giovanni Brusca, for example, has recounted that he "helped lots of people recover their cars." If the stolen vehicle had already been taken apart, his men would steal another that was the same model and color, in order to satisfy whoever had asked for Cosa Nostra's help (Lodato 1999: 73).

Whenever the chiefs of the Sicilian mafia consortium deem it appropriate, gangsters and criminals are punished for violating rules of the mafia legal order, not only when their own honor and property are at stake (as we have seen above), but even if none of their specific interests is damaged. Around the mid-1970s, for example, a Czech female dancer touring in Palermo was slashed on her face while her bag was being snatched. This was presented with great uproar in the local press. A few days later, the body of the young bag-snatcher was found in the back of a car with a piece of cardboard tied around his neck, reading: "Any vermin disgracing Sicily must die like this" (Grasso 1998; TrPA 1989: 18–19). Several *pentiti* have reported that this action was carried out by Cosa Nostra. Likewise, in 1986 it murdered the killer of a boy called Claudio Domino, who had been killed because he had by chance observed an extramarital liaison. Domino's death outraged Cosa Nostra members so much that they not only punished his murderer but Giovanni Bontade (a high-ranking member of the Palermitan Santa Maria del Gesù group) also unwillingly provided proof of the association's existence. During one of the hearings of the first Palermitan *maxiprocesso*, when the investigating judges were still trying to demonstrate the existence of Cosa Nostra, Bontade read a statement in the name of Cosa Nostra disavowing any involvement in Domino's murder (Lodato 1999: 64).

The Administration of Justice

In the past, when many mafia norms were entrenched in local customs, the *capimafia* represented a genuine judicial authority functioning as an alternative to the state and, as such, they were often called to solve the conflicts arising within their communities. As late as the 1950s the judges presiding over the court in Locri, Calabria, protested against the usurping of their responsibilities by the mafiosi: "Everywhere else agrarian disputes are discussed before a court and are resolved with a judicial sentence; instead, here in Siderno and Locri, people usually resort to Macrì's occult abilities" (qtd. in Ciconte, 1996: 43–44). Nor can the services provided by Antonio Macrì, the leader who was morally responsible for the 'Ndrangheta for more than two decades, simply be attributed to a rural mafia tradition that had died out much earlier everywhere else.

The same activities of mediation were carried out—at least up to the mid-1970s—by the chiefs of important urban *cosche*, such as Pippo Calderone and Paolino Bontade. Calderone, who represented Cosa Nostra in Catania (Sicily's second largest city) until 1978, used to hear a large array of friends and clients every day, devoting much of his time to satisfying their requests (TrPA 1987a). In the same way, in the 1950s and 1960s the chief of the powerful Santa Maria del Gesù mafia family, don Paolino Bontade, embodied the role of "the traditional *capomafia* who intervenes directly in all the matters in his area, arbitrating private disputes, assuming the role of great protector of his citizens, infiltrating public offices and private companies, exercising his influence through sly and hidden intimidation systems covered up by formally correct and respectful behavior" (TrPA [1965] 1981: 728).

In fact, many of the prescriptions contained in mafia legal orders were widespread among the people of southern Calabria and western Sicily, and because of this, mafia *cosche* enjoyed consistent popular legitimacy at least up to the end of the last world war. Due to this consensus and the weakness of state authorities, the administration of justice and maintenance of order was often entrusted to high-ranking mafiosi. "The mafia," noted Corrado Stajano in his book about Africo, a Calabrian village on the Aspromante, "was rooted in the village, it governed misery and poverty, regulating disagreements and resolving the quarrels that so often tore the peasant world apart because of the use or abuse of pastures, the violation of boundaries, and cattle rustling. The 'Ndrangheta behaved as a government authority, it used violence and diplomacy, threat or the art of compromise" (1979: 37; see also Sabetti 1984).

In particular, members of the two consortia were entrusted with the enforcement of the norms forming the code of honor, which were not only at the core of the mafia "subuniverse of meaning," but were also widespread in society at large (though they were not recognized by the state legal order). The *capimafia* of the past liked to picture themselves as defenders of the traditional moral imperatives deriving from the code of honor and thus strengthen their legitimacy. Hence, they frequently intervened in order to restore the violated honor of a woman who had been seduced or to preserve her virginity. Here is, for instance, Henner Hess's account of an episode, taken up and recounted by Giuseppe Lo Schiavo in his novel *Gli inesorabili*:

> Peppino Bellía . . . has seduced Rosina dell'Aria . . . and refuses to marry the girl. Rosina, an orphan, asks for help from a relation . . . who is a client of Don Salvatore Sparaino, the old *capo-mafia* of Gangi. The latter summons Peppino and his father, Disma Bellía . . . to his house. Asked what a father should do if his daughter is seduced with a subsequently broken promise of marriage, Disma Bellía, who believes one of his own daughters has been seduced, replies: "*Oh! Santo di pantanone! Gli sparerei in fronte se in quarantott'ore non riparasse!*" ["Oh, my holy God! I would shoot him in the front, if he did not repair the damage within forty-eight hours!"]. Sparaino thereupon discloses to him the true state of affairs and very discreetly implies a threat by putting himself in the role of father: "*Rosina è un'orfana e io sono il padre di tutti*" ["Rosina is an orphan and I am everybody's father"]. (Hess 1973: 137–38; see also Ciconte 1992: 220–22)

Mafia enforcement of the norms deriving from the traditional code of honor is also recalled by defectors. According to Francesco Marino Mannoia, for example, as late as the 1970s Father Giacinto of the Monastery of Santa Maria del Gesù was murdered by associates of the local *cosca* "because he was a whoremonger" (TrPA 1989: 18–19, 130). *Pentiti*, however, also admit that the prescriptions concerning the sexual sphere are no longer systematically enforced as they used to be. Now that these norms are no longer widely shared and are followed only superficially even by many "men of honor," mafia families only rarely make sure that they are respected even within their village or neighborhood. If the families' intervention is required, however, they do not hesitate to intervene. A few years ago in Reggio Calabria, for example, the Labates intervened to dissuade an overly passionate boyfriend from continuing a relationship, since the girl's father did not like him (TrRC 1994a; see also CPM 2000: 76).

Even nowadays, where the mafia is most strongly rooted, Cosa Nostra and the 'Ndrangheta families still represent themselves as full-fledged alternatives to state power. Among the *cosche* of the province of Trapani, for example, the longstanding claim to exercise territorial sovereignty has been institutionalized through the division of roles between "internal" and "external" members. "The task of the internal member," recalls Pietro Scavuzzo, a former affiliate of the Vita family located near to the provincial capital, is the total control of the territory through the continuous presence in the village and the complete availability vis-à-vis the villagers for all their needs, even the smallest ones, such as, for example, the settlement of bureaucratic procedures or relations with the city hall. At the same time, through the family's "financial company," he handles small loans and bill discounts, exploiting the bureaucratic slowness of the government, which it virtually opposes and substitutes.

The external member, instead, deals more directly with the family's illicit activities and, hence, risks more personally; however, he is more generally advantaged and likely to access to leadership. As soon as he is ritually affiliated, the internal member is entitled to a salary which is about two and half million every month. The external, instead, is paid no salary, because he runs the illicit trades and, therefore, he finances himself and, indeed, finances the family itself. (TrPA 1994a: 104)

... NOR STATES

With Italy's postwar modernization and the consequent decline of traditional subculture, the gap between the mafia legal order and the values and norms subscribed by society at large has grown progressively wider and, especially in Sicily, the *cosche* have partially lost the "judicial" functions that were theirs for so long. In the place of this kind of control, territorial sovereignty is now increasingly exercised through what can be described as a "protection tax"—the so-called *pizzo*.[6] All the families associated with Cosa Nostra and the 'Ndrangheta force—by fair means or foul—many (if not most) of both the licit and illicit enterprises that are active in their area of control to pay this on a regular basis.

Protection Rackets

There are many different ways of paying the *pizzo*, though this usually takes the form of a (forced) transfer of money (known as a *tangente*, a kickback). This can also be a payment in kind, for example, by forcing a company to take on a *guardiania* (protection services) that is then paid for by putting a "man of honor," or a client of his, on the company's payroll, or the acquisition of supplies from firms controlled by the mafiosi. Sometimes the company subjected to extortion is also forced to accept the participation of mafia members or their associates in jobs for which it has a contract (PrPA 1993c: 219; TrRC 1994a; see also Cazzola 1992).

Contrary to what has often been assumed, mafia groups have not always demanded the payment of a "protection tax" on all the economic activities in their zone. In the past, the mafiosi often forced their *guardianie* only onto large companies or the properties of rich landowners, but did not usually ask for money from shopkeepers, craftsmen, and small businesses. On this, Buscetta recalls, "While I was in Palermo [the late 1960s], we did not ask for 'contributions' from the managers of commercial activities; indeed, this would have been incompatible with the fundamental principles of Cosa Nostra. When I came back to Italy [in the early 1980s], I realized . . . that it was now general practice to ask for a *mesata* [that is, a monthly contribution] from all those who ran a commercial activity in the territories of the respective families" (TrPA 1984, II: 59–60). Until the early 1960s, the financial requirements of the families associated with Cosa Nostra and the 'Ndrangheta were relatively limited. That is to say, mafia groups did not pay regular salaries to their members, most of whom had regular jobs in the legal or informal economy, where they earned the predominant part of their income (see also Falcone 1993: 116–19).

Lying behind this expansion and widespread diffusion of extortion practices is the growing importance assigned to wealth and its rapid accumulation. Extortion is undoubtedly an easy way of making money: it does not require any high initial investments, it carries low managing costs and, in areas where state protection is not regarded as adequate or reliable, it is also a low-risk operation, because people at large usually prefer to pay a low kickback than go to the police. Indeed, it is now viewed as so "normal" that a simple phone call is often sufficient to ensure the transfer of cash. In some cases, the entrepreneurs have actually been reported as having asked to whom they were to pay their kickback even before receiving an explicit request (Ministero dell'Interno 1994a: 187). In some of the areas where Cosa Nostra and the 'Ndrangheta do not have complete control over the territory, youth gangs and pseudomafia criminal groups also often demand money from local businesses, precisely because it is so easy to get.

For mafia families in both Calabria and Sicily, the protection racket has thus come to be an easy and relatively stable financial source used to pay the growing "fixed costs" of managing the *cosca*. Kickbacks are, in fact, used: (1) to provide salaries for the "soldiers" who, unlike before, now rarely have a regular job; (2) to pay the legal expenses of imprisoned mafia members and to assist their families (this particular need has risen consistently since the early 1980s); and (3) to finance the group's "military" activities, particularly when all normal trading activities are suspended, as during a war, or when the pressure of the law enforcement agencies is particularly high.

Only a minimal portion of the extortions carried out in Sicily and Calabria is reported to the police, as is evident from the data in figure 4.3. Far from reliably estimating the extension of the phenomenon, the number of reported episodes is principally an indication of people's trust (or lack of trust) in state institutions. Especially in the high-mafia density regions, the increase in their reporting should be considered a positive sign—for example, this happened in

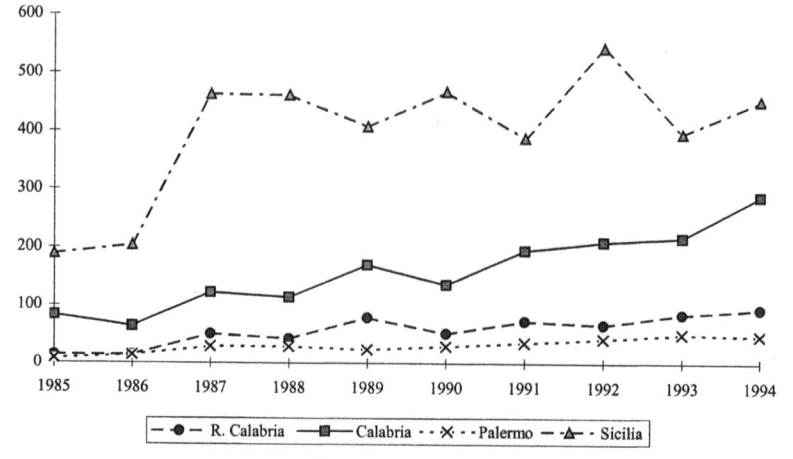

	1985	1986	1987	1988	1989	1990	1991	1992	1993	1994
R. Calabria	14	14	51	43	79	52	73	67	85	94
Calabria	83	64	122	114	170	136	195	210	217	288
Palermo	8	14	29	29	24	30	36	43	51	48
Sicily	189	204	463	462	408	468	389	544	396	453

Source: ISTAT, several years

FIGURE 4.3. Extortions reported in the provinces of Palermo and Reggio Calabria and in the regions of Sicily and Calabria, 1985–1994. *Source*: ISTAT, several years.

Sicily at the beginning of the early 1990s. Nonetheless, even during this period the Commissione Parlamentare Antimafia of the Eleventh Legislature (1992–94) estimated that reports accounted for less than 10 percent of all the extortions actually carried out (CPM 1994b). Despite the founding of numerous anti-racket associations in several Sicilian and Calabrian cities and the approval of an ad hoc law by parliament in 1991, there is no good reason to assume that the picture has changed in any way substantially since then.

According to the attorney general of Reggio Calabria, "all business activities in towns or provinces are subjected to the extortion racket: industrial firms, commercial businesses, farms, and even the professions" (CPM 1993f: 8). In both regions, in particular, the *cosche* claim a percentage on every building project carried out on their territory. "The rule," *pentito* Leonardo Messina states, "is that any firm starting a job on the territory of a family must contact a man of honor of that family, in order to establish either the percentage to be paid to the mafia family, considering the overall value of the work to be accomplished, or the payment of a kickback—so as to say—'in kind'" (PrPA 1992: 60).

In the building sector, the *cosche* do not usually content themselves with the extraction of a sum of money. The "payments in kind" that Messina mentions are frequent, one of their functions also being to maintain the power of the organizations. Since the 1950s, for example, the Calderone brothers of Catania protected the building companies run by the Costanzo brothers and, in addition to receiving a million *lira* monthly kickback (about $1,600 in the 1950s and early 1960s) gave work to thousands of people in the Costanzo's building yards (CPM 1992b: 333–34). Even in Palermo the enforced employment of one or more people—often presented as the provision of protection services—has been widespread ever since the end of the Second World War. "Mafiosi or elements controlled by the mafia," noted the investigating judges of the Palermo court in a report written in 1965, "are generally the guardians of the building sites, areas, deposits, plants, suburb houses, and country estates" (TrPA [1965] 1981: 663–64).

Together with corrupt politicians and public officials, some Palermitan mafia families made large financial as well as nonmonetary profits from what has been called the "Sack of Palermo," the savage building expansion that changed the face of the city both rapidly and dramatically from the mid-1950s to the end of the 1960s (Chubb 1982; Cancila 1988: 525–42). Initially taking orders from the politicians, the *cosche* contented themselves with extortion money. Soon, however, some of them set up their own companies and pressed claims to become directly involved in both small and large building sites. By the early 1970s, Judge Falcone noted, the building industry in the city of Palermo was almost entirely in the hands of the mafia: "Mafia organizations entirely control the building sector in Palermo—the quarries where aggregates are mined, site clearance firms, cement plants, metal depots for the construction industry, wholesalers for sanitary fixtures, and so on" (Falcone and Turone 1982).

Starting in the mid-1960s, the same kind of development also took place in Calabria. Toward the end of the decade, Calabria—which had previously been largely excluded from the projects of "extraordinary intervention" launched by the central government to foster southern Italy's industrialization—was finally given some of the funds distributed by the Cassa per il Mezzogiorno, a governmental agency set up in the 1950s to run the projects. This occurred when a Calabrian politician, Giacomo Mancini, became the minister for public works and held the position for almost five years. During this period he promoted the construction of the Salerno–Reggio Calabria highway and the expansion in the number of railway tracks from Reggio Calabria to Battipaglia in Apulia (Tino 1985). The national building companies that won these tenders were immediately targeted by the mafia *cosche* responsible for those pieces of territory, which claimed the payment of a "protection tax" through intimidation and threats. Realizing the high potential of this area of business to generate money, mafia families did not restrict themselves to only collecting the *pizzo*, but also demanded more direct participation in the work itself. For example, they set up small building firms to gain subcontracts for the site clearances (PrRC 1995: 279ff.).

This development was greatly accelerated by the Colombo Package, named after its creator, who was then prime minister. This was a plan of extraordinary investments in the Reggio Calabria province, which was issued in 1970 to placate the anger of the people of Reggio Calabria, who had revolted against the decision to make Catanzaro the new official seat of regional administration (Tino 1985: 857–78; Gambino 1976: 31–53).[7] The biggest single item of the Colombo Package was the construction of the Fifth Steelwork Center together with the necessary infrastructure on the Gioia Tauro plain on the Tyrrhenian coast. Though in actual fact only the port was ever built, and this was first used only in 1995, the investments provided for were huge and the 'Ndrangheta families soon mobilized to obtain subcontracts for the realization of the port and basic infrastructures. "In September 1974," wrote the investigating judge Agostino Cordova in the indictment against Paolo De Stefano and fifty-nine others,

> the three leading mafia *cosche* of the province, headed respectively by don Antonio Macrì, the Piromalli and De Stefano brothers, met at Gioia Tauro to discuss the projected development of the industrial port and of the Fifth Steelwork Center. It would seem that all the participants agreed to reject the proposal made by the companies concerned, which offered a 3 percent payment in return for being left in peace. It was in the mafia's interest to make sure that they got the subcontracts, so as to insert its own people and to control the whole project. (TrRC 1978: 121; see also Sciarrone 1993)

Cities and Countryside

From the early 1970s on, the *tangenti* provided by building companies and, more generally, the infiltration of the building sector and the manipulation of public contract bidding, have represented one of the most important sources of revenue for all mafia groups and, indeed, over the last few decades, the most important source for many of the families in Cosa Nostra. Large-scale enterprises, such as supermarkets, are also systematically targeted (see Ministero dell'Interno 2001e: 14–16). Petty extortions are, on the other hand, generally carried out on economic actors indiscriminately only in the larger urban centers, primarily Reggio Calabria, Palermo, and Catania.

In addition to the political-entrepreneurial strategies of each *cosca*, such diversification reflects the economic specificities of the different areas. Since the "Sack of Palermo" came to an end, city centers have only rarely been the seat of large building projects and, consequently, the revenues that the local families can extract from the sector are occasional and limited in size. On the other hand, urban agglomerations host many hundreds of commercial activities of all sizes, which can be easy prey for mafia rackets. Meaningfully, the Sicilian *cosca* that has developed the most complex and capillary system of this kind of extortion is the Madonia family, which exercised—and still exercises—its "sovereignty" over the richest and most highly commercially developed areas of Palermo. In the early 1990s, the police found a ledger containing a detailed account of what the shopkeepers in the most elegant Palermitan streets, Via Maqueda, Viale della Libertà, and Via Notarbartolo, had to pay on a monthly basis.[8]

In nonurban areas the racket has never spread to such an extent: "In the countryside villages," explains Giovanni Brusca, the former leader of the San Giuseppe Jato *cosca* in the Palermitan inland, "shopkeepers do not pay a *pizzo*; this is paid only by companies" (Lodato 1999: 77). At any rate, revenues from shops are lower, and most of the families probably believe that it is not worth the effort of putting them under pressure when larger and safer profits can be achieved by extorting from companies that have won public tenders and are involved in the building sector. By abstaining from extorting retail enterprises, furthermore, *capimafia* increase their legitimacy, demonstrating magnanimity and wealth. Emblematic in this respect are the opinions expressed by Giuseppe Farinella, for many years the uncontested *dominus* of the Madonie, a large mountainous district northeast of Palermo. "Don Peppino," a victim of his maintains, "did not want his men to extort a *pizzo* from the shopkeepers because the latter, in contrast to the entrepreneurs, did not carry out any speculative activity and then because he ... thought that asking shopkeepers for a *tangente* seemed like begging for alms" (PrPA 1994a: 71).

No matter who the victims are, families belonging to Cosa Nostra and the 'Ndrangheta still consider that raising a more or less regular "tax" on the main productive activities of their areas is an undeniable right of theirs stemming from their territorial dominion. Proof of this can be seen in the rigorous division of the kickbacks when state construction involves the territory of more than one family. When the railway between Reggio Calabria and Melito Porto Salvo, a town only some thirty kilometers away, was turned into a two-line track, the *tangente* corresponding to 8 percent of the whole value of the project was divided proportionately among all the *locali* whose territory was touched by the works (TrRC 1993b). The families receiving higher revenues sometimes cede a quota to the poorer *cosche*, but they do it at their own discretion because they are sovereign on their own territory and are entitled to all the revenue they may extract from it. According to Giovanni Brusca, this sharing policy was a longstanding tradition followed by the Madonia group. "But nobody," the new *pentito* quickly pointed out, "had the right to claim this money. I would like to explain this matter with an example. If in my neighborhood there is the Fiat [factory], I can pocket all the *pizzo* that this eventually pays and nobody can advance claims of any sort. Maybe in the next neighborhood there is only a small firm with five workers. The men of honor of this area must content themselves with what they can recover from that firm" (Lodato 1999: 75). Even subcontracts for the construction of the Fifth Steelwork Center in Gioia Tauro, whose total value reached the astronomic amount of 2,526,291,632 million *lire* (over $3,800 billion at the exchange rate of the time) were largely distributed on the basis of territorial criteria. More than half the contracts were, in fact, granted to a single *cosca*, the Piromalli family, which dominated the area where the Steelwork Center was supposed to be (but, in reality, was never) built (TrRC 1978: 226).

It is hence not surprising that the extortion racket is, without exception, the only economic activity run by the group as a whole and whose profits are mainly exploited for the achievement of collective goals, or are else divided, more or less equally, among the members. This is because racketeering is not primarily an economic activity. In other words, for mafia members it represents the due collection of a tribute by a political organization acting as an alternative to the state.

The fundamentally political nature of the mafia extortion system is shown clearly by the sanctions imposed upon those who refuse to comply with the *cosche*'s requests. Far from reflecting the often limited entity of the sums at stake, the penalties inflicted by the Cosa Nostra and the 'Ndrangheta families are frequently very severe. It is not so much the financial loss that sets off mafia reaction, but the will to make mafia sovereignty respected. For this reason, those who do not pay the requested tribute are sometimes punished with death. Between 1978 and 1984, at least twenty-four entrepreneurs were murdered in the province of Palermo, and in the following decade, the death toll reached thirty (Santino 1991: 217; Centorrino and Signorino 1993). Among these was Libero Grassi, the courageous entrepreneur of Palermo who was killed in the summer of 1991 because he had refused to pay a *pizzo* to the Madonias. Commenting on the heated debate that his murder generated in both Sicilian and national public opinion, one of the mafiosi responsible allegedly stated more or less the following: "Patience, we will overcome even this [fuss]; but if we did not shoot this *cornuto* [cuckold], all the others would have followed his example. We must make ourselves felt from time to time" (TrPA 1993d).

Political Communities That Are Not Fully Institutionalized

Despite the fact that the goals of mafia associations differ substantially from those of modern states, recognition of their political dimension cannot be denied. In this respect, what Weber stated at the beginning of the twentieth century still holds: it is impossible to define a political organization with reference to its goals, because there are very few goals that historical political institutions have not, at some time, pursued. The "political" character of an organization can be defined only in terms of the means that are specific to it: namely, its use of force (1978: 55). Furthermore, mafia families and the modern political organization par excellence, the state, share what is considered the minimal goal of politics even by those who deny the possibility of a teleological definition of the state (see for example Bobbio 1990; Nozick 1974): that is, the maintenance of order within the social group and defense against outside attacks.

Like all analogies, however, that between mafia associations and the modern state—though useful to highlight the political dimension of the former—cannot be drawn too far without running the risk of clouding the specific characteristics of this research object. Although Cosa Nostra and 'Ndrangheta families consider themselves political communities with the right of dominion over a territory and over people within it, the simplistic equation with the state, advanced by some observers since the late nineteenth century (see Schneegans 1980) and recently proposed by some Palermitan prosecutors with reference to the Sicilian mafia phenomenon (PrPA 1993a and 1993c; Lo Forte 1996), is misleading. As noted in chapter 3, the legal orders of Cosa Nostra and the 'Ndrangheta have long been respected by their members and some of their prescriptions (most notably concerning honor) have frequently enjoyed a higher degree of effectiveness and legitimation in wide sectors of the local population than the state legal orders. Nonetheless, it is a serious analytical mistake to overestimate the comprehensiveness and stability of mafia normative statutes, since they remain incomparably simpler and less sophisticated than those developed by modern states.

In this respect, it is probably helpful to remember that—even in the Old World—the functions typical of a political organization have only gradually stopped being carried out intermittently in reaction to an external threat and been centralized in a superordinate and separate community: a community that has with time become permanent and has progressively been strengthened by the belief, held by its members, in its legitimacy (Poggi 1991). In other historical phases, however, the minimal functions of a political community—namely, the external defense of and internal domination over a territory—have been accomplished by a variety of other institutions: kinship groups, neighborhood associations, warrior associations, groups primarily oriented toward economic interests, and, as anthropological research shows, even secret societies (Weber 1978: 901ff.). Secret groups, in particular, perform important political and judicial functions in numerous simple societies, supplementing or even supplanting the governmental activities of the rulers (Webster 1932).

Along such a path mafia families can thus be located in an intermediate position between the ideal-typical poles represented by the most primitive forms of political power and the opposite one of the modern state. "One might imagine a continuum running from anarchy to banditry to mafia to routine government.

The defining feature of that continuum is the extent to which control over the use of force is concentrated in a single organization" (Tilly 1988: xx; see also Poggi 1991: 11–31). That is, mafia associations represent cases of a political community that is not yet fully institutionalized. They act as a political body toward their own members but throughout their history they have been struggling—with varying degrees of success—to force their own primordial legal order onto the entire population of their territory and to endow it with legitimacy. They have never succeeded, however, in neutralizing all the rival centers of power. "Sicily's problem," Charles Tilly paradoxically notes, "is not a shortage, but a surfeit, of government." Mafia families constitute many small proto-states, none of which has succeeded in conquering and legitimizing its monopoly of physical force. Tilly posits, "If one mafia network managed to extend its control all over Sicily, all concerned would begin to describe its actions as 'public' rather than 'private,' the national government would have to come to terms with it, outsiders and insiders alike would begin to treat its chiefs as the legitimate authority. It would be a government; it would resemble a state. With outside recognition of its autonomy, plus the development of differentiated and centralized instruments of control, it would *be* a state" (ibid.: xxiii; see also Tilly 1985).

The Mixture of Politics and Economy

Like the actors who played an important part in the creation of oceanic commerce in the sixteenth century, mafia associations cannot be classified as exclusively governmental or business enterprises. In fact, profit- and power-oriented activities are present and closely intertwined in both clusters of actors. "The way," noted the historian Frederick Lane, "in which force was applied to secure gain determined the economic success or failure of many innovating enterprises that created oceanic commerce" (1966: 402). Nor is violence a marginal element in the action of mafia groups, given that the success of both consortia's entrepreneurial activities depends on the employment of such a resource.

It is mainly due to violence that mafia families or single high-ranking members have managed to gain control over scarce resources in local contexts since the nineteenth century. Wheat, sulfur, citrus fruits, petrol, bus companies, public works, votes, and contacts with national politicians: these are only some of the resources managed, in different historical moments and geographical places, by the members of the two mafia associations examined here. And violence has also been a key resource to enter and stay on international illegal markets. This is clear in the above-mentioned example of the chiefs of the Palermitan mafia families who, in the early 1970s, managed to enter the international tobacco smuggling trade only because they forced the main Palermitan and Neapolitan smugglers who had run the business for many years to accept them (TrPA [1985] 1992: 90–96).

Despite the manifold and intense involvement of most contemporary state apparatuses in the economy, we are still used to thinking that government and business have always existed as separate organizations. However, up until the beginning of the modern period, neither governments nor business enterprises were formed in any of the ways that are now familiar to us. Joseph Schumpeter, for example, has noted that our concepts of "state" and "private" enterprise cannot be applied to the institutions of feudalism without creating a distorted view of those institutions (1976: 169, 201). This is because under feudalism the state was in a certain sense the private property of a prince, just as the fief was the private property of a vassal. While fulfilling political functions, such as the provision of internal order and protection against external enemies and the administration of justice, the feudal vassals were also expected to make profits from the management of the fief, part of which had to be ceded to the sovereign: "In the feudal system a fief holder was expected to manage his fief with an eye to profit. The successful baron might disdain bourgeois haggling over merchandise, but he was an expert in using military and governmental means of making money" (Lane 1966: 418; see also Poggi 1991).

The separation of force-using enterprises from the profit-seeking enterprises that we now call business enterprises occurred at different times in different areas of Europe. Southern Italy was one of the districts where it occurred later, for in the nineteenth century the vestiges of feudal structures were still clearly visible and the spirit and legal forms of feudalism shaped most social relationships, especially in the countryside (Sereni 1968).

In the case of mafia associations, this process of differentiation has taken place only to a minimal extent even nowadays. Mafia groups came into being in a context where this separation had not yet been fully achieved, and they were subsequently hindered from taking part in the successive process of functional differentiation that has invested all modern societies (Giesen 1991: 76–79, 1989) because of their criminalization by state institutions. For the members of mafia groupings, violence thus became not only an effective means through which to gain power, profits, and social prestige—through strengthening their commitment to secrecy, exclusion from the legal community also compelled mafia associations to maintain this use of violence in order to back their internal normative code and to defend themselves from the attacks of state agencies and underworld competitors.

The families associated with Cosa Nostra and the 'Ndrangheta are certainly political organizations. As we saw above, within their communities they claim to exercise territorial sovereignty and to levy more or less regular tributes from most revenue-producing subjects. Nonetheless, it is reductive to classify Sicilian and Calabrian *cosche* as "power syndicates" specialized in the sale of protection and, with reference to Alan Block's dichotomy (1983), to oppose them to "enterprise syndicates," which merely provide illegal goods and services. Though this interpretation has found several supporters over the last few years (Lupo 1993: 192–200; Catanzaro 1994a, 1994b; Siebert 1994: 182–83), it is a false counterposition. No matter what is said, mafia groups do not operate only as power syndicates; "the secret of mafia continuity lies in the peculiar combination of profit-making activities and the control of the territory" (Becchi and Rey 1994: 75). Far from merely "selling" protection, mafia groups and their members are actively involved in a plurality of business activities: they not only trade in a variety of illegal commodities, but they also exploit violence and intimidation to occupy some of the important spaces in the legitimate economy.

The mixture of these two types of action is well exemplified by the activities undertaken by Cosa Nostra and the 'Ndrangheta in the building sector, and specifically in the market of construction for the state. The matrix was, at least initially, fundamentally political. As we saw above, the entry of the *cosche* into the building sector originated in their claim to levying a tribute from all the main productive activities located in their territory. This political objective was, however, soon complemented by economic interests. According to Giacomo Lauro, for example, the planned construction of the Fifth Steelwork Center in Gioia Tauro and the public works financed in Calabria in the aftermath of the Reggio Calabria revolt galvanized the Reggio Calabria *cosche*. As soon as he heard the news, "Ciccio Canale . . . people said, got very excited and jumped up from his chair in the living room of De Stefano's villa in Archi at the seaside. Not to mention Domenico Tripodo, Natale Iamonte, Natale Iannò, and Pietro Pirrello. This last, people said, had already signed bills saying that he would soon become very rich. Likewise, the Frascati brothers and hundreds of other people suddenly felt as if they were truck drivers or entrepreneurs, whereas up to a day before they had sold fruit and vegetables" (PrRC 1995: 4734).

Since the 1960s firms owned by mafiosi have systematically resorted to making undercover agreements with politicians and civil servants in order to win tenders, and—as the Clean Hands investigations proved (Della Porta 1992; Della Porta and Vannucci 1994; Magatti 1996)—this practice has long been common to building companies all over Italy. The novelty of the 1980s and 1990s was, indeed, represented by the involvement of mafia representatives in the *comitati d'affari*, originally formed of politicians and entrepreneurs, which had controlled the bidding processes of large-scale public works all over the country for many years. One example of this was the case of the plan to build a power plant on the site of the unfinished Fifth Steelwork Center (with an estimated budget of five trillion *lire* [about $3.7 billion], a fifth of which was supposed to be spent on subcontracts). In the late 1980s, when the plan began to be implemented, it soon became very clear that the mafia *cosche* would no longer be content with *tangenti* and subcontracts. "With reference to the construction of the ENEL Power Plant in Gioia

Tauro,"[9] the Palmi judges wrote in a 1993 warrant of arrest, "the mafia has not only infiltrated into subcontracting, but into the direct management of the works ... through liaison elements linking the private [building] firms, the state company afflicted by party kickback policies, politicians, and the representatives of *imprese a partecipazione mafiosa* [companies in which mafiosi had a share]" (PrPL 1993: 1987–88).

Thus mafia conditioning no longer took place only "downstream," at the end of the economic process of public investment (subcontracts and extortions), but also "upstream," at the beginning of the process, with decisions taken jointly by mafia representatives together with the state agencies and the large building companies that were particularly interested in obtaining large contracts for public works (ibid.). In western Sicily, for example, a sort of "duopoly" was established in the late 1980s: the public works market was subject to the complete top-down control of two strong subjects—Cosa Nostra and the *comitati d'affari*—that had joined forces in a kind of symbiosis cemented by silence and complicity (TrPA 1991, 1993b, 1998; Ministero dell'Interno 2001e: 15–16).

It may well be—as Diego Gambetta and Peter Reuter maintain (1995; see also Gambetta 1993 and Reuter 1987)—that Cosa Nostra and 'Ndrangheta members stabilized these illegitimate cartel agreements by providing credible enforcement; as the former mayor of Baucina, near Palermo put it, local mafiosi "oversaw the fair distribution of contracts among firms participating in bids" (*La Repubblica*, April 14, 1990, qtd. in Gambetta and Reuter 1995, 26). There are no doubts, however, that the cartel agreements run by the *comitati d'affari* preexisted mafia involvement and had proved to be resilient even without mafia enforcement. The Clean Hands investigations launched by the Milan prosecutor's office in 1992 and subsequently furthered by the prosecutors of other Italian cities have, in fact, proved that secret agreements between politicians and entrepreneurs were widespread in the rest of the country as well, and operated efficiently even without the *cosche*'s mediation (Magatti 1996).

Lacking in both know-how and experience, mafiosi would never have become involved at increasingly higher levels of the public work adjudication system if they had not been supported, especially in the early phases, by the *cosca*'s military potential. And it is indeed the ability to use violence—an exquisitely political feature—that differentiates them from nonmafia firms. Though it is not always necessary, the selection of firms that are directly or indirectly controlled by a mafia *cosca* or their members in a public work project can always be guaranteed as a result of violence and intimidation. Likewise, it is thanks to its ability to command violence and its reputation for effective execution of threats that the mafia can stabilize cartel agreements.

Cosa Nostra and 'Ndrangheta families do not limit themselves to threats or bomb attacks, even though these are obviously the most frequent types of intervention. If it is worth it, they do not hesitate to physically eliminate whoever hinders their plans. At the end of the 1980s, when 600 billion *lire* ($444 million) were allocated for modernization of Reggio Calabria, the local *cosche* had no hesitation in murdering a Christian Democrat politician, Ludovico Ligato, the former president of the Ferrovie dello Stato [state railway]. Returning to Reggio Calabria after twenty years in Rome, Ligato demanded a 10 percent bribe on the whole project, thus jeopardizing agreements that had already been reached between the local politicians and the city's main mafia groups (TrRC 1992; PrRC 1995: 1880–82; Ciconte 1994; Licandro and Varano 1993).

As in feudal institutions, the overlap between force-using and profit-seeking enterprises is paralleled by a lack of clear boundaries between the private and public spheres. The mafia family is managed by its chief as a flexible tool to simultaneously foster his own and the group's interests, and it is up to each leader to find a balance between different, sometimes diverging, interests. Emblematic in this respect is the management of the group finances. The rule states that the proceeds of the illicit enterprises run by the *cosca* have to be shared among members: it is, however, the chief who decides how the family turnover should be divided. Most important are the monthly salaries and fixed running costs (such as lawyers' expenses and welfare contributions for the families of killed or imprisoned "men of honor"). The chief is then free to divide the rest, either by rewarding himself and his blood family or by distributing the money among the most worthy, needy, or trustworthy members.

The confusion between public and private property is reinforced by the provisions usually taken by mafia leaders to hide the proceeds of criminal activities from the eyes of law enforcement officials. In order to do so, properties and assets are fraudulently registered to front men. Initially, these were relatives of the *capomafia* but recently, due to the increasing sophistication of investigations, unrelated persons and limited companies are preferred. This practice weakens the claim that the mafia boss and his blood family may exercise upon the goods and, especially in the case of the boss's death, may render the family's inheritance difficult. In the event of the disappearance or the deposition of the *cosca* chief, the properties that are not registered in his or a family relative's name become the property of his successor. "From what I learned in mafia circles and particularly from Silvio Badalamenti," recalls Angelo Siino, the Corleonesi's ambassador in the public work market for more than ten years, "the camping site called AZ-10 belonged to Gaetano Badalamenti, most probably through front men. Once Badalamenti was deposed and suspended from Cosa Nostra, it was 'inherited' by Bernardo Provenzano, who runs it through Pino Lipari" (TrPA 1998: 300).

From what has been said above, it is clear that the features of the families associated with Cosa Nostra and the 'Ndrangheta cannot be constrained within concepts such as those of "state" and "enterprise," which "always maintain the perfume of a specific institutional framework" (Schumpeter 1976: 201). The only way to recognize their multiplicity and complexity of goals and functions is to consider them as multifunctional entities, which have always attempted to exercise political dominion over their communities of settlement.

5

Mafia, State, and Society

The point is that in any society there must be some people who adjust situations when they become complicated, and this is usually the task of state officials. But when the state is not there or is not sufficiently strong, private individuals do so.
—I. MONTANELLI,
 Pantheon minore (1973)

This statement—made in the 1950s by Calogero Vizzini, one of the most famous postwar mafiosi—underlines a fundamental point about mafia structures: that their power has always been matched by the weakness of state structures. Thus the development and existence of Sicilian and Calabrian mafia associations over the last hundred and fifty years cannot be explained without mentioning the longstanding incapacity of state institutions to guarantee order and public security over wide areas of the Mezzogiorno through the monopoly of force, and thus to gain full legitimacy in the eyes of the local population. Filling a power void left by the state, the mafia has for many years represented a "wild self-government" (Alongi [1886] 1977: 11) and, as even Judge Giovanni Falcone admitted a year before he was killed, "for many years it has done its bit to stop Sicilian society from disintegrating into complete chaos" (1993: 124).

The power ceded to mafia associations has prevented the strengthening of state power and has sharply slowed the state's acceptance by large portions of the southern Italian population. Mafia *cosche* have thus become deeply antithetical to the modern state-building process and have rendered the process far less advantageous than would normally be the case for the local population in those areas where mafiosi have exercised their dominion. This anomalous division of power has also been consolidated by the activity of numerous state officials and representatives who have entered into alliance with the mafiosi, either to foster some superior collective interest or, more frequently, to foster their own. This state of affairs has strengthened the *capimafia*'s power and authority within local societies, thus perpetuating the existence of mafia groups. In relation to this point, Calabrian mafia witness Giacomo Lauro is very clear: "The mafia cannot exist without complicity or middlemen. In Calabria, these take the form of entrepreneurs acting as middlemen, corrupt politicians, deviant Freemasonry, and members of the secret services. There cannot be any mafia without such support. Likewise, there is no police without mafia informants and collaborators. This is what it is like"(PrRC 1995: 227; see also Varano 1996).

COMPETITION AND COMPLEMENTARITY

A key issue agreed upon by all the scholars who have carried out research on the mafia since the early 1960s is that the origins of the mafia phenomenon—whether it be considered an attitude or an organization—cannot be understood unless the forms and pace of the state-building process in the Mezzogiorno are taken into account. In Charles Tilly's words, the mafia is "an outgrowth of the particular form that the process of state formation took in Italy" (1988: xxi). That is to say, the mafia developed because the national system of power expanded without fully subordinating local systems of power. Indeed, it was obliged to actually rely on these—constituted by landlords who still wanted to be the feudatory and mafia organizations—if it wanted to govern at all in the larger areas of southern Italy. A vicious circle was consequently set in motion, one which has been described very clearly by Henner Hess: "The chronic weakness of the state resulted in the emergence of self-help institutions and the exclusive power positions of informal groups made it impossible for the state to win the loyalty of the public, while its resultant weakness again strengthened the family, the clientele and *mafioso* positions" (1973: 25).

The Power Vacuum

The mafia developed and consolidated in a power vacuum left empty by the Bourbons, who dominated southern Italy up to 1860, and by the Italian state, which was created in 1861 under the leadership of the Piedmontese Savoia dynasty. Weakened by the absence of an absolutist state tradition, the Bourbons were unable to steer the disintegration of the feudal political and economic system in the Kingdom of the Two Sicilies. Feudalism was formally abolished in the continental Mezzogiorno in 1806, under French dominion, and in Sicily by the Bourbons themselves in 1812, under the pressure of the British government, which then protected the island. On paper, the Bourbons, who were fully restored to power after the 1815 Vienna Congress, officially completed the transition from feudal institutions to those typical of an administrative monarchy by the end of the 1820s. In reality, the change from the old to the new system was much more contradictory: the new state structures proved to have only a weak territorial grip and to be largely ineffective in exercising social regulation (see Pezzino 1992a). In both Sicily and Calabria, furthermore, the formal abolition of feudalism was largely insufficient to disrupt the system of large estates (called *latifundia*) and succeeded only partially in providing incentives for a new modern landowning bourgeoisie willing to abandon the old and unproductive agricultural techniques. In Sicily the sale of former feudal property began only after 1860 (Sereni 1968; Bevilacqua 1985).

For many years after unification, the new Italian government fared even worse. It quickly managed to alienate southern sympathies and to prevent the development of any trust in the new state institutions as a result of both the weakness inherent to the system it had set up and the sudden outbursts of indiscriminate and barbarous repression to which it was liable. Especially in Sicily, incorporation into the national kingdom of Italy was thus largely perceived as yet another invasion by a foreign power. As the Sicilian socialist intellectual Napoleone Colajanni passionately declaimed, "Those who were supposed to restore the law, to promote liberty, and to be educators in the noble sense of the word began to alienate the sympathy and trust . . . of the masses, who felt as though they were treated as members of an inferior and *conquered* race" (1900: 52).

Provisions designed to ensure the penetration of these new state institutions instead gave rise to dissatisfaction and hostility. For example, the first draft triggered very strong indignation: by tradition the men of the Kingdom of the Two Sicilies were not liable to compulsory military conscription. As a result, thousands of young people ignored the government's call to arms, preferring to go into the mountains and become bandits (see Riall 1998: 163–78). In addition, the introduction of a new taxation system, taxing income on labor and not only on landed property and rents, also produced widespread discontent. In Palermo, furthermore, unification also entailed an immediate reduction in the bureaucratic apparatus and the abolition of hundreds of administrative jobs and functions, which had come to be seen as inviolable rights by those practicing them.

The effects of the state's suppression of religious corporations in 1866 were even more dramatic: not only did it leave numerous employees without work and a swarm of mediators with nothing to do, but it also unexpectedly wiped out a system of social assistance that had functioned as the primary means of survival for the large Palermitan *Lumpenproletariat*. The property seized from the Church and monasteries was not even used to satisfy the claims for land of landless peasants. Most of the expropriated land was given to the more financially competitive landowners, thus provoking further disillusion among the lower strata of the population. Finally, both in Sicily and in Calabria, many economic activities were— together with a series of bad harvests—heavily affected by reforms on customs duties, which suddenly left them unprotected from external competition and thus alienated the new government from the sympathy of all southern entrepreneurs, large and small (Hess 1973: 14–33; Renda 1984: 183–205; Marino 1986: 91ff.).

Despite the legislative and administrative instruments brought in from northern Italy, the structures of the newborn Italian state were long unable to penetrate large parts of the South or to guarantee public safety effectively. One example of this could be seen in the public perception of policemen and officials in the Carabinieri; their law-keeping role was virtually rejected by the population, which only very rarely cooperated with them. The lack of an adequate road system and the high rate of illiteracy also prevented the government machine from permeating Sicily and Calabria. As Leopoldo Franchetti put it, late-nineteenth-century western Sicily "was a society whose orders were all founded on the assumption that no public authority exists" ([1876] 1993: 14); the same considerations can also be extended to southern Calabria. Likewise, Pasquale Turiello spoke about "a barbaric intolerance" on the part of the South for the legal and impersonal dominion of the state ([1889] 1980). Diffidence, fear, and resentment dominated the attitudes of the masses in relation to state power, which had not improved their social and economic situation but had simply placed heavy financial and material burdens on them, as well as appearing distant from their needs and unable to protect them.

Police authorities representing the national government had such scarce authority that, according to Alongi, "most people believed that a private *vendetta* was the best way to assert rights, that laws and courts were an administrative pleonasm, an irony; that the government and rich people had become allies so as to tyrannize the poor, for whom the only chance left was to become *facinorosi* [violent], thieving, and cruel to gain protection and impunity for misdeeds, thereby improving their economic situation" ([1886] 1977: 16; see also Lorenzoni 1910: 678–85). The key prescription of the code of honor—the right and duty to do justice oneself—was thus underwritten by a large part of the population, and whoever was able to use or command violence enjoyed respect in all social strata. Indeed, violence was abundant at all levels, as in neither Sicily nor Calabria was the dissolution of feudalism followed by the effective establishment of a centralized political authority capable of exercising an effective monopoly of physical force. Thus, far from decreasing private violence, the abolition of feudalism ended up by making it more widespread and "democratic." As Leopoldo Franchetti put it,

> Since the abolition of feudalism had changed positive law, the latter's conformity with the factual conditions and with the juridical sense of the population ended completely. On the one hand, positive law no longer recognized violent acts of any kind in either theory or in practice, and considered them all as criminal. . . . On the other, the factual conditions were modified by the change in positive law and society was encouraged to become more

democratic, by leaving the way open to everybody to use the forces existing in it. However, since private domineering action [*prepotenza*] was one of the few forces which the society recognized, when this took the shape of violence, the reform had the simple effect of opening up the way for a larger number of people to use violence. ([1876] 1993: 93–94)

From the beginning of the nineteenth century on, a variety of figures in both regions exploited the power vacuum produced by the incapacity of state institutions to monopolize violence. Landowners and the aristocracy used it to maintain their feudal privileges, challenged as these were by the ongoing modernization of the country. The *civili*, the bourgeoisie, instead used it to support their social ascent, as did the lower classes, for whom violence represented the only alternative to poverty and a means of rapid enrichment (Pezzino 1987: 909). During the last fifty years of the twentieth century, the actions of all these three social groups has been labeled *mafioso*. Contrary to assumptions long dominant in the scientific debate, however, it is important to recognize that these subjects did not always act alone, embodying "a heroic and anarchical form of individualism" (Novacco 1972: 45). Whereas landowners, particularly in Sicily, surrounded themselves with groups of violent *campieri* in order to defend their declining semifeudal authority, the exponents of the second and third subgroups set up associations and gangs of various types, all of which promoted their common interests. As noted in chapter 1, some of these groups, and particularly those that succeeded in consolidating, are the direct ancestors of the *cosche* associated with Cosa Nostra and the 'Ndrangheta.

Consensus and Authority

In a context where violence constituted an open resource, mafia associations have long been the only entities that have succeeded in regulating its use on a local basis, largely through replacing barons whose feudal authority was declining. Presenting themselves as political organizations alternative to the state, mafia associations provided services of protection, mediation, and social integration that neither the Bourbon nor the Italian state officials were able to accomplish. Thus, though they promoted the affiliates' interests, the *cosche* ended up responding to the otherwise unanswered needs of all social classes, serving their interests in different measure:

> For the weak—the peasants and the miners—[the mafia] provided at least some guarantee that obligations between them would be kept, some guarantee that the usual degree of oppression would not be habitually exceeded. . . . It might even, on occasions, have provided the framework of revolutionary or defensive organization. . . . For the feudal lords it was a

means of safeguarding property and authority: for the rural middle class a means of gaining it. For all, it provided a means of defense against the foreign exploiter—the Bourbon or Piedmontese government—and a method of national or local self-assertion. (Hobsbawm 1974: 41)

It is indeed for this reason that, both in Sicily and in Calabria, mafia *cosche* long enjoyed the consensus—or at least, the tolerance—of large strata of the local population, whose cultural codes they repeated and manipulated (see chapters 2 and 3). Unlike the state, at least up to the 1950s, mafia power thus succeeded in transforming itself into authority, as several sources of the nineteenth and twentieth century describe. In an article published in the *Corriere della Sera* in 1955, for example, the Calabrian writer Corrado Alvaro recalled the presence of the mafia in his youth in the following way:

> The Fibbia, *'ndrina, 'ndranghita*, the Onorata Società, in short, the mafia, so much talked about these days, is something I have known about ever since I could reason. One precise memory is when, having come home for the holidays, my mother, running toward me, told me that my father was busy in the room upstairs with those of the association. Pleased, I said: "Is there finally an association in this village?" Having just finished my studies, I thought that it was an association for the promotion of local interests. My mother immediately disillusioned me: "It is the delinquent association." I don't know what my father was doing with those people, but I was not surprised. Nobody in the village considered them people to avoid, and not out of fear, but because they represented one kind of ruling class. Given our confused ideas on justice and injustice, wrong and right, legal and illegal, for the true or presumed abuses carried out by those who in some way held power, we did not find it improper to go out with a *'ndranghitista*. (1955b)

The legitimacy of the mafia *cosche* was increased by the fact that they often gave the impression of being a religious association or political party. On this, Alongi noted that "even confraternities are really in most cases mafia groups. Opposed to each other, they gain profits and influence from feasts, from the collectivism of retaliation, and from vendettas" ([1886] 1977: 99; see also Fiume 1984).[1]

To strengthen their legitimacy, up to the decades following the Second World War mafia groups in Sicily and Calabria also resorted to populist appeals that presented the mafiosi as champions of justice and defenders of the weak and the oppressed. For example, here is how Calogero Vizzini, the legendary mafia chief of the 1950s from Villalba, depicted himself in a self-portrait recently discovered by the historian Giuseppe Marino:

> Some journalists of the Voices told me that I am a mafioso. I have asked myself this question more than once and I must admit that I have always

given it a positive answer: I am a mafioso and I present myself to you, Sicilian communists, as such. I stress that you are Sicilian and do not come from another region, because you are the only ones who can understand me when I speak about the *maffia*. I am a person who has always had compassion for other people's sorrows, for their material miseries, and I have always committed myself in order to relieve them. I must confess that I often came back home with no money in my pockets, since I had given it all to those who had asked me on the street.

I have always opposed those who wanted to impose on me and on this matter I have never made exceptions: as I respect all my fellow companions, I also want to be respected. I have always stood up, whenever I realized that weak people were oppressed and maltreated, even if I did not personally know them. . . . As you see, I am a mafioso in our way, in the Sicilian way, giving what I can to those in need, respecting and making myself respected, not tolerating bullying against the weak, respecting the honor of others, and ensuring my own be respected. (Marino 1986: 281–82)

The tenets of *sicilianismo* also proved to be very handy for Sicilian mafiosi to make themselves respected and accepted by the local population. As already mentioned, *sicilianismo* is an ideology developed by the Sicilian dominant classes in order to rebut the accusations of backwardness and complicity with evildoers and to claim their right of inclusion, from 1860 onward, in the national elite. Imbued by the confused feelings of solidarity and victimism that constitute its core, Sicilian "men of honor" have frequently justified the existence of mafia associations by repeating and adapting the reasonings of *sicilianismo*. Tommaso Buscetta maintains, "The only idea really felt by men of honor is the Sicilianist one. We feel it really close, congenial. The old members inside Cosa Nostra told me that the association of men of honor was born to protect Sicily, because we Sicilians have felt neglected, abandoned by foreign governments and even by the Roman one. For this reason, Cosa Nostra, instead of the state, has been law on the island" (Arlacchi 1994: 15–16).

In the early twentieth century, the creativity of Luigi Natoli provided Sicilian mafiosi with an even more immediate tool of legitimation. Under the pseudonym of William Galt, in fact, Natoli published—first in installments in a Palermitan newspaper in 1908–9 and later as a book—the novel *I Beati Paoli* ([1903–9] 1993), which obtained enormous success and was read by all social classes from the aristocracy to the landless peasants (La Duca [1971] 1993). The plot, which drew from rich folk material,[2] was about a secret sect—the Beati Paoli—active in the early eighteenth century, which administered justice in a situation of weakness and corruption of public authorities, a sort of collective Robin Hood that opposed short-sighted legalistic conceptions and avenged the sufferings of oppressed people (Eco [1971] 1993). Since the publication of Natoli's novel, Sicilian mafiosi love to portray themselves as the successors of the Beati Paoli, and Cosa Nostra traces its origin to this secret sect.[3]

No such novel or tailor-made ideology developed by the regional elite was available for Calabrian mafiosi to justify their deeds and power. As the 'Ndrangheta's bonds with the privileged classes have always been weaker than in Sicily, mafia legitimation claims in Calabria have often presented the 'Ndrangheta as a champion of popular strata against the privileges of the aristocracy and bourgeoisie. This embryonic class awareness emerges, for example, with great clarity from the account of the association history provided by *pentito* Francesco Fonti:

> The 'Ndrangheta is a rural phenomenon and rose in opposition to the excess power *[strapotere]* of the rich landowners who exploited the peasants and bent the law for their own convenience. The Mano Nera [Black Hand, here presented as a forerunner of the 'Ndrangheta] developed to defend the peasants from this constant menace. With threats, it extorted money from the landowners to give a better chance to poorer people. Its members also organized wheat and cattle thefts and then divided the booty among friends and relatives. By doing so, some of these Mano Nera leaders achieved the reputation of fair men and defenders of the weak. (PrRC 1995: 4427)[4]

In both Sicily and Calabria, mafia claims were so persuasive that, according to several nineteenth-century observers, their members did not exclusively include those who wanted to promote their social ascent through violence. Mafia associations also grouped people from different social strata who, feeling unprotected by official authorities, sought security in a brotherhood capable—if necessary—of defending their rights with violence. "In Oppido and the nearby villages," according to a local magistrate who was questioned by the Catanzaro Court of Appeal in 1902, "there were two classes of *picciotti*. The sectarian affiliates belonged to the first, the action group, which committed thefts and *camorre* and afterward divided the profit among themselves. The second, the group of the contributors, was composed of honest and upright citizens, who even paid a monthly tax with the twofold scope of avoiding damage by the *picciotti* of action and of being protected by the latter" (Nicaso 1990: 80). Likewise, as early as 1838 the Bourbon official Calà Ulloa noted that even in Sicily "many landowners . . . have judged it more convenient to become oppressors than oppressed and so have enrolled in the parties" ([1838] 1961).

To reinforce their standing in the local community, furthermore, the chiefs of the *cosche* used violence sparingly. "The Palermitan *mafioso*," noted Antonino Cutrera at the end of the nineteenth century, "does not kill anybody, he imposes his influence with his moral force and only exceptionally does he resort to acts of violence" ([1900] 1988: 54). Even in their requests for extortion, the mafia members treated their targets courteously and carefully avoided depending excessively on threats. By playing on the individual's sense of his worth as a man, they reinforced their victims' feeling of *omertà* and assured them that, by not seeking state protection, they too would gain in respect. "For many it was a positive honor to be well treated by a proven *mafioso*, regardless of the sacrifice involved" (Schneider and Schneider 1976: 194).

Thus, by exploiting widespread cultural values and fulfilling real and otherwise unsatisfied needs, mafia groups succeeded in consolidating their power, contemporaneously blocking that of the state: "The powers and the influences which the law is supposed to fight are stronger than the organization aiming to impose the law.... Public opinion observes this extralegal social system; the mass of the population admits, recognizes, and justifies the existence of those forces that would elsewhere be judged illegitimate and also the means by which they are imposed. Therefore, those who eventually want to stand on the side of law must fear not only vendetta, but also public condemnation, that is, dishonor" (Franchetti [1876] 1993: 14).

Cohabitation

In the years immediately following the unification of the country, the Italian state machine repeatedly tried—with indiscriminate repressive campaigns—to monopolize violence and to destroy all alternative centers of power, coopting only those representatives of the southern aristocracy and bourgeoisie who were willing to back the government's repressive action. The overwhelming victory of the Left in the 1874 elections, which led to the "parliamentary revolution" of March 1876, marked the failure of this policy and the defeat of the "Historical Right" that had governed the country from 1860 (Pezzino 1987: 913ff., 1990a: 134–50; Brancato 1986: 126–69; Davis 1988: 290ff.; Alatri 1954). Facing accusations of collusion with mafiosi and evildoers, made by northern politicians and observers, the Sicilian ruling class united to reject them and to claim inclusion in the highest spheres of national politics, denying the existence of a specific mafia problem in Sicily.

To achieve such inclusion, the Sicilian elites and, to a lesser extent, those in Calabria, were even ready to come to terms with the leaders of mafia groups. Thus, parallel to the consolidation of the Sicilianist movement, they relied increasingly on local *capimafia* not only to maintain order on their properties, but also to gather the votes they needed to enter the national parliament. The turning point was represented by the extension of suffrage in 1882, which gave the right to vote to all literate males and thus increased the candidates' reliance on the mafiosi's services. "Mafia *cosche*," noted the Sicilian political scientist Gaetano Mosca at the beginning of the twentieth century, "immediately understood the great advantage that they could draw from their participation in the political and administrative elections. This participation become more effective and active after the law widened the suffrage and gave the right to vote to the members of the *cosche* and to the classes in which they had greater influence and enjoyed prestige" ([1900] 1949: 243).

The clienteles organized by the *capimafia*—their nuclei formed by mafia groups—mingled with a wider network of clientelistic relationships through which the central government integrated southern upper classes into the national political system and secured their support for government majorities. From 1876 on, the Mezzogiorno deputies become the mainstay of the "transformist" project initiated by Prime Minister Agostino Depretis and continued by his successors until the outbreak of the First World War, in order to defend the northern bourgeoisie's hegemony, which was threatened by peasants' protests and the urban masses. In such a context, "the mafia clientele was the specific application of a more general system. Its peculiarity distinguished itself in the fact that in this case one used the extremist methods of armed threat and suppression of the antagonist and the opponent" (Romano 1963: 161).[5]

In the early twentieth century, these votes became virtually indispensable when the further extension of suffrage and the rise of the Popular and Socialist parties threatened to break the traditional supremacy of the liberal political class. Indeed, the dynamics of the prewar period—often termed Giolitti's Era, because he was prime minister almost uninterruptedly from 1903 to 1914—favored the strengthening of mafia structures, which were organized as political machines to gather votes for liberal clienteles and notables, and promoted their legitimation. The action of mafia clienteles was, in fact, openly supported by the state authorities at all levels, including even the prefects—the direct representatives of the central government in the single provinces. In 1909 Gaetano Salvemini described Giolitti's action in the following way:

> Giolitti exploits the miserable conditions of the Mezzogiorno in order to link the mass of southern deputies to himself: he gives them "carte blanche" in the local administrations; during elections he provides them with the services of the underworld and the Questura; he ensures them and their clients the most unconditioned impunity; he lets the electoral trials become statute-barred and intervenes with amnesties at the right moment; he leaves the mayors condemned for electoral crimes in office; he gives decorations to the guilty; he never punishes delinquent delegates; he deepens and consolidates violence and corruption, where they originate spontaneously from local miseries; he introduces them officially in the villages where they were before ignored. The Hon. Giolitti is certainly not the first Italian statesman who has considered the Mezzogiorno a conquered land, open to all evil.

But none has ever been so brutal, so cynical, so unscrupulous as he in founding his political power on the exploitation, the perversion and scorn of the Italian Mezzogiorno; in the elections in Mezzogiorno, none has made more systematic and open use of any sort of violence and crime. (1963: 137–38)

The inclusion of mafia associations within political-electoral circuits was facilitated by the working attitude adopted by most *capimafia*, especially in Sicily. Notwithstanding the antagonism intrinsic to the two types of organization, only very rarely did the bosses openly oppose state institutions or publicly foster noncompliance with state laws. No matter how they had begun their career, the leaders of a mafia group did not consider themselves to be bandits or outlaws. Indeed, they portrayed themselves as men who favored law and order, even showing formal deference to state authority.

Government agencies formally condemned mafia violence and occasionally fiercely repressed its most violent manifestations, especially when they were directed against the persons or the properties of landowners. As a rule, however, they came to terms with the representatives of mafia power and de facto delegated to the latter the maintenance of public order over wide areas of western Sicily and southern Calabria, where the authority of the central government was scarce and even the personal safety of state officials was in danger. At least up to the mid–nineteenth century, many historical *capimafia* enjoyed the open protection of the political-administrative establishment and exercised their power with the full conviction of acting in the name of legality. As the Parliamentary Anti-mafia Commission finally acknowledged in 1993, "In practice, the relationships between the institutions and mafia took place, for many years, in the form of relationships between two distinct sovereignties: neither would attack the other, as long as each remained within its own boundaries. . . . The state attacked only when the Cosa Nostra attacked and after that it would go back to the cohabitation" (CPM 1993c).

Political and judicial authorities themselves legitimated mafia power in a plurality of ways, as soon as it shed its subversive potential and gave up formal opposition to the state. In 1944, for example, Giuseppe Genco Russo, who had been accused between 1920 and 1942 of eleven murders, several attempted murders, and a very high number of robberies, thefts, and extortions, was rehabilitated by the Caltanissetta Court of Appeal for his only definitive conviction (CPMS 1976a: 45). In 1958, two months before dying in a mafia ambush, Michele Navarra, uncontested chief of the Corleone mafia family, was granted the honorary title of Cavaliere dell'Ordine al Merito della Repubblica Italiana [Knight of the Esteemed Order of the Italian Republic] (Prefettura di Palermo [1971] 1981). Both before and after the Fascist dictatorship, similar honors were bestowed upon other mafia chiefs, such as Calogero Vizzini, Giuseppe Genco Russo, and Santo Flores.

The "legalization" of mafia power was sometimes enacted to such an extent that the mafiosi were called on to represent the central government in a local context. As the main character of a novel written by the Calabrian writer Saverio Strati maintains, "They all know who these mafiosi, these courageous men are. They are public characters: they occupy places in the City Hall as commissioners or even as mayors. Protected by the politicians—people whisper that even a minister was present at a plenary meeting of the regional mafia" (1977: 9). For example, in Marineo, a village forming part of the Palermitan Conca d'Oro, the notary Filippo Calderone became mayor in 1879 and held this position until 1892, though he headed a *cosca* of evildoers that threatened his political rivals and extorted money from the whole village (Cirillo Rampolla [1889] 1986; Fiume 1986). In Raffadali, a village inland from Agrigento, the functions of justice of the peace [*giudice conciliatore*] were entrusted for over a decade to Vincenzo Di Carlo, the head of the local mafia group (CPMS 1971: 276–77). Even the Allied Military Government of the Occupied Territories (AMGOT), which occupied southern Italy in 1943, appointed numerous *capimafia* as mayors of towns and villages in western Sicily and the province of Reggio Calabria. In fact, the latter represented the only authority that had not been swept away by the collapse of the Fascist regime in a power vacuum that the AMGOT was unable to fill (Mangiameli 1987; CPMS 1976a: 113–33; Renda 1987: 15–97).

As late as 1955, the complementary nature of mafia and state power was acknowledged by one of Italy's most influential magistrates. When Calogero Vizzini died, the chief prosecutor in the Corte di Cassazione, Giuseppe Guido Lo Schiavo, wrote, "It has been said that the mafia despises the police and the judiciary, but this is incorrect. The mafia has always had respect for the judiciary and for justice, it has accepted its sentences, and has not obstructed judges in their work. In the pursuit of bandits and outlaws it even sided with the forces of law and order. . . . Today, we hear the name of an authoritative successor in the position held by don Calogero Vizzini in the secret consortium. May his action aim to the respect of state laws and to the social improvement of all" (1955).

The relationship between mafia and state power was slightly less symbiotic in Calabria, especially along the Ionic coast of the province of Reggio Calabria. There, most 'ndranghetisti had few contacts with government parties; indeed, many of them became members of the Italian Communist Party (PCI) during the Second World War and in the successive decades were even elected as mayors to their own villages on the Communist ticket (Ciconte 1992: 261–79; Cervigni 1956). Different political sympathies were sometimes found even within the same *locale*. "In Africo, for example," a former mafia affiliate recalls, "two opposing tendencies coexisted as far as both political and mafia interests were concerned: the Bruzzanitis supported the Left, the PCI; the priest, don Stilo, instead, represented the DC [Christian Democracy] and both 'lived together' in the Onorata Società" (PrRC

1995: 4755). Such a plurality of orientations was favored by the widespread conviction that closer alliance with the ruling parties at the national level would not lead to any particularly significant advantages for the *cosche*. This point is clearly made by the *pentito* Giovanni Gullà, who explains as follows why many *'ndranghetisti* neglected the Christian Democracy and moved to the Communist Party after the Second World War:

> Even if it may seem strange, there was a historical moment when in many Calabrian villages, not to say in many areas, there were true zones of superimposition between the environment of the Onorata Società and the Communist environment, since there was no unified political line in the 'Ndrangheta. Each of us went according to his own tendencies, his sympathies, not so much following economic interests, because there were no real economic interests in that period, when the criminal level was primitive. There was no close relationship with the public administration. The predominant economic sector was the agricultural one and the transformation of some products, such as citrus fruits. Hence there were no very important interests. At that time the 'Ndrangheta nursed agrarian interests, such as the *sensalia* [mediation] and the *guardiania* [imposed protection]. Everything turned out into a "systematic" extortion of these agricultural activities, given that there was only a little bit of construction, it was still too early. (PrRC 1995: 343)

In larger centers, however, mafia groups were most frequently allied with established power, even in Calabria. For instance, the prefect of Reggio Calabria wrote the following in 1955: "The underworld controls local activities and quite often political activity (given that in these cities it is impossible to enter and stay in the public administration without the support and favor of representatives of the local underworld), which is reciprocated with both tolerant and abusive considerations." Thanks to such control, the mafiosi were able to exercise "systematic intervention . . . in rents, public tenders, service, concessions, the collection of civic rights, and so on, from which they earn illicit profits" (qtd. in Ciconte 1992: 262).

To better accomplish the functions of mediation and integration delegated to them by the state and to direct the local electorate's vote toward the candidates representing the government parties, the mafiosi were often allowed to hold positions not only within the local administrations but also in the newly created bodies of the *parastato* (state-funded companies and cooperatives working in a variety of economic sectors) from the late 1940s on. The latter, in particular, was one of the ways in which the state compensated Sicilian "men of honor" for their important contribution in repressing the peasant protests calling for an agrarian reform under the aegis of the Communist and Socialist parties. In the 1950s, we thus find members of mafia organizations leading agrarian and the reclamation consortia, peasant health insurance services, and the Ente Riforma Agraria Siciliana, the body that was in charge of implementing the agricultural reform and dividing the great estates. Giuseppe Genco Russo, for example, was for many years the vice president of the Consorzio di Bonifica del Tumarrano [Tumarrano Reclamation Agency], which operated over an area of about 100,000 hectares with a budget of more than 40 billion *lire* (over 64 million dollars; Fed. PCI-CL [1964] 1976: 662). Again, Diego Gioia, the well-known *capomafia* of Canicattì, was president of the local health insurance offices on which all the peasants depended for medical assistance. In his turn, the mafia boss Vincenzo Guzzo was not only the vice mayor of his own city, Licata in the Agrigento province, for several years, but was also a leading figure on the local agricultural council and president of the Unione Provinciale delle Cooperative (Fed. PCI-AG [1964] 1976: 714–16, 743–44). On the plain of Gioia Tauro, the 'Ndrangheta *cosche* occupied the cooperative that dealt with most of the citrus production and became the distributing seat of the subsidies granted by the state to farmers (Piselli and Arrighi 1985: 442–58).

In exchange for their electoral support to local notables and for maintaining order in local contexts, the mafiosi obtained all kinds of favors for themselves and their clients: the concession of an arms license or a building permit; the amendment of a police report; the transfer of an overly efficient state official; and, last but not least, protection from judicial investigations. The most important gain was, however, symbolic: thanks to collusion with state apparatuses, the mafiosi's power, which had been conquered with violence, consolidated and was consecrated by official legitimation.

MAFIA AND POLITICS IN REPUBLICAN ITALY

The establishing of the republic and the rise of mass parties after the Second World War were not enough to destroy the clientelistic channels through which much of the southern Italian population was integrated into the national political system. From the 1950s onward, there was merely a transformation from the traditional "vertical" clientelism, based on notables, to a "horizontal" or "bureaucratic" type. This occurred because relationships with the electorate were overseen no longer by single politicians, but by a variety of ad hoc secondary organizations, such as the Catholic union CISL, the Christian Association of Italian Workers (ACLI), the Coldiretti (the farmers' Catholic union), and some others (Tarrow 1967; see also Fantozzi 1993). In a system of mass patronage of this kind, the associates of mafia families secured a role no less important than the one they had had vis-à-vis traditional notables, as competition with left-wing parties made the votes gathered by mafia groupings more valuable than ever. At the same time, the occupation of government posts by the majority party, the Christian Democrats, and the channeling of huge resources to the South in order to industrialize it, multiplied the possibilities of clientelistic exchange (see Gribaudi 1980; Mastropaolo 1993).

Initially semiofficial, from the mid-1960s on these relationships and exchanges between *capimafia* and state representatives became more reserved and secret until, by the end of the twentieth century, they were increasingly viewed as damaging for reputations and careers. This has come about as a result, especially from the 1970s onward, of the fact that the Cosa Nostra *cosche* and, to a lesser extent, the 'Ndrangheta have undergone a process of delegitimation. Initially prompted by enlightened minorities, this change is consequent to the wider modernization process which—though inconsistently and with contradictions—has invested the entire country over the last fifty years.

Continuities . . .

In the 1950s and 1960s the mediation of the *capimafia* between the local population and national political representatives was favored by the consensus that the *cosche* continued to enjoy in many communities: "Call it as you like, Honorary Society, *fibbia, 'ndragata*, the Just One, it is a criminal association only in the face of the law, but not in the consciences of some of the Aspromonte popular strata" (Adelfi 1955). In those years, traditional images and myths maintained their grip over a wide pool of young people among whom mafia families found their new recruits. Even Judge Paolo Borsellino recalled that, as a young boy, he envied some of his schoolmates who were the sons or relatives of "men of honor" (Lucentini 1994; Stille 1995: 26–27). Nor was the acceptance of mafia power limited to the lower strata: in those years, some Cosa Nostra members were often seen in the most exclusive clubs of the Palermitan bourgeoisie, such as the Circolo della Stampa [Press Club] and the Circolo di Tiro a Volo [Clay-Pigeon Shooting Club] (TrPA 1995a, 1995b; see also Stille 1995: 27).

The Catholic Church, too, contributed to the legitimation of mafia power and, indeed, according to several sources, some priests were ritually affiliated to mafia groups (Stajano 1979; Mignosi 1993). Even in the decades following the end of the Second World War, many priests protected "men of honor," sometimes openly, and up to the late 1980s, few voices were raised within the Catholic hierarchies to denounce mafia violence and abuse (Cascio 1998; Roccuzzo 1998; Lodato 1994b; Mignosi 1993; Scordato 1997; Cavadi 1993).

Despite the precise reports made by some left-wing politicians during the 1950s and early 1960s, national public opinion showed only a very limited awareness of the mafia phenomenon. The word *mafia* hardly ever appeared in Italian newspapers, and a dismissive attitude was widespread among law enforcement officers (with very few exceptions), journalists, and politicians. The prevailing attitude was described very well by Vittorio Nisticò, the director of *L'Ora*, a courageous Palermitan newspaper that provided the first detailed descriptions of mafia violence in the 1950s (and whose printing press was, in revenge, destroyed with a bomb):

> The word *mafia* or *mafioso* had almost disappeared from the reports of police stations and from the vocabulary of many judicial courts. For a long while merely mentioning the topic of mafia was like putting one's hands on electricity: there was always somebody powerful ready to get angry. . . . Obtaining some useful information from the *questure* was an almost impossible enterprise for a newspaper; there were no few cases when the mafia motive was officially excluded for crimes which in fact bore the signature of this or that *cosca* quite clearly. (Nisticò 1964: 24; see also Chilanti 1971: 43–45; Di Lello 1994)

The few mafiosi who had problems with the judiciary could hide comfortably at home, without taking any special precautions. As late as the 1970s, despite a pending arrest warrant, Gaspare Mutolo continued to live in his Palermitan neighborhood, a few meters away from his official address, and sent his children to the local school, registering them with his real surname and giving the teachers his current address and telephone number (CPM 1993b: 1234–35, 1260). Likewise, as a fugitive, Buscetta lived in Palermo at his son's house for long periods, and, though this address was known to the police authorities, nobody ever came to look for him (CPM 1992c: 365–66). Even more open, if that is possible, was the complicity in smaller towns and villages. In 1955, the fugitive Vincenzo Romeo, from Bova on the Aspromonte mountain, even succeeded in marrying publicly in his own town church, inviting "all the chiefs of the Honored Society" to his reception (Ciconte 1992: 245–94). According to a former member of the San Cataldo family, Leonardo Messina, "in every town, the mayor, the [Carabinieri] marshal, and the *capomafia* command. The three of them are told about the presence of a fugitive on their territory; policemen and Carabinieri meet him, but they turn around" (CPM 1992d: 532).

Empowered by popular consensus and the benign neglect of law enforcement agencies, members of Cosa Nostra and the 'Ndrangheta met with little difficulty in accomplishing their roles as brokers and pursuing their own goals of power and wealth. In Sicily, many "men of honor" supported the separatist movement following the Second World War, but within a few years' time they were all coopted within the Christian Democrats' ranks. The DC, in fact, offered larger political and economic returns and remained, for over forty years, the party closest to the Sicilian mafia consortium. As Salvatore Cancemi, former chief of the Porta

Nuova family, put it, "Cosa Nostra's orientation has always been to vote for the Christian Democratic Party. Certainly in Cosa Nostra we have never voted for the Communists or the Fascists. If somebody preferred the exponents of smaller parties to the Christian Democrats, this was allowed" (PrPA 1995a, III: 35). According to a recent estimate (based on the politicians mentioned by mafia witnesses in the indictment against former Prime Minister Giulio Andreotti), from 40 to 75 percent of Christian Democrat members of parliament and about 40 percent of all those elected in western Sicily between 1950 and 1992 were openly supported by Cosa Nostra (Arlacchi 1995: 15–17; see also Montanaro and Ruotolo 1995; and Lupo 1996a).

Especially in Sicily, many "men of honor" were actively involved in political life and held important political positions at the city, regional, and even national levels. Among those who succeeded in combining the two "careers," Tommaso Buscetta remembers the following:

> The Monarchic Giuseppe Guttadauro (*rappresentante* of the Corso dei Mille family), the Christian Democrat Giuseppe Trapani (*consigliere* of my own family), Antonino Sorci (belonging to the Villagrazia di Palermo family, a namesake of the cousin called *Ninu lu Riccu*), Giuseppe Cerami (who would go on to become a senator and was a member of the Santa Maria del Gesù family). These last two Christian Democrats were councilors on the Palermo city council at the time when Salvo Lima was mayor and Vito Ciancimino the commissioner for public works.
>
> At that time, furthermore, many men of honor were on both the city and provincial councils, and I can easily indicate them, as soon as I have the list of the people elected in that period. I even remember that a sort of motion or resolution against the mafia was once voted in the Palermo provincial council, which was unanimously approved. Immediately afterward, almost half of the councilors hurried over to explain to us, men of honor, that it was unavoidable, because otherwise they would have brought suspicion upon themselves. Obviously men of honor were also on the regional assembly—though there were fewer of them. (PrPA 1995a, I: 103–5)

Politicians active at the national level were also in the mafia ranks: for example, the lawyers Giuseppe Cerami and Francesco Barbaccia, who was famous for being elected without ever having made a campaign speech (TrPA 1995a, 1995b; PrPA 1995a, 1995b). As late as November 2000, the former Christian Democrat senator, Palermo's vice mayor and commissioner Vincenzo Inzerillo, was sentenced to a nine-year conviction as a "made" member of the Brancaccio Palermitan *cosca* (*Gazzetta del Sud*, November 22, 2000).

The pool of politicians that was not ritually affiliated, but whom the Cosa Nostra families were able to influence, was much wider. Among them was Salvo

Lima, who was mayor of Palermo between the 1950s and the 1960s, and Vito Ciancimino, who was first commissioner for public works in Lima's administration and then took over as mayor when Lima was elected as a member of the national parliament in 1968 (Vasile 1994; Santino 1997). Together with Giovanni Gioia, these two men were the leading Sicilian figures of a new generation of Christian Democrat politicians who—under the aegis of Amintore Fanfani—resorted to vertical clientelism and systematically occupied the public administration and the *parastato* (state companies and agencies) positions to gain power and foster their political careers. For these politicians, mafia families fulfilled the crucial functions of safeguarding political support and running party branches—these had, under the leadership of the *fanfaniani* (members of Fanfani's faction), become "the keystone for control of the party because it is there that the *tesseramento* takes place" (Chubb 1982: 64). Within the DC, in fact, ruling offices were assigned through elections for which only the *tesserati* (those who had a party card) were eligible. Thus, those controlling the process of recruitment at the local level exerted a considerable influence in the selection of the party leadership even at the national and regional level. It was for precisely this reason that mafia families continued to maintain their powerful leverage over all the Christian Democrat politicians. Though the local politicians' power was enhanced by their relationship with the center and, most notably, by their access to state patronage resources, "the means by which that power is generated are predominantly local" (ibid.: 78).[6]

Apparently there was a considerable disparity of power, as the *giovani turchi* (young Turks, as the *fanfaniani* were called) controlled all the fundamental levers of economic and political power in those years. Nonetheless, they remained vulnerable to mafia requests. "The lists of candidates," recalls the first politician and "man of honor" to become a mafia witness, "were decided by Lima, Pennino [chief of the Brancaccio family], and Brandaleone [one of Lima's followers, commissioner in the Palermo City Hall and member of the Porta Nuova mafia family]" (TrPA 1995a: 80). Furthermore, according to Buscetta, Pennino's house was "the natural seat of the DC" (ibid.: 54).

Cosa Nostra's strong influence did not merely involve the city's political life, but extended to include at least the regional administration, which (unlike most other Italian regions) had been established as early as 1946 to weaken the separatist movement and which enjoyed considerable legislative and financial autonomy. Cosa Nostra *cosche*, for example, openly supported the Milazzo government, which ruled the regional administration at the end of the 1950s, backed by a heterogeneous coalition of center and left-wing parties. It was in those years that the cousins Ignazio and Nino Salvo, "men of honor" belonging to the Salemi family in the province of Trapani, gained control over the private concession for collecting taxes in Sicily, including extremely favorable conditions for doing so. As opposed to the 3.3 percent national average, they were allowed to keep 10 percent of all they collected. Moreover, the Sicilian parliament granted them very generous expense reimbursements and prolonged delays (called *tolleranze*) in delivering the tax revenue to the government, and the Salvos were thus able to invest the collected sums in profitable activities at no cost. To consolidate this privilege, the two cousins had no scruples about withdrawing their support from the Milazzo government and making an alliance with those Christian Democrat politicians who had been excluded from the autonomist experience and who wanted to tighten their grip over the regional administration (TrPA 1985, XXXII: 6826–59). From then until the mid-1980s, when they were prosecuted by the first anti-mafia pool, the Salvos were among the most powerful characters in the economic, political, and social life of Sicily—not only thanks to their wealth, but also due to their iron control over the Trapani Christian Democracy branch, which guaranteed them great influence over all the decisions taken by Italy's largest party at the regional level (CPMS 1976c: 601–3).

. . . and Changes

Even when the superimposition of roles was not total, relations between Sicilian "men of honor" and the more entrepreneurial politicians became closer and more equal beginning in the mid-1950s. This movement was favored by the common social origins and shared will of these men to conquer power by all means available. Between politicians and mafiosi there was no longer a gap in social extraction, education, and lifestyle—factors that had separated most of the latter from liberal notables. In fact, the politicians who reached the top in the parties and local administrations in the postwar period were *homines novi* coming from medium to low, if not humble, backgrounds, like most members of mafia groups—and like the mafiosi they wanted to make careers at any cost. Unlike the politicians of the liberal epoch, they did not dispose of family properties to allow them to live "for politics," leaving aside any monetary profit they could draw from it. To refer to Weber's famous dichotomy, people like Lima, Salvo, Gioia, and Ciancimino had to live "from politics." A political career for them constituted the main instrument to conquer status, power, and wealth, and their whole personal success depended on its outcome (Weber 1994; see Pizzorno 1992: 21–26).

During this period, then, relations between government politicians and members of mafia families were a constant *do ut des*, where each side needed the other. The politicians depended on the mafiosi to gather votes and to run the party branches. Thanks to the politicians, the mafiosi increased their power and guaranteed themselves immunity from law enforcement investigations. Their relationship was cemented by some common and traditional values and a common weltanschauung, but it was at the same time constantly in the balance, as each side was strongly dependent on the other and neither of them managed to conquer a definitive edge.

The instability of the political-mafia link was, moreover, emphasized by the slow but inexorable decline of its legitimation and by the rise of political and social subjects—especially the unions and left-wing parties—that repeatedly made public their abuses of power. For many years these groups had had very little impact on national decision making. Nonetheless, the leaders of the majority parties holding government posts could not ignore these reports when they had an indisputable empirical base. Although they were ready to close an eye—and sometimes even two—toward the techniques employed in southern Italy to gather votes, the DC's national leaders had no interest in sharing the state powers with the representatives of mafia associations permanently. The mafia had been appropriately exploited to suppress the peasant movement and banditry that had openly challenged state sovereignty after the Second World War (see Barrese and D'Agostino 1997; Chilanti 1952) but now had—in the opinion of Alcide De Gasperi and Mario Scelba (prime minister and minister of the interior in Italy's first postwar cabinets) and their successors—to fall into line again, remaining in a subordinate position. This was the reason underlying the severe repression following the Ciaculli massacre of June 30, 1963—despite the close relationships of friendship and common interest between Sicilian politicians and "men of honor." In the following years, all the leading figures of the Sicilian mafia found themselves in prison, in compulsory exile in northern Italy, or forced to emigrate. At the end of that same decade, however, most of them were freed for lack of evidence by the Catanzaro and Bari courts, which held the two most important trials because of presumed partiality on the part of the Palermitan court.

Following the bomb explosion in Ciaculli that killed seven policemen, the Parliamentary Commission to Investigate the Mafia Phenomenon in Sicily (usually known as the Anti-mafia Commission) finally managed to get off the ground, becoming the most authoritative—though often powerless—seat to denounce mafia-political collusion. It had been created for the first time in 1962, after fifteen years of unsuccessful requests by Communist and Socialist members of parliament. Two days after formally installing the commission, however, the parliament was dismissed, and this bicameral committee would probably not have been reestablished if the explosion had not drawn the attention of national public opinion to the problem of the mafia in Sicily (CPMS 1976a: 3–39; Barrese 1988: 5–54).

The Ciaculli massacre also represented a turning point in the relations between politicians and mafiosi in another respect. "Before 1963," noted the first parliament's Anti-mafia Commission in its final report in 1976, "many mafiosi paraded their relationships with politicians and local administrators—and vice versa. At polling stations, the mafiosi were impudent and aggressive. Nowadays it is rare to see links between mafiosi and politicians so openly manifested" (CPMS 1976a: 581). Though it was by no means a clear-cut or generalized trend, from the mid-1960s onward the mafia—especially in large urban centers—began to be discussed and condemned, and open relationships with mafiosi began to be a handicap for politicians.

Consolidation and Degeneration

In Calabria, the intermingling between mafia and political elites took place later than in Sicily. "The historical phase of mafia subordination to politics" (PRPL 1993: 1688–89) ended only with the 1970 national elections, which were held a few months after the end of the Reggio Calabria revolt. In these elections, the Reggio Calabrians supported the Movimento Sociale Italiano (MSI, the former Fascist Party), which had taken over leadership of the revolt, severely punishing the Christian Democracy and the Socialist Party, which had ordered its repression with tanks. An important, though not officially declared, goal of the plan of extraordinary investments in the Reggio Calabria province, which was launched after that election (the so-called Colombo Package), was thus to reconquer these lost votes and, with this aim, the local representatives of the DC and PSI struggled to reestablish clientelistic relationships with the 'Ndrangheta, whose city branches, headed by the De Stefano brothers, had backed the revolt and entered into alliance with the MSI. This soon became clear to the managers of the northern companies that won the first tenders for the construction of the Gioia Tauro port. On the matter, witness Giacomo Lauro recalls, "When some entrepreneurs visited the Reggio Calabria prefect, *questore*, and chief prosecutor of the time and raised the problem that the mafia would undoubtedly put its hands on the 'pie,' they received an easy answer: 'We have to make everybody happy, otherwise we will not be able to reestablish democracy and will fall back into serious disorder'" (PrRC 1995: 4734).

Electoral and business pacts between *capimafia* and state representatives were often underwritten in the shadow of the Freemasonry, into whose lodges—both the official and the secret, parallel ones (the latter being labeled "deviated" in Italian)—the 'Ndrangheta bosses entered massively after 1970. With the establishment of the Santa, in fact, the higher-ranking affiliates were authorized to join a Masonic lodge; indeed, most of them did so to the point that, according to Pasquale Barreca, a former high-ranking member of the De Stefano coalition, "in Calabria the 'Ndrangheta and Freemasonry have become a 'single thing'" (PrRC 1995: 5722; see Forgione and Mondani 1994). As the prosecutors of the Reggio Calabria Direzione Distrettuale Antimafia note, the entrance into the Freemasonry allowed the mafiosi simultaneously to reach economic, political, and legal goals:

> The ['Ndrangheta's] entrance into previously existing or ad hoc constituted Masonic lodges was the way to establish links with those social strata which

traditionally adhered to the Freemasonry, that is, members of the liberal professions (physicians, lawyers, and notaries), entrepreneurs and politicians, representatives of government institutions, including judges, prosecutors, and police officials. Through this link, the 'Ndrangheta was able to find not only new opportunities for its economic investments, but also previously inconceivable political outlets and above all, "cover-up," which was accomplished in various ways and at various levels (diversions, lack of investigations, attacks of every kind on incompliant prosecutors and judges, adjustments of trials, etc.). This produced a substantial impunity, characteristic of this criminal organization, rendering it almost "invisible" to institutions, to such an extent that it was only a couple of years ago that it came to the attention of national public opinion and the most highly qualified investigative bodies. (PrRC 1995: 4980–81; see also CPM 2000a: 79–91, 117–31)[7]

Thanks to the powers of mediation of the Freemasonry, even in Calabria the pacts between politicians and mafiosi became—as in Sicily from the 1950s—more "equal." The power of the politicians was apparently much stronger than that of the *capimafia* and basically consisted in their ability to condition the allocation process of state resources. In order to do so, however—and it was in this that their intrinsic weakness lay—they needed the votes that the mafiosi gathered for them during electoral competitions. In this respect, the 'Ndrangheta's blackmailing power is still today particularly high, even higher than that of Cosa Nostra. It has, in fact, been estimated that in the small and medium-sized southern Calabrian municipalities, the ruling mafia family can control up to 40 percent of the votes, while this percentage decreases to 15 to 20 percent in the larger towns (Arlacchi 1988: 137–40; Ciconte 1994: 6). This assessment was also confirmed by the former mayor of Reggio Calabria, Agatino Licandro: in his opinion, among the members of the city council "there are at least 10 to 15 percent who are consciously elected with mafia votes" (CPM 1993a: 58).

The votes activated by the 'Ndrangheta often determine not only local elections, but also regional and national ones. It is no coincidence that in the early 1990s, when the relationships between mafia and politics started to be judicially investigated, the Reggio Calabrian prosecutor's office requested parliamentary authorization to proceed against four Calabrian members of parliament (Hon. Riccardo Misasi, Hon. Sandro Principe, Hon. Paolo Romeo, and Sen. Sisinio Zito) on the grounds of suspected criminal mafia association. Additionally, the investigation on the *voto di scambio* [exchange vote] initiated by the chief prosecutor of Palmi, who seized electoral material from the homes of well-known mafia bosses during the political elections of April 5, 1992, confirmed the mafiosi's interest in engaging in electoral campaigns so as to elect candidates who will offer protection and support for their criminal activities (Forgione and Mondani 1994). Despite enormous difficulties, some of the criminal investigations taking place over the following years were won when brought to trial. In October 2000, for example, the former member of parliament Paolo Romeo was sentenced to five years of imprisonment for being a member of a criminal association of mafia type (*Gazzetta del Sud,* October 10, 2000). On the basis of this and other charges, the former regional counselor of the Partito Socialdemocratico Italiano (PSDI) Pino Tursi Prato was convicted with a nine-year sentence in January 2001 (*Gazzetta del Sud,* January 25, 2001). The Reggio Calabrian MP Amedeo Matacena was also convicted in March 2001 for his external support to the 'Ndrangheta.[8]

From the early 1980s on, the two power structures forming mafia and political elites have increasingly unified. Instead of supporting external politicians, the major 'Ndrangheta families have often mobilized their electoral weight to back mafia members standing for office, or people linked by close kinship ties to the family chief or high-ranking members. This solution has the advantage of simplifying relations with the official power, eliminating the need to set up negotiations, agreements, and alliances with politicians outside the mafia family. The disadvantages of this superimposition of roles consist in the excessive visibility of the mafia group's leaders and an undue concentration of power in the hands of a few individuals, which may become counterproductive at critical moments when the mafia consortia are attacked by law enforcement institutions and public opinion. The outcome of this trend has been described very clearly by Roberto Pennisi, a prosecutor of the Reggio Calabrian Procura della Repubblica in a hearing before the Parliamentary Anti-mafia Commission:

> Often when we talk about the relationship between the mafia and "pieces" of the state, politics, and the professions (doctors, lawyers, engineers, and so on), we think that the mafia is on one side and all these others on the other and that these relationships are almost like rivers set up between these two entities.... But there are no rivers, because it is the same thing. The mafia has its own physicians, its own lawyers, its own politicians and, perhaps, its own "pieces" of state institutions. There is no need to imagine a relationship. ... The mafia has all these characters within it; it shapes them, they are its own, it does not need to get close to them or to entrap them, in order to get, and consequently do, favors. (CPM 1993a: 122–23)

The men leading the De Stefano *cosca* since the mid-1980s exemplify very clearly this phenomenon, which has been described as "the internalization of representation" (Arlacchi 1988: 176–77). Since Paolo De Stefano's death in 1985, this *cosca,* the largest in Reggio Calabria, has been headed by his cousin, the lawyer Giorgio De Stefano, who represented the Christian Democrats on the city council for many years, and Paolo Romeo, a member of parliament for the PSDI for several legislatures (PrRC 1993c). Likewise in Gioia Tauro, blood relatives of Girolamo Mazzaferro, Giuseppe Piromalli, and Saverio Mammoliti long represented the interests of the local mafia groups—perhaps the 'Ndrangheta's most powerful ones—in the city council (CPM 2000: 35).

In contrast, in Cosa Nostra, the overlapping of relations between the mafia and politics, which had been common practice from the time of Fanfani's leadership on, progressively broke down with the balance going mainly in the favor of the mafia until the early 1990s. Emboldened by the billions accumulated through heroin trafficking, Cosa Nostra chiefs increased their demands on politicians from the late 1970s on, trying to control the decisions of the public administration in an increasingly pressing and arrogant way and claiming favors of all kinds at the national level. And for the first time they also began to kill the politicians who did not honor the pacts underwritten with them, to punish their betrayal and to warn the remaining referents. The first to be killed was Michele Reina, the secretary of the Palermitan DC, in March 1979. A few months later, Piersanti Mattarella, the DC president of the Sicilian regional administration, was murdered; after having received mafia votes, he had been trying to free himself from its conditionings and to launch a moralizing campaign inside his own party (PrPA 1995b).

This open use of violence revealed not only a growing mafia arrogance, but also the deteriorating quality of relations between the mafia and political power. That is to say, postwar socioeconomic and cultural modernization processes fostered the dissolution of a broad mafia subculture that was previously shared by both mafiosi and politicians. Consequently, the shared cultural humus that typified relations between these two groups of actors began to erode, leading to a new paradigm of behavior based on utilitarian calculations. In other words, before entering a deal, each side now carefully assesses the financial, electoral, or judicial gains that it could draw from the other.[9] This change was accompanied, in Sicilian mafia families, by a growing distrust and lack of respect toward the political class.

This changing attitude is clearly documented by the following statements, which refer to two phases of the relationship between the mafia and politics over a span of about thirty years. According to Gioacchino Pennino, the relationship between Salvo Lima and his uncle, also called Gioacchino, chief of the Brancaccio mafia family, "was of a great affinity on both a personal and a political level. Tommaso Buscetta and the La Barbera brothers were closely linked to both: they met each other very, very often" (TrPA 1995a: 80). The exchange of favors thus formed part of a long-term relationship which, being based on friendship and mutual respect, went far beyond calculated ends. Thirty years later, however, the relationships between *capimafia* and politicians are portrayed in a very different light. According to Balduccio di Maggio, the man who helped to capture Riina, Riina "personally told me more than once that it is not possible for a politician, at any level, to become a man of honor. It is not even possible for a man of honor to start a political career. On the basis of this rule, which was expressed to me in categorical terms, there is a substantial contempt on the part of Cosa Nostra toward politicians, who are not regarded as serious enough to become part of the organization" (PrPA 1995a, II: 66).

All the same, this new attitude has not led to looser relationships with politicians, because Cosa Nostra men are only too aware that they cannot afford it. "Politicians' behavior," Di Maggio goes on, "might sometimes give rise to 'disappointments,' but their function was particularly important for Cosa Nostra and, hence, there was an 'obligation' for all men of honor to vote for the Christian Democrats. The unanimous conviction was that we could usefully influence, through politicians, the courts' action and, furthermore, that the function of Sicilian politicians was imperative for 'Roman politics' concerning Sicilian matters and, especially, involving Cosa Nostra" (ibid., III: 15).

Nowadays, Cosa Nostra leaders are ready to bribe a politician to get what they want, and, indeed, monetary rewards occasionally compensate for the weakening strength of subcultural values. However, to consolidate their power, the *capimafia* have mainly begun to resort to intimidation and violence. Their aim is to force whoever has asked for their help even once to remain "at the *cosche*'s disposal," ready—either for personal advantage or, more often, the result of fear—to satisfy any of their requests. The new attitude is again synthesized by Di Maggio: "We obviously give votes to politicians of our choice and after making an agreement with them, but they have to do what we say, otherwise we break their horns" (PrPA 1995a, II: 66). In 1992, for example, Cosa Nostra leaders had no scruples about murdering two of their closest and longest standing political allies, Salvo Lima and Ignazio Salvo, who had been unable to "swing" a revision of the *maxiprocesso*. To revenge this judicial decision, which condemned many "men of honor" to spend the rest of their lives in prison, they even went as far as planning the murder of one of Giulio Andreotti's sons, since Andreotti, heading the DC faction to which Lima and Salvo belonged, had been expected to intervene in favor of Cosa Nostra. While his Sicilian "lieutenants" enjoyed Cosa Nostra's electoral support for more than two decades, Andreotti in fact tried to distance himself from it, fostering several anti-mafia provisions while he was prime minister between 1989 and 1992, in order to end his long political career with a final crowning success: election as president of the republic (PrPA 1995a; see also the declarations of the latest *pentito*, Antonino Giuffrè, up to April 2002 Bernardo Provenzano's closest aide, who confirms both Di Maggio's assessment of politicians and Andreotti's collusion with Cosa Nostra, as reported in *Corriere della Sera*, November 29, 2002: 9).[10]

A DIFFICULT LIBERATION

The deterioration of relations between the mafia and politics is the result of a slow process of delegitimation that has invested mafia power during the whole postwar period, but has recorded a sharp acceleration from the early 1980s onward. This process is rooted in the deep socioeconomic and cultural transformations that have taken place in the country as a whole since the end of the Second World War. In the last two decades, however, it has been actively promoted by growing minorities of citizens, quite often southerners themselves, who in different seats and ways have started to fight the arrogance and violent ways of the mafia in Sicily and other regions of the Mezzogiorno.

Anti-Mafia Movements

A crucial role in the ethical and political movement of the anti-mafia rebellion has been played by the new generation of law enforcement officials who were trained during and after the 1968 cultural revolution (Ginsborg 1998: 356ff.). Breaking with their institutions' traditional acquiescence to the dominant political and economic centers of power (including, in Sicily and Calabria, the mafia), some of these new judges, prosecutors, and police officials began to investigate southern Italian mafia associations, their infiltration into the legal economy, and their political and institutional protection. Members of this group were, for example, Giovanni Falcone, Paolo Borsellino, and the other investigating judges of the Palermitan anti-mafia pool who wrote the indictment for the first *maxiprocesso* under the leadership of Antonino Caponnetto.[11]

As a direct result of their courage and determination, many of the Sicilian (by birth or adoption) representatives of this generation fell victim to mafia violence from the late 1970s on. In barely four years, for example, between 1979 and 1983 all the following were killed: the chief of the Palermitan *squadra mobile* [police investigative squad], Boris Giuliano; the judge Cesare Terranova, who was to take over the Investigating Office [Ufficio Istruzione] of the Palermo court; the chief prosecutor Gaetano Costa; Pio La Torre, head of the Communist Party in Sicily, who had just presented the first anti-mafia bill in Parliament; the Palermo prefect Carlo Alberto Dalla Chiesa; the Trapani prosecutor Giangiacomo Ciaccio Montalto; and the chief of the Palermo Investigating Office and Terranova's successor, Rocco Chinnici (Lupo 1993: 216–17).

After a period of calm during the late 1980s, another season of shocking murders started again in 1992. This was the direct result of the confirmation by the Corte di Cassazione of most of the convictions and the investigating judges' reconstruction of Cosa Nostra history in the first Palermitan *maxiprocesso* — the Corleonesi murdered the two magistrates who were held primarily responsible for the outcome of the trial. Giovanni Falcone and Paolo Borsellino were slaughtered two months apart, along with Falcone's wife and eight policemen from their escorts, in two huge bomb explosions in the summer of 1992.

These two clearly perceptible periods of mafia action against the state triggered the rise of a popular anti-mafia movement which—above all in Palermo, but also in other southern cities—accompanied and supported the actions of the new generation of law enforcement officials. For the first period in the early 1980s, the turning point was represented by the murder of General Carlo Alberto Dalla Chiesa on September 2, 1982. A hero in the fight against left-wing terrorism, the general was killed with his young wife and driver after only three months in Palermo as prefect of the province and high commissioner against the mafia (see Dalla Chiesa 1984). Shocked by this murder, the citizens of Palermo took part in unprecedented public demonstrations, including a spontaneous candlelight procession in honor of his memory.

Two weeks after the Dalla Chiesa murder, an important anti-mafia act was approved by parliament. Based on the proposal presented by the Communist member of parliament Pio La Torre a few months before his death, the new bill introduced the crime of "membership in a mafia-type delinquent association" [*associazione a delinquere di stampo mafioso*] (Art. 416bis of the Penal Code) and authorized the seizure and forfeiture of illegally acquired property for those suspected of being members of mafia groups (Ingroia 1993; Turone 1984, 1995). It was on this provision that the Palermitan anti-mafia pool built its judicial offensive against Cosa Nostra in the mid-1980s.

During the following years, a "protean and multifaceted anti-mafia movement" developed in Palermo (Schneider and Schneider 1994). This was promoted by some fairly stable associations and groups that were founded with the specific aim of fighting the mafia, understood as both a collective entity and the attitudes and behavior of individuals. Even the city administration was invested by this wind of change. In 1985, Leoluca Orlando, a member of a reformist left-wing faction of the Christian Democrats who had taken a clear stance against the mafia, began to serve as mayor. During his first administration, which lasted until 1990, the city hall became a focal point for the condemnation of mafia and its supportive political culture. For the multiplicity of activities that accompanied Palermo's *maxiprocesso*, the mid-1980s were labeled as "Palermo's springtime."

After a period of retreat and disillusion in the late 1980s, the anti-mafia movement recovered energy and vitality in the early 1990s and, particularly after the killings of the summer of 1992, attracted a large number of people and associations over the whole country. A march organized in memory of Giovanni Falcone thirty days after his murder brought an estimated 500,000 people to Palermo. In the following months and years a new generation of politicians, who made the fight against the mafia the defining issue of their programs, were elected mayors in many Sicilian towns and villages (including some Cosa Nostra strongholds, such as Corleone and San Giuseppe Jato) and, to a lower extent, in Calabria as well (see Ministero dell'Interno 1995b; and CPM 2001: 25–33).[12]

As in the early 1980s, state institutions also reacted to the new mafia aggression with a strong counterattack, which, though relying on a series of emergency measures, rapidly produced significant results (for a detailed overview, see Jamieson 2000: 40–126). In August 1992 a new anti-mafia bill was passed, whose most effective provision was the introduction of a special detention system for the leaders of mafia associations (Art. 41*bis* of the Act No. 354/75). In the following twelve months, thirteen of those undergoing this kind of prison treatment decided to become mafia witnesses (Ministero dell'Interno 1994b). Another measure that proved very successful was the decision to send seven thousand army troops to Sicily to set up roadblocks, guard judges and politicians, and enable the police to concentrate on investigative work. Though a provisional and largely conciliatory measure, the so-called Operation Sicilian Vespers gave Sicilian citizens visible evidence of state support.

Within a few months, many mafia chiefs, some of whom had been on the run for decades, were captured. On January 8, 1993, the Carabinieri arrested Totò Riina, who had evaded capture for more than twenty-two years. The twenty-six Direzioni Distrettuali Antimafia set up in early 1992 by Giovanni Falcone initiated important inquiries concerning the chiefs and members of many mafia groups and, thanks to the contributions of mafia witnesses, discovered within only a few months who had ordered and carried out the Capaci and Via D'Amelio killings, in which Giovanni Falcone and Paolo Borsellino were killed (see TrCL 1994; Bianconi and Savatteri 1998; Tescaroli 2000).

Parallel to the corruption investigations of the Clean Hands Pool in Milan (see Magatti 1996; Della Porta and Vannucci 1994), several inquiries—mostly in Sicily, but to a lesser extent also in Calabria—started to reveal the extent of collusion of state representatives with Cosa Nostra and the 'Ndrangheta. Between 1991 and 1995 more than half the deputies of the Sicilian regional parliament and seventeen Sicilian members of the national parliament were targeted with charges of mafia association and corruption (see Cazzola and Morisi 1996). Criminal proceedings, in particular, were started for all the leaders of Andreotti's Sicilian supporters who had not been killed by the mafia or had not already died of natural causes (Arlacchi 1995). Indeed, even Andreotti, one of the most important politicians in the postwar period (he has been a member of parliament since 1948, prime minister seven times, and a government minister countless times), was brought to trial in Palermo on charges of belonging to a mafia-type delinquent association, while the prosecutor's office in Perugia accused him of having ordered the murder of journalist Mino Pecorelli in 1979 (PrPA 1995a). In autumn 1999, however, the former Christian Democrat statesman was acquitted of both charges because the highest courts of both cities regarded the proof presented by the two prosecutors' offices as insufficient (*La Repubblica*, September 25 and October 24, 1999; see Tranfaglia 2001). The Palermitan ruling was confirmed by an appeals court in May 2003 (*La Repubblica*, May 3, 2003: 1). In November 2002, instead, an appeals court in Perugia overturned Andreotti's second acquittal and sentenced him to twenty-four years in jail for ordering Pecorelli's murder (*The Economist*, November 23, 2002: 29).

Anti-mafia investigations also targeted state officials, including some high-ranking ones. In 1993 the former head of the first section of the Corte di Cassazione, Corrado Carnevale, one of Italy's highest-ranking judges, was prosecuted and brought to trial for favoring mafia bosses in his sentences (he was long nicknamed *ammazzasentenze*, "sentence-killer"). Though acquitted by the first-degree court, Carnevale was subsequently found guilty by the Palermitan court of appeals in June 2001 and sentenced to six years of imprisonment (*Corriere della Sera*, June 30, 2001: 1). In October 2002, however, the Corte di Cassazione overturned his conviction (*Corriere della Sera*, November 1, 2001: 1).

Anti-mafia investigations have not only focused on national politicians and high-ranking state officials; they also cover local contexts, where the mafia influence on the public administration's decision making is usually stronger than at the supraregional level. One act in particular, Act No. 221/91, has proved to be a very effective instrument for dismantling mafia-political pacts, which have sometimes been very strong. This authorizes the dismissal of the city, provincial, and regional councils when it is proved that they have been "polluted" or conditioned by the mafia. From May 1991 to December 2000, and with special frequency in 1992 and 1993, more than 110 city councils were dismissed, in particular 30 in Sicily and 22 in Calabria (Ministero dell'Interno 1999a, 2000a: 42, 2001a: 186; see Parini 1999; see table 5.1).

The investigations concerning the political-criminal nexus were first institutionally recognized in April 1993, when the Parliamentary Anti-mafia Commission of the XI legislature, headed by MP Luciano Violante, published a report on "mafia and politics" (CPM, 1993c). This was the first official document to recognize the relationship existing between Cosa Nostra and vast sectors of the political and institutional establishment. After many years of isolated complaints on

TABLE 5.1. City councils dismissed according to Act. No. 221/1991, 1991–2000

	1991	1992	1993	1994	1995	1996	1997	1998	1999	2000
City councils dismissed	21	21	34	4	3	8	7	6	6	4
in Sicily	6	8	9	—	—	1	2	—	4	—
in Calabria	6	4	2	—	2	2	2	1	—	3

Source: Ministry of the Interior

the part of few public officials and opposition members, the *pactum sceleris* between the *cosche* and state representatives was finally targeted by judicial inquiries and the attention of national public opinion.

Counterattacks and Mistakes

To protest against the repressive campaign, warn their political referents of possible retaliations, and reassure the "men of honor" undergoing the special detention system, in 1993 Cosa Nostra chiefs launched an open challenge to state sovereignty, staging alarming acts of terrorism in several cities of central-northern Italy. On May 14, 1993, a car bomb was exploded in Via Ruggero Fauro in Rome in an attempt to kill the TV journalist Maurizio Costanzo, who luckily survived. Two weeks later, on May 27, an even more devastating blast destroyed buildings in Via dei Georgofili, in Florence's historical center, seriously damaging some halls of the adjacent Museo degli Uffizi and killing five people. Finally, on the night of July 27–28, three bombs rapidly exploded one after the other near the Basilica of San Giovanni in Laterano, the ancient church of San Giorgio in Velabro in Rome, and in the gardens of the municipal villa in Via Palestro in Milan, causing the death of six people, wounding many others, and seriously damaging the facades of the two sacred places (see Vigna 1996).

Disappointed by the unfulfilled promises of Christian Democrat politicians and worried about the effectiveness of the state anti-mafia campaign, in the following months Cosa Nostra and 'Ndrangheta chiefs planned a separatist project. Their aim was to create an independent state in southern Italy, or at least in Sicily, which could be tightly controlled by mafia associations. According to some *pentiti*, Cosa Nostra's terrorist strategy also served the implementation of this project and the creation of a new political order in Italy. High-ranking mafia defectors also say that Cosa Nostra's open challenge to the state was fostered by superior, hidden instigators (see Buscetta 1999: 158–66 and Cancemi's statements in Tescaroli 2000). Though taking these hypotheses seriously, the Caltanissetta and Florence prosecutor's offices (which were respectively in charge of the investigations concerning the Capaci and Via D'Amelio 1992 killing and on the 1993 bomb explosions in mainland Italy) have so far been unable to find conclusive evidence (Tescaroli 2000; Travaglio 2001).

Whether or not linked to Cosa Nostra's 1992 and 1993 bombs, the separatist project went through the first implementation stages, with some initial signs of success. Several small parties supporting the federalist project sponsored by the northern Italian Lega Nord were created in southern Italy as well, often under the auspices of Licio Gelli, the head of a secret Masonic lodge, the P2. At the election for the renewal of the Catania provincial council in January 1994, a separatist ticket called Sicilia Libera, created by Tullio Cannella acting on the orders of the Corleonesi, gained about 9 percent of the consensus. Initiatives to support such a plan were also taken by the chiefs of the Calabrian mafia consortium (interview 10; *La Repubblica* May 24, 1998: 8; Abbate and Gomez 2001; Vitale 2001).

The plan, however, came to a sudden halt, as the leaders of the two mafia confederations thought their interests could be better represented at the national level by a new alliance of center-right parties. This started to take shape in 1993 under the leadership of TV tycoon Silvio Berlusconi, who won the national elections in March 1994. Directly after the elections, the Calabrian *pentito* Cesare Polifroni stated the following: "At this moment the prevalent attitude is to wait for the politics of the new government. I may say in this respect that all the organizations in Sicily, Calabria, and Campania were ordered to vote either for Berlusconi or for Pannella, with the certainty that they were going to be the winning group. We believe that the new government will dismantle all the repressive legislation and go back to the 'free state'" (PrRC 1995: 5071). Despite repeated attempts to discredit the *pentiti* and to reform the anti-mafia legislation, Berlusconi's first government, lasting only few months, did not succeed in fulfilling mafia expectations. Notwithstanding the absence of sensational legislative changes, however, Cosa Nostra and the 'Ndrangheta did manage—during and after the cabinet headed by Berlusconi—to achieve their main goal: the weakening and progressive delegitimization of the repressive campaign that had begun after the 1992 killings.

Several factors contributed to such a turn. Among these, it is necessary to mention—as well as the prima donna behavior of some prosecutors and judges—the inefficiency and incompetence of several sectors of public institutions, above all the legislative and executive bodies. As soon as the phase of large anti-mafia demonstrations and declarations of principles came to an end, the politicians were unable to plan and implement "anti-mafia strategies worth their name" (Caselli 1998: 20). Not even the left-wing coalitions that for the first time in the history of Italy's republic governed the country from 1996 to 2001 were able to develop effective strategies against the mafia and corruption. Although the Communist Party and its successors (first called Partito Democratico della Sinistra [Democratic Party of the Left] and then Democratici di Sinistra [Democrats of the Left]) had for decades denounced the Christian Democrats' collusion with the mafia and long supported law enforcement action, left-wing politicians seemed to forget their long-standing anti-mafia commitment as soon as they got into office.

One example of the legislative and bureaucratic inefficiency is the case of the anti-racket law, approved in February 1992 following the protests initiated by the shopkeepers in Capo d'Orlando (a town in the province of Messina), which stimulated the growth of a nationwide anti-racket movement (Grasso 1992). Blocked by complicated procedures and bureaucratic shackles, the "Solidarity Fund for Extortion Victims" set up by the law did not provide effective support for the several hundreds of entrepreneurs who yearly report the extortion of which they have been victim.[13] The normative was so ineffective that in February 1999 a new bill was passed (Grasso 1998; *La Repubblica,* February 4, 1999: 21). In the meantime, however, the number of reports made had sharply lowered and the whole movement of popular protest had been weakened. Fewer than ten Palermitan entrepreneurs and shopkeepers, for example, attended the ceremony to celebrate the birth of the first city anti-racket association in March 1999 (*Corriere della Sera,* March 17, 1999: 10).

National state institutions have also proved incapable of providing law enforcement officials working in "border" areas with safe conditions and effective means to work. In Reggio Calabria, for example, the large-scale investigations started by the prosecutor's office and the police forces have been partially cancelled by the lack of staff in the local courts. In April 1998, the Reggio Calabria court was obliged to free 62 of the 280 defendants in the penal proceeding known as Olimpia, as the period for preventive detention had elapsed (Boemi 1998; see also CPM 2000a: 47–51).

Even the management of mafia witnesses has been inadequate, and only thanks to the extraordinary commitment of single law enforcement officials have structural deficiencies been at least partially offset (interviews 12, 14, and 20). Lacking personnel and means, the Servizio Centrale Protezione [Central Protection Agency] has often not managed to guarantee people admitted to the protection program the safety and benefits foreseen by the law, nor has it been able to control efficiently all the witnesses who were allowed to serve their imprisonment sentences in secret hiding places out of jail. Hence, while bureaucratic shackles have turned out to be an objective disincentive to judicial cooperation, national public opinion has been repeatedly confused by the escapes, retractions, and declarations "by installment" of a minority of *pentiti,* some of whom have again begun to commit crimes and even murders (including Baldassare Di Maggio, the *mafioso* who helped the police arrest Riina). These episodes have nurtured the more or less disinterested criticisms of wide sectors of the legal profession and the party system, which lament a compression of individual rights for the sake of the fight against the mafia. In January 2001, a new bill to reform the whole area was finally approved by the parliament, limiting the benefits granted to the mafia witnesses and forcing them to refer all they know within a time span of six months (*Corriere della Sera,* February 8, 2001; see also Spataro 2000; Ingroia 2001b; and Re 2001).

Constitutional and legislative reforms to improve defendants' rights (the so-called *giusto processo,* due process) were also passed by the left-wing cabinets that came to power as a result of the Olive Tree coalition's victory in spring 1996. These reforms, however, did not take the peculiarities of mafia organized crime into due account and, by invalidating all the witnesses' declarations that could not be confirmed at the trial stage, witnesses, particularly mafia defectors, were rendered vulnerable to mafia intimidation and threats (Di Matteo, Imbergamo, and Tescaroli 2001).

Last but not least, the weakening of popular support for investigations beginning after the 1992 killings has been aided by the intrinsic limits of an antimafia campaign that has been exclusively entrusted to law enforcement agencies and has not been supported by a comprehensive program to foster the social, economic, and cultural development of the South. Indeed, in the early 1990s all ad hoc measures (*intervento straordinario*) for the development of southern Italy came to a brusque halt. The Department and Agency for the Mezzogiorno, which had replaced the Cassa per il Mezzogiorno created in the 1950s, were both closed in May 1993 and their activities entrusted to an official receiver, whose job was to transfer the functions of the suppressed bodies to the agencies of ordinary state administration. Nor was the break in extraordinary funding replaced by the consolidation of ordinary aid programs for depressed areas of the national territory. "A heavy anti-southern mortgage," produced by the scarce results of thousands of billions of Italian *lire* spent over previous decades to stimulate southern Italian development, prevented for many years the conversion into law of bills necessary to regulate new supportive ordinary intervention and to coordinate the action of the different public bodies involved (SVIMEZ 1995). At the same time, to reduce Italy's huge public debt and to foster its entrance into the European Monetary Union, public investments were brusquely reduced (from 3.3 percent of the GDP in 1989 to 2.1 percent in 1995) and the whole welfare system was drastically cut, with the paradoxical result that yearly social expenses per inhabitant are today higher in northern Italy (about 8.6 million *lire*, corresponding to $5,000) than in the South (about 6.3 million, or $3,700; SVIMEZ 1998; Trigilia 1994).

These measures have produced a slowing down of economic growth in southern Italy and, particularly, in most of Sicily and Calabria, though some areas show an opposite trend. Due to the initiatives of some entrepreneurs, the wisdom of local administrators or the favorable structural conditions, some local contexts have recorded positive growth rates, attracting investments from northern Italy and from abroad and creating hundreds of jobs. Examples of this new trend are the so-called Etna Valley on the outskirts of Catania, which is in the process of becoming a high-tech pole, and the port of Gioia Tauro, which has become the largest container port of the Mediterranean. The average statistical data, however, point to a sharp negative trend. It is enough to say that between 1991 and 1997 the GDP of the Mezzogiorno grew by only 1.7 percent, whereas in the Center-North a 7.7 percent growth was recorded (SVIMEZ 1998). In Sicily and Calabria a quarter of the active population has been unemployed for many years. According to SVIMEZ, the unemployment rate is as high as 35 percent in the province of Enna, 29.7 percent in Catania, and 29 percent in Palermo, while in Calabria the number of unemployed people increased by 8 percent between 1993 and 1999, reaching 28 percent (Volpi 1999; Regione Calabria 1999: 6). In the latter region, juvenile unemployment was as high as 66 percent in 1999, with a peak of 71 percent in the Reggio Calabria province (CPM 2000a). Only in the late 1990s did the effects of the structural reforms initiated in the mid-1990s—and, particularly, the shake-up of the Italian public administration attempted by the Minister Franco Bassanini and the 2000–2006 plan of public investments and incentives for the Mezzogiorno developed by the Italian treasury under the leadership of Carlo Azeglio Ciampi (Barca 2001)—begin to be perceived. By then, however, the fight against the mafia had already lost much of its active popular support in the South.

It is, above all, the lasting problem of unemployment that has sharply contributed to the weakening of the popular anti-mafia movement. Many of those who marched in 1992 in Palermo to protest against the mafia today feel betrayed by the broken promises of national politicians, especially those belonging to left-wing parties that governed the country from 1996 to early 2001. In the political elections of May 2001, southern voters thus overwhelmingly supported the right-wing parties, most notably Berlusconi's Forza Italia. This last, for example, won parliament seats in all of Sicily's sixty electoral districts. Excellent results were also gained by the right-wing parties in the subsequent regional elections, as well as those for the Palermitan city council. Not only did Leoluca Orlando, Palermo's former anti-mafia mayor, fail to be elected president of the Sicilian region, but the left-wing parties also lost their majority and the mayoral seat on the Palermitan city council.

It is far from certain whether Berlusconi, who was reelected as Italy's prime minister in June 2001, will be able to fulfill his electoral promises and provide hundreds of thousands of jobs. The recession that has plagued Italy and the world's other nations since September 2001 has made the fulfillment of Berlusconi's promises, in the short term at least, quite difficult. In the meanwhile, in order to survive, hundreds of long-term unemployed have no choice but to find a job in the flourishing underground or criminal economy. According to the budget office of the Calabria region, the sphere of "irregular employment" stands at about 200,000 labor units, corresponding to approximately 42 percent of all the employees of the production sector compared with 13 percent in the Center-North (Regione Calabria 1999: 6).

This represents a powerful factor of legitimization for the *cosche*, which are still, in some contexts, one of the main employers. Especially outside the larger cities, in villages and towns, where the civil society was only superficially involved in the ethical-political protest movement of the early 1990s, "men of honor" may again become life models. They are feared because of their readiness to use violence, and respected because they are the repository of the last hopes that a person might have to find a job (interview 8).

Blackmailing and Underestimation

Aided by the mistakes and inefficiencies of the public administration, the delegitimation of the anti-mafia campaigns has also been actively promoted by politicians and state officials colluding with the mafia or sharing mafiosi's judicial interests. Notwithstanding the disappearance of the Christian Democracy—the privileged reference of southern Italian mafia associations for over fifty years—Sicilian and Calabrian mafia families still control quite a few state representatives and employees. Of course, throughout the 1990s secret pacts with "men of honor" became riskier for whoever had a public image to defend, and mafia and pseudo-mafia groups of all the Mezzogiorno found it increasingly difficult to find politicians willing to make long-term pacts with the mafia (Lodato and Grasso 2001: 74). Though new recruits are on the decrease, the strength of mafia blackmailing still conditions a considerable number of politicians and public officials. To save their apparent respectability (if not their lives), they are obliged to keep on serving the *cosche*'s interests. These, furthermore, coincide with their own to a large extent, since their political (and physical) safety—like the mafiosi's—depend on the dismissal of the anti-mafia and anti-corruption judicial activity which started in 1992.

Colluding politicians include not only representatives of the old guard, but also members of parties founded after the outbreak of the Clean Hands season. It is meaningful, for example, that Silvio Berlusconi's former right-hand man and member of parliament for Forza Italia, Marcello Dell'Utri, is facing trial in Palermo on charges of being member of a mafia-type delinquent association (PrPA 1997a). Berlusconi himself has been suspected of investing and laundering Cosa Nostra's money at the beginning of his career, hiring a "man of honor" to protect his children, regularly paying a two hundred million *lira* (about $175,000 in the early 1980s) "contribution" to Cosa Nostra bosses, and colluding with the mafia in various ways. The investigation by the Palermitan Prosecutor's Office was, however, subsequently closed for the lack of any conclusive evidence (Veltri and Travaglio 2001; Travaglio 2001). Even if *pentiti*'s statements on Berlusconi's accounts had no empirical basis, there is an objective convergence of interests between this media tycoon–turned-politician and the mafiosi. Ever since he officially entered the political game in early 1994, Berlusconi has been trying to block the anti-corruption and anti-mafia investigations that targeted him and several of his associates by staging delegitimation campaigns against law enforcement officials (who are all dubbed "Communists" or *toghe rosse*, red gowns), calling their impartiality into question and consistently supporting legislative measures that sharpened defendants' rights and made investigations and trials more burdensome, slower, and less efficient.

Whereas a direct mafia link could not yet be proved in Berlusconi's case, lower-ranking politicians in his party, Forza Italia, were less lucky. As already mentioned, in March 2001 the Reggio Calabria court condemned Amedeo Matacena for giving his external support [*concorso esterno*] to some 'Ndrangheta *cosche*. Matacena—the son of the man who owns the main private company running the ferries between Calabria and Sicily—was, from 1994 to 2001, a member of the national parliament in Forza Italia's lists (*Corriere della Sera*, March 14, 2001). Another member of parliament for Forza Italia and one of the leaders of Berlusconi's party in Sicily, Gaspare Giudice, is now also facing trial on the charge of mafia association, after the Palermitan prosecutor's office asked the House of Deputies, unsuccessfully, to allow them to arrest him in 1998 (*La Repubblica*, July 16, 1998; *Gazzetta del Sud*, June 6, 2001). Filiberto Scalone, a former senator belonging to the post-Fascist Alleanza Nazionale (a party forming part of Berlusconi's coalition) was also convicted to nine years of imprisonment in January 2001 for collusion with Cosa Nostra and fraudulent bankruptcy (*Gazzetta del Sud*, January 28, and August 5, 2001).

Judicial investigations do not concern only politicians from the right-wing coalition. They also touch members of the increasingly heterogeneous left-wing alliance, as investigations concerning the former treasury undersecretary Stefano Cusumano and other members of the small Unione Democratica per la Repubblica (UDR) party on charges of bid-rigging [*turbativa d'asta*] and mafia-type delinquent association go to show. The UDR's entrance into the government majority enabled the creation of the executive headed by Massimo D'Alema in October 1998 and the survival of the left-wing government coalitions up to the elections in spring 2001 (*Corriere della Sera*, April 27, 1999: 8). In the aftermath of the April 2001 national elections, an investigation of the Procura di Agrigento hypothesizes that at least one candidate (Alfonso Lo Zito) of the second-largest left-wing party, Margherita, bribed mafiosi to gain their electoral support (*La Repubblica*, July 3, 2001).

The enfeeblement of the state anti-mafia campaign has, however, not been exclusively due to openly colluded politicians. In fact, they represent a minority of all the people's representatives sitting in the national parliament and in regional and local councils. As soon as the bombs and the dynamite explosions came to a halt, a much wider number of members of all the political parties have been willing to muffle the political-criminal aspects of the as yet unresolved southern question. Most of them are not blackmailed by mafia associations; indeed, the majority is moved by noble intentions, either because they want to convince Italian and foreign entrepreneurs to invest in southern Italy or because they want to defend abstract libertarian principles to the highest degree possible.

In a political system in which the survival of both national and local cabinets often depends on a few votes, many politicians, including some belonging to left-wing parties, have also rediscovered the old habit of "holding one's nose" and accepting the support of colleagues who defend mafia interests, sometimes even to promote apparently good and disinterested goals (such as, for example, the fight against unemployment or the industrialization of southern Italy or some parts of it). Even in parties that have distinguished themselves for their anti-mafia commitment, a conviction like that of Giovanni Giolitti (perhaps the most influential Italian prime minister in the early twentieth century) seems to have spread that the development of the country—and, deep down, the maintenance of one's own power—justifies the adoption of clientelistic methods and alliance with mafia-tarnished subjects.

It is on these *Realpolitiker* as well as on openly colluded politicians and government officials and the disillusion of growing sections of the southern Italian population that Cosa Nostra and the 'Ndrangheta families count to reconquer their lost terrain and halt their decline.

Mafia Decline and Its Dependency on Politics

That there has been a decline is undeniable. Despite weakening popular support for the repressive action of law enforcement agencies and the increasing difficulties the agencies have encountered, since 1992 the *cosche* have undergone a process of debilitation and delegitimation. This was allegedly acknowledged even by Bernardo Provenzano, Totò Riina's successor at the head of Cosa Nostra. According to an informant, in fact, in the mid-1990s Provenzano said that he was convinced that Cosa Nostra would need at least five to seven years to recover from the serious crisis into which it had plunged and to improve its economic situation, which was at that point precarious (Ministero dell'Interno 2001e: 10).

Even in Calabria, where the civil society is to a large extent "inert, if not complacent" (Boemi 1998: 29), mafia groups have undergone strong limitations. In January 1999, at the end of the hearings concerning the Olimpia-1 Operation, the Reggio Calabria court handed down 62 life sentences and 141 sentences amounting to over 1,380 years of imprisonment, while another three hundred defendants are involved in the three following parts of the inquiry (TrRC 1999; *Gazzetta del Sud*, January 20, 1999). Likewise, the ninety-nine defendants of the Tirreno maxi-trial, which took place in Palmi against the greatly feared Piromalli and Molè *cosche*, were sentenced to eighty-nine life sentences and 731 years of imprisonment by the local first-degree court. The investigations did not focus only on the core families of the province of Reggio Calabria, but also involved their ramifications in central and northern Italy. In Milan, for example, between 1994 and 1998 more than a thousand members of the 'Ndrangheta faced trial in about twenty *maxiprocessi*, all of which ended with convictions and heavy sentences (Benedusi 1997; *Panorama*, March 25, 1999: 57; see TrMI 1996a, 1996b, 1997a, 1997b, 1997c, 1998).

The attacks against Cosa Nostra have been even stronger. With the exception of Bernardo Provenzano, all the leading figures in the 1980s and 1990s, some of whom had been in hiding for decades, were arrested in the space of a few years, and none of them will survive their prison sentences. Furthermore, Sicilian law enforcement authorities have, even more than their Calabrian counterparts, carried out inquiries on what is sometimes called the "third level": namely, the political and judicial protection mafia groups enjoyed for decades (*Panorama*, September 1999, 17: 46–49). The imprisoned chiefs are so discouraged that in early 2001 some of them allegedly proposed a deal to state institutions: they would confess their own crimes, without involving other mafia members, in exchange for a reduction in their convictions and the abolition of the special detention system (*La Repubblica*, February 6, 2001: 15).

Even the financial drain on the two organizations has been heavy. During the Olimpia trial, for example, the Reggio Calabria court seized properties for over 150 billion *lire* and confiscated goods for over 40 billion definitively (respectively, 88 and 24 million dollars; *Gazzetta del Sud* January 20, 1999). According to the prefect of Reggio Calabria, assets worth 1.5 trillion *lire* (almost 900 million dollars) have been seized in the province since 1990 (CPM 2000a: 51). Indeed, some mafia families now seem to be virtually bankrupt as a result of seizures and sentences. The Latella *cosca*, for example, was "hit to death"—to use the colorful expression of a police official—after forty-two of its members received life sentences and another sixty members and flankers received heavy sentences. According to several law enforcement investigators, in the mid-1990s many mafia groups, both in Palermo and in Reggio Calabria, stopped paying the monthly salary to the families of the convicted "men of honor," thus ending one of the most important principles of the mafia legal order because they no longer have liquidity (ibid.: 58; interview 30).

It is, above all, to condition the outcome of the pending trials, to amend heavy first-degree sentences in appeal trials, and to improve the detention conditions of the imprisoned members that the Cosa Nostra and 'Ndrangheta families need politicians and public officials to comply with them. The manipulation of state decision making processes, however, does not merely have judicial goals, as mafia families count on their ramification in the state administration to improve their financial lot as well.

With the exception of the Cuntrera-Caruana family, in fact, the Cosa Nostra *cosche* have been marginalized from the large transcontinental heroin and cocaine trade since the 1980s (even though there are still a few "men of honor" who import or deal in narcotics alone or in partnership with others). Several factors have prevented them from maintaining the good market positions Sicilian mafiosi had in the early 1980s. Among them, the success of several joint operations carried out by American and Italian law enforcement agencies should be recognized, such as the Pizza Connection and the Iron Tower cases (Jacobs, Panarella, and Worthington 1994: 129–66; Blumenthal 1988). Another decisive element was the outcome of the second "mafia war" in Sicily in the early 1980s. That is to say, that in the struggle for power between Sicilian mafia families, the winning coalition managed only partially to maintain the position held by the losing families, whose members and extensive contacts in North America had proved to be instrumental for the wholesale heroin trade. As a result, since the mid-1980s the families forming the internal nucleus of the Corleonesi coalition seem to have gained most of their proceeds from the extortion and bid-rigging of large public work contracts in Sicily, neglecting drug trafficking (TrPA 1991, 1993b, 1998; Ministero dell'Interno 2000c, 2001d, 2001e; see Lodato 1999). As noted in a recent report of the Direzione Investigativa Antimafia, "The following situation . . . is proved by all judicial investigations of a certain level carried out in Sicily: Cosa Nostra families essentially live from extortions, while their chiefs draw more substantial profits from the public work sector" (Ministero dell'Interno 2001e: 15).

The marginalization of mafia families from heroin processing and wholesale export in the United States must also be placed within the framework of a long-term process that today has become evident: the progressive concentration of illegal drug processing in the production countries. As in other markets, the production of the final product—heroin and cocaine—and of the semi-manufactured products—morphine, heroin base, and coca paste and base—tends today to be carried out in developing countries, where production and labor costs are lower (Lewis 1985: 15).

Cosa Nostra families also pay a price for their peripheral location, which keeps them far away not only from drug production areas but also and above all from large retail markets in Europe and the United States. Most of the heroin sold in European markets is nowadays imported by a multiplicity of Turkish, Kurd, and, more recently, Albanian family firms, which dispose of direct contacts in production areas, are located in strategic transit points, or can exploit the weakness of their state institutions (Paoli 1999b, 2000a, 2000b). Likewise, the numerous Colombian clans, which today process about 70 percent of the cocaine bound for export, are often themselves in charge of the drug transportation in Europe or, at any rate, sell it to a plurality of small and large intermediaries. Contrary to the most pessimistic forecasts, Cosa Nostra men do not dispose of any right of exclusivity and, indeed, the investigations carried out during the 1990s demonstrate that most smuggling operations outpass Sicily and Cosa Nostra families. Seizure data, in particular, show that the preferred destinations for smuggling cocaine into Europe are Spain and the Netherlands (EMCDDA 1997: 37, 2001: 21). In Spain, Colombian traffickers are aided by speaking Spanish and by the presence of a consistent community of conationals. In the Netherlands, whose ports are the most trafficked in Europe, cocaine imports can be more easily hidden within legitimate trade flows. In neither of these countries has a systematic involvement of Italian Cosa Nostra members been proved.

Thanks to their wider links in central and northern Italy and in several European countries, the 'Ndrangheta *locali* held important positions in the international cocaine trade at least up until the mid-1990s, as proved by the seizure of over five thousand kilograms of cocaine in 1994. They have also operated predominantly as wholesale distributors on the domestic market for heroin and hashish, occasionally also importing large lots of these substances (see PrMI 1997; TrMI 1997c; Maggi 1996). In their homeland, particularly in the Gioia Tauro plain as well as in northern Calabria, *'ndranghetisti* and their acolytes have also started to cultivate cannabis, sometimes adopting sophisticated irrigation methods: in 1999, for example, over 600,000 cannabis plants were seized by the police (CPM 2000: 40). Even Calabrian mafia groups, however, are considerably weakened by the judicial inquiries that have disrupted their settlements in the Center-North and at all levels of the drug distribution system they have to face the competition of new, flexible, and changing criminal enterprises. In a study carried out in Milan at the turn of the century, the 'Ndrangheta's share of the local drug market appeared to have decreased substantially since the early 1990s (Paoli 2000b; see also 1999b, 1998c).

The families associated with Cosa Nostra and the 'Ndrangheta also find it very difficult to enter other illegal markets, either because their normative code does not allow trade in certain goods or because they do not possess the necessary contacts and know-how. The prohibition on exploiting prostitution, for example, which exists in both confederations (Falcone 1993: 115; as well as in the American La Cosa Nostra, see U.S. Senate 1988: 237), has blocked the entrance of the Sicilian and Calabrian *cosche* into what has become one of the most profitable illicit trades: the smuggling of humans and the exploitation of migrants in the sex industry or the informal economy.

The lack of competencies and contacts as well as recruitment restrictions (see chapter 3) also hinder the organizations from entering any other illegal sectors, such as the illegal markets in arms, gold, and dirty money, which constitute only a small appendix to the much wider legal markets (see Naylor 1987, 1995, 1996; Ruggiero 1996). And though there are a few exceptions, most Cosa Nostra and 'Ndrangheta men have to date been unable to participate personally in this kind of trafficking. On the matter, the Palermitan prosecutor, Ignazio De Francisci, noted:

> It is not true that the Cosa Nostra "surfs the Internet," or "is in Milan," or "works with software" (these are all statements that have been made by Sicilian politicians). . . . Cosa Nostra still smells of stables and sheep. The "men of honor"'s basic DNA is that of the shepherd's and, partially, the peasant's. These are the roots of Cosa Nostra. The current leaders of the organization are more at ease in a *mannara* (in Sicilian dialect, sheepfold) than

in a living-room, they reason like shepherds because they were born shepherds. (De Francisci 1996: 14–15)

Because of the growing difficulties in international marketplaces, the families of both mafia consortia have for many years invested much energy in extorting all the productive activities under their areas of competence, where they operate under a virtual monopoly regime and face no competition (see Ministero dell'Interno 2001d; Becchi and Rey 1994). Thus, far from profiting from Cosa Nostra and 'Ndrangheta's entrepreneurial difficulties, people and companies of high-density mafia districts are today exploited by the mafiosi more than ever, as they are called to make up for the failed earnings from drug or other illegal trades.

It is significant, for example, that the Piromalli family has managed to heavily condition the management of the new container port in Gioia Tauro. This began to be active in the mid-1990s and in only three years became the largest in the Mediterranean, moving over 2 million containers in 1998 (Lasco 1999). Since 1994, when Contship Italia first asked to rent the port area to start transshipment activity and the Medcenter Container Terminal was set up thanks to 138 billion *lire* in state financing (about $86 million), the action of the Piromallis' referents has had a twofold aim. First, they aimed to "oblige the Medcenter company, through its vice president Walter Lugli, and the Contship company, through its president Enrico Ravano, to pay a kickback of 1.50 U.S. dollars for each transshipped container, a sum which corresponded to about half the net profits earned by the two companies" (Lasco 1999).

Dissatisfied by its merely parasitic role, the Piromallis additionally wanted to get contracts, subcontracts, and jobs in the two firms that run the port and in the others that have grown up and will grow in the surrounding area thanks to generous public funding. Despite subscribing to a legality pact, the managers of both Contship and Medcenter gave in to mafia requests. The arrest warrant issued in January 1999 against members of the Piromalli mafia group states that the two companies have inserted "firms indicated by the defendants (and in some cases belonging to the latter) in the port-servicing activities" and have hired people recommended by the mafia sodality, thus contributing to reinforcing the latter's power in the Gioia Tauro plain (Feo 1999; Sciarrone 1999; CPM 2000a: 151–87).

Like the Piromallis in Gioia Tauro, all the Sicilian and Calabrian mafia families place their hopes for economic recovery in gaining public contracts, which have just started to be distributed once more, especially in the South, after the sharp drop following the Tangentopoli ("Bribesville," initially an allusion to Milan) inquiries. Between 2000 and 2006, Sicily and Calabria will respectively dispose of 18,000 and 10,000 billion *lire* coming from the European Union funds of Agenda 2000 (respectively, $8,600 and $4,800 million; Volpi 1999; Regione Calabria 1999). Apparently, the *cosche* intend to acquire—directly and through front men—a substantial portion of these funds and of the sums being distributed by the central government and the local administrations. Unaware of being wiretapped, a "man of honor" recently stated: "They say we should not make any fuss, they recommend that we all avoid making noise and attracting attention, because we have to get all this Agenda 2000" (*La Repubblica*, February 6, 2001: 15; see also CSM 2001: 13–15; Ministero dell'Interno 2001e: 16). In order to do so, the chiefs are relying on the large number of state and party officials who are ready—as a result of their ambitions, convictions, or fear—to cooperate with the mafia.

What is at stake was clearly singled out in the report on the DIA's activities in the second half of 2000: "If Cosa Nostra relies on seizing the public funds intended for large-scale construction works in order to recover definitively, preventing it from implementing this project could plunge it into one of the most serious crises it has ever known" (Ministero dell'Interno 2001d: 16). Unfortunately, this awareness does seem to shared by the ministers of the cabinet set up in June 2001 and headed by Silvio Berlusconi. As minister for public work Pietro Lunardi officially stated a few months afterward, while talking about the huge public investments foreseen for the construction of a bridge over the Messina strait, "In southern Italy there is the mafia and we need to come to terms with it" (*La Repubblica*, August 23, 2001, and Vitale 2001; see also Ingroia 2001a). Incompetence or mafia collusion? It is hard to say. There can be no doubt, however, about the following point: even more than in the past, the survival of the *cosche* now seems to depend on how their relationships with politics and different sectors of the public administration are set up in the future.

Conclusions

The picture is now clear: Cosa Nostra and the 'Ndrangheta are secret and multifunctional brotherhoods each composed of about a hundred units. Though these are usually called families by their members, they are clearly distinct from the latter's blood families. They rely instead on bonds of artificial kinship created through the ceremony of initiation of new members. In both consortia, the single *cosche* enjoy wide autonomy and have their own ruling bodies, but are united, according to Durkheim's principle of mechanical solidarity, by sharing the same symbolic, ritual, and normative apparatus and a single collective identity.

Initially favored by the emulation of bourgeois revolutionary societies, the pledge to secrecy has since the mid–nineteenth century become a necessity for the groups of Cosa Nostra and the 'Ndrangheta in order to avoid state law enforcement action. Their longstanding use of violence, in fact, places the two confederations outside the state legal order, even though repressive public activity has been neither constant nor effective and more or less shady compromises between the state and the mafia power have been frequent ever since the unification of Italy in 1861.

Exploiting secrecy and violence, the families of Cosa Nostra and the 'Ndrangheta have traditionally employed the strength of mafia bonds to pursue a plurality of goals and to carry out numerous different functions, so much so that it is impossible to identify any one that is exclusive. The *cosche* are neither economic enterprises aiming at the maximization of profits nor an industry for private protection. Empowered by the flexibility guaranteed by fraternization contracts, the *capimafia* dispose of their subordinates' labor force—and even lives—to reach the collective or personal aims that they select. Historically, one of the most important among these has been the exercise of political dominion within their communities, which is mainly expressed today in the extraction of a financial contribution from all productive activities that take place in a family's domain. In the past, however, the mafia also imposed some rules belonging to its own legal order on the general population.

For more than a century, mafia groups have supplemented the activity of state institutions in their villages and neighborhoods, thus also preventing the state's rooting and legitimation. By manipulating the codes and rites of traditional Sicilian and Calabrian subculture and answering otherwise unsatisfied needs, they have enjoyed the consensus of large numbers of the local population. Only in the mid-1980s did this pillar of mafia power begin to waver.

Following the processes of economic and cultural modernization that occurred all over Italy after the Second World War, the mafia "subuniverse of meaning" (Berger and Luckmann 1967)—the set of rites, symbols, and norms explaining and justifying the existence and organization of the two mafia associations both to "men of honor" themselves and to members of their local communities—has progressively lost its attractive and explicative power. For the *cosche* it has become increasingly difficult to transmit the role of "men of honor" to new adherents, to enable them to regard their associates as brothers, or to convince them to subordinate their personal interests to the mafia family ones. At the same time, more and more Sicilian and Calabrian citizens find it difficult to sanction the values embodied by the mafiosi.

To maintain social status and respect, during the last thirty years the families of Cosa Nostra and the 'Ndrangheta have resorted to violence, secrecy, and the strength of mafia fraternization bonds to gain wealth. They have participated increasingly frequently in trade in illegal goods and services and have imposed their companies on the local economic competition through force. The entrepreneurial transformation, however, has not been complete nor has it meant giving up their claim to exercise political dominion. It is the apparatus of mafia legitimation—which constituted a major strength of the two mafia associations for so many years—that has prevented this change and even today sharply conditions the *cosche*'s economic performance. Unable to diversify their personnel, mafia families now find it increasingly difficult to maintain their market positions in some sectors of the illegal economy (above all, drug trafficking), while they have not succeeded in entering others (such as the arms trade) because they lack the necessary contacts and competencies. This is because the bonds of brotherhood and tradition still prevail over the exigencies of the organization of production factors and hence the enhancement of production, marketing, and finance functions (Becchi and Rey 1994: 76).

Far from expanding toward the outside, Cosa Nostra groups and, to a lesser extent, even those of the 'Ndrangheta have in the last fifteen years receded into their territories, avoiding international competition. Today they obtain a growing and preponderant quota of their revenues by manipulating the tendering process of public works and imposing generalized extortive regimes on all the economic enterprises of their areas. Instead of creating stable "enterprise syndicates" (Block 1983) capable of operating on international illegal markets, both Sicilian and Calabrian *cosche* tend to fuse entrepreneurial action with the action typical of "power syndicates" and thus to concentrate on those profit-making activities that are more directly advantaged by the control of a territory and collusion with politicians and government officials. Though the relationship with the latter has lost its rooting in a common weltanschauung and is accepted by shrinking portions of public opinion, Cosa Nostra and 'Ndrangheta families have become even more dependent on the decisions made by public, local, and central administrations. These administrators are thus today largely arbiters of both the judicial and the economic-financial lots of mafia coalitions.

Bearing in mind the long history and recent evolution of the two mafia confederations, we need to ask if they can be regarded as an ideal type of organized crime (see Paoli 1999a). This question can be answered in the affirmative if—as occurs routinely in Italy—organized crime is identified with large-scale, stable, and structured organizations that are either illegal per se or are routinely involved in activities prohibited by the local state apparatus. Such a concept, however, is not widespread in the scientific debate that developed in the United States in the 1950s and which has expanded to involve scholars from many other nationalities, nor is it reflected in the official definitions of organized crime adopted by most countries and at the international level.[1]

The Italian conception of organized crime can be considered a "demystified" version of the position that was held for many years by U.S. law enforcement agencies and congressional committees and popularized by the media worldwide. From the 1950s on, in fact, the U.S. official standpoint identified organized crime with a nationwide, centralized criminal organization, headed by and to a great extent consisting of members of Italian (and specifically Sicilian) origin and dominating the most profitable illegal markets. Ever since Joe Valachi's testimony before the Permanent Subcommittee on Investigations of the U.S. Senate in 1963, this criminal organization has been known as La Cosa Nostra or, more correctly, Cosa Nostra (U.S. Senate 1951, 1957, 1963; see also Blakey 1986 and Smith 1975).

The idea of an alien conspiracy polluting the economic and social life of the country has been rejected by the majority of American social scientists since the 1960s. They have accused this theory of being ideological, serving personal political interests, and lacking in accuracy and empirical evidence (Smith 1975, 1976;

W. Moore 1974; Hawkins 1969). At the same time, a different conceptualization has been proposed that focuses on the most visible and noncontroversial aspect of organized crime: the supply of illegal products and services. In order to eradicate the ethnic stereotypes of crime and to focus direct attention on the marketplace, several authors have put forward the expression "illicit" or "illegal enterprise" as a substitute for the ethnically loaded term "organized crime" (Smith 1975, 1976, 1980; Haller 1990). As Dwight Smith, one of the earliest proponents of the new approach, expressed it, "Illicit enterprise is the extension of legitimate market activities into areas normally proscribed—i.e. beyond existing limits of law—for the pursuit of profit and in response to a latent illicit demand" (1975: 335).

More often, however, organized crime has been equated with the provision of illegal goods and services. According to Alan Block and William Chambliss, for example, "organized crime [should] be defined as (or perhaps better limited to) those illegal activities involving the management and coordination of racketeering and vice" (1981: 13). Organized crime has thus become a synonym for illegal enterprise. Indeed, according to a review of definitions carried out by Frank Hagan (1983) in the early 1980s, consensus now exists among American criminologists that organized crime involves a continuing enterprise operating in a rational fashion and focused on obtaining profits through illegal activities. In most of these definitions no minimum requirement is set as far as the size, organization, or stability of the groups involved are concerned. The focus is, instead, on the illegal activities themselves, regardless of how or by whom they are carried out.

This conception of organized crime has been imported into Europe, with particular success in those countries with little or no direct experience of the mafia phenomenon. As early as the mid-1970s, Hans-Jürgen Kerner and John Mack (1975) talked about a "crime industry," and, in an earlier report written in German, Kerner subscribed even more explicitly to the view of organized crime as an enterprise (1973). This emphasis on illegal market activities has remained unchallenged ever since. Hence, for example, according to Dick Hobbs, "Organized crime ... [is] referred to in terms of its relationship to the marketplace" (1994: 442). Likewise, the Dutch scholar Petrus van Duyne points out that organized crime results from illegal market dynamics: "What is organized crime without organizing some kind of criminal trade; without the selling and buying of forbidden goods and services in an organizational context? The answer is simply nothing" (1997: 203).

This "entrepreneurial" conception of organized crime—focusing on the provision of illegal goods and services regardless of the degree of organization shown by the actors—has shaped official definitions of organized crime in many European countries. Hence, for example, the definition adopted by the German State Ministries of Justice and the Interior in 1990 maintains that:

Organized crime is the planned violation of the law for profit or to acquire power, whose offences are each, or together, of a major significance and are carried out by more than two participants who cooperate within a division of labor for a long or undetermined time span using at least one of the following: commercial or commercial-like structures; violence or other means of intimidation; influence on politics, media, public administration, justice, and legitimate economy. (BKA 1995)[2]

This means that the German definition of organized crime can be applied not only to the members of a criminal organization in a strict sense, but also to relatively small and loose partnerships and teams set up for the pursuit of profit-oriented offences. Very low requirements are also set by the United Nations Convention on Transnational Organized Crime, which was opened for signature in December 2000 in Palermo. In this, an organized criminal group is defined as "a structured group of three or more persons existing for a period of time and acting in concert with the aim of committing one or more serious crimes or offences established pursuant to this Convention, in order to obtain, directly, or indirectly, a financial or other material benefit" (UNGA 2000).

Notwithstanding these "minimalist" definitions, in the public discourse organized crime is still equated with highly structured, octopus-like criminal organizations, and the southern Italian mafia—specifically, the Sicilian Cosa Nostra—is considered an archetype of organized crime worldwide. Indeed, the general public (but also several scholars and a larger number of practitioners) still tends to assume that the southern Italian mafia associations—together with the most rooted nonterrorist organizations, such as the American Cosa Nostra, the Chinese Triads, and the Japanese Yakuza—dominate world illegal markets and represent a model for all actors dealing with illegal goods and commodities (see, e.g., Sterling 1990, 1994; Williams and Florez 1994; UNESC 1994).

The preceding pages demonstrate very clearly that—at least as far Cosa Nostra and the 'Ndrangheta are concerned—this hypothesis has no empirical backing. The two southern Italian mafia consortia cannot be considered a universally valid ideal type of organized crime if it is understood as the provision of illegal goods and services. In reality, their units are not the product of illegal market dynamics, nor do the development of illegal entrepreneurial activities and profit maximization represent the main goal of their action even today.

Moreover, empirical research shows that the great majority of illegal exchanges in Western countries are carried out by numerous relatively small and often ephemeral enterprises. This is because all illegal market actors are subject to the constraints deriving from the illegal status of the products they sell. These constraints have to do with the fact that illegal market entrepreneurs are obliged to operate both without and against the state.

First, since the goods and services they provide are prohibited, illegal market suppliers cannot resort to state institutions to enforce contracts and have violations of contracts prosecuted, nor does the illegal arena host an alternative sovereign power to which a party may appeal for redress of injury. As a result, property rights are poorly protected, employment contracts cannot be formalized, and the development of large, formally organized, enduring companies is strongly discouraged (Reuter 1983, 1985).

Second, all suppliers of illegal commodities are forced to operate under the constant threat of arrest and confiscation of their assets by law enforcement institutions. Participants in criminal trades will thus try to organize their activities in such a way as to assure that the risk of police detection is minimized. Incorporating drug transactions into kinship and friendship networks and reducing the number of customers and employees are two of the most frequent strategies illegal entrepreneurs employ to reduce their vulnerability to law enforcement moves (ibid.; M. Moore 1974: 15–31).

Even southern Italian mafia families are subjected to the constraints deriving from the illegal status of products and, when they deal in drugs or other illegal commodities, they do not operate as monolithic productive and commercial units. On the contrary, their members frequently set up short-term partnerships with some other mafia affiliates, or even nonmembers, to carry out illegal transactions (see Paoli 2000b). In other words, on the illegal markets of most industrialized countries ruled by relatively strong and efficient state apparatuses, the dominant model is not organized crime, but—following the title of a famous book by Peter Reuter—"disorganized crime" (1983). This realization led Henner Hess to conclude that "the mafia is a power structure and, as such, completely different from what is commonly called organized crime (and which is usually a cooperation aimed at gaining material advantages)" (1995: 63).

Even if Hess's position can be judged as being too extreme, it is clear that mafia families cannot be considered firms. Cosa Nostra and 'Ndrangheta's ritual and organizational apparatus may help create the trust necessary to establish economic partnerships, but more often than not it strongly hinders the families and their members' economic activities, as we saw in the preceding chapters. Indeed, it is interesting to note that the main mafia groups of Sicily and Calabria are not the only large-scale criminal organizations now facing difficulty operating in international illegal markets. The decline of the American Cosa Nostra and the exclusion of its members from the most profitable illegal trades is today recognized even by U.S. law enforcement agencies (Reuter 1995; Jacobs and Gouldin 1999). Likewise, empirical studies demonstrate that the illegal trades connecting Asia to the United States and Europe are far from being monopolized by the much dreaded Chinese Triads (Chin 1990, 1996; Booth 1990). Just like Cosa Nostra and the 'Ndrangheta, the Triads are secret and multifunctional associations that create bonds of artificial kinship among their members and neither can nor want to transform themselves into illicit enterprises whose only goal is profit (Murray 1994; Ownby and Somers Heidues 1993; Fong 1981). As a result, the smuggling of drugs and migrants from Asia is carried out by a plurality of small and medium-sized enterprises, and only a minority of these groups is affiliated to the Triads (Chin 1999). In the last few years, even the groups belonging to the segmentary society of the Japanese Yakuza are facing the increasingly fierce competition of nontraditional criminal entrepreneurs (*International Herald Tribune*, June 18, 1999).

Believing that the above-mentioned criminal organizations detain a monopolistic position on domestic and international illegal markets and that all illegal enterprises tend to imitate their configuration not only lacks empirical support but is also dangerous. This is because it confuses even further an already confused public debate, in which different and opposing conceptions of organized crime clash and are superimposed on each other. It is significant, for example, that agreeing on a suitable definition of organized crime turned out to be the most difficult task of all for the negotiators of the new United Nations Convention on the topic (Joutsen 1998), and in the end a very broad definition, based on a least common denominator, was adopted.

As the expression "organized crime" has been attributed, since the 1950s, with various and sometimes contrasting meanings, it is now impossible to avoid the polysemy that it creates; indeed, its recent success in the international political debate is very likely due to its multivocality. However, when considering this wide range of phenomena in detail we must highlight the distinctions and differences in its uses—the alternative being to fall back into the night described by Hegel in which "all cows are black."

Avoiding doing so leads, above all, to negative consequences for understanding and analysis. Moreover, if we do not distinguish between the different forms of crime that are labeled "organized," we are unable to find out their different "causes" and, thus, may end up adopting undifferentiated preventive and repressive policies, which, while effective with some offenders, are totally ineffective with others.

This risk of confusion does not affect only the international and foreign debate, but also—and even more strongly—the Italian one. As in other contexts in the early and mid–twentieth century, Italian illegal markets have over the last twenty years become increasingly multiethnic. Today—all over North America and Europe—illegal goods and services are sold and exchanged by a multiethnic variety of people. Side by side with local criminals, we find illicit entrepreneurs coming from a variety of different countries who have no access to the legal economy and hence use crime as a "queer ladder of social mobility" (Bell 1965; see also Light 1977).

In too many cases, then, these subjects are labeled as mafia and believed to be organized in the same way as Cosa Nostra and the 'Ndrangheta (see, for example, Ministero dell'Interno 2000a). Sooner or later—in Italy and elsewhere—we will have to discuss seriously these assumptions and the opportunity of employing the instruments developed in anti-mafia campaigns in the fight against this "other" form of organized crime, which—if we take the Italian definition of the concept as a parameter—is not as organized as it is very often made out to be.

Notes

Introduction

1. Founded by and long composed of immigrants from Naples and surroundings, the Chicago mafia family was heavily influenced by the camorra tradition (for more information on the Neapolitan camorra, see note 3 in this chapter), which does not forbid prostitution (U.S. District Court 1994: 7; Nelli 1976: 163–78, 239–41).

2. The Racketeer Influenced and Corrupt Organizations (RICO) Act was passed by Congress in 1970 to attack the organizational structure of criminal groupings and to address the infiltration of legitimate industries by organized crime. It is not limited to organized crime, but rather extends to all forms of "enterprise" criminality. The RICO Act makes it a crime to acquire an interest in, to participate in the affairs of, or to invest the profits acquired from an enterprise through a pattern of racketeering activity. Criminal RICO penalties are severe: a defendant may be sentenced to a maximum imprisonment of twenty years, and to twenty additional years if a RICO conspiracy is proved. RICO also provides for massive fines and for mandatory forfeiture of the portion of the defendant's wealth that can be traced to the proceeds of the racketeering activity. The RICO Act also contains two civil remedial provisions. The first provision has become very popular (and controversial) in commercial litigation, as it gives private victims the right to sue racketeers for triple damages. The second provision, which allows the government to sue racketeers for injunctions, restraining orders, and other equitable remedies to prevent the defendants from further racketeering, has proved to be a very effective tool for purging mafia presence from labor unions and industries (for comprehensive discussion of RICO, see Lynch 1987).

To the frustration of RICO drafter and law professor G. Robert Blakey, it took a decade for federal prosecutors to begin using RICO. It was, in fact, only in the late 1970s that Blakey was able to convince law enforcement officials to pursue evidence of crimes and associations connected to a RICO enterprise and to focus on the entire criminal group rather than on individuals (see Bonavolonta and Duffy 1996). Since then RICO criminal provisions have been very successfully used against organized crime and, specifically, Cosa Nostra families, but also political corruption, white-collar crime, and violent groups (Blakey and Roddy 1996, particularly 1612ff.; Jacobs, Panarella, and Worthington 1994).

Despite its effectiveness, RICO has been variously criticized for being vague and too broad, for subjecting defendants to double jeopardy, and for violating due process (Lynch 1990; Kenney and Finckenauer 1995: 319–23). To date, the statute has withstood all constitutional challenges.

3. Historically, the Neapolitan camorra used to be considered Italy's second most important criminal organization after the Sicilian mafia. Judicial investigations have, however, shown that the more than one hundred gangs currently operating in Naples and its surroundings are no longer part of a single association. To promote their cohesion and social standing, these gangs—in varying degrees—all refer to the camorra tradition, which goes back to the early nineteenth century and has also influenced the Calabrian 'Ndrangheta. Unlike the Cosa Nostra and 'Ndrangheta families, however, the Neapolitan crime groups today operate in full autonomy, frequently fight each other, and do not consider themselves bound in even a loose confederation (see Sales 1993; Monzini 1999).

4. "Family" is the term Cosa Nostra members most frequently use to indicate the single groups constituting this mafia confederation. 'Ndrangheta affiliates refer to the bands as family as well, though they also use the expression *locale*, which means "place" in Italian. In the past, Sicilian mafia members also used to employ the term *borgata* [neighborhood] (TrPA 1984, I: 4), but contemporary *pentiti* hardly mention it. The latter term or its American translations—"brugad" or "brigade"—are also mentioned by American Cosa Nostra defectors (see Alfonso D'Arco's declaration in U.S. District Court 1994 and Vincent Cafaro's testimony in U.S. Senate 1988: 223).

Ever since the nineteenth century, the word *cosca*, which means "artichoke" in Sicilian dialect, has been employed by external observers to refer to mafia groupings. Although it is now currently used by mafia members too, it is not clear whether it originally formed part of mafia terminology.

5. Conversely, these themes attract only the marginal interest of the prosecutors and judges who carry out interrogations with the *pentiti*. This constitutes a major research drawback, since the witnesses' declarations and resulting criminal cases represent the main source of information for social scientists. In fact, with very few exceptions, social scientists are not usually granted direct access to mafia turncoats. In Italy, Pino Arlacchi is one of the few who has been authorized to talk directly with two of the first and most important witnesses of Cosa Nostra, Antonino Calderone and Tommaso Buscetta. On the basis of these conversations he wrote two books (Arlacchi 1993 and 1994). Several journalists have also been allowed to speak to witnesses (Biagi [1986] 1990; Bettini 1994; Colaprico and Fazzo 1995; Nicotri 1996; Lodato 1999), while others have helped the mafiosi to write their memoirs (Gentile 1993; Castagna 1967).

Chapter 1

1. For instance, in the southwest Sicilian provinces of Caltanissetta and Agrigento a rival confederation of criminal groups, called the Stidda ("star" in Sicilian dialect), began to emerge in the second half of the 1980s and to seriously challenge the supremacy of Cosa Nostra there. Originally formed by "men of honor" who had been expelled from Cosa Nostra, the Stidda imitated its organization and cultural apparatus. However, the *stiddaioli*'s power lessened markedly from 1993 onward as a result of internal conflicts, defections, and betrayals, as well as actions taken against it by both local Cosa Nostra families and law enforcement agencies (TrPA 1993a; Ministero dell'Interno 1994: 202–11, 1995a: 37–39, 1995b, 2001a: 110, 117–28, 2001e: 13).

2. In 1992 two new provinces were established in Calabria: Vibo Valentia and Crotone. However, since the data concerning criminal groups in these new administrative districts are not comparable with intelligence information, the text refers to the old territorial boundaries.

3. For a description of southern Italian mafia settlements in northern Italy, see the report published by the Parliamentary Anti-mafia Commission on this topic (CPM 1994a). The report was also published as a book by the rapporteur, Carlo Smuraglia (1994). For additional information, see also CPM 1988; Portanova et al. 1996; Ciconte 1998; Sciarrone 1998; and Massari 1998 and 2001. For a general overview of the international ramifications of Italian organized crime, see Jamieson 1994.

4. These accounts were confirmed in the early 1990s by Paolo Pezzino, who analyzed the records of the judicial hearings and the final sentence in the criminal case against the members of the Fratellanza. According to these judicial sources, the association based in Favara had other associated groups in several neighboring towns and counted about five hundred associates, divided into smaller groups. These were usually formed by about five to fifteen members and were headed by a *capo decina* responsible to the *capo testa* who ruled the whole organization (1990a: 205–18; see also Crisantino 2000, which analyzes the criminal case against the *stoppagghieri* of Monreale).

5. By reflecting upon the substitution of the title "father" with that of "boss" in the American Cosa Nostra of the 1930s, Joseph Bonanno described very clearly a transformation that also took place in Sicily during the postwar period: "The title 'boss' represented a corruption of the title 'Father.' It's regrettable that in America the term 'boss' became the more popular of the two. The terms are not interchangeable. 'Father' describes a paternal, kinship-oriented relationship between a leader and his followers. 'Boss' connotes a relationship between a master and his servants or his workers. The growing use of the word 'boss' when referring to 'Father' was one of the earliest indications that in America relationships between a leader and his followers had more of a business than a kinship base" (Bonanno 1983: 85).

6. According to Humbert Nelli, democratic principles were formally observed but—as in the Sicilian Cosa Nostra—constantly violated by even the mafia-type associations that developed in Italian American immigrant communities in the early twentieth century: "Like the Old World models, the groups were run (in theory, at least) along democratic lines, each member having a voice in specifying the (illegal) activities of the organization and also a vote in the election of the leaders. In practice, shrewd, effective and ruthless *Capos* and others in the gang's hierarchy, once entrenched, came to view their positions as

permanent and not subject to the whims of an electorate. Over time, subordinates also came to share this view: rank-and-file members accepted their lot as inferiors, at least in part because of economic realities" (1976: 138–39). During Prohibition, in fact, some of the group leaders made huge profits with the direct management and the extortion of bootlegging ventures, thus increasing the gap between leaders and their followers. Nonetheless, as in the Sicilian Cosa Nostra, the huge wealth did not prevent the first-generation Italian-born mafia leaders from being challenged (and defeated) by younger, even shrewder criminals, who were born (or at least grew up) in the United States.

7. The distinction between blood and mafia family is further stressed by the 'Ndrangheta normative code. Despite the frequent exceptions, this prescribes that the affiliation of a new member can be neither decided nor performed by his relatives. On this point Antonio Zagari maintains: "'Ndrangheta's rules absolutely prohibit that the 'baptism,' the rite of affiliation, is officiated by persons linked to the candidate by kinship bonds. Relatives and kin may assist the rite, but they cannot intervene to express favorable or opposing opinions. As a rule, a Calabrian *mafioso*, even at the top of the organization, should not even decide whether his own son is or is not to be affiliated. From their birth, however, the sons of Calabrian men of honor are, by right, considered *giovani d'onore*" (Zagari 1992: 26; TrMI 1994a: 133).

8. Several other documents of that time, containing analogous descriptions, have been published by Nicaso (1990). It is interesting to notice that the same internal division and ranks were described by several late nineteenth century sources in reference to the Neapolitan camorra (see Monnier [1863] 1994; Alongi 1890; Monzini 1999).

9. According to the description provided by Joe Valachi in the early 1960s (U.S. Senate 1963; Maas 1969) and confirmed by several other witnesses, the American Cosa Nostra's commission was set up in the 1930s and is formally composed of the chiefs of all U.S. mafia families. For security reasons, however, it hardly meets in this plenary form and its decisional powers are permanently entrusted to a smaller body (see Cressey 1969). As of the 1980s and early 1990s, this body was made up of the chiefs of four of the five New York families and the head of the Chicago family. They could occasionally invite other bosses when problems concerning specific areas were discussed (see Angelo Lonardo's and Vincent Cafaro's statements in U.S. Senate 1988: 86–88 and 250–51 as well as Alfonso D'Arco's declarations in U.S. District Court 1994: 4–5). It is not clear whether the commission still exists and how much authority it has today (Jacobs and Gouldin 1999: 135–37).

10. It is worth stressing that the provincial commission's existence and internal organization, as described by mafia witnesses, have been confirmed by the wiretappings of several conversations between mafiosi. Among them, the most important are those between Antonino Gioè and Gioacchino La Barbera, two members of the Altofonte family (Palermo province), which were intercepted in autumn 1992 in a Palermitan flat (PrPA 1993b: 108–20; for a list of all the most meaningful intercepted conversations between Sicilian mafiosi, see PrPA 1993b: 91–94).

11. In the Sicilian dialect, a *lupara* is a sawed-off shotgun used by shepherds to protect their flock from wolves *[lupi]*. A "white *lupara*" is a "clean," "bloodless" murder in which the victim's body is never found.

12. Leonardo Messina recalls that, in order to strengthen his control of the mafia families outside the Palermo province, in the mid-1980s Riina introduced a new role: the "ambassador," a direct representative of the Corleonesi in the different provincial contexts. The ambassador was not bound to hierarchies and could personally contact the members of single families, to give them orders or to gather information, even without informing their leader (CPM 1992d).

13. The role played by the Sicilians in this process was definitively confirmed by the investigations conducted after the killing of Antonio Scopelliti, prosecutor at the Corte di Cassazione (the Italian supreme court of appeal), carried out in a small outlying ward of Reggio Calabria in August 1991. As the first-degree sentence issued in May 1996 clarifies, the Sicilian mafia demanded the death of Scopelliti—the prosecutor in the revision of the first-degree sentence handed down at the Palermo maxitrial—as "payment" for its peace-promoting intervention in the conflict between the 'Ndrangheta families (*La Repubblica* 1996; TrRC 1993c, 1993b: 39–40).

14. It is interesting to note that the same process of centralization has also been taking place in the Japanese "mafia," the Yakuza. According to the very precise estimates of the Japanese police, in 1992 the Yamaguchi-gumi syndicate included almost 40 percent of Yakuza affiliates and presided over thirteen hundred smaller groups, while in 1980 it had held a share of only 11 percent. As in the Italian Mezzogiorno, the main reason for this process seems to have been the growing pressure exercised by law enforcement bodies: this favored the development of mechanisms to regulate violence and coordinate criminal activities and an increased level of secrecy (National Police Agency 1989; Japanese Embassy in Rome 1993).

15. Interestingly, according to some defectors, the same trend would affect the American Cosa Nostra commission as well (see U.S. Senate 1988: 253).

Chapter 2

1. The only partial exception is represented by the British historian Eric Hobsbawm, who presented symbols and ritual behavior as a constitutive element of all premodern social movements in his book on primitive forms of social protest, a chapter of which is devoted to the mafia (1974). However, the recognition of their relevance in the case of the mafia is only indirect, given that no explicit reference to mafia symbols and rituals can be found in the book.

2. For example, at the end of a long volume in which the mafia is presented as an industry of private protection, Diego Gambetta is unable to explain the reasons for life choices of this kind: "This trade is extremely uncertain: it includes being chased by police and hounded by violent rivals, having to rely on criminals for customers. In addition, owning a protection firm can prove to be a nightmare, if only because of the evanescence of property rights. On these grounds alone no sensible parent would recommend a career in the mafia to his or her children (but, as we know, in the world of the mafia, one cannot trust even one's parents). Those who choose to enter such a trade must therefore enjoy special competitive advantages and suffer from a lack of preferable alternatives.... In short, if one is not an insider by birth or a clever psychopath, one is unlikely to choose to become a mafioso" (Gambetta 1993: 246).

3. The same ritual of initiation and oath are still used in American Cosa Nostra families, at least in those that have remained more faithful to the tradition. In his hearing before the Senate's Permanent Subcommittee on Investigations in 1988, Vincent Cafaro recalled his affiliation to the mafia with the following words: "I remember the day I became a member of the Genovese family. Tony Salerno had told me and Patty Jerome to meet him and Buckaloo one morning. When we arrived, Buckaloo took me to the El Cortile restaurant on Mulberry Street, where we met with Funzi Tieri, the *brugad*'s underboss, and Fat Tony, who at that time was the *consigliere*. I knew what I was there for when I saw a gun, a knife, a pin, alcohol and tissue laying out on the table. Funzi asked me if I wanted to become a member of the family. He said I could accept or not accept, and there would be no hard feelings. But he also said that 'once you accept you belong to us. We come first. Your family and home come second. We come first, no matter what.' And I accepted. Funzi then showed me the gun and the knife, and says 'This is the gun and the knife, you live with the gun and die by the knife.' He told me that Fat Tony had sponsored me, and gave me a piece of paper to let burn in my hand while I took the oath. 'If I betray the Cosa Nostra, I shall burn like this paper.' He then pricked my trigger finger with the pin and told me, 'Now you are *amico nostra* [*sic*], you have been born over again. Now you are a man; you belong to us'" (U.S. Senate 1988: 224; see also Angelo Lonardo's testimony before the same subcommittee as well as Joe Valachi's and Sammy "the Bull" Gravano's accounts in Maas 1969 and 1997). A very similar rite was recorded in 1989 by the FBI with the aid of an eavesdropping device, in Medford, Massachusetts, when four men were admitted into New England's Patriarca family (Jacobs and Gouldin 1999: 138). The following year, turncoat George Fresolone wore a recording device that allowed FBI agents to record his affiliation into the Bruno-Scarfo family in Philadelphia (Fresolone and Wagman 1994). A few defectors, however, deny having undergone a formal ceremony of initiation (see, for instance, Teresa 1973).

4. To reach the high rank of *santista*, the liminal phase usually lasts several days. Significantly called the "*santa* of the purgatory," this transition is symbolized by a golden key that, according to the legend, is buried at the bottom of the sea and may be picked up only by new *santisti*. The key is given symbolically to each newly initiated member, while he is waiting for the definitive approval of his promotion by the family that is said to lead all the 'Ndrangheta, the *locale* of San Luca on the Aspromonte mountain. Once approval has been granted, the new member has to give the key back at a meeting of seven *santisti*, who are metaphorically in charge of putting it back at the bottom of the sea (PrRC 1995: 5726).

5. Up to 1979 the average annual exchange rates between the Italian *lira* and the U.S. dollar are drawn from Ciocca and Ulizzi (1990: 360–62). The later data were kindly provided by Luigi Federico Signorini of the Bank of Italy's Ufficio Studi.

6. Mafia ceremonies of initiation also have powerful legitimating functions. Through repetition, they confirm the authority of the officiant, who under normal circumstances is the chief of the family. No matter by what means or on what basis he has achieved his ruling position inside the society, his authority as chief is powerfully reasserted with each restaging of the affiliation ritual. Furthermore, in the 'Ndrangheta the rites of passage staged to mark the transition from one rank to another reaffirm the legitimacy of the internal stratification system.

7. From the late nineteenth century on, even the Neapolitan camorra drew its boundaries according to the code of honor, and the language of honor traditionally played a key role in distinguishing affiliates from nonaffiliates (see Marmo 1989 and 1988, which draws on sources of the time).

8. The most radical position is held by Michael Herzfeld (1980, 1987), who went so far as to provocatively state that honor is a false category created by anthropologists. This is not, however, the right place to discuss this controversy, which has been enormous, since it questions the existence of a cultural unity around the Mediterranean (see Fiume 1989).

9. Having committed a murder used to be a precondition for admission in the American Cosa Nostra as well, but this criterion has not been strictly observed since the early 1970s. Angelo Lonardo, for example, recalls that in the late 1940s, "to be proposed for membership in Cosa Nostra, you would have to have killed someone and stood up to the pressure of police scrutiny. Today, you do not have to kill to be a member, but just prove yourself worthy by keeping your mouth shut or by being a 'stand-up' guy." In southern Italy as in the United States, however, if a "made" man is instructed to kill, he has no choice but to obey: as Lonardo puts it, "If you are called upon to kill someone, you have to be prepared to do it" (U.S. Senate 1988: 86 and 257).

10. The weaker expressions "friend of ours" or "*amico nostra* [*sic*]," referring to a formal member of an Italian American mafia family, are common within the American Cosa Nostra. The expressions "made member" and "wiseguy" are also used (U.S. Senate 1988: 229).

11. In the 'Ndrangheta the unity and the communion of the whole mafia association are also emphasized by resort to a metaphorical image. According to several *pentiti*, the Calabrian mafia association is symbolically depicted as a big leafy tree, the "tree of science," whose main sections correspond to the major 'Ndrangheta ranks. The roots represent the family chief; the trunk the *camorristi di sgarro*; the branch structure the *camorristi*. The single branches stand for the *picciotti*, that is, the lowest ranking members and the flowers represent the *giovani d'onore*, young sons of mafia affiliates. Finally, the leaves stand for the *contrasti onorati*, the nonmembers who are considered worthy of affiliation, while the falling leaves represent the betrayers, "those who must die because of infamous things" (PrMI 1993: 194–99; TrMI 1994a: 119). Once again, an analogy directly transmits meaning between the "subsidiary" and the "principal" subjects. In particular, the biological and functional unity of the "subsidiary subject"—in this case, the tree—is attributed to the mafia organization (Black 1962).

12. The *pentito* Giuseppe Marchese was denied such authorization, because the parents of his girlfriend were divorced. His brother, who was also an affiliate, suggested that he "wash his dirty linen in the family"—that is, that he marry an orphan, and not a daughter of divorcees. "I understood what I had to do: to kill Rosaria's father.... I went along, taking time, then there was no longer any time left. My brother faced me and said: 'So, Pino, shall we all beat our heads against the wall? With this marriage you are wearing yourself out and wearing out your own family. If you don't kill him, we'll kill him.' I immediately broke off my relationship with Rosaria" (*La Repubblica*, January 10–11, 1993).

13. Further proof of this claim can be seen in the murder of Giovanni Fici, "man of honor" of the Ciaculli family, which took place in the mid-1980s. After having miraculously escaped a previous murder attempt, during which he was wounded, Fici

became very cautious and hardly ever left his house or its immediate surroundings. Filippo La Rosa, another affiliate who, being Fici's cousin, enjoyed his trust, was entrusted with the task of getting close to him and bringing him to where the murder could be carried out. La Rosa managed to convince Fici to see a doctor to treat his wounds and, as planned, near the doctor's office, the Ciaculli family hit squad shot him (PrPA 1993c: 197–99).

14. Equality among members is a trait common to all those forms of sociability based on fraternization contracts. According to Otto von Gierke, a feeling of brotherly equality also inspired German guilds: "All guilds were, like the old fellowships, associations of men each of whom was equal to the others, united by a bond of personal affinity. For they were fellowships and their members fellows and *pares*" ([1868] 1990: 22). Likewise, Weber highlighted the same feeling among the members of Protestant sects: "Internally," he wrote, "among the sect members, the spirit of early Christian brotherliness prevailed" (1946: 318).

15. In turn, the Catania witness, Antonino Calderone, recalls that the "tax collectors" Nino and Ignazio Salvo "were powerful and untouchable outside Cosa Nostra. But inside the society we were equal, indeed we [the *pentito* himself and his brother Pippo] were in a certain way above them, because Ignazio was the representative of a small town like Salemi, and I represented a big city, whereas Pippo was the provincial representative and secretary of the Region [Cosa Nostra's regional commission]" (Arlacchi 1993: 76).

16. This categorization of humanity has some affinities with the famous typology of men presented by don Mariano, the main character of Leonardo Sciascia's novel, *Il giorno della civetta* [The day of the owl]: "Men, half-men, sub-men, (with all the due respect), cuckolds, and *quaraquaquà*. . . . Men are very few; half-men are few, so much that I'd be happy if the human race went no lower than half-men. . . . But no, it sinks lower to sub-men; they're like kids who think they're big, monkeys who imitate grown up people's actions. . . . And lower still, to the cuckolds—there's getting to be an army of them, nowadays. . . . And at last you get the *quaraquaquà*: they ought to live in puddles like ducks, since their lives have no more meaning or feeling than a duck's" (1994: 109).

17. It was exactly for this reason that "Riina went crazy" (PrPA 1995a, III: 49) on January 30, 1992, when the Corte di Cassazione definitively confirmed the first-degree sentence of the Palermo *maxi-processo* [maxitrial] involving more than four hundred Sicilian "men of honor." To reaffirm his legitimate right to rule and to reassure the Cosa Nostra members who had been imprisoned, he ordered the murder of the two politicians—Salvo Lima and Ignazio Salvo—who had failed to manipulate the judicial outcome of the trial and the two investigating judges—Giovanni Falcone and Paolo Borsellino—who had been most influential in the case (see chapter 5).

18. The meetings officially start when the chief of each *società* pronounces a long and complicated formula containing references both to religious figures and to the mythical founders of the three major southern Italian criminal organizations. Several versions of this formula are known. In all cases, however, the final words are invariably the same: "Silver cup, consecrated host, with these words of humility the society is formed" (TrMI 1994e: 149; Malafarina 1986: 89). The function of these symbolic references is clear: to reassert the group legitimacy, in both religious and traditional terms, at each family gathering. On these occasions, the symbolic and effective equality among the members is also

reaffirmed. In fact, the member holding the position of *mastro di giornata* has to seize the arms of all those present, following a ritual procedure (Castagna 1967: 33–34).

19. Only one mafia witness, who was affiliated to a peripheral and traditionalist *cosca*, reports that the assemblies of his family are opened by pronouncing a ritual formula before the image of a saint (PrPA 1992: 140–41).

20. For a detailed account of the so-called second mafia war in Calabria, see TrRC 1993b and 1999 and Ciconte 1996.

21. Even longer selection and education times are imposed by the Italian American Cosa Nostra: few seem to enter the families belonging to this association before their late thirties, while in Sicily and Calabria members enter in their twenties. The longer waiting times are also due to the fact that in America the initiation of the new members is centrally regulated by the commission. Since the 1930s this body has often "put a freeze" on the making of any new members, except for those replacing a member who died or retired from active membership (see Angelo Lonardo's testimony in U.S. Senate 1988: 86–87, and Sam Gravano's recollections in Maas 1997). As a result of the above policy, the ratio between "made" members and associates is much higher in the United States than in Sicily or Calabria: according to Alfonso D'Arco, for example, in the early 1990s the Chicago family had only fifty "made" members, but thousands of associates (U.S. District Court 1994).

22. Ten years earlier, other clans of the Cosa Nostra had also had to face considerable financial losses after entrusting their money to the Sicilian banker Michele Sindona. See Commissione Sindona 1982a, 1982b; Commissione P2 1984; TrMI [1986] 1994; Spero 1980; Stajano 1991.

Chapter 3

1. The origins of the Carbonari as well as the channels by which they penetrated into Italy are still obscure. According to most Carbonari legends, France was the birthplace of the association, but various sources place it in Scotland or England, while other scholars refer to the German sect of the Illuminati. There are also some researchers who consider the Carboneria an indigenous Italian organization.

    Consequently, the Neapolitan exiles of 1799, the Bourbon Restoration, the British troops via Malta and Sicily, the French troops, and Joachim Murat have all been suggested as possible reasons for the introduction and spread of the sect in Italy. However, according to John Rath, who carefully reviewed the literature on this subject, the most accredited version presents the Carbonari as an emanation of the Freemasons. "In other words," he states, "the Carbonari were a 'popular' Freemasonry created by liberal anti-Napoleonic Masons to serve as a vehicle to arouse the uneducated masses in Southern Italy against the French" (1964: 356). Nonetheless, after the Restoration, the Carbonari began to oppose the Bourbon regime and rapidly increased their ranks in the Kingdom of the Two Sicilies, where they played a primary role in the rebellion of July 1820, as well as in the northern states.

2. The *pentito* Leonardo Messina reports, however, that his family had a written collection of mafia rules, which he called the "bible" (PrPA 1992: 42).

3. According to several nineteenth-century sources, the prisoners of the main Palermi-

tan prison, which hosted mafiosi and criminals of all kinds, also had a slang of their own, which was called—as in Calabria—*bacchiaggiu* (Pitrè [1889] 1993: 317–31; Cutrera [1900] 1988: 81–87). This word is still currently used by Cosa Nostra members. However, it no longer refers to a form of slang, but to the short, incomplete, and metaphorical way of talking often adopted by "men of honor," especially the older ones (Bettini 1994).

4. According to several historical sources, membership in a mafia group, or at least mafiosi attitudes, was often indicated by a special way of dressing and acting. In an essay written at the end of the nineteenth century, Francesco Melari gives us the following description of a member of the Calabrian Honored Society: "The young man, who entered the Society at the level of *picciotto*, wears trousers tight to the thigh and large at the inferior extremes, which are called 'bell bottoms,' a handkerchief knotted around his neck, bent collars, a round small hat, under whose brims one can see the tuft of the *bravi*, which stands out horizontally on his left temple. Dressed like this, the *picciotto* has a bold, provocative air" (1885; see also Nicaso 1990). Some of these clothes were used by Calabrian mafiosi well after the end of the Second World War (Alvaro 1955b). The Sicilians, instead, have stopped using them—if they ever did, as some sources deny it (Cutrera [1900] 1988)—since Italy's unification, "when they realized that the new government was not stupid and would persecute them" (Alongi [1886] 1977: 54).

5. The *copiata* is composed of two parts. The first varies with each rank and is revealed to the affiliate, whenever he is promoted to a new rank. The second is permanent and lists the name of the *mafioso*'s five godfathers, who are usually chosen among the most representative members of his own family and the neighboring ones (PrRC 1995: 376). The *copiata* thus has a double function. First, it is used to identify the 'Ndrangheta members; second, it allows higher-ranking *'ndranghetisti* to identify the position held by their younger counterparts.

6. Ritual formulas of recognition were once also widespread in western Sicily, as both Giuseppe Alongi ([1886] 1977: 102–3) and Antonino Cutrera ([1900] 1988: 120–24) report. See also Lupo 1993: 110–11.

7. The same rule is also valid in the Italian American Cosa Nostra (see Maas 1997).

8. In the United States as well, the American Cosa Nostra's commission was primarily set up to interrupt the long chain of murders which kept attracting the attention of the law enforcement forces (see U.S. Senate 1988: 250).

9. In mafia slang, the expression *mamma santissima* is used to refer to mafia chiefs. It literally means "most holy mother," referring to Holy Mary, regarded as the protector of the 'Ndrangheta (PrRC 1995: 5735).

10. The adoption of Masonic references and rituals has not led to the abandonment of traditional religious figures and formulas in either the Santa or the higher ranks. Despite the well-known anti-Christian position of the Freemasonry, the two phenomena come together in the 'Ndrangheta in a way that is colorful and contradictory. According to the mafia witness Fonti, for example, "the religious figures associated with the rank of *vangelo* are all the Apostles and Holy Peter and Paul, the historical ones are Mazzini [a well-known Mason as well as a hero of Italy's fight for independence in the mid–nineteenth century], as founder and promoter of the secret society generally speaking, and Cavour [the first prime minister of unified Italy], as a supreme example of statesman" (ibid.: 5727).

11. Since the late 1970s, the growing number of members and the creation of higher ranks have to some extent weakened the original characteristics of the Santa, which was initially meant to be a secret nucleus of the Calabrian mafia organization. For this reason, the *dote* of santista and the higher ranks are considered normal ranks of the *società maggiore* by some former affiliates of the 'Ndrangheta who were not born in Calabria, such as Calogero Marcenò (TrMI 1994e).

12. The murder of Giuseppe Greco "Scarpa" [the shoe], the bold and bloodthirsty chief of the Ciaculli district and an old ally of the Corleonesi, is a good example of this. Greco's murder was ordered by Totò Riina in autumn 1985, when the former's charisma and power started to represent a danger to the latter's personal supremacy. To weaken Greco's prestige, Riina ordered the "massacre of piazza Scaffa." A few months before his murder, eight people were killed within the Ciaculli *mandamento*. Greco was not informed of this, a deliberate strategy to enable him to be accused of a lack of effective power over the territory under his jurisdiction. Difficulties in circulating information inside the Sicilian mafia association were also exploited to delay and weaken the reactions of his followers. The news of Greco's murder was kept secret for a long time, while the rumor that he had fled abroad to escape law enforcement pressure was spread deliberately (PrPA 1993c: 242–56).

13. Only in 1993, for example, was it discovered that Salvatore Biondino, the man who was with Riina on the day of his arrest, had belonged to the Cosa Nostra since 1978 and headed the San Lorenzo *mandamento* in Palermo since the mid-1980s, replacing his imprisoned chief, Giacomo Giuseppe Gambino. His membership within the Cosa Nostra was known only to a very limited number of "men of honor" outside his family (TrCL 1993, 1994a; PrPA 1995a, III: 34).

14. From the mid-1920s on, Fascist propaganda portrayed the mafia as a "state within the state," with its own laws, tribunals, and taxes. As the "Iron Prefect" Cesare Mori wrote in his memoirs, the mafia had created "a state within a state, and a regime within a regime: that is, the mafia regime, with its laws, its monetary and blood tributes, and its penal sanctions which fully invested and exploited the island, damaging the state in particular, and especially to the detriment of the population. This last had no freedom of choice between the rightful, distant, and inactive state and the other state, nearby, well defined, and fully operative, and had to bow down before the latter and accept its dominion" (1993: 147). As a result, the mafia was declared incompatible with Fascism and acts of indiscriminate repression were justified (Duggan 1989; see also Lo Schiavo 1964).

15. The only exceptions to this so far can be found in some comments made by Mariano Meligrana (1983), an article published by Giovanni Fiandaca (1994), and by a short chapter in the second edition of Lupo's *Storia della mafia* (1996b: 36–41). Additionally, in the late 1950s, Antonio Pigliaru applied Romano's conception to the Sardinian banditry in a work called *La vendetta barbaricina come ordinamento giuridico* (1959).

16. Several scholars of independent disciplines have shown that the centrality of sovereignty in the definition of law was determined by the historical framework in which such a conception developed. Modern states, struggling to affirm their superiority over powerful centers of power represented by the Church and feudal lords, needed an explicit theory of imperium in order to eliminate these parallel jurisdictions and to legitimate a

secular structure of centralized administration. The best answer to these political needs was provided by the theory of natural law, which was developed in the sixteenth century by Grotius and Hobbes. It was, in particular, in Hobbes's reflections that the concept of imperium or sovereignty acquired pivotal importance and became inseparable from those of law and state. Consequently, the legal validity of any corporation not explicitly created or recognized by the state was denied. Hobbes's theory became the consequent justification of absolute power (Bobbio 1958; Smith 1974; Foucault 1980).

17. For a review of the most recent publications concerning legal anthropology, see Snyder 1993.

18. Before the consolidation of modern states, every group of people linked by objective situations—such as birth, political, religious or ethnic membership, lifestyle, or job—or created by an explicit fraternization procedure could establish its own legal order. As Weber maintains, "in the Medieval *imperium* every man was entitled everywhere to be judged by that tribal law by which he 'professed' to live by. The individual carried his *professio iuris* wherever he went. Law was not a *lex terrae* . . . but rather the privilege of the person as a member of a particular group" (1978: 696). This point was clearly made by the ninth-century Archbishop of Lyon, quoted by Marc Bloch: "When in Frankish Gaul five persons happened to gather together, it was no occasion for surprise if each of them—a Roman perhaps, a Salian Frank, a Ripuarian Frank, a Visigoth and a Burgundian—obeyed a different law" (1975, I: 111).

19. This rule goes back to the nineteenth century, as a short story by Antonino Cutrera confirms. At the end of the century, the Amoroso brothers, who headed the mafia family of the Porta Montalto neighborhood in Palermo, were standing trial, charged with the murder of their cousin. According to the prosecutors, the brothers had killed the cousin, who had done military service in the Carabinieri corps, "because they were ashamed to have a former *sbirro* [policeman] for a relative" (Cutrera [1900] 1988: 158–59).

20. The emulation of state courts is promoted to such an extent that in the trials of the 'Ndrangheta a member is chosen to act as defense lawyer, a role called "mother of charity" in mafia jargon. According to Fonti, "this is not a fixed role, but changes every time. We just make sure that it is entrusted to an affiliate with particularly good rhetorical skills" (PrRC 1995: 4439–40).

21. According to several *pentiti*, the functions of adjudication are still formally entrusted to the *consigliere* of each family. None of them, however, has provided concrete examples of this role.

22. Balduccio Di Maggio later became a mafia witness and gave information that allowed for Riina's arrest in 1993, after twenty-two years of hiding.

Chapter 4

1. The political dimension of southern Italian mafia associations is increasingly being recognized by several scholars: Santino 1994b; Paoli 1997; Santoro 1998, 2000.

2. The same considerations are put forward even by several American Cosa Nostra defectors who testified for the U.S. government. Asked what he gained from being a member, Vincent Cafaro—a member of the powerful Genovese family in New York, who made over 2 billion dollars a year in the number business—did not mention the money,

but answered as follows: "You gain honor, respect: that is what you gain. Honor and respect ... within the community and all over the city. Five boroughs, I would say." When Senator Nunn persisted and asked him how an organized crime that carried out all sorts of criminal activities including murder could be considered honorable, Cafaro replied as an old-style Sicilian mafioso would have done: "Well, in our way of thinking and our way of life, that is what it is to us. Being honorable, and respect. That is the way we are brought up. That is the way you are born and raised in these big Italian neighborhoods" (U.S. Senate 1988: 236). Likewise, in another testimony before the Permanent Subcommittee of Investigations, Angelo Lonardo, the former underboss of the Cleveland mafia family stated that he had become a member because people "show more respect for you," though he admitted that he "also got money for it later." When he was asked whether he considered his membership part of a business-making operation, he had no doubts: "No," he replied (ibid.: 111).

3. In both everyday language and scientific discourse the adjective "political" is also applied to groups that have no direct relationship with the use of force, but which attempt to influence the activities of political organization: parties are the main representatives of this category. This type of social action is called "politically oriented" action by Max Weber (1978: 54) and his distinction is maintained here.

4. In Calabria, the bond between each mafia group and its territory is so close that, according to the mafia witness Francesco Fonti, the basic unit of the 'Ndrangheta, the *locale*, as the *'ndranghetisti* call it, "forms and activates only on its own territory." Only "the Society [that is, the assembly of affiliates belonging to different *locali*] may meet in any other place and specifically in prisons" (PrRC 1995: 4430).

5. The principle of territoriality is respected to such an extent that Sicilian "men of honor" usually ask for the authorization of the competent family head before buying a house or a piece of land on the territory of another *cosca*. This was what Salvatore Contorno did in the early 1980s, when he wanted to buy a plot of land in Ciaculli, which was then part of Michele Greco's undisputed territory. Only after receiving Greco's permission did Contorno conclude the deal (TrPA [1985] 1992: 72–73). Mannoia, too, tells how he followed the same *iter* before building his house in the territory of Ciaculli, viewing it "as a rightful act of respect" (TrPA 1989: 148).

6. Literally a "beakerful," the word *pizzo* originally referred to the right of the overseer to scoop from the grain being threshed by the peasants (see Fentress 2000: 163).

7. For a history of the Reggio Calabria revolt, which began as a popular protest and was taken over by right-wing parties, see Lombardi Satriani 1971; D'Agostini 1972; and Walston 1988: 207–15.

8. It is worth recalling that even after the discovery of the ledger, many of the shopkeepers involved continued to deny having paid a *tangente* and were finally prosecuted for false testimony. Given the certainty of mafia revenge, the risk of being convicted by state authorities is still perceived as the lesser of two evils (interview 26).

9. ENEL is the acronym of the Italian Electrical Company, which held a monopoly over the Italian supply of electricity until the partial liberalization of the utility sector in the late 1990s.

Chapter 5

1. Even in the United States mafia groups sometimes originated from—or coincided with—legitimate mutual-benefit societies. Among the latter, the most famous was the Unione Siciliana, which was set up in Chicago in 1895 to provide for insurance and fraternal needs of unskilled immigrant laborers and was subsequently exploited by local mafiosi for criminal purposes. Mafia infiltration was so extensive that the name "Unione Siciliana" was used during the 1920s to identify mafia groups in Chicago, New York, and other American cities (Nelli 1976: 199).

2. In *I Beati Paoli. Storia, letteratura e leggenda* (1991), Renda collected and analyzed all the documents previous to Natoli's book that referred to the legend of the Beati Paoli. The oldest reference dates back to 1767.

3. The plot of Natoli's romance is much alive in today's mafia culture and its main characters are still employed as models of ideal-typical sets of attitudes and behavior. In one of their first public confrontations, for example, Totò Riina and the witness Gaspare Mutolo turned upon each other by referring to the characters of the novel.

4. The popular "soul" of the 'Ndrangheta is confirmed by the diffusion of the double militancy in the mafia association and the Communist Party (PCI) after the Second World War. Whereas Cosa Nostra always opposed the Communist Party, refusing to vote for the PCI and setting an incompatibility between the mafia and Communist membership, in Calabria, especially in the villages on the Ionic coast, "membership in the PCI was not incompatible with that in the Honored Society" (PrRC 1995: 4726–27). At the end of the Second World War, many *'ndranghetisti* came back to their hometowns after having served years of forced residence on small islands during the Fascist regime, indoctrinated by communist companions and proudly wearing "hammer and sickle" tattoos. The postwar communist mayors of the villages of Cardeto, Africo, Canolo, Platì, and Caulonia were "men of honor," and the mafia families Bruzzaniti and Maviglia in Africo, Catanzariti in Platì, and D'Agostino in Canolo were well known for their active support of the PCI (PrRC 1995: 4726–27; see also Ciconte 1992: 265–71).

5. On the rise of the Italian clientelistic system, see Graziano 1973, 1978, 1980; Boissevain 1974; and Fantozzi 1993. The relationships between mafia and politics in Sicily and Calabria is well described in Barone 1987, Chubb 1989, Pezzino 1996, Tranfaglia 2001, and Piselli 1988.

6. The importance of the local rooting of political power is also demonstrated by the outcome of the struggle between Lima and Giovanni Gioia, who had been the leader of the *fanfaniani* wing in Sicily and Lima's sponsor for many years. When the latent rivalry between the two exploded during the 1968 national elections, Lima defeated his former patron, though Gioia's prestige and contacts at the national level far surpassed those of Lima. Thanks to his control over local levers of power, however, and to his ramified networks of personal loyalties, Lima, who was then virtually unknown outside Palermo, came first among all the DC candidates in the constituency of western Sicily, outdistancing government ministers and undersecretaries, including Gioia himself. After this election he formally broke his partnership with Gioia and founded Andreotti's faction in Sicily, which attracted a great number of Gioia's supporters (Chubb 1982; Vasile 1994).

7. Many Sicilian "men of honor" have also become members of the Freemasonry

since the 1970s. On the matter see TrPA 1993c; CPM 1993c: 60–66; Bonsanti, De Luca, and Stajano 1995; Cipriani 1993.

8. In many other cases, however, as in Sicily, the Calabrian prosecutors have had difficulty in proving secret and illegal pacts between politicians and mafiosi, as the courts have refused to rely exclusively on the declarations made by *pentiti*. Hence, for example, Giacomo Mancini, the former national secretary of the Socialist Party and mayor of Cosenza, was condemned to three years and six months imprisonment for external support of mafia associations (*concorso esterno*) in March 1996, but was then found not guilty by the Catanzaro Court in October 1999 (*Corriere della Sera*, November 20, 1999).

9. As early as the late 1920s this same change was pointed out by John Landesco with reference to Italian American organized crime: "The most powerful factor of all in the decline in the popular participation in funerals is, in all probability, the profound change that is taking place in the nature of the relations of organized crime and machine politics. The old basis in friendly relations is being superseded by a cash nexus. Political protection for the powerful financial interests of organized crime is coming to rest less and less upon friendship and more and more upon pecuniary considerations" ([1929] 1979: 295).

10. The most important anti-mafia provisions of the last Andreotti government included the laws concerning extortive kidnappings and the protection of witnesses (Acts No. 82/19 and 203/91); the bill that allowed the dissolution of city and provincial councils polluted by mafia infiltration (Act No. 221/91); and the provisions that established "a supporting fund for the victims of extortive requests" (Act. No. 172/92); the Direzione Investigativa Antimafia, a police agency specializing in the fight against organized crime, and the Direzione Nazionale Antimafia, which coordinates the activity of twenty-six Direzioni Distrettuali Antimafia located in the prosecutor's offices of the major Italian cities and specializing in anti-mafia investigations (Act No. 8/92) (see Violante 1994: 210ff.).

11. For biographies of Giovanni Falcone and Paolo Borsellino, see respectively La Licata 1993 and Lucentini 1994. Caponnetto published his memoirs in 1993. The work of the first Palermitan anti-mafia pool has been reconstructed in Lodato 1994a, Rossi 1992, and Stille 1995.

12. It goes beyond the scope of this work to describe and analyze the manifold manifestations and faces of the Sicilian and national anti-mafia movements: however, see Cavadi 1994, 1998; Alajmo 1994; Casarrubea and Blandano 1991, 1993; Siebert 1994: 267–453; Puglisi 1990; Schneider and Schneider 1994; Renda 1993; Costantino 1993; Ramella and Trigilia 1994; Santino 2000b; Jamieson 2000: 127–58; and, most recently, Schneider and Schneider 2003.

13. During its first five years of activity, the fund accepted less than a hundred out of the over five hundred requests for compensation that were presented and distributed less than ten billion *lire* (about $6.3 million) to extortion victims, though it had available more than 150 billion *lire* ($94 million; Grasso 1998).

Conclusions

1. For a synthesis of the American and international debate on organized crime, see Paoli 2002.

2. The influence of the illegal enterprise paradigm on the German conception of

organized crime is also confirmed by practitioners. This is, for instance, what Peter Korneck, a Frankfurt prosecutor with many years of experience in the field, has to say on the matter: "Experts who work not only theoretically but also practically maintain that [organized crime] implies the activities of persons who commit serious offences in an enduring cooperation founded on the principle of the division of labor with the aim of maximizing profits. If you omit the reference to 'serious offences,' you are left with the description of an activity that in Germany and in all the Western world is usually described as entrepreneurial activity" (Raith 1989: 268).

References

Judicial Documents

Corte di Cassazione. 1992. *Sentenza sui ricorsi proposti da Calò Giuseppe ed altri avverso la sentenza del 14.3.1992 della Corte d'Assise d'Appello di Firenze.* November 24.

PrCT, Procura della Repubblica di Catania. Direzione Distrettuale Antimafia. 1993. *Richiesta di applicazione di misure cautelari nei confronti di Santapaola Benedetto + 155.* November 27.

———. 1995. *Richiesta di applicazione di misure cautelari nei confronti di Cultrera Felice + 8.* March 19.

PrCZ, Procura della Repubblica di Catanzaro. Direzione Distrettuale Antimafia. 1995. *Richiesta di applicazione di misure cautelari nei confronti di Giampà Francesco + 43.* June 14.

PrMI, Procura della Repubblica di Milano. 1990. *Richiesta di applicazione di misure cautelari nei confronti di La Rosa Gaetano + 11.* May 2.

———. Direzione Distrettuale Antimafia. 1993. *Richiesta di applicazione di misure cautelari nei confronti di Flachi Giuseppe + 138.* June 7.

———. 1997. *Requisitoria del P.M. Maurizio Romanelli nella causa penale contro Agnifili + altri.* Procedimento n. 16 + 19 + 20/94. 6 + 11 + 12 + 14/95.

PrPA, Procura della Repubblica di Palermo. Direzione Distrettuale Antimafia. 1992. *Verbali di interrogatorio reso dal collaboratore di giustizia, Leonardo Messina.* N.d.

———. 1993a. *Richiesta di applicazione di misure cautelari nei confronti di Agate Mariano + 57.* February 20.

———. 1993b. *Richiesta di applicazione di misure cautelari nei confronti di Agrigento Giuseppe + 60.* May 20.

———. 1993c. *Richiesta di applicazione di misure cautelari nei confronti di Abbate Luigi + 87.* December 23.

---. 1994a. *Richiesta di applicazione di misure cautelari nei confronti di Adorno Francesco + 19.* N.d.

---. 1994b. *Richiesta di applicazione di misure cautelari nei confronti di Arnone Umberto + 14.* N.d.

---. 1995a. *Memoria depositata dal pubblico ministero nel procedimento penale n. 3538/94, instaurato nei confronti di Andreotti Giulio.* N.d.

---. 1995b. *Memoria depositata dal pubblico ministero nel procedimento penale n. 3162/89 a carico di Greco Michele ed altri, relativa ai c.d. 'omicidi politici' (cioè agli omicidi di Michele Reina, Piersanti Mattarella, Pio La Torre e Rosario Di Salvo).* N.d.

---. 1996a. *Richiesta di applicazione di misure cautelari nei confronti di Accardo Antonino + 82.* January 13.

---. 1996b. *Richiesta di applicazione di misure cautelari nei confronti di Aragona Salvatore + 29.* February 20.

---. 1997a. *Memoria depositata dal pubblico ministero nel procedimento penale n. 4578/96, instaurato nei confronti di Dell'Utri Marcello.* March.

---. 1997b. *Memoria depositata dal pubblico ministero nel procedimento penale n. 1866/93, instaurato nei confronti di Carnevale Corrado.* July.

PrPL, Procura della Repubblica di Palmi. 1993. *Richiesta di rinvio a giudizio, di misure cautelari e di archiviazione nei confronti di Galluzzo Vincenzo Rosario + 81.* November 15.

PrRC, Procura della Repubblica di Reggio Calabria. Direzione Distrettuale Antimafia.

1992a. *Richiesta di applicazione di misure cautelari nei confronti di Mammoliti Saro + 12.* July 31.

---. 1992b. *Richiesta di applicazione di misure cautelari nei confronti di Barbaro Antonio + altri.* August 1.

---. 1992c. *Richiesta di applicazione di misure cautelari nei confronti di Morabito Giuseppe + 5.* October 21.

---. 1992d. *Richiesta di applicazione di misure cautelari nei confronti di Strangio Francesco + 9.* October 27.

---. 1993a. *Richiesta di rinvio a giudizio e di archiviazione nei confronti di Barbaro Francesco + 52.* July 16.

---. 1993b. *Richiesta di applicazione di misure cautelari nei confronti di Morabito Giuseppe + 161.* November 5.

---. 1993c. *Domanda di autorizzazione a procedere in giudizio contro il deputato Paolo Romeo.* Rome: Camera dei Deputati, doc. IV, no. 465, XI Legislature.

---. 1995. *Richiesta di ordini di custodia cautelare in carcere e di contestuale rinvio a giudizio nel procedimento contro Condello Pasquale + 477.* July.

TrAG, Tribunale di Agrigento. Ufficio Istruzione. [1986] 1988. *Ordinanza-sentenza di rinvio a giudizio nei confronti di Ferro Antonio + 43.* February 2. Selected parts reprinted in *La mafia di Agrigento. Gli atti del processo di Villaseta. I boss—Gli insospettabili—I politici—Gli imprenditori*, ed. G. Arnone. Cosenza: Il filo d'Arianna.

TrCL, Tribunale di Caltanissetta. Ufficio del Giudice per le Indagini Preliminari. 1993. *Ordinanza di custodia cautelare in carcere nei confronti di Agrigento Giuseppe + 17.* November 11.

---. 1994a. *Ordinanza di custodia cautelare in carcere nei confronti di Aglieri Pietro + 18.* April 11.

---. 1994b. *Ordinanza di custodia cautelare in carcere nei confronti di Occhipinti Gianfranco.* April 20.

TrCT, Tribunale di Catania. Ufficio del Giudice per le Indagini Preliminari. 1994. *Ordinanza di custodia cautelare in carcere nei confronti di Cocuzza Antonino + 44.* N.d.

———. 1995. *Ordinanza di custodia cautelare in carcere nei confronti di Cannizzo Giovanni.* N.d.

TrLO, Tribunale di Locri. 1993. *Ordinanza di custodia cautelare in carcere nei confronti di Filippone Salvatore + 12.* October 30.

TrMA, Tribunale di Marsiglia. 1987. *Verbali di interrogatorio reso dal collaboratore di giustizia, Antonino Calderone.*

TrMI, Tribunale di Milano. Ufficio Istruzione Processi Penali. [1986] 1994. *Ordinanza-sentenza di rinvio a giudizio nei confronti di Michele Sindona.* July. Selected parts reprinted in Sindona. *L'atto di accusa dei giudici di Milano.* Rome: Editori Riuniti.

———. 1989. *Ordinanza-sentenza di rinvio a giudizio per la bancarotta del Banco Ambrosiano emessa dai giudici istruttori Antonio Pizzi e Renato Bricchetti.* April 7.

TrMI, Tribunale di Milano. Ufficio del Giudice per le Indagini Preliminari. 1993. *Ordinanza di custodia cautelare in carcere nei confronti di Agil Fuat + 164.* October 2.

———. 1994a. *Ordinanza di custodia cautelare in carcere nei confronti di Zagari Antonio + 155.* January 12.

———. 1994b. *Ordinanza di custodia cautelare in carcere nei confronti di Alberga Nicola + altri.* May 23.

———. 1994c. *Ordinanza di custodia cautelare in carcere nei confronti di Flachi Giuseppe + 207.* May 27.

———. 1994d. *Ordinanza di custodia cautelare in carcere nei confronti di Cirelli Lucia + 16.* June 3.

———. 1994e. *Ordinanza di custodia cautelare in carcere nei confronti di Abys Adriano + 394.* June 6.

———. 1994f. *Ordinanza di custodia cautelare in carcere nei confronti di Di Modica Luigi + 78.* October 3.

TrMI, Tribunale di Milano. Sezione Penale. 1996a. *Sentenza nella causa penale contro Avalos Osorio Jorge Enrique + 23.* February 17.

———. 1996b. *Sentenza nella causa penale contro Dilek Mustekabi + 16.* February 28.

TrMI, Tribunale di Milano. Corte d'Assise. 1997a. *Sentenza nella causa penale a carico di Annacondia Salvatore + 143.* April 27.

———. 1997b. *Sentenza nella causa penale a carico di Agil Fuat + 132.* June 11.

———. 1997c. *Sentenza nella causa penale a carico di Agnifili + altri.* September 4.

———. 1998. *Sentenza nella causa penale a carico di Merico Bruno + 2.* September 29.

TrPA, Tribunale di Palermo. Ufficio Istruzione Processi Penali. [1964] 1981. *Ordinanza-sentenza di rinvio a giudizio nei confronti di La Barbera Angelo + 42.* June 23. Reprinted in *Documentazione allegata alla relazione conclusiva,* ed. Commissione Parlamentare d'inchiesta sul fenomeno della mafia in Sicilia, doc. XXIII, no. 1/XI, vol. IV, tome XVII: 461–594. Rome: Camera dei Deputati.

———. [1965] 1981. *Ordinanza-sentenza di rinvio a giudizio nei confronti di Torretta Pietro + 120.* May 8. Reprinted in *Documentazione allegata alla relazione conclusiva,* ed. Commissione Parlamentare d'inchiesta sul fenomeno della mafia in Sicilia, doc. XXIII, no. 1/XI, vol. IV, tome XVII: 595–817. Rome: Camera dei Deputati.

TrPA, Tribunale di Palermo. Sezione Prima. [1968] 1980. *Sentenza contro Garofalo Francesco + 16 imputati di associazione a delinquere.* June 25. Reprinted in *Documentazione allegata alla relazione conclusiva,* ed. Commissione Parlamentare d'inchiesta sul fenomeno della mafia in Sicilia, doc. XXIII, no. 1/VIII, vol. IV, tome XIV: 1075–140. Rome: Camera dei Deputati.

TrPA, Tribunale di Palermo. Ufficio Istruzione Processi Penali. [1973] 1980. *Ordinanza-sentenza di rinvio a giudizio nei confronti di Albanese Giuseppe ed altri 113*. Reprinted in *Documentazione allegata alla relazione conclusiva*, ed. Commissione Parlamentare d'inchiesta sul fenomeno della mafia in Sicilia, doc. XXIII, no. 1/VIII, vol. IV, tome XIV: 1171–445. Rome: Camera dei Deputati.

———. 1982. *Ordinanza-sentenza di rinvio a giudizio nei confronti di Rosario Spatola + 119*. N.d.

———. 1983–85. *Verbali di interrogatorio reso dal collaboratore di giustizia, Vincenzo Sinagra*.

———. 1983–85. *Verbali di interrogatorio reso dal collaboratore di giustizia, Stefano Calzetta*.

———. 1984. *Verbali di interrogatorio reso dal collaboratore di giustizia, Tommaso Buscetta*.

———. 1984–85. *Verbali di interrogatorio reso dal collaboratore di giustizia, Vincenzo Marsala*.

———. 1984–85. *Verbali di interrogatorio reso dal collaboratore di giustizia, Salvatore Contorno*.

———. 1985. *Ordinanza-sentenza di rinvio a giudizio nei confronti di Abbate Giovanni + 706*. November 8.

———. 1987a. *Verbali di interrogatorio reso dal collaboratore di giustizia, Antonino Calderone*.

TrPA, Tribunale di Palermo. Corte di assise. 1987b. *Sentenza nei confronti di Abbate Giuseppe + altri*. December 16.

TrPA, Tribunale di Palermo. Ufficio Istruzione Processi Penali. 1989. *Verbali di interrogatorio reso dal collaboratore di giustizia, Francesco Marino Mannoia*.

TrPA, Tribunale di Palermo. Ufficio del Giudice per le Indagini Preliminari. 1991. *Ordinanza di custodia cautelare in carcere nei confronti di Morici Serafino + 4*. July 9.

TrPA, Tribunale di Palermo. Ufficio Istruzione Processi Penali. [1985] 1992. *Ordinanza-sentenza di rinvio a giudizio nei confronti di Abbate Giovanni + 706*. November 8. Selected parts reprinted in *Mafia: L'atto d'accusa dei giudici di Palermo*, ed. Corrado Stajano. Rome: Editori Riuniti.

TrPA, Tribunale di Palermo. Ufficio del Giudice per le Indagini Preliminari. 1992. *Ordinanza di custodia cautelare in carcere nei confronti di Riina Salvatore + 23*. October 20.

———. 1993a. *Ordinanza di custodia cautelare in carcere nei confronti di Puzzangaro Gaetano + 52*. March 8.

———. 1993b. *Ordinanza di custodia cautelare in carcere nei confronti di Riina Salvatore + 24*. May 18.

———. 1993c. *Ordinanza di custodia cautelare in carcere nei confronti di Accordino Alessandro + 44*. July 17.

———. 1993d. *Ordinanza di custodia cautelare in carcere nei confronti di Madonia Salvatore + 2*. October 10.

———. 1993e. *Ordinanza di custodia cautelare in carcere nei confronti di Ferraro Pietro + 9*. December 16.

———. 1994a. *Ordinanza di custodia cautelare in carcere nei confronti di Accardi Gaetano + 73*. March 25.

———. 1994b. *Ordinanza di custodia cautelare in carcere nei confronti di Capizzi Benedetto + 7*. October 20.

———. 1994c. *Ordinanza di custodia cautelare in carcere nei confronti di Alberti Gerlando + 14*. December 12.

———. 1994d. *Ordinanza di custodia cautelare in carcere nei confronti di Mandalari Giuseppe + 1.* December 17.

———. 1995a. *Ordinanza di custodia cautelare in carcere nei confronti di Mannino Giuseppe.* February 13.

———. 1995b. *Ordinanza di custodia cautelare in carcere nei confronti di Inzerillo Vincenzo.* February 14.

———. 1998. *Ordinanza di custodia cautelare in carcere nei confronti di Buscemi Antonino + 9.* N.d.

TrPL, Tribunale di Palmi. Corte di Assise. 1986. *Sentenza a carico di Pesce Giuseppe ed altri.* June 9.

TrRC, Tribunale di Reggio Calabria. Ufficio Istruzione Processi Penali. 1978. *Ordinanza-sentenza di rinvio a giudizio nei confronti di Paolo De Stefano + 5.* N.d.

———. 1988. *Ordinanza-sentenza di rinvio a giudizio nei confronti di Albanese Mario + 190.* N.d.

TrRC, Tribunale di Reggio Calabria. Ufficio del Giudice per le Indagini Preliminari. 1990. *Ordinanza di custodia cautelare in carcere nei confronti di Imerti Antonino + 44.* November 28.

TrRC, Tribunale di Reggio Calabria. Ufficio Istruzione Processi Penali. 1991. *Ordinanza-sentenza di rinvio a giudizio contro De Stefano Domenico + 22.* April 24.

TrRC, Tribunale di Reggio Calabria. Ufficio del Giudice per le Indagini Preliminari. 1992. *Ordinanza di custodia cautelare in carcere nei confronti di Battaglia Piero + 10.* December 1.

———. 1993a. *Ordinanza di custodia cautelare in carcere nei confronti di Archinà Rocco Carlo + 44.* January 8.

———. 1993b. *Ordinanza di custodia cautelare in carcere nei confronti di De Stefano Giorgio, + 18.* March 5.

———. 1993c. *Ordinanza di custodia cautelare in carcere nei confronti di Riina Salvatore + 20.* April 20.

———. 1994a. *Ordinanza di custodia cautelare in carcere nei confronti di Labate Pietro + 17.* January 7.

———. 1994b. *Ordinanza di custodia cautelare in carcere nei confronti di Biafore Rodolfo + 12.* November 2.

TrRC, Tribunale di Reggio Calabria. Corte d'Assise. 1999. *Sentenza nella causa penale contro Condello, Pasquale + 282.* January 19.

TrRO, Tribunale di Roma. Ufficio Istruzione Processi Penali. 1992. *Ordinanza di rinvio a giudizio e sentenza istruttoria di proscioglimento contro Carboni Flavio ed altri.* April 29.

TrTO, Tribunale di Torino. Ufficio del Giudice per le Indagini Preliminari. 1993. *Ordinanza di custodia cautelare in carcere nei confronti di Marando Pasquale + 51.* October 15.

———. 1994. *Ordinanza di custodia cautelare in carcere nei confronti di Belfiore Salvatore + altri.* June 23.

TrTP, Tribunale di Trapani. Ufficio Istruzione Processi Penali. 1990. *Ordinanza-sentenza di rinvio a giudizio contro Agate Mariano + 59.* October 19.

TrVV, Tribunale di Vibo Valentia. Ufficio Istruzione Processi Penali. 1985. *Ordinanza-sentenza di rinvio a giudizio contro Mancuso Francesco + 200.* N.d.

Parliamentary Hearings and Reports

Commissione P2, Commissione parlamentare d'inchiesta sulla loggia massonica P2. 1984. *Relazione di maggioranza e Relazioni di minoranza,* doc. XXIII, IX Legislature. Rome: Camera dei Deputati.

Commissione Sindona, Commissione Parlamentare d'inchiesta sul caso Sindona e sulle responsabilità politiche ed amministrative ad esso eventualmente connesse. 1982a. *Relazione di maggioranza* (relatore Azzaro), doc. XXIII, no. 2–*sexies*, VIII Legislature. Rome: Camera dei Deputati.

———. 1982b. *Relazione di minoranza* (relatore Teodori), doc. XXIII, no. 2, VIII Legislature. Rome: Camera dei Deputati.

CPM, Commissione Parlamentare d'inchiesta sul fenomeno della mafia e sulle altre associazioni similari. 1988. *Relazione sulle risultanze del gruppo di lavoro incaricato di svolgere indagini sulla criminalità organizzata e, in particolare, sul riciclaggio di proventi illeciti in provincia di Milano*, doc. XXII, no. 34, X Legislature. Rome: Camera dei Deputati.

———. 1989. *Relazione sulle risultanze dell'indagine del gruppo di lavoro della Commissione incaricato di svolgere accertamenti sullo stato della lotta alla mafia nella provincia di Reggio Calabria*, doc. XXIII, no. 6, X Legislature. Rome: Camera dei Deputati.

———. 1990a. *Relazione di minoranza presentata dall'On. Luciano Violante ed altri*, doc. XXIII, no. 12–*bis*/1, X Legislature. Rome: Camera dei Deputati.

———. 1990b. *Relazione sulle vicende connesse alla costruzione della centrale termoelettrica di Gioia Tauro*, doc. XXIII, no. 24, X Legislature. Rome: Camera dei Deputati.

———. 1992a. *Relazione Annuale*, doc. XXIII, no. 47, X Legislature. Rome: Camera dei Deputati.

———. 1992b. *Audizione del collaboratore di giustizia Antonino Calderone*. November 11, XI Legislature. Rome: Camera dei Deputati.

———. 1992c. *Audizione del collaboratore di giustizia Tommaso Buscetta*. November 16, XI Legislature. Rome: Camera dei Deputati.

———. 1992d. *Audizione del collaboratore di giustizia Leonardo Messina*. December 4, XI Legislature. Rome: Camera dei Deputati.

———. 1993a. *Audizioni in Calabria*. January 29, XI Legislature. Rome: Camera dei Deputati.

———. 1993b. *Audizione del collaboratore di giustizia Gaspare Mutolo*. February 9, XI Legislature. Rome: Camera dei Deputati.

———. 1993c. *Relazione sui rapporti tra mafia e politica con note integrative*, doc. XXIII, no. 2, XI Legislature. Rome: Camera dei Deputati.

———. 1993d. *Forum su Economia e Criminalità*. May 14–15, XI Legislature. Rome: Camera dei Deputati.

———. 1993e. *Audizione del Procuratore della Repubblica di Palmi Agostino Cordova*. July 9, XI Legislature. Rome: Camera dei Deputati.

———. 1993f. *Relazione sulla situazione della criminalità in Calabria, con nota integrativa*, doc. XXIII, no. 8, XI Legislature. Rome: Camera dei Deputati.

———. 1993g. *Prima relazione annuale, con note integrative*, doc. XXIII, no. 9, XI Legislature. Rome: Camera dei Deputati.

———. 1994a. *Relazione su insediamenti e infiltrazioni di soggetti ed organizzazioni di mafiose in aree non tradizionali*, doc. XXIII, no. 11, XI Legislature. Rome: Camera dei Deputati.

———. 1994b. *Relazione conclusiva*, doc. XXIII, no. 14, XI Legislature. Rome: Camera dei Deputati.

———. 1995. *Relazione sul "caso Cordopatri,"* doc. XXIII, no. 5, XII Legislature. Rome: Camera dei Deputati.

———. 1998. *Relazione sui sequestri di persona a scopo di estorsione*, doc. XXIII, no. 14, XIII Legislature. Rome: Camera dei Deputati. Available online: www.camera.it/chiosco_parlamento.asp?content=/_bicamerali/antimafia/home.htm. Accessed March 2002.

———. 1999. *Relazione sull'infiltrazione mafiosa nei Cantieri Navali di Palermo*, doc. XXIII, no. 21, XIII Legislature. Rome: Camera dei Deputati. Available online: www.camera.it/chiosco_parlamento.asp?content=/_bicamerali/antimafia/home.htm.

———. 2000a. *Relazione sullo stato della lotta alla criminalità organizzata in Calabria*, doc. XXIII, no. 42, XIII Legislature. Rome: Camera dei Deputati. Available online: www.camera.it/chiosco_parlamento.asp?content=/_bicamerali/antimafia/home.htm. Accessed March 2002.

———. 2000b. *Relazione sulla criminalità organizzata in Campania*, doc. XXIII, no. 46, XIII Legislature. Rome: Camera dei Deputati. Available online: www.camera.it/chiosco_parlamento.asp?content=/_bicamerali/antimafia/home.htm. Accessed January 2002.

———. 2001. Relazione conclusiva, doc. XXIII, no. 57, XIII Legislature. Rome: Camera dei Deputati. Available online: www.camera.it/chiosco_parlamento.asp?content=/_bicamerali/antimafia/home.htm. Accessed January 2002.

CPMS, Commissione Parlamentare d'inchiesta sul fenomeno della mafia in Sicilia. 1971. *Relazione sull'indagine riguardante casi di singoli mafiosi*, doc. XXIII, no. 2–*quater*, V Legislature. Rome: Camera dei Deputati.

———. [1972] 1976. Sintesi delle conclusioni cui era pervenuto nel corso della V Legislatura il comitato per le indagini sui casi dei singoli mafiosi, sul traffico di stupefacenti e sul legame tra fenomeno mafioso e gangsterismo americano. Supplement to *Relazione sul traffico mafioso di tabacchi e stupefacenti nonché sui rapporti tra mafia e gangsterismo italo americano. Relatore: Zuccalà*, doc. XXIII, no. 2, VI Legislature: 447–93. Rome: Camera dei Deputati.

———. 1976a. *Relazione conclusiva. Relatore: Carraro*, doc. XXIII, no. 2, VI Legislature: 1–328. Rome: Camera dei Deputati.

———. 1976b. *Relazione sul traffico mafioso di tabacchi e stupefacenti nonché sui rapporti tra mafia e gangsterismo italo americano. Relatore: Zuccalà*, doc. XXIII, no. 2, VI Legislature: 329–567. Rome: Camera dei Deputati.

———. 1976c. *Relazione di minoranza. Relatori: La Torre, Benedetti, Malagugini, Adamoli, Chiaromonte, Lugnano, Maffioletti, Terranova*, doc. XXIII, no. 2, VI Legislature: 569–956. Rome: Camera dei Deputati.

———. 1976d. *Relazione di minoranza. Relatori: Nicosia, Pisanò, Giuseppe Niccolai*, doc. XXIII, no. 2, VI Legislature: 959–1247. Rome: Camera dei Deputati.

Fed. PCI-AG, Federazioni del P.C.I. di Agrigento e di Sciacca. [1964] 1976. Memoriale per la Commissione Parlamentare Antimafia. Supplement to Commissione Parlamentare d'inchiesta sul fenomeno della mafia in Sicilia. *Relazione di minoranza. Relatori: La Torre, Benedetti, Malagugini, Adamoli, Chiaromonte, Lugnano, Maffioletti, Terranova*, doc. XXIII, no. 2, VI Legislature: 691–779. Rome: Camera dei Deputati.

Fed. PCI-CL, Federazione del P.C.I. di Caltanissetta. [1964] 1976. Memoriale per la Commissione Parlamentare Antimafia. Supplement to Commissione Parlamentare d'inchiesta sul fenomeno della mafia in Sicilia. *Relazione di minoranza. Relatori: La Torre, Benedetti, Malagugini, Adamoli, Chiaromonte, Lugnano, Maffioletti, Terranova,* doc. XXIII, no. 2, VI Legislature: 613–90. Rome: Camera dei Deputati.

Reports of Other Italian State Agencies

Archivio Centrale dello Stato. 1968–69. *L'inchiesta sulle condizioni sociali ed economiche della Sicilia (1875–76).* Ed. S. Carbone and R. Crispo. Bologna: Cappelli.

Comitato provinciale stupefacenti di Roma. [1971] 1980. Relazione del 24 maggio 1971 del dott. Giorgio Staffieri, dirigente la Sezione Narcotici del Comitato provinciale stupefacenti di Roma su mafia, contrabbando di tabacchi e traffico di stupefacenti nella provincia di Roma. Reprinted in *Documentazione allegata alla relazione conclusiva,* ed. Commissione Parlamentare d'inchiesta sul fenomeno della mafia in Sicilia, doc. XXIII, no. 1/VIII, vol. IV, tome XIV: 1005–13. Rome: Camera dei Deputati.

CSM, Consiglio Superiore della Magistratura. 2001. *Verifica della evoluzione delle forme organizzativo-dirigenziali di Cosa Nostra al fine di un'eventuale elaborazione di proposte per attuare strategie di contrasto. Risoluzione approvata dall'Assemblea Plenaria nella seduta antimeridiana del 7 giugno 2001.* Relatore: G. Natoli.

Criminalpol, Direzione Centrale della Polizia Criminale. 1989. *Indagini sull'organizzazione mafiosa siciliana denominata "Cosa Nostra." Rapporto riepilogativo dell'attività investigativa svolta su Cuntrera Pasquale ed altri.* November 9.

———. 1995. *Punti di situazione a livello provinciale,* unpublished report.

DIA, Direzione Investigativa Antimafia. 1993a. *Cosche di Cosa Nostra della provincia di Agrigento,* unpublished report.

———. 1993b. *Cosche di Cosa Nostra della provincia di Catania,* unpublished report.

———. 1993c. *Cosche di Cosa Nostra della città di Palermo,* unpublished report.

———. 1993d. *Cosche di Cosa Nostra della provincia di Trapani,* unpublished report.

———. 1993e. *Famiglia di Carini,* unpublished report..

———. 1993f. *Profili della criminalità organizzata nell'Italia settentrionale e centrale,* unpublished report.

———. 1994. *Espansione territoriale e devianze della 'Ndrangheta,* unpublished report.

Gruppo Interforze. 1991. *Profili strutturali delle organizzazioni criminali calabresi.* Rome: Guardia di Finanza.

———. 1993a. *Bozza relativa alle famiglie mafiose della provincia di Palermo redatta dal gruppo interforze di quella città e consegnata in via informale,* unpublished report.

———. 1993b. *Bozza relativa alle famiglie mafiose della città di Palermo redatta dal gruppo interforze di quella città e consegnata in via informale,* unpublished report.

Guardia di Finanza. [1971] 1980a. Relazione dell'11 giugno 1971 del maggiore Bernardo Angelozzi del Comando Generale della Guardia di Finanza su mafia e traffico di stupefacenti. Reprinted in *Documentazione allegata alla relazione conclusiva,* ed. Commissione Parlamentare d'inchiesta sul fenomeno della mafia in Sicilia, doc. XXIII, no. 1/VIII, vol. IV, tome XIV: 1015–32.

———. [1971] 1980b. Relazione dell'11 giugno 1971 del capitano Pietro Soggiu del Comando Generale della Guardia di Finanza su mafia e contrabbando di tabacchi.

Reprinted in *Documentazione allegata alla relazione conclusiva*, ed. Commissione Parlamentare d'inchiesta sul fenomeno della mafia in Sicilia, doc. XXIII, no. 1/VIII, vol. IV, tome XIV: 1035–66.

Ministero dell'Interno.1989. *Sequestri di persona a scopo di estorsione*. Rome: Ministero dell'Interno.

———. 1992. *Relazione semestrale sull'attività svolta e i risultati conseguiti dalla Direzione Investigativa Antimafianel primo semestre del 1992*. Rome: Ministero dell'Interno.

———. 1993a. *Rapporto sul fenomeno della criminalità organizzata per il 1992*. Rome: Ministero dell'Interno.

———. 1994a. *Rapporto sul fenomeno della criminalità organizzata per il 1993*, doc. XXXVIII-*bis*, no. 1, XII Legislature. Rome: Camera dei Deputati.

———. 1994b. *Relazione semestrale sull'attività svolta e i risultati conseguiti dalla Direzione Investigativa Antimafia nel secondo semestre del 1993*. Rome: Ministero dell'Interno.

———. 1995a. *Rapporto sul fenomeno della criminalità organizzata (anno 1994)*. Rome: Ministero dell'Interno.

———. 1995b. *Relazione semestrale sull'attività svolta e i risultati conseguiti dalla Direzione Investigativa Antimafia nel secondo semestre del 1994*. Rome: Ministero dell'Interno.

———. 1996a. *Rapporto sul fenomeno della criminalità organizzata (anno 1995)*, doc. XXXVIII-*bis*, no. 1, XIII Legislature. Rome: Camera dei Deputati.

———. 1996b. *Relazione sui programmi di protezione, sulla loro efficacia e sulle modalità generali di applicazione per coloro che collaborano alla giustizia—I semestre 1996*. Doc. XCI, no. 1, XIII Legislature. Rome: Senato della Repubblica.

———. 1997a. *Rapporto sul fenomeno della criminalità organizzata (anno 1996)*. Doc. XXXVIII-*bis*, no. 2, XIII Legislature. Rome: Camera dei Deputati.

———. 1997b. *Relazione sui programmi di protezione, sulla loro efficacia e sulle modalità generali di applicazione per coloro che collaborano alla giustizia—II semestre 1996*. Doc. XCI, no. 2, XIII Legislature. Rome: Senato della Repubblica.

———. 1998a. *Rapporto sul fenomeno della criminalità organizzata (anno 1997)*. Doc. XXXVIII-*bis*, no. 3, XIII Legislature. Rome: Camera dei Deputati.

———. 1998b. *Relazione sui programmi di protezione, sulla loro efficacia e sulle modalità generali di applicazione per coloro che collaborano alla giustizia—I semestre 1998*. Doc. XCI, no. 5, XIII Legislature. Rome: Senato della Repubblica.

———. 1999a. *Consigli comunali sciolti ai sensi del decreto legge 31 maggio 1991, n. 164, convertito in legge 22 luglio 1991, no. 221*, unpublished report.

———. 1999b. *Relazione semestrale sull'attività svolta e i risultati conseguiti dalla Direzione Investigativa Antimafia nel secondo semestre del 1998*. Rome: Ministero dell'Interno. Available online: www.interno.it/dip_ps/dia/semestrali.htm. Accessed January 2002.

———. 1999c. *Relazione semestrale sull'attività svolta e i risultati conseguiti dalla Direzione Investigativa Antimafia nel primo semestre del 1999*. Rome: Ministero dell'Interno. Available online: www.interno.it/dip_ps/dia/semestrali.htm. Accessed January 2002.

———. 2000a. *Rapporto sul fenomeno della criminalità organizzata (anno 1999)*. Rome: Camera dei Deputati. Available online: www.poliziadistato.it/pds/online/documentazione.htm. Accessed January 2002.

———. 2000b. *Relazione semestrale sull'attività svolta e i risultati conseguiti dalla Direzione Investigativa*

Antimafia nel secondo semestre del 1999. Rome: Ministero dell'Interno. Available online: www.interno.it/dip_ps/dia/semestrali.htm. Accessed January 2002.

———. 2000c. *Relazione semestrale sull'attività svolta e i risultati conseguiti dalla Direzione Investigativa Antimafia nel primo semestre del 2000*. Rome: Ministero dell'InternoAvailable online: www.interno.it/dip_ps/dia/semestrali.htm. Accessed January 2002.

———. 2001a. *Rapporto sul fenomeno della criminalità organizzata (anno 2000)*. Rome: Camera dei Deputati. Available online: www.poliziadistato.it/pds/online/documentazione.htm. Accessed January 2002.

———. 2001b. *Relazione al Parlamento sull'attività della sicurezza pubblica nel territorio nazionale—Anno 2000*. Rome: Ministero dell'Interno. Available online: www.interno.it/sezioni/dipartimento/. Accessed January 2002.

———. 2001c. *Relazione al Parlamento sui programmi di protezione, sulla loro efficacia e sulle modalità generali di applicazione per coloro che collaborano alla giustizia—1 luglio–31 dicembre 2000*. Rome: Ministero dell'Interno. Available online: www.poliziadistato.it/pds/online/documentazione.htm. Accessed January 2002.

———. 2001d. *Relazione semestrale sull'attività svolta e i risultati conseguiti dalla Direzione Investigativa Antimafia nel secondo semestre del 2000*. Rome: Ministero dell'Interno. Available online: www.interno.it/dip_ps/dia/semestrali.htm. Accessed January 2002.

———. 2001e. *Relazione semestrale sull'attività svolta e i risultati conseguiti dalla Direzione Investigativa Antimafia nel primo semestre del 2001*. Rome: Ministero dell'Interno. Available online: www.interno.it/dip_ps/dia/semestrali.htm. Accessed January 2002.

Prefettura di Palermo. [1971] 1981. Fascicolo trasmesso il 5 giugno 1971 relativo alla concessione dell'onorificenza di Cavaliere al merito della Repubblica italiana al dottor Michele Navarra. Reprinted in *Documentazione allegata alla relazione conclusiva*, ed. Commissione Parlamentare d'inchiesta sul fenomeno della mafia in Sicilia, doc. XXIII, no. 1/XI, vol. IV, tome XVII: 343–66. Rome: Camera dei Deputati.

Regione Calabria. Assessorato al Bilancio, Programmazione e Politiche Comunitarie. Comitato Regionale per la Programmazione dei fondi strutturali 2000–2006. 1999. *Rapporto Interinale*. Catanzaro: Regione Calabria.

Reports of International and Foreign Bodies

Australian Federal Police. National Assessment Unit. Strategic Branch. Intelligence Division. 1990. *La criminalità organizzata italiana e l'Australia*, Italian translation of the original report. Rome: Ministero dell'Interno.

BKA, Bundeskriminalamt. 1992. *La criminalità organizzata italiana*, Italian translation of the original report. Rome: Ministero dell'Interno.

———. 1995. *Lagebild Organisierte Kriminalität Bundesrepublik Deutschland 1994*. Wiesbaden: BKA.

EMCDDA, European Monitoring Centre for Drugs and Drug Addiction. 1997. *Annual Report on the State of the Drugs Problems in the European Union. 1997*. Luxembourg: Office for Official Publications of the European Communities.

———. 2001. *Annual Report on the State of the Drugs Problems in the European Union. 2001*. Luxembourg: Office for Official Publications of the European Communities. Available online: annualreport.emcdda.org/en/download/index.html. Accessed January 2002.

Japanese Embassy in Rome. 1993. *Data Provided to the Italian Ministry of the Interior*, unpublished report.
New York State Organized Crime Task Force. 1988. *Corruption and Racketeering in the New York City Construction Industry.* Ithaca, N.Y.: ILR Press.
National Police Agency. 1989. *White Paper on Police: Organized Crime Control Today and Its Future Task.* Tokyo.
PCOC, President's Commission on Organized Crime. 1983. *Organized Crime: Federal Law Enforcement Perspective.* Record of Hearing I. Washington, D.C.: U.S. Government Printing Office.
——. 1985. *Organized Crime and Gambling.* Record of Hearing VII. Washington, D.C.: U.S. Government Printing Office.
——. 1986a. *The Impact: Organized Crime Today.* Washington, D.C.: U.S. Government Printing Office.
——. 1986b. *The Edge: Organized Crime, Business, and Labor Unions.* Washington, D.C.: U.S. Government Printing Office.
Task Force on Organized Crime. The President's Commission on Law Enforcement and Administration of Justice. 1967. *Task Force Report: Organized Crime.* Washington, D.C.: U.S. Government Printing Office.
UNESC, United Nations Economic and Social Council. 1994. *Problems and Dangers Posed by Organized Transnational Crime in the Various Regions of the World.* Background Document for the World Ministerial Conference on Organized Transnational Crime, E/CONF.88/2. August 18.
UNGA, United Nations General Assembly. 2000. *Crime Prevention and Criminal Justice: Report of the Ad Hoc Committee on the Elaboration of a Convention against Transnational Organized Crime on the Work of Its First to Eleventh Sessions.* 55th sess., A/55/383. November 2.
U.S. District Court, Northern District of Illinois, Eastern Division. 1994. *United States of America v. Laborers' International Union of North America, AFL-CIO, et al. Declaration of Alfonso D'Arco.* July 19.
U.S. Senate. 1951. *Third Interim Report of the Special Committee to Investigate Organized Crime in Interstate Commerce (Kefauver Committee).* 81st Cong., 2d sess. Washington, D.C.: U.S. Government Printing Office.
——. Judiciary Committee. 1957. *Investigations on Improper Activities in the Labor or Management Field.* Hearings. Washington, D.C.: U.S. Government Printing Office.
——. Committee on Government Operations. 1963. *Hearings of Joseph Valachi before the Permanent Subcommittee on Investigations of the Committee on Government Operations.* Washington, D.C.: U.S. Government Printing Office.
——. Permanent Subcommittee on Investigations of the Committee on Governmental Affairs. 1988. *Organized Crime: Twenty-Five Years After Valachi.* Hearings. 100th Congress, 2d Session. Washington, D.C.: U.S. Government Printing Office.

Secondary Sources

Abadinsky, H. 2000. *Organized Crime.* 6th ed. Belmont, Calif.: Wadsworth.
Abbate, L., and P. Gomez. 2001. Da "Sicilia Libera" a "Forza Italia". *Micromega* 4: 229–33.
Adelfi, N. 1955. Il mondo tenebroso dell'onorata società. *La Nuova Stampa*, September 22.

Alajmo, R. 1994. *Un lenzuolo contro la mafia*. Palermo.
Alatri, P. 1954. *Lotte politiche in Sicilia sotto il governo della Destra (1866–74)*. Torino: Einaudi.
Albini, J. L. 1971. *The American Mafia: Genesis of a Legend*. New York: Appleton Century Crofts.
Alongi, G. [1886] 1977. *La Maffia*. Reprint, Palermo: Sellerio.
———. 1890. *La camorra. Studio di sociologia criminale*. Turin: Bocca.
———. 1904. *La Mafia*. 2d rev. ed. Palermo.
Alvaro, C. 1930. *Gente di Aspromonte*. Milan: Treves.
———. 1953. Il canto di Cosima. In *L'amata alla finestra*, 137–42. Turin: Buratti.
———. 1955a. I briganti. *Corriere della Sera*, May 18.
———. 1955b. La fibbia. *Corriere della Sera*, September 17.
Anderson, A. G. 1979. *The Business of Organized Crime: A Cosa Nostra Family*. Stanford, Calif.: Hoover Institutions Press.
Anonimo. 1990. *Uomo di rispetto*. Milan: Mondadori.
Arlacchi, P. 1988. *Mafia Business: The Mafia Ethic and the Spirit of Capitalism*. Oxford: Oxford University Press.
———. 1993. *Men of Dishonor: Inside the Sicilian Mafia: An Account of Antonino Calderone*. New York: William Morrow.
———. 1994. *Addio Cosa Nostra. La vita di Tommaso Buscetta*. Milan: Rizzoli.
———. 1995. *Il processo. Giulio Andreotti sotto accusa a Palermo*. Milan: Rizzoli.
Asprea, L. 1971. *Il previtocciolo*. Milan: Feltrinelli.
Banfield, E. C. 1958. *The Moral Basis of a Backward Society*. Glencoe, Ill.: Free Press.
Barca, F. 2001. New Trends and Policy Shifts in the Italian Mezzogiorno. *Daedalus* 130 (2): 93–113.
Barone, G. 1987. Egemonie urbane e potere locale (1812–1913). In *La Sicilia*, ed. M. Aymard and G. Giarrizzo, 157–371. Turin: Einaudi.
Barone, L. 1989–90. L'ascesa della 'Ndrangheta negli ultimi due decenni. *Meridiana* 7–8: 249–69.
Barrese, O. 1988. *I complici. Gli anni dell'antimafia*. Cosenza: Rubbettino.
Barrese, O., and G. D. Agostino. 1997. *La guerra dei sette anni. Dossier sul bandito Giuliano*. Soveria Mannelli: Rubbettino.
Battaglia, L. 1999. *Passion, Justice, Freedom: Photographs of Sicily*. New York: Aperture.
Becchi, A., and G. M. Rey. 1994. *L'economia criminale*. Bari: Laterza.
Becchi, A., and M. Turvani. 1993. *Proibito? Il mercato mondiale della droga*. Rome: Donzelli.
Bell, D. [1953] 1965. Crime as an American Way of Life. In *The End of Ideology: On the Exhaustion of Political Ideas in the Fifties*. New York: Free Press.
Benedusi, A. 1997. Cifre: Tutti i processi di mafia a Milan. *Omicron* 2: 5–6.
Benton, L. 1994. Beyond Legal Pluralism: Towards a New Approach to Law in the Informal Sector. *Social and Legal Studies* 3: 223–42.
Berger, P. L., and T. Luckmann. 1967. *The Social Construction of Reality: A Treatise in the Sociology of Knowledge*. New York: Anchor Books.
Bettini, M. 1994. *Pentito. Storia di mafia*. Turin: Bollati Boringhieri.
Bevilacqua, P. 1985. Uomini, terre, economie. In *La Calabria*, ed. P. Bevilacqua and A. Placanica. Turin: Einaudi.
Biagi, E. [1986] 1990. *Il boss è solo*. Milan: Oscar Mondadori.
Bianconi, G., and G. Savatteri. 1998. *L'attentatuni. Storie di sbirri e di mafiosi*. Milan: Baldini and Castoldi.

Billington, J. 1980. *Fire in the Minds of Men: Origins of the Revolutionary Faith*. New York: Basic Books.
Black, M. 1962. *Models and Metaphors: Studies in Language and Philosophy*. Ithaca, N.Y.: Cornell University Press.
Blakey, G. R. 1986. Definition of Organized Crime in Statutes, and Law Enforcement Administration. In *The Impact: Organized Crime Today. Report to the President and the Attorney General*, ed. President's Commisssion on Organized Crime. Washington, D.C.: U.S. Government Printing Office.
Blakey, G. R., and K. P. Roddy. 1996. Reflections on *Reeves v. Ernst & Young*: Its Meaning and Impact on Substantive, Accessory, Aiding, Abetting and Conspiracy Liability Under RICO. *American Criminal Law Review* 33: 1345–702.
Bloch, M. 1975. *Feudal Society*. London: Routledge and Kegan Paul.
Bloch, M. 1973. The Long Term and the Short Term: the Economic and Political Significance of the Morality of Kinship. In *The Character of Kinship*, ed. J. Goody. New York: Cambridge University Press.
Bloch, M., and S. Guggenheim. 1981. Compadrazgo, Baptism, and the Symbolism of a Second Birth. *Man* 16: 376–86.
Block, A. A. 1983. *East Side—West Side: Organizing Crime in New York (1930–1950)*. New Brunswick, N.J.: Transaction Books.
Block, A. A., and W. J. Chambliss. 1981. *Organizing Crime*. New York: Elsevier.
Blok, A. 1972. The Peasant and the Brigand: Social Banditry Reconsidered. *Comparative Studies in Society and History* 14: 494–503.
———. 1984. Rams and Billy-Goats: A Key to the Mediterranean Code of Honour. In *Religion, Power, and Protest in Local Communities: The Northern Shore of the Mediterranean*, ed. E. R. Wolf. Berlin: Mouton.
———. 1988. *The Mafia of a Sicilian Village, 1860–1960: A Study of Violent Peasant Entrepreneurs*. New York: Polity.
Blumenthal, R. 1988. *Last Days of the Sicilians: At War with the Mafia—The FBI Assault on the Pizza Connection*. New York: Times Books.
Bobbio, N. 1958. *Teoria della norma giuridica*. Turin: Giappichelli.
———. 1960. *Teoria dell'ordinamento giuridico*. Turin: Giappichelli.
———. 1977. Teoria e ideologia nella dottrina di Santi Romano. In *Dalla struttura alla funzione. Nuovi studi di teoria del diritto*, ed. N. Bobbio. Milan: Comunità.
———. 1990. Politica. In *Dizionario di Politica*, directed by N. Bobbio, N. Matteucci, and G. Pasquino. Milan: TEA.
Boemi, S. 1998. Libertà di mafia. *Micromega* 3: 24–32.
Bohannan, P. 1967. The Differing Realms of the Law. In *Law and Warfare: Studies in the Anthropology of Conflict*, ed. P. Bohannan. Garden City, N.Y.: Natural History Press.
Boissevain, J. 1974. *Friends of Friends: Networks, Manipulators, and Coalitions*. Oxford: Basil Blackwell.
Bok, S. 1984. *Secrets: On the Ethic of Concealment and Revelation*. New York: Oxford University Press.
Bolzoni, A., and G. D'Avanzo. 1993. *Il capo dei capi. Vita e carriera criminale di Totò Riina*. Milan: Mondadori.
Bonanno, J., with S. Lalli. 1983. *A Man of Honor: The Autobiography of Joseph Bonanno*. New York: Simon and Schuster.

Bonavolonta, J., with B. Duffy. 1996. *The Good Guys: How We Turned the FBI Round—And Finally Broke the Mob*. New York: Simon and Schuster.

Bonsanti, S., M. De Luca, and C. Stajano. 1995. *Il caso Mandalari*. Rome: Libera.

Booth, M. 1990. *The Triads: The Chinese Criminal Fraternity*. London: Grafton.

Bourdieu, P. 1991. *Language and Symbolic Power*. Cambridge: Polity.

Brancaccio di Carpino, F. 1901. *Tre mesi nella Vicaria di Palermo nel 1860*. Naples: Ruggiano.

Brancato, F. 1986. *La mafia nell'opinione pubblica e nelle inchieste dall'Unità d'Italia al fascismo. Studio storico elaborato per incarico della Commissione Parlamentare d'inchiesta sul fenomeno della mafia in Sicilia*. Cosenza: Pellegrini.

Buscetta, T., with S. Lodato. 1999. *La mafia ha vinto. Intervista di Saverio Lodato*. Milan: Mondadori.

Brögger, J. 1968. Conflict Resolution, and the Role of Bandit in Peasant Society. *Anthropological Quarterly* 41: 228–40.

Calabrò, M. A. 1991. *Le mani della mafia. Vent'anni di finanza e politica attraverso la storia del Banco Ambrosiano*. Rome: Edizioni Associate.

Calà Ulloa, P. [1838] 1961. Considerazioni sull stato economico e politico della Sicilia, Riservatissima al Ministro della Giustizia Parisio in Napoli. Reprinted in *Il riformismo borbonico nella Sicilia del Sette e dell'Ottocento. Saggi storici*, ed. E. Pontieri. Naples: Edizioni scientifiche italiane.

Cancila, O. 1984. *Così andavano le cose nel secolo sedicesimo. Quando la mafia non si chiamava mafia*. Palermo: Sellerio.

———. 1988. *Palermo*. Bari: Laterza.

Caponnetto, A. 1993. *I miei giorni a Palermo. Storie di mafia e di giustizia raccontate a Saverio Lodato*. Milan: Garzanti.

Casarrubea, G., and P. Blandano. 1991. *L'educazione mafiosa*. Palermo: Sellerio.

———. 1993. *Nella testa del serpente. Insegnanti e mafia*. Molfetta: La Meridiana.

Cascio, R. 1998. La Chiesa del silenzio. *Micromega* 1: 69–80.

Caselli, G. 1998. Il silenzio è complice. *Micromega* 3: 13–23.

Castagna, S. 1967. *Tu devi uccidere*. Ed. A. Perria. Milan: Il Momento.

Catanzaro, R. 1986. Impresa mafiosa e sistemi di regolazione sociale: Appunti sul caso siciliano. In *La legge antimafia tre anni dopo. Bilancio di un'esperienza applicativa*, ed. G. Fiandaca and S. Costantino, 177–93. Milan: Angeli.

———. 1991. *Il delitto come impresa. Storia sociale della mafia*. Milan: Rizzoli.

———. 1992. *Men of Respect. A Social History of the Sicilian Mafia*. New York: Free Press.

———. 1994a. La mafia tra mercato e stato: Una proposta di analisi. In *La mafia, le mafie*, ed. G. Fiandaca and S. Costantino. Bari: Laterza.

———. 1994b. Violent Social Regulation: Organized Crime in the Italian South. *Social and Legal Studies* 3: 267–79.

Cavadi, A., ed. 1993. *Il Vangelo e la lupara*. 2 vols. Bologna: Centro editoriale dehoniano.

———. 1994. *A scuola di antimafia*. Palermo: Centro siciliano di documentazione Giuseppe Impastato.

———. 1998. *Volontari a Palermo. Materiali per gli operatori del Centro sociale "S. Francesco Saverio."* 2d. rev. ed. Palermo: Centro siciliano di documentazione Giuseppe Impastato.

Cazzola, F. 1992. *L'Italia del pizzo. Fenomenologia della tangente quotidiana*. Turin: Einaudi.

Cazzola, F., and M. Morisi. 1996. *La mutua diffidenza. Il reciproco controllo tra magistrati e politici nella prima Repubblica*. Milan: Feltrinelli.

Centorrino, M. 1986. *L'economia mafiosa*. Soveria Mannelli: Rubbettino.

———. 1989. La mafia come impresa. *Politica ed economia* 9.

———. 1993a. Mafia e sviluppo locale. *Politica ed economia* 2.

———. 1993b. *I conti della mafia*. Soveria Mannelli: Rubbettino.

Centorrino, M., and D. Signorino. 1993. Criminalità e modelli di economia locale. In *Mercati illegali e mafie. L'economia del crimine organizzato*, ed. S. Zamagni, 75–92. Bologna: Il Mulino.

Cervigni, G. 1956. Antologia della "fibbia." *Nord e Sud* (May): 59–76.

Chilanti, F. 1952. *Da Montelepre a Viterbo*. Rome: Croce.

———. 1993. Nota per la direzione di Paese Sera del 14 giugno. In *Vita di capomafia. Memorie raccolte da Felice Chilanti*, by N. Gentile. Rome: Crescenzi Allendorf.

———. 1971. *La mafia su Roma*. Milan: Palazzi Editore.

Chin, K.-L. 1990. *Chinese Subculture and Criminality*. New York: Greenwood.

———. 1996. *Chinatown Gangs: Extortion, Enterprise, and Ethnicity*. New York: Oxford University Press.

———. 1999. *Smuggled Chinese: Clandestine Immigration to the United States*. Philadelphia: Temple University Press.

Chubb, J. 1982. *Patronage, Power, and Poverty in Southern Italy: A Tale of Two Cities*. Cambridge: Cambridge University Press.

———. 1989. *The Mafia and Politics: The Italian State under Siege*. Ithaca, N.Y.: Cornell University Press.

Ciconte, E. 1992. *'Ndrangheta dall'Unità ad oggi*. Bari: Laterza.

———. 1994. Ludovico Ligato. In *Cirillo, Ligato e Lima. Tre storie di mafia e politica*, ed. N. Tranfaglia. Bari: Laterza.

———. 1996. *Processo alla 'Ndrangheta*. Bari: Laterza.

———. 1998. *Mafia, camorra e 'Ndrangheta in Emilia-Romagna*. Rimini: Panozzo.

Ciocca, P., and A. Ulizzi. 1990. I tassi di cambi nominali e "reali" dell'Italia dall'Unità nazionale al sistema monetario europeo (1861–1979). In *Ricerche per la storia della Banca d'Italia*. Bari: Laterza.

Cipriani, G. 1993. *I mandanti. Il patto strategico tra massoneria, mafia e poteri politici*. Rome: Editori Riuniti.

Cirillo Rampolla, G. [1889] 1986. *Suicidio per mafia*. Reprint, Palermo: La Luna.

Clawson, M. A. 1989. *Constructing Brotherhood: Class, Gender, and Fraternalism*. Princeton, N.J.: Princeton University Press.

Cohen, A. 1974. *The Two-Dimensional Man: An Essay on the Anthropology of Power and Symbolism in Complex Society*. London: Routledge and Kegan Paul.

Colacino, T. V. 1885. La Fratellanza. Associazione di malfattori. *Rivista di discipline carcerarie in relazione con l'Antropologia, col Diritto Penale e con la Statistica* XV (5–6): 177–89.

Colajanni, N. 1900. *Nel regno della mafia. Dai Borboni ai Sabaudi*. Rome: Rivista popolare.

Colaprico, P., and L. Fazzo. 1995. *Manager calibro 9. Vent'anni di malavita a Milano nel racconto del pentito Saverio Morabito*. Milan: Garzanti.

Cornwell, R. 1983. *God's Banker: An Account of the Life and Death of Roberto Calvi*. London: Victor Galleancz.

Costantino, S. 1993. *A viso aperto. La resistenza antimafiosa di Capo d'Orlando*. Palermo: La Zisa.
Cressey, D. 1969. *Theft of the Nation*. New York: Harper and Row.
Crisantino, A. 2000. *Della segreta e operosa associazione. Una setta alle origini della mafia*. Palermo: Sellerio.
Crupi, P. 1992. *L'anomalia selvaggia. Camorra, mafia, picciotteria e 'Ndrangheta nella letteratura calabrese del Novecento*. Palermo: Sellerio.
Cutrera, A. [1900] 1988. *La mafia e i mafiosi: Origini e manifestazioni. Studio di sociologia criminale*. Reprint, Cerchio: Polla editore.
D'Agostini, F. 1972. *Reggio Calabria: i moti del luglio 1970–febbraio 1971*. Milan: Feltrinelli.
D'Alessandro, E. 1959. *Brigantaggio e mafia in Sicilia*. Messina: D'Anna.
Dalla Chiesa, N. 1978. *Il potere mafioso. Economia e ideologia*. Milan: Mazzotta.
———. 1984. *Delitto imperfetto. Il generale—la mafia—la società italiana*. Milan: Mondadori.
Da Passano, M., ed. 1981. *I moti di Palermo del 1866. Verbali della Commissione parlamentare d'inchiesta*. Rome: Camera dei Deputati.
Davis, J. 1977. *People of the Mediterranean: An Essay in Comparative Social Anthropology*. London: Routledge and Kegan Paul.
Davis, J. A. 1988. *Conflict and Control. Law and Order in Nineteenth-Century Italy*. London: Macmillan.
De Francisci, I. 1996. L'atteggiarsi delle associazioni mafiose sulla base delle esperienze professionali acquisite. Report presented to the conference organized by the Consiglio Superiore della Magistrura: "I delitti di criminalità organizzata: Profili criminologici, sostanziali e processuali." Frascati, December 12.
Della Porta, D. 1992. *Lo scambio occulto. Casi di corruzione politica in Italia*. Bologna: Il Mulino.
Della Porta, D., and A. Vannucci. 1994. *Corruzione politica e amministrazione pubblica. Risorse, meccanismi, attori*. Bologna: Il Mulino.
De Mauro, M. 1962a. La confessione del dott. Melchiorre Allegra: Come io, medico, diventai mafioso. *L'Ora*, January 22–23.
———. 1962b. La confessione del dott. Melchiorre Allegra: La mafia mi ordinò di entrare in politica. *L'Ora*, January 23–24.
———. 1962c. La confessione del dott. Melchiorre Allegra: Tutti gli uomini della cosca. *L'Ora*, January 24–25.
Di Bella, M. P. 1980. Note sul concetto di onore nelle società mediterranee. *Rassegna Italiana di Sociologia* 4: 607–16.
———. 1983. L'onore in Sicilia e dell'onore nella mafia. Convergenze e divergenze. In *Mafia e potere. Società civile, organizzazione mafiosa ed esercizio dei poteri nel Mezzogiorno contemporanee*, ed. S. Di Bella. Soveria Mannelli: Rubbettino.
Di Forti, F. 1982. *Per una psicoanalisi della mafia*. Verona: Bertani.
Di Lello, G. 1994. *Giudici*. Palermo: Sellerio.
Di Lorenzo, S. 1996. *La Grande Madre Mafia. Psicoanalisi del potere mafioso*. Parma: Pratiche Editrice.
Di Maria, F., and G. Lavanco. 1995. *A un passo dall'inferno. Sentire mafioso e obbedienza criminale*. Florence: Giunti.
Di Matteo, A., F. Imbergamo, and L. Tescaroli. 2001. Perché mai un mafioso dovrebbe pentirsi? *Micromega* 2: 203–15.

Duggan, C. 1989. *Fascism and the Mafia.* New Haven, Conn.: Yale University Press.

Durkheim, E. 1964. *The Division of Labor in Society.* New York: Free Press.

———. [1899–1900] 1984. Deux lois de l'évolution pénale. *L'année sociologique* 4: 65–95. Reprinted as The Evolution of Punishment, in *Durkheim and the Law*, ed. S. Lukes and A. Scull. London: Basil Blackwell.

Duyne, P. C. van. 1997. Organized Crime, Corruption, and Power. *Crime, Law, and Social Change* 26: 201–38.

Eco, U. [1971] 1993. "Beati Paoli" e l'ideologia del romanzo "popolare." Introduction to L. Natoli (W. Galt), *I Beati Paoli.* Reprint, Palermo: Flaccovio.

Eisenstadt, S. N. 1956. Ritualized Personal Relations: Blood Brotherhood, Compadre, etc.: Some Comparative Hypotheses and Suggestions. *Man* 96: 90–95.

———. 1971. *Traditional Patrimonialism and Modern Neopatrimonialism.* Beverly Hills: Sage.

Eisenstadt, S. N., and B. Giesen. 1995. The Construction of Collective Identity. *Archives Europeénnes de Sociologie* XXXVI: 72–102.

Eisenstadt, S. N., and L. Roniger. 1980. Patron-Client Relationship as a Model of Structuring Social Exchange. *Society for Comparative Study of Society and History*: 42–77.

———. 1984. *Patrons, Clients, and Friends: Interpersonal Relations and the Structure of Trust in Society.* Cambridge: Cambridge University Press.

Eliade, M. 1959. *Initiation, rites, sociétés secrètes. Naissances mystiques.* Paris: Gallimard.

Evans-Pritchard, E. E. [1933] 1963. Zande Blood-Brotherhood. In *Essays in Social Anthropology*: 131–61. London: Faber and Faber.

Falcionelli, A. 1937. *Les societies secretès italiennes.* Paris: Payot.

Falcone, G. 1989. Intervista di Giovanna Fiume. *Micromega* 5: 199–209.

———, with Padovani, M. 1993. *Men of Honour: The Truth about the Mafia.* London: Warner.

Falcone, G., and G. Turone. 1982. Tecniche di indagine in materia di mafia. Report presented to the conference "Riflessioni ed esperienze sul fenomeno mafioso," organized by the Consiglio Superiore della Magistrura. Castelgandolfo, June 4–6.

Falcone, G. 1983. Strutture organizzative, rituali e *"baccagghiu"* della 'Ndrangheta. In *Mafia e Potere. Società civile, organizzazione mafiosa ed esercizio dei poteri nel Mezzogiorno contemporaneo,* ed. S. Di Bella. Soveria Mannelli: Rubbettino.

Falk Moore, S. 1978. *Law as Process: An Anthropological Approach.* London: Routledge and Kegan Paul.

Falzone, G. 1987. *Storia della mafia.* Palermo: Flaccovio.

Fantozzi, P. 1993. *Politica, clientela e regolazione sociale. Il Mezzogiorno nella questione politica italiana.* Soveria Mannelli: Rubbettino.

Feo, F. 1999. Fronte del porto. *Narcomafie* 7(2): 4–7.

Fiandaca, G. 1994. La mafia come ordinamento giuridico. Utilità e limiti di un paradigma. *Segno* 155: 23–35.

Fiandaca, G., and S. Costantino. 1990. La mafia negli anni '80, Il fenomeno mafioso tra vecchi e nuovi paradigmi. *Sociologia del diritto* 3: 75–96.

Fiume, G. 1984. *Le bande armate in Sicilia (1819–49). Violenza ed organizzazione del potere.* Palermo: Annali della Facoltà di Lettere e Filosofia dell'Università di Palermo.

———. 1986. Introduzione to G. Cirillo Rampolla. *Suicidio per mafia,* ed. G. Fiume. Palermo: La Luna.

———. 1991. Bandits, Violence, and the Organization of Power in Sicily in the Early Nineteenth Century. In *Society and Politics in the Age of the Risorgimento, Essays in Honour of Denis Mack Smith*, ed. J. A. Davis and P. Ginsborg. Cambridge: Cambridge University Press.

———, ed. 1989. *Onore e storia nelle società mediterranee*. Palermo: La Luna.

Fong, M. L. 1981. *The Sociology of Secret Societies: A Study of Chinese Secret Societies in Singapore and Peninsular Malaysia*. Oxford: Oxford University Press.

Forgione, F., and P. Mondani. 1994. *Oltre la cupola, Massoneria, mafia, politica*. Milan: Rizzoli.

Fortes, M. 1962. Ritual and Office in Tribal Society. In *Essays on the Ritual of Social Relations*, ed. M. Gluckmann. Manchester: Manchester University Press.

———. 1970. *Kinship and the Social Order. The Legacy of Lewis Henry Morgan*. London: Routledge and Kegan Paul.

Fortes, M., and E. E. Evans-Pritchard, eds. 1940. *African Political Systems*. London: Oxford University Press.

Foster, G. M. 1953. Cofradìa and Compadrazo in Spain and Spanish America. *Southwestern Journal of Anthropology* 9 (spring): 1–28.

Foucault, M. 1980. *Power/Knowledge: Selected Interviews and Other Writings (1972–1977)*, ed. C. Gordon. New York: Pantheon.

Franchetti, L. [1876] 1993. *Condizioni politiche ed amministrative della Sicilia*. Reprint, Rome: Donzelli.

Fentress, J. 2000. *Rebels and Mafiosi: Death in a Sicilian Landscape*. Ithaca, N.Y.: Cornell University Press.

Fresolone G., and R. J. Wagman. 1994. *Blood Oath*. New York: Simon and Schuster.

Gambetta, D. 1993. *The Sicilian Mafia: The Business of Private Protection*. Cambridge: Harvard University Press.

Gambetta, D., and P. Reuter. 1995. Conspiracy among the Many: The Mafia in Legitimate Industries. In *The Economics of Organized Crime*, ed G. Fiorentini and S. Peltzman. New York: Cambridge University Press.

Gambino, S. 1975. *La mafia in Calabria*. Reggio Calabria: Edizioni Parallelo 38.

———. 1976. *Mafia. La lunga notte della Calabria*. Serra San Bruno: Edizioni quaderni Calabria-oggi.

———. 1977. Il carcere non mangia gli uomini. Biografia giudiziaria di Don Mico Tripodo. *Quaderni del Mezzogiorno e delle isole* 42–43: 91–100.

Gennep, A., van. 1960. *The Rites of Passage*. Chicago: University of Chicago Press.

Gentile, N. 1993. *Vita di capomafia. Memorie raccolte da Felice Chilanti*. Rome: Crescenzi Allendorf.

Georgiou, P. 1973. The Goal Paradigm and Notes Toward a Counter Paradigm. *Administrative Science Quarterly* 18: 291–310.

Giannini, M. S. 1988. Le società segrete. In *Trattato di criminologia, medicina criminologica e psichiatria forense*, ed. F. Ferracuti, vol. IX: *Forme di organizzazioni criminali e terrorismo*. Milan: Giuffré.

Giarrizzo, G. 1989. La Sicilia dal Cinquecento all'Unità d'Italia. In *La Sicilia dal Vespro all'Unità d'Italia*, ed. V. D'Alessandro and G. Giarrizzo: 99–783. Turin: UTET.

———. 1994. *Massoneria e Illuminismo nell'Europa del Settecento*. Venice: Marsilio.

von Gierke, O. [1868] 1990. *Community in Historical Perspective. A Translation of Selections from "Das deutsche Genossenschaftsrecht," Principally from vol. I: "Rechtsgeschichte der deutschen Genossenschaft,"* ed. A. Black. Cambridge and New York: Cambridge University Press.

Giesen, B. 1989. Symbolic, Institutional, and Social-Structural Differentiation. In *Social Structure and Culture*, ed. H. Haferkamp, 67–87. Berlin: De Gruyter.

———. 1991. *Die Entdinglichung des Sozialen. Eine evolutionstheoretische Perspektive auf die Postmoderne.* Frankfurt am Main: Surkhamp.

———. 1993. *Die Intellektuellen und die Nation.* Frankfurt am Main: Surkhamp.

———. 1995. Kollektive Identität und Exclusion. In *Soziale Welt und Soziologische Praxis. Soziologie als Beruf und Programm*, ed. D. Bögenhold, D. Hoffmeister, C. Jasper, E. Kemper, and G. Solf. Göttingen: Otto Schwartz.

Ginsborg, P. 1998. *L'Italia del tempo presente. Famiglia, societa civile, Stato, 1980–1996.* Turin: Einaudi.

Gouldner, A. W. 1960. The Norm of Reciprocity: A Preliminary Statement. *American Sociological Review* 25: 161–78.

Grasso, T. 1992. *Contro il racket. Come opporsi al ricatto mafioso.* Bari: Laterza.

———. 1998. I fondi antiusura e antiracket. In *I soldi della mafia. Rapporto '98*, ed. L. Violante. Bari: Laterza.

Graziano, L. 1973. Patron-Client Relationship in Southern Italy. *European Journal of Political Research* 1: 3–34.

———. 1978. Center-Periphery Relations and the Italian Crisis: The Problem of Clientelism. In *Territorial Politics in Industrial Nations*, ed. S. Tarrow, P. J. Katzenstein, L. Graziano. New York: Praeger.

———. 1980. *Clientelismo e sistema politico. Il caso dell'Italia.* Milan: Angeli.

Gribaudi, G. 1980. *Mediatori. Antropologia del potere democristiano nel Mezzogiorno.* Turin: Rosenberg and Sellier.

Guderman, S. 1973. Spiritual Relationships and Selecting a Godparent. *Man* 10: 221–37.

Habermas, J. 1989. *The Structural Transformation of the Public Sphere: An Inquiry into a Category of Bourgeois Society.* Cambridge: MIT Press.

Hagan, F. 1983. The Organized Crime Continuum: A Further Specification of a New Conceptual Model. *Criminal Justice Review* 8 (spring): 52–57.

Hahn, A. 1997. Geheimnis. In *Vom Menschen. Handbuch Historische Anthropologie*, ed. C. Wulf. Basel: Beltz.

Halevi, R. 1984. *Les loges maçonniques dans la France de l'Ancien Régime aux origines de la sociabilité démocratique.* Paris: Armand Colin.

Haller, M. 1970. Urban Crime and Criminal Justice: The Chicago Case. *Journal of American History* 57: 619–35.

———. 1990. Illegal Enterprise: A Theoretical and Historical Interpretation. *Criminology* 28(2): 207–35.

Hart, H. L. A. 1994. *The Concept of Law.* 2d ed. Oxford: Clarendon.

Hawkins, G. 1969. God and the Mafia. *Public Interest* 14 (winter): 24–51.

Herzfeld, M. 1980. Honor and Shame: Problems in the Comparative Analysis of Moral Systems. *Man N.S.* 15(2): 339–51.

———. 1987. *Anthropology through the Looking-Glass: Critical Ethnography in the Margins of Europe.* Cambridge: Cambridge University Press.

Hess, H. 1973. *Mafia and Mafiosi: The Structure of Power.* Farnborough: Saxon House.

———. 1995. Parastato e capitalismo corsaro. La mafia siciliana dal 1943 al 1993. *Incontri meridionali* ?: 41–71.

Hobbs, D. 1994. Professional and Organized Crime in Britain. In *The Oxford Handbook of Criminology*, ed. M. Maguire, R. Morgan, and R. Reiner. Oxford: Clarendon Press.

Hobsbawm, E. J. 1974. *Primitive Rebels: Studies in Archaic Forms of Social Movement in the Nineteenth and Twentieth Centuries.* Manchester: Manchester University Press.

Hocart, A. M. 1935. Blood-Brotherhood. *Man* 35 (August): 126–28.

Hoebel, E. A. 1954. *The Law of Primitive Man.* Cambridge: Harward University Press.

Ianni, F., with E. A. Reuss-Ianni. 1973. *Family Business: Kinships and Social Control in Organized Crime.* New York: Russell Sage Foundation.

Ingroia, A. 1993. *L'associazione di tipo mafioso.* Milan: Giuffré.

———. 2001a. Convivere con la mafia? *Micromega* 4: 234–9.

———. 2001b. Legge sui pentiti: Luci e ombre. *Narcomafie* 9(3): 19–20.

Ishino, I. 1953. The *Oyabun-Kobun*: A Japanese Ritual Kinship Institution. *American Anthropologist* 55: 695–707.

Istituto Nazionali di Statistica Annuel. Annuario statistiche giudiziarie penali. Rome: Istat.

Jacob, M. C. 1991. *Living the Enlightenment: Freemasonry and Politics in Eighteenth Century Europe.* Oxford: Oxford University Press.

Jacobs, J. B. 1999. *Gotham Unbound: How New York City Was Liberated from the Clutches of Cosa Nostra.* New York: New York University Press.

Jacobs, J. B., and L. P. Gouldin. 1999. Cosa Nostra: The Final Chapter? In *Crime and Justice: A Review of Research*, vol. 25, ed. M. Tonry. Chicago: University of Chicago Press.

Jacobs, J. B., C. Panarella, and J. Worthington. 1994. *Busting the Mob.* New York: Oxford University Press.

Jamieson, A. 1994. The Transnational Dimension of Italian Organized Crime. *Transnational Organized Crime* 1(2): 151–72.

———. 2000. *The Antimafia: Italy's Fight against Organized Crime.* Basingstoke: Macmillan.

Jones, M. 1967. Freemasonry. In *Secret Societies*, ed. N. Mackenzie. London: Aldus.

Joutsen, M. 1998. Options for the (Draft) United Nations Convention Against Transantional Organized Crime. Paper presented at the Multidiscplinary Meeting of Academics on the Subject of Organized Crime in Europe. Brussels, May 18–19.Kefauver, E. 1951. *Crime in America.* New York: Doubleday.

Kefauver, E. C. 1951. *Crime in America.* Garden City, N.Y.: Doubleday.

Kelly, R. J. 1999. *The Upperworld and the Underworld: Case Studies of Racketeeering and Business Infiltrations in the United States.* New York: Kluwer Academic and Plenum.

Kenney, D. J., and J. O. Finckenauer. 1995. *Organized Crime in America.* Belmont, Calif.: Wadsworth.

Kerner, H. J. 1973. *Professionelles und Organisiertes Verbrechen. Versuch einer Bestandsaufnahme und Bericht über neuere Entwicklungstendenzen in der Bundesrepublik Deutschland und in der Niederlanden.* Wiesbaden: BKA.

Kerner, H. J., and J. A. Mack. 1975. *The Crime Industry.* Lexington, Mass.: Lexington Books.

Kertzer, D. I. 1988. *Ritual, Politics, and Power.* New Haven, Conn.: Yale University Press.

Knight, S. 1985. *The Brotherhood.* London: Panther.

Koselleck, R. 1988. *Critique and Crisis: Enlightenment and the Pathogenesis of Modern Society.* London: Berg.

Labate, V. 1909. *Un decennio di Carboneria in Sicilia (1821–31)*. Rome: Società Editrice Dante Alighieri.

La Duca, R. [1971] 1993. Storia e leggenda de "I Beati Paoli." Historical and Bio-Bibliographical Notes to L. Natoli (W. Galt), *I Beati Paoli*. Reprint, Palermo: Flaccovio.

La Fontaine, J. 1985. *Initiation*. Harmondsworth: Penguin.

La Licata, F. 1993. *Storia di Giovanni Falcone*. Milan: Rizzoli.

Landesco, J. [1929] 1968. *Illinois Crime Survey 1929*—Part III, reprinted as *Organized Crime in Chicago*. Chicago: University of Chicago Press.

Lane, F. C. 1966. *Venice and Its History, The Collected Papers of F. C. Lane*. Baltimore: John Hopkins University Press.

Lasco, F. 1999. Attenti a quel duopolio. *Narcomafie* 7(2): 13–16.

Lestingi, F. 1880. La mafia in Sicilia. *Archivio di psichiatria, antropologia criminale e scienze penali* 1: 362–66.

———. 1884. L'associazione della Fratellanza nella provincia di Girgenti. *Archivio di psichiatria, antropologia criminale e scienze penali* 5: 452–63.

Lewis, R. 1985. Serious Business: The Global Heroin Economy. In *Big Deal: The Politics of the Illicit Drug Business*, by A. Henman, R. Lewis, and T. Malyon. London: Pluto.

Licandro, A., and Varano, A. 1993. *La città dolente. Confessione di un sindaco corrotto*. Turin: Einaudi.

Li Causi, L., and M. Cassano. 1993. Antropologia, mafia e scienze sociali. Riflessioni dall'esterno. *Ossimori* 3: 10–19.

Light, I. 1977. The Ethnic Vice Industry, 1880–1944. *American Sociological Review* 42 (June): 464–79.

Llewellyn, K. N., and E. A. Hoebel. 1941. *The Cheyenne Way: Conflict and Case Law in Primitive Jurisprudence*. Norman: University of Oklahoma Press.

Lodato, S. 1994a. *Quindici anni di mafia. La guerra che lo Stato può ancora vincere*. Milan: Rizzoli.

———. 1994b. *Dall'altare contro la mafia*. Milan: Rizzoli.

———. 1999. *Ho ucciso Giovanni Falcone. La confessione di Giovanni Brusca*. Milan: Mondadori.

Lodato, S., and P. Grasso. 2001. *La mafia invisibile: La nuova strategia di Cosa Nostra*. Milan: Mondadori.

Lo Forte, G. 1996. L'atteggiarsi delle associazioni mafiose sulla base delle esperienze processuali acquisite: La mafia siciliana. Report presented to the conference organized by the Consiglio Superiore della Magistrura: "I delitti di criminalità organizzata: Profili criminologici, sostanziali e processuali." Frascati, May 13–17.

Lombardi Satriani, L. 1971. *Reggio Calabria. Rivolta e strumentalizzazione*. Vibo Valentia: Qualecultura.

Lombroso, C. 1878. *L'uomo delinquente in rapporto all'antropologia, giurisprudenza e alle discipline carcerarie*. Turin: Bocca.

Lorenzoni, G. 1910. Relazione del delegato tecnico professor Giovanni Lorenzoni. In *Inchiesta parlamentare sulle condizioni dei contadini nelle province meridionali e in Sicilia*, vol. 6: *Sicilia*, tome 1. Rome: n.p.

Lo Schiavo, G. G. 1955. Nel regno della mafia. *Processi* 5 (January): 21–25.

———. 1964. *Nel regno della mafia*. Rome: Bianco.

Lowrie, K. 2001. Eastern European Organized Crime Conditions in the United States.

Paper presented at the "High-Level Expert Meeting on East European Organized Crime." Europol: The Hague, November 29–30.

Lucentini, U. 1994. *Paolo Borsellino: Il valore di una vita*. Milan: Mondadori.

Luhmann, N. 1970. *Soziologische Aufklärung*. Stuttgart: Westdeutscher.

———. 1979. *Trust and Power: Two Works*. Chichester: Wiley.

———. 1990. The Paradox of System Differentiation and the Evolution of Society. In *Differentiation Theory and Social Change: Comparative and Historical Perspectives*, ed. C. A. Jeffrey and P. Colomy. New York: Columbia University Press.

Lupo, S. 1988. "Il tenebroso sodalizio." Un rapporto sulla mafia palermitana di fine Ottocento. *Studi storici* 29(2): 463–89.

———. 1993. *Storia della mafia dalle origini ai giorni nostri*. Rome: Donzelli.

———. 1994. Pentitismo, ieri ed oggi. In *La mafia, le mafie*, ed. G. Fiandaca and S. Costantino. Bari: Laterza.

———. 1996a. *Andreotti, la mafia, la storia d'Italia*. Rome: Donzelli.

———. 1996b. *Storia della mafia dalle origini ai giorni nostri*. Rev., and exp. ed. Rome: Donzelli.

Lupsha, P. A. 1985. La Cosa Nostra in Drug Trafficking. Unpublished paper.

Lynch, G. E. 1987. RICO: The Crime of Being a Criminal. *Columbia Law Review* 87: 661–764, 920–84.

———. 1990. A Conceptual, Practical, and Political Guide to RICO Reform. *Vanderbilt Law Review* 43(3): 769–803.

Maas, P. 1969. *The Valachi Papers*. New York: Bantam.

———. 1997. *Underboss: Sammy the Bull Gravano's Story of Life in the Mafia*. New York: HarperCollins.

Mack Smith, D. 1968. *History of Modern Sicily*. London: Chatto and Windus.

Mackenzie, N. 1967. Introduction to *Secret Societies*, ed. N. Mackenzie. London: Aldus.

Magatti, M. 1996. *Corruzione politica e società italiana*. Bologna: Il Mulino.

Maggi, M. A. 1996. *Dall'impresa familiare all'organizzazione complessa: Il caso di un'azienda criminale nella città di Milano*. Tesi di laurea presentata alla Facoltà di Scienze Politiche dell'Univerisità degli Studi di Milano.

Maine, H. S. 1887. *Ancient Law: Its Connection with the Early History of Society and Its Relations to Modern Ideas*. 11th ed. London: John Murray.

Malafarina, L. 1983. 'Ndrangheta ieri ed oggi: Dalla chiusura della "vallate" al superprocesso dei 260 della mafia della Piana di Gioia Tauro. In *Mafia e Potere. Società civile, organizzazione mafiosa ed esercizio dei poteri nel Mezzogiorno contemporaneo*, ed. S. Di Bella. Soveria Mannelli: Rubbettino.

———. 1986. *La 'Ndrangheta. Il codice segreto, la storia, i miti, i riti e i personaggi*. Reggio Calabria: Casa del Libro.

Malinowski, B. 1961. *Crime and Custom in Savage Society*. London: Kegan Paul.

Mangiameli, R. 1987. La regione in guerra (1943–50). In *La Sicilia*, ed. M. Aymard and G. Giarrizzo. Turin: Einaudi.

———. 1990. Banditi e mafiosi dopo l'Unità. *Meridiana* 7–8: 73–118.

Maniscalco, M. L. 1994. Mafia e segretezza, Meccanismi sociali della segretezza e criminalità organizzata. *Quaderni di Sociologia*: 93–109.

March, J. G. 1981. Decisions in Organizations and Theories of Choice. In *Perspectives on*

Organization Design and Behavior, ed. A. H. Van de Ven and W. F. Joyce. New York: Wiley.

Marino, G. C. 1986. *L'opposizione mafiosa. Mafia politica stato liberale.* Palermo: Flaccovio.

———. 1988. *L'ideologia sicilianista.* Palermo: Flaccovio.

Marmo, M. 1988. La camorra e lo stato liberale. In *Camorra e criminalità organizzata in Campania*, ed. F. Barbagallo. Naples: Liguori.

———. 1989. L'onore dei violenti, l'onore della vittime. Un'estorsione camorrista del 1862 a Napoli. In *Onore e storia nelle società mediterranee*, ed. Giovanna Fiume. Palermo: La Luna.

Martino, P. 1983. Storia della parola 'ndranghita. In *Le ragioni della mafia. Studi e ricerche di "Quaderni calabresi,"* by F. Faeta et al. Milan: Jaca.

———. 1988. *Per la storia della 'Ndrangheta.* Rome.

Massari, M. 1998. Gli insediamenti mafiosi nelle aree "non tradizionali." *Quaderni di sociologia* 42(18): 5–27.

———. 2001. La criminalità mafiosa nell'Italia centro-settentrionale. In *Mafie nostre e mafie loro. Criminalità organizzata italiana e straniera nel Centro-Nord*, ed. S. Becucci and M. Massari. Milan: Comunità.

Mastropaolo, A. 1993. Tra politica e mafia. Storia breve di un latifondo elettorale. In *Far politica in Sicilia. Deferenza, consenso, protesta*, ed. M. Morisi. Milan: Feltrinelli.

Mauss, M. 1990. *The Gift: The Form and Reason for Exchange in Archaic Societies.* London: Routledge.

McClennan, J. 1962. *Crime without Punishment.* New York: Duell, Sloane, and Pearce.

Melari, F. 1885. *Il ventre di Reggio. Osservazioni sull'igiene pubblica e proposta di risanamento della città di Reggio Calabria.* Reggio Calabria: n.p.

Meligrana, M. 1983. Giuridicità popolare e potere mafioso. L'istituto della vendetta. In *Mafia e potere. Società civile, organizzazione mafiosa ed esercizio dei poteri nel Mezzogiorno contemporaneo*, ed. S. Di Bella: 239–250. Soveria Mannelli: Rubbettino.

Mendelson, E. M. 1967. Primitive Secret Societies. In *Secret Societies*, ed. N. Mackenzie. London: Aldus.

Michels, R. [1912] 1962. *Political Parties: A Sociological Study of the Oligarchical Tendencies of Modern Democracies.* New York: Free Press.

Mignosi, E. 1993. *Il signore sia coi boss. Storie di preti fedeli alla mafia e di padrini timorosi di Dio.* Palermo: Arbor.

Mintz, S. W., and E. R. Wolf. 1950. An Analysis of Ritual Co-parenthood (*Compadrazgo*). *Southwestern Journal of Anthropology* 6 (winter): 341–68.

Monnier, M. [1863] 1994. *La camorra. Notizie storiche raccolte e documentate.* Reprint, Lecce: Argo.

Montalto, S. 1973. *La famiglia Montalbano.* Chiaravalle Centrale: Frama's Edizioni.

Montanaro, S., and S. Ruotolo, eds. 1995. *La vera storia d'Italia. Interrogatori, testimonianze, riscontri, analisi. Giancarlo Caselli e i suoi sostituti ricostruiscono gli ultimi venti anni di storia italiana.* Naples: Liguori.

Montanelli, I. 1973. *Pantheon minore.* Milan: Mondadori.

Monzini, P. 1997. L'estorsione nei sistemi di criminalità organizzata. *Quaderni di sociologia* 60(11): 134–60.

———. 1999. *Gruppi criminali a Napoli e a Marisglia. La delinquenza organizzata nella storia delle due città (1820–1990).* Catanzaro: Meridiana Libri.

Moore, M. H. 1974. *The Effective Regulation of an Illicit Market in Heroin*. Lexington, Mass.: Lexington Books.

Moore, W. H. 1974. *The Kefauver Committee and the Politics of Crime, 1950–1962*. Columbia: University of Missouri Press.

Morgan, G. 1986. *Images of Organization*. Beverly Hills: Sage.

Mori, C. 1993. *Con la mafia ai ferri corti*. Naples: Flavio Pagano Editore.

Mosca, G. [1900] 1949. Che cosa è la mafia. In *Partiti e sindacati nella crisi del regime parlamentare*. Bari: Laterza.

Murray, D., in cooperation with Q. Baoqi. 1994. *The Origins of the Tiandihui. The Chinese Triads in Legend and History*. Stanford, Calif.: Stanford University Press.

Natoli, L. [1908–9] 1993. *I Beati Paoli*. Reprint, Palermo: Flaccovio.

Naylor, R. T. 1987. *Hot Money and the Politics of Debt*. New York: Simon and Schuster.

———. 1995. Loose Cannons: Cover Commerce and Underground Finance in the Modern Arms Black Market. *Crime, Law, and Social Change* 22: 1–57.

———. 1996. The Underworld of Gold. *Crime, Law, and Social Change* 25: 191–241.

Nelken, D. 1995. Review of *The Sicilian Mafia: The Business of Private Protection*, by D. Gambetta. *British Journal of Criminology* 35(2): 287–89.

Nelli, H. S. 1976. *The Business of Crime: Italians and Syndicate Crime in the United States*. New York: Oxford University Press.

Nicaso, A. 1990. *Alle origini della 'Ndrangheta. La picciotteria*. Soveria Mannelli: Rubbettino.

Nicastro, S. 1961. *Dal Quarantotto al Sessanta*. Trapani: Vento.

Nicotri, P. 1996. *Mafioso per caso. Carmelo Mutoli: Dalla "fuitina" nel cuore della mafia alla perdita del figlio per "infamia."* Rome: Kaos Edizioni.

Nisticò, V. 1964. Introduction to *Rapporto sulla mafia*, by F. Chilanti and M. Farinella. Palermo: Flaccovio.

Novacco, D. 1972. *Mafia ieri, mafia oggi*. Milan: Feltrinelli.

Nozick, R. 1974. *Anarchy, State, and Utopia*. Oxford: Blackwell.

Ownby, D. 1996. *Brotherhoods and Secret Societies in Early and Mid-Qing China: The Formation of a Tradition*. Stanford: Stanford University Press.

Ownby, D., and M. Somers Heidhues, eds. 1993. *"Secret Societies" Reconsidered: Perspectives on the Social History of Modern South China and Southeast Asia*. Armonk: M. E. Sharpe.

Paoli, L. 1993. Criminalità organizzata e finanza internazionale. *Rassegna Italiana di Sociologia* 34(3): 391–423.

———. 1994. An Underestimated Criminal Phenomenon: The Calabrian 'Ndrangheta. *European Journal of Crime, Criminal Law, and Criminal Justice* 2(3): 212–38.

———. 1996. The Integration of the Italian Crime Scene. *European Journal of Crime, Criminal Law and Criminal Justice* 3(3): 131–62.

———. 1997. The Pledge to Secrecy: Culture, Structure, and Action of Mafia Associations. Ph.D. diss., European University Institute.

———. 1998a. The *Pentiti*'s Contribution to the Conceptualization of the Mafia Phenomenon. In *The New European Criminology: Crime and Social Order in Europe*, ed. V. Ruggiero, N. South, and I. Taylor. London: Routledge.

———. 1998b. Associazioni mafiose e contratti di status. *Quaderni di sociologia* 62(18): 73–95.

———. 1998c. Droga-Traffici. In *Mafia: 150 anni di storia e storie*, ed. Cliomedia Officina. CD-ROM. Rome: La Repubblica.

———. 1999a. Die italienische Mafia: Paradigma oder Spezialfall der organisierten Kriminalität? *Monatliche Zeitschrift für Kriminologie und Strafrechtreform* 6: 425–40.

———. 1999b. The Future of Sicilian and Calabrian Organized Crime. In *Organized Crime: Uncertainties and Dilemmas*, ed. S. Einstein and M. Amir. Chicago: Office of International Criminal Justice.

———. 2000a. Il crimine organizzato in Italia e in Germania. In *Il crimine organizzato come fenomeno transnazionale: Manifestazioni empiriche, prevenzione e repressione in Italia, Germania e Spagna*, ed. V. Militello, L. Paoli, and J. Arnold. Freiburg: Edition Iuscrim.

———. 2000b. *Pilot Project to Describe and Analyse Local Drug Markets—First Phase Final Report: Illegal Drug Markets in Frankfurt and Milan*, Lisbon: EMCDDA. Available online: www.emcdda.org/multimedia/project_reports/situation/local_drug_report.pdf. Accessed November 2001.

———. 2001a. *Illegal Drug Trade in Russia: A Research Project Commissioned by the United Nations Office for Drug Control and Crime Prevention*. Freiburg: edition iuscrim.

———. 2002. The Paradoxes of Organised Crime. *Crime, Law, and Social Change* 37 (1): 51–97.

Parini, E. G. 1999. *Mafia, politica e società civile. Due casi in Calabria*. Soveria Mannelli: Rubbettino.

Peristiany, J. G. 1974. Introduction to *Honour and Shame: The Values of Mediterranean Society*, ed. J. G. Peristiany. Chicago: Midway Reprint.

Perrow, C. 1961. The Analysis of Goals in Complex Organizations. *American Sociological Review* 26: 854–66.

Peterson, V. W. 1983. *The Mob: Two Hundred Years of Organized Crime in New York*. Ottawa, Ill.: Green Hill.

Pezzino, P. 1987. Stato violenza società. Nascita e sviluppo del paradigma mafioso. In *La Sicilia*, ed. M. Aymard and G. Giarrizzo. Turin: Einaudi.

———. 1988. Onorata società o industria della violenza? Mafia e mafiosi tra realtà storica e paradigmi sicilianisti. *Studi storici* 29(2): 437–62.

———. 1990a. *Una certa reciprocità di favori. Mafia e modernizzazione violenta nella Sicilia postunitaria*. Milan: Angeli.

———. 1990b. La tradizione rivoluzionaria siciliana e l'invenzione della mafia. *Meridiana* 7–8: 45–71.

———. 1992a. *Il Paradiso abitato dai diavoli. Società, élites, istituzioni nel Mezzogiorno contemporaneo*. Milan: Angeli.

———. 1992b. *La congiura dei pugnalatori. Un caso politico-giudiziario alle origini della mafia*. Venice: Marsilio.

———. 1993. La mafia siciliana come "industria della violenza." Caratteri storici ed elementi di continuità. *Dei delitti e delle pene* 2: 67–79.

———. 1996. Mafia e politica una questione nazionale. *Passato e presente* XIV (38): 7–23.

———. 1997. La mafia. In *I luoghi della memoria. Strutture ed eventi dell'Italia unita*, ed. M. Isnenghi. Bari: Laterza.

———, ed. 1995. *Mafia: Industria della violenza. Scritti e documenti inediti sulla mafia dalle origini ai giorni nostri*. Florence: La Nuova Italia.

Pigliaru, A. 1959. *La vendetta barbaricina come ordinamento giuridico.* Milan: Giuffré.
Piselli, F. 1988. Circuiti politici mafiosi nel secondo dopoguerra. *Meridiana* (January): 125–66.
Piselli, F., and G. Arrighi. 1985. Parentela, clientela e comunità. In *La Calabria*, ed. P. Bevilacqua and A. Placanica. Turin: Einaudi.
Pistone, J. D., with R. Woodley. 1988. *Donnie Brasco: My Undercover Life in the Mafia.* New York: New American Library.
Pitrè, G. [1889] 1993. *Usi e costumi, credenze e pregiudizi del popolo siciliano.* Reprint, Catania: Clio.
Pitt-Rivers, J. 1968. Honor. In *International Encyclopedia of the Social Sciences*, ed. D. L. Sills, vol. 6. London: Macmillan and Free Press.
———. 1973. The Kith and the Kin. In *The Character of Kinship*, ed. J. Goody. New York: Cambridge University Press.
Pizzorno, A. 1987. I mafiosi come classe media violenta. *Polis* 1(2): 195–204.
———. 1992. La corruzione nel sistema politico. Introduction to *Lo scambio occulto. Casi di corruzione politica in Italia*, by D. della Porta. Bologna: Mulino.
Poggi, G. 1991. *The State: Its Nature, Development, and Prospect.* Stanford, Calif.: Stanford University Press.
Popitz, H. 1990. *Fenomenologia del potere.* Bologna: Il Mulino.
Portanova, M., G. Rossi, and F. Stefanoni. 1996. *Mafia a Milano. Quarant'anni di affari e delitti.* Rome: Editori Riuniti.
Pospísil, L. 1974. *Anthropology of Law. A Comparative Theory.* New Haven, Conn.: HRAF Press.
Puglisi, A. 1990. *Sole contro la mafia.* Palermo: La Luna.
Puzo, M. 1969. *The Godfather.* New York: Putnam.
Raith, W. 1989. *Mafia: Ziel Deutschland. Vom Verfall der politischen Kultur zur Organisierten Kriminalität.* Köln: Kösler.
Ramella, F., and C. Trigilia. 1994. Associazionismo e mobilitazione contro la criminalità organizzata. In *La mafia, le mafie*, ed. G. Fiandaca e Salvatore Costantino. Bari: Laterza.
Rath, J. 1964. The Carbonari: Their Origins, Initiation Rites, and Aims. *American Historical Review* 69: 353–70.
Re, K. 2001. Sei mesi per dire tutto. *Narcomafie* 9(3): 35–38.
Recupero, A. 1987a. La Sicilia all'opposizione (1848–74). In *La Sicilia*, ed. M. Aymard and G. Giarrizzo. Turin: Einaudi.
———. 1987b. Ceti medi e "*homines novi*": alle origini della mafia. *Polis* 2: 307–28.
Renda, F. 1984. *Storia della Sicilia dal 1860 al 1970*, vol. 1, *I caratteri originari e gli anni della unificazione italiana.* Palermo: Sellerio.
———. 1985. *Storia della Sicilia dal 1860 al 1970*, vol. 2, *Dalla caduta della Destra al fascismo.* Palermo: Sellerio.
———. 1987. *Storia della Sicilia dal 1860 al 1970*, vol. 3, *Dall'occupazione militare alleata al centrosinistra.* Palermo: Sellerio.
———. 1993. *Resistenza alla mafia come movimento nazionale.* Cosenza: Rubbettino.
Reuter, P. 1983. *Disorganized Crime: The Economics of the Visible Hand.* Cambridge: MIT Press.
———. 1985. *The Organization of Illegal Markets: An Economic Analysis.* Washington, D.C.: National Institute of Justice.
———. 1987. *Rackteering in Legitimate Industries. A Study in the Economics of Intimidation.* Prepared

for the National Institute of Justice, U.S. Department of Justice. Santa Monica, Calif: Rand.

———. 1995. The Decline of the American Mafia. *Public Interest* 120 (summer): 89–99.

Riall, L. 1998. *Sicily and the Unification of Italy: Liberal Policy and Local Power, 1959–1866.* Oxford: Clarendon.

Rizzo, W., N. Savoca, and A. Sciacca. 1994. *Il governo della mafia. L'alleanza tra uomini d'onore, politici e imprenditori a Catania. I ricatti ai gruppi Agnelli e Berlusconi, Le intimidazioni a Pippo Baudo e il tentativo di rapirlo.* Palermo: Arbor.

Roccuzzo, A. 1998. Baciamo le mani, Monsignore. *Micromega* 1: 81–92.

Romano, S. F. 1963. *Storia della mafia.* Milan: Sugar.

Romano, S. 1977. *L'ordinamento giuridico.* Florence: Sansoni.

Rossi, L. 1992. *I disarmati. Falcone, Cassarà e gli altri.* Milan: Mondadori.

Roth, G. [1968] 1971. Personal Rulership, Patrimonialism, and Empire Building. In *Scholarship and Partisanship: Essays on Max Weber,* by R. Bendix and G. Roth. Berkeley: University of California Press.

Ruggiero, V. 1996. *Organized and Corporate Crime in Europe: Offers That Can't Be Refused.* Aldershot: Dartmouth.

Sabetti, F. 1984. *Political Authority in a Sicilian Village.* New Brunswick, N.J.: Rutgers University Press.

Sahlins, M. D. 1972. *Stone Age Economics.* Chicago: Aldine Atherton.

Sales, I. 1993. *La camorra. Le camorre.* Rome: Editori Riuniti.

Salvemini, G. 1962. *Il ministro della mala vita e altri scritti sull'Italia giolittiana.* Milan: Feltrinelli.

Santino, U. 1988. The Financial Mafia: The Illegal Accumulation of Wealth and the Financial-Industrial Complex. *Contemporary Crises* 12: 203–43.

———. 1990. Introduction to *L'impresa mafiosa. Dall'Italia agli Stati Uniti,* by U. Santino and G. La Fiura. Milan: Angeli.

———. 1991. L'omicidio mafioso. Dinamica della violenza ed evoluzione del fenomeno mafioso dagli anni '60 ad oggi. In *La violenza programmata. Omicidi e guerre di mafia a Palermo dagli anni '60 ad oggi,* by G. Chinnici and U. Santino. Milan: Angeli.

———. 1994a. *La borghesia mafiosa. Materiali di un percorso di analisi.* Palermo: Centro siciliano di documentazione Giuseppe Impastato.

———. 1994b. *La mafia come soggetto politico.* Palermo: Centro siciliano di documentazione Giuseppe Impastato.

———. 1997. *L'alleanza e il compromesso. Mafia e politica dai tempi di Lima e Andreotti ai giorni nostri.* Soveria Mannelli: Rubbettino.

———. 2000a. *La cosa e il nome: Materiali per lo studio dei fenomeni premafiosi.* Soveria Mannelli: Rubbettino.

———. 2000b. *Storia del movimento antimafia. Dalla lotta di classe all'impegno civile.* Rome: Editori Riuniti.

Santino, U., and G. La Fiura. 1990. *L'impresa mafiosa. Dall'Italia agli Stati Uniti.* Milan: Angeli.

Santoro, M. 1995. La mafia e la protezione. Tre quesiti e una proposta. *Polis* 9(2): 285–99.

———. 1998. Mafia, cultura e politica. *Rassegna italiana di sociologia* 39(4): 441–76.

———. 2000. Oltre lo stato, dentro la mafia: Note per l'analisi culturale di una istituzione politica. *Teoria politica* 16 (2): 97–117.

Sbriccoli, M. 1988. Fonti giudiziarie e fonti giuridiche. Riflessioni sulla fase attuale degli studi di storia del crimine. *Studi storici* 29(2): 491–501.

Scarpinato, R. 1992. Mafia e politica. In *Mafia. Anatomia di un regime*. Rome: Librerie Associate.

Schelling, T. 1967. Economics and Criminal Enterprise. *Public Interest* 7: 61–78.

———. 1971. What Is the Business of Organized Crime? *American Scholar* 40 (autumn): 643–52.

Schneegans, A. 1890. *La Sicilia nella natura, nella storia e nella vita*. Florence: Barbera.

Schneider, J. 1971. Of Vigilance and Virgins: Honor, Shame, and Access to Resources in Mediterranean Societies. *Ethnology* 10(1): 1–24.

Schneider, J. C., and P. T. Schneider. 1976. *Culture and Political Economy in Western Sicily*. New York: Academic Press.

———. 1984. Mafia Burlesque: The Profane Mass as Peace-Making Ritual. In *Religion, Power and Protest in Local Communities: The Northern Shore of the Mediterranean*, ed. E. R. Wolf, 117–33. Berlin and New York: Mouton.

———. 1994. Mafia, Antimafia, and the Question of Sicilian Culture. *Politics and Society* 22(2): 237–58.

———. 2003. *Reversible Destiny: Mafia, Antimafia, and the Struggle for Palermo*. Berkeley: University of California Press.

Schneider, P. 1969. Honor and Conflict in a Sicilian Town. *Anthropological Quarterly* 42: 130–54.

Schumpeter, J. A. 1976. *Capitalism, Socialism, and Democracy*. 5th ed. London: Allen and Unwin.

Sciarrone, R. 1993. Il rapporto tra mafia ed imprenditorialità in un'area della Calabria. *Quaderni di sociologia* 37(5): 68–92.

———. 1998. *Mafie vecchie e mafie nuove. Radicamento ed espansione*. Rome: Donzelli.

———. 1999. Uno Stato nello Stato. *Narcomafie* 7(2): 8–12.

Sciascia, L. 1994. *Il giorno della civetta*. Milan: Adelphi.

Scordato, C. 1997. Chiesa e mafia. In *Mafia e società italiana. Rapporto '97*, ed. L. Violante. Bari: Laterza.

Scott, R. W. 1987. *Organizations: Rational, Natural, and Open Systems*. Englewood Cliffs, N.J.: Prentice-Hall.

Sereni, E. 1968. *Il capitalismo nelle campagne (1860–1990)*. Turin: Einaudi.

Sergi, P. 1991. *La "Santa" violenta*. Cosenza: Periferia.

Siebert, R. 1994. *Le donne, la mafia*. Milan: Il Saggiatore.

Silvestri, F. 1999. Dynasty nella Piana. *Narcomafie* 7(2): 17–19.

Simmel, G. 1950. The Secret and the Secret Society. In *The Sociology of Georg Simmel*, trans. and ed. K. H. Wolff. London: Free Press.

Smith, D. C., Jr. 1975. *The Mafia Mystique*. New York: Basic Books.

———. 1976. Mafia: The Prototypical Alien Conspiracy. *The Annals of the American Academy* 423 (January): 75–88.

———. 1980. Paragons, Pariahs, and Pirates: A Spectrum-Based Theory of Enterprise. *Crime and Delinquency* 26: 358–86.

Smith, M. G. 1974. *Corporations and Society*. [London]: Duckworth.

Smuraglia, C. 1994. *La mafia al Nord*. Soveria Mannelli: Rubbettino.

Snyder, F. 1993. Law and Anthropology: A Review. Working Paper. No. 93/4. San Domenico: European University Institute.

Spataro, A. 2000. Ragione e pentimento. *Micromega* 1: 57–67.

Spero, J. E. 1980. *The Failure of the Franklin National Bank: Challenge to the International Banking System*. New York: Columbia University Press.

Stajano, C. 1979. *Africo: Una storia italiana di governanti e governati, di mafia, di potere e di lotta*. Turin: Einuadi.

———. 1991. *Un eroe borghese. Il caso dell'avvocato Giorgio Ambrosoli assassinato dalla mafia politica*. Turin: Einaudi.

Sterling, C. 1990. *Octopus: The Long Reach of the International Sicilian Mafia*. New York: Norton.

———. 1994. *Thieves' World: The Threat of the New Global Network of Organized Crime*. New York: Simon and Schuster.

Stille, A. 1995. *Excellent Cadavers: The Mafia and the Death of the First Italian Republic*. London: Jonathan Cape.

Strati, S. 1957. *La Teda*. Milan: Mondadori.

———. 1960. *Mani vuote*. Milan: Mondadori.

———. 1977. *Il selvaggio di Santa Venere*. Milan: Mondadori.

———. 1979. *Il diavolaro*. Milan: Mondadori.

———. 1986. *Conca degli aranci*. Milan: Mondadori.

SVIMEZ, Associazione per lo sviluppo dell'industria nel Mezzogiorno. 1995. *Rapporto 1995 sull'economia del Mezzogiorno*. Bologna: Il Mulino.

———. 1998. *Rapporto 1998 sull'economia del Mezzogiorno*. Bologna: Il Mulino.

Tarrow, S. G. 1967. *Peasant Communism in Southern Italy*. New Haven, Conn.: Yale University Press.

Tefft, S. K. 1980. Secrecy, Disclosure, and Social Theory. In *Secrecy: A Cross-Cultural Perspective*, ed. S. K. Tefft. New York: Human Sciences Press.

Tegnaeus, H. 1952. *Blood-Brothers. An Ethno-Sociological Study of Blood-Brotherhood with Special Reference to Africa*. New York: Philosophical Library.

Teresa, V. C., with T. C. Renner. 1973. *My Life in the Mafia*. Garden City, N.Y.: Doubleday.

Tessitore, G. 1985. Emergenza e garantismo nella legislazione antimafia. Profili storici dall'Unità d'Italia al Fascismo. *Nuovi Quaderni del Meridione* 23(92).

———. 1997. *Il nome e la cosa. Quando la mafia non si chiamava mafia*. Milan: Angeli.

Tescaroli, L. 2000. *Perché fu ucciso Giovanni Falcone*. Soveria Mannelli: Rubbettino.

Tilly, C. 1985. War Making and State Making as Organized Crime. In *Bringing the State Back In*, ed. P. B. Evans, D. Rueschemeyer, and T. Skocpol. Cambridge: Cambridge University Press.

———. 1988. Foreword to *The Mafia of a Sicilian Village, 1860–1960: A Study of Violent Peasant Entrepreneurs*, by A. Blok. New York: Polity.

Tino, P. 1985. L'industrializzazione sperata. In *La Calabria*, ed. P. Bevilacqua and A. Placanica. Turin: Einaudi.

Titone, V. 1964. *Storia, mafia e costume in Sicilia*. Milan: Edizioni del Milione.

Tranfaglia, N. 2001. *La sentenza Andreotti. Politica, mafia e giustizia nell'Italia Repubblicana*. Milan: Garzanti.

Travaglio, M., ed. 2001. Berlusconi e le stragi. *Micromega* 4: 240–54.

Trigilia, C. 1994. *Sviluppo senza autonomia. Effetti perversi delle politiche nel Mezzogiorno.* Bologna: Il Mulino.

———. 1999. Capitale sociale e sviluppo locale. *Stato e mercato* 59: 419–431.

Turiello, P. [1889] 1980. *Governo e governati in Italia*, ed. P. Bevilacqua. Reprint, Turin: Einaudi.

Turner, V. W. 1967. *The Forests of Symbols.* Ithaca, N.Y.: Cornell University Press.

———. 1992. *Blazing the Trail: Way Marks in the Exploration of Symbols*, ed. E. Turner. Tucson: The University of Arizona Press.

———. 1995. *The Ritual Process: Structure and Anti-structure.* Chicago: Aldine.

Turone, G. 1984. *Le associazioni di tipo mafioso.* Milan: Giuffrè.

———. 1995. *Il delitto di associazione mafiosa.* Milan: Giuffrè.

Turrisi Colonna, N. 1864. *Cenni sullo stato attuale della sicurezza pubblica in Sicilia.* Palermo.

Unger, M. R. 1976. *Law in Modern Society, Towards a Criticism of Social Theory.* New York: Free Press.

Varano, A. 1996. 'Ndrangheta, neofascismo e massoneria deviata. In *Mafia e antimafia. Rapporto '96*, ed. L. Violante. Bari: Laterza.

Vasile, V. 1994. Salvo Lima. In *Cirillo, Ligato e Lima. Tre storie di mafia e politica*, ed. N. Tranfaglia. Bari: Laterza.

Veltri, E., and M. Travaglio. 2001. *L'odore dei soldi. Origini e misteri delle fortune di Silvio Berlusconi.* Rome: Editori Riuniti.

Vigna, P. 1996. Le tracce di chi ordinò le stragi. In *Mafia e antimafia. Rapporto '96*, ed. L. Violante. Bari: Laterza.

Villari, P. [1875] 1972. *Le lettere meridionali ed altri scritti sulla questione sociale in Italia.* Ed. L. Chiti. Turin: Loescher.

Violante, L. 1994. *Non è la priovra. Dodici tesi sulle mafie italiane.* Turin: Einaudi.

Vitale F. 2001. Devolution in salsa mafiosa. *Micromega* 4: 221–28.

Volpi, G. 1999. Sicilia: Passi avanti ma lo sviluppo non fa sconti. *Il Sole—24 Ore—Rapporti: Sicilia* 14 (June): 1, 12.

Walston, J. 1988. *The Mafia and Clientelism: Roads to Rome in Post-War Calabria.* London and New York: Routledge.

Warren, C., and B. Laslett. 1980. Privacy and Secrecy: A Conceptual Comparison. In *Secrecy: A Cross-Cultural Perspective*, ed. S. K. Tefft. New York: Human Sciences Press.

Weber, M. 1946. The Protestant Sects and the Spirit of Capitalism. Reprinted in *From Max Weber*, ed. H. H. Gerth and C. W. Mills. New York: Free Press.

———. 1978. *Economy and Society*, ed. G. Roth and C. Wittich. Berkeley: University of California Press.

———. 1981. *General Economic History.* New Brunswick, N.J.: Transaction Books.

———. 1994. Politik als Beruf. In *Studienausgabe der Max Weber Gesamtausgabe Band I/17*, ed. W. J. Mommsen and W. Schluchter. Tübingen: J. C. B. Mohr (Paul Siebeck).

Webster, H. 1932. *Primitive Secret Societies, A Study in Early Politics and Religion.* 2d rev. ed. New York: Macmillan.

Wikan, U. 1984. Shame and Honor: A Contestable Pair. *Man N.S.* 19(4): 635–52.

Williams, P., and C. Florez. 1994. Transnational Criminal Organizations and Drug Trafficking. *Bulletin on Narcotics* 46(2): 9–24.

Yates, F. 1975. *The Rosicrucian Enlightenment.* London: Paladin.

Zagari, A. 1992. *Ammazzare stanca. Autobiografia di uno 'ndranghetista pentito.* Cosenza: Periferia.

Names Index

Abadinsky, H., 9
Abbate, G., 13
Abbate, L., 208
Adelfi, N., 192
Adelfio, F., 75
Agate, M., 138, 139
Alajmo, R., 243 n. 12
Alatri, P., 186
Albanese, G., 16, 59, 134
Albini, J. L., 3
Albrecht, H. J., xii
Allegra, M., 14, 41, 52
Alongi, G., 24, 34, 39, 86, 109, 110, 111, 147, 161, 178, 181, 183, 232 n. 8, 238 n. 4
Alvaro, C., 37, 38, 183, 238 n. 4
Amorosos, 34, 240 n. 19
Anderson, A. G., 4, 7
Andreotti, G., 4, 194, 202, 205, 206, 242 n. 6, 243 n. 10
Annacondia, S., 154
Anonimo, 149
Anselmo, V., 80

Arlacchi, P., ix, 10, 15, 19, 25, 31, 41, 53, 57, 64, 68, 72, 80, 84, 87, 94, 105, 106, 111, 126, 130
Arrighi, G., 31, 191
Asciutto-Grimaldis, 62
Asprea, L., 38, 70, 84
Austin, J., 123

Badalamenti, G., 53, 54, 176
Badalamentis, 88, 146
Bagarella, L., 119
Banfield, E. C., 82
Barbaccia, F., 194
Barbaros, 145
Barca, F., 211
Barone, G., 39, 144, 242 n. 5
Barone, L., 51
Barreca, P., 31, 61, 198
Barrese, O., 197
Basile, E., 136
Bassanini, F., 211
Battaglia, L., xi

Becchi, A., 152, 174, 218, 221
Bell, D., 226
Bellìa, D., 163
Bellìa, P., 163
Benedusi, A., 214
Benestare, A., 89
Benton, L., 124
Berger, P. L., 66, 67, 96, 119, 221
Berlusconi, S., 12, 14, 208, 211, 212, 213, 219
Bertolini, F., 160
Bettini, M., 79, 93, 95, 97, 111, 120, 125, 230 n. 5, 238 n. 3
Bevilacqua, P., 39, 180
Biagi, E., 81, 104, 150, 230 n. 5
Bianconi, G., 56, 205
Billington, J., 104
Biondino, S., 239 n. 13
Black, M., 235 n. 11
Blakey, G. R., 222, 230 n. 2
Blandano, P., 243 n. 12
Bloch, Marc, 76, 131, 240 n. 18
Bloch, Maurice, 21, 22, 77, 83
Block, A. A., 5, 7, 173, 222, 223
Blok, A., 15, 25, 36, 66, 73, 74, 92, 147
Blumenthal, R., 215
Boarzi, A., 49
Bobbio, N., 122, 123, 125, 127, 131, 240 n. 16
Boemi, S., x, 209, 214
Bohannan, P., 127, 131
Boissevain, J., 147, 242 n. 5
Bok, S., 102
Bolzoni, A., 46
Bonanno, J., 7, 44, 53, 88, 231 n. 5
Bonannos, 10, 20
Bonavolonta, J., 230 n. 2
Bonsanti, S., 243 n. 7
Bontade, G., 161
Bontade, P., 162
Bontade, S., 43, 44, 54, 148, 149
Bontades, 88, 146
Booth, M., 225
Borsellino, P., 14, 139, 192, 203, 204, 205, 236 n. 17, 243 n. 11

Bourdieu, P., 72
Brancaccio di Carpino, F., 103
Brancato, F., 14, 186
Brandaleone, 195
Briolotta, S., 160
Brögger, J., 36
Bruno-Scarfos, 234 n. 3
Brusca, G., 119, 159, 161, 169
Bruzzanitis, 189, 242 n. 4
Buckaloo, 234
Buscetta, T., xii, 13, 14, 24, 27, 41, 53, 57, 68, 75, 80, 81, 87, 95, 99, 104, 105, 111, 119, 130, 132, 137, 149, 150, 151, 165, 184, 193, 194, 195, 201, 207, 230 n. 5

Cafaro, V., 5, 230 n. 4, 232 n. 9, 234 n. 3, 240 n. 2
Calà Ulloa, P., 33, 185
Calabrò, M. A., 92
Calcara, V., 93
Calderone, A., 57, 68, 72, 84, 99, 106, 147, 148, 149, 151, 230 n. 5, 236 n. 15
Calderone, F., 189
Calderone, P., 56, 162, 236 n. 15
Calò, P., 146
Campo, P., 96, 97
Cancemi, S., 117, 193, 207
Cancila, O., 35, 167
Cannella, T., 207
Capogreco, A., 93
Capone, A., 9
Caponnetto, A., 203, 243 n. 11
Caprarotta, F., 138, 139
Carnevale, C., 206
Casarrubea, G., 243 n. 12
Cascio, R., 192
Caselli, G., x, 208
Cassano, M., 66
Castagna, S., 15, 65, 67, 70, 72, 75, 81, 86, 105, 128, 230 n. 5, 237 n. 18
Cataldos, 62
Catanzaritis, 242 n. 4
Catanzaro, R., 15, 22, 25, 116, 142, 174
Cavadi, A., x, 192, 243 n. 12

NAMES INDEX

Cavour, C. Benso Conte di, 238 n. 10
Cazzola, F., 164, 205
Centorrino, M., 15, 142, 170
Cerami, G., 194
Cervigni, G., 189
Chambliss, W. J., 223
Chilanti, F., 82, 193, 197
Chin, K. L., 225, 226
Chinnici, R., 203
Chubb, J., 167, 195, 242 n. 6
Ciaccio Montalto, G., 203
Ciampi, C. A., 211
Ciancimino, V., 194, 195, 196
Ciconte, E., 29, 36, 37, 59, 68, 86, 112, 113, 129, 162, 163, 176, 189, 190, 193, 199, 231 n. 3, 237 n. 20, 242 n. 4
Ciocca, P., 234 n. 5
Cipriani, G., 243 n. 7
Cipriani, P., x
Chilanti, F., 82, 193, 197
Clawson, M. A., 76
Coco Trovato, F., 154, 155
Cohen, A., 67
Colacino, T., 34, 40, 68, 81
Colajanni, N., 180
Colaprico, P., 87, 91, 132, 134, 230 n. 5
Colletti, C., 96, 97
Colonna Turrisi, N., Barone of, 33
Commissos, 62
Condello, G., 88
Condello, P., 101
Condellos, 88, 89
Contorno, S., 13, 99, 146, 241 n. 5
Coppola, F. F., 3
Cordìs, 62
Cordopatri, Baronessa of, 154
Cordopatri, F., Barone of, 154
Cornwell, R., 92
Costa, G., 46, 61, 112, 115, 116, 136, 203
Costantino, S., 21, 243 n. 12
Costanzo, M., 207
Costanzos, 167
Costas, 62
Cressey, D., 4, 16, 65, 124, 134, 232 n. 9

Crisantino, A., 231 n. 4
Crupi, P., 37, 113
Cuntrera-Caruanas, 32, 215
Cursotis, 29
Cutrera, A., viii, 34, 36, 38, 40, 69, 77, 86, 87, 101, 128, 185, 238 n. 3, 240 n. 19

D'Agostini, F., 241 n. 7
D'Agostino, G., 197
D'Agostinos, 62, 242 n. 4
D'Alema, M., 213
D'Alessandro, E., 35, 36
Dalla Chiesa, C. A., 203, 204
Dalla Chiesa, N., 25, 110, 204
D'Amico, F., 138
D'Amico, V., 138, 139
Da Passano, M., 36
D'Arco, A., 230, 232 n. 9, 237 n. 21
D'Avanzo, G., 46
Davis, J., 73, 152
Davis, J. A., 186
De Francisci, I., x, 161, 217, 218
De Gasperi, A., 197
De Gennaro, G., x
Della Porta, D., 174, 205
Dell'Utri, M., 212
De Luca., M., 243 n. 7
De Mauro, M., 14, 41, 52, 68
De Nava, G., 37
Depretis, A., 187
De Stefano, G., 63, 200
De Stefano, O., 89
De Stefano, P., 88, 89, 168, 200
De Stefanos, 50, 51, 60, 61, 89, 115, 153, 168, 198, 200
Diana, B., 81
Di Bella, M. P., 74
Di Carlo, V., 189
Di Forti, F., 78
Di Lello, G., 193
Di Maggio, B., 139, 202, 209, 240 n. 22
Di Maria, F., 21
Di Matteo, A., 210
Di Matteo, M. S., 118, 210

Domino, C., 161
Drago, G., 120
Duffy, B., 230 n. 2
Duggan, C., 239 n. 14
Durkheim, E., 16, 19, 52, 78, 89, 98, 130, 220
Duyne, P. van, 223

Eco, U., 185
Eder, C., xi
Eisenstadt, S., xi, 45, 67, 77, 78, 89, 90, 92, 96
Eliade, M., 110
Evans-Pritchard, E. E., 52, 82
Evola, G., 139

Faia, S., 160
Falcionelli, A., 103
Falcone, G., 13, 14, 24, 42, 44, 56, 66, 68, 73, 75, 112, 165, 167, 178, 203, 204, 205, 217, 236 n. 17, 243 n. 11
Falzone, G., 103
Fanfani, A., 195, 201
Fantozzi, P., 191, 242 n. 5
Farinella, G., 169
Fazzo, L., 87, 91, 132, 134, 230 n. 5
Felman, D., xii
Fentress, J., 36, 40, 241 n. 6
Feo, F., 218
Ferro, V. C., 149
Fiandaca, G., 21, 123, 133, 239 n. 15
Fici, G., 235, 236 n. 13
Filastò, A., 107
Filippo, V., 37
Filippone, G., 151
Finckenauer, J. O., 230 n. 2
Fiume, G., 33, 35, 36, 183, 189, 235 n. 8
Flachi, G., 154
Flores, S., 188
Florez, C., 147, 224
Fong, M. L., 226
Fonti, F., 29, 87, 101, 129, 185, 240 n. 20, 241 n. 4
Forgione, F., 198, 200

Fortes, M., 21, 42, 52, 82
Foster, G. M., 77
Foucault, M., 240
Franchetti, L., 19, 33, 74, 109, 141, 181, 186
Frascatis, 153, 174
Fresolone, G., 5, 234 n. 3
Funzi, T., 234 n. 3

Gambetta, D., 19, 99, 121, 142, 143, 160, 175, 233 n. 2
Gambino, G. G., 239 n. 13
Gambino, S., 50, 112, 168
Gambinos, 6
Ganci, C., 79
Ganci, R., 54
Garibaldi, G., 116
Gelli, L., 207
Genco Russo, G., 136, 149, 188, 191
Gennep, A. van, 67, 72
Genoveses, 6, 7, 234 n. 3, 240 n. 2
Gentile, N., 14, 41, 73, 82, 134, 230 n. 5
Georgiou, P., 143
Giannini, M. S., 103
Giarrizzo, G., 103, 104
Gierke, O. von, 77, 236 n. 14
Giesen, B., xi, 64, 67, 84, 96, 173
Ginsborg, P., 203
Gioè, A., 232 n. 10
Gioffrè, F. A., 153
Gioia, D., 191
Gioia, G., 195, 242 n. 6
Gioias, 196
Giolitti, G., 187, 214
Giudice, G., 213
Giuffrè, A., 202
Giuliano, B., 203
Gomez, P., 208
Gouldin, L. P., 4, 5, 6, 7, 225, 232 n. 9, 234 n. 3
Gouldner, A. W., 81
Grassi, L., 170
Grasso, P., x, 12, 32, 63, 64, 100, 160, 161, 208, 209, 212, 243 n. 13
Gravano, S., 234 n. 3, 237 n. 21

Graziano, L., 242 n. 5
Greco, G., 239 n. 12
Greco, M., 57, 241 n. 5
Greco, P., 120
Greco, S., 53
Gribaudi, G., 192
Grotius, H., 240 n. 16
Guderman, S., 77
Guggenheim, S., 77
Gullà, G., 114, 116, 190
Guttadauro, G., 194
Guzzo, V., 191

Habermas, J., 104
Hagan, F., 223
Hahn, A., xi, 102
Halevi, R., 104
Haller, M., 3, 222
Hänsch, A., xi
Hart, H. L. A., 126, 127
Hauriou, M., 122
Hauschild, T., xi
Hawkins, G., 3, 223
Heidues Somers, M., 226
Herzfeld, M., 235
Hess, H., xi, 15, 25, 35, 66, 74, 84, 149, 150, 152, 163, 179, 181, 225
Hobbes, T., 240 n. 16
Hobbs, D., 223
Hobsbawm, E., 35, 101, 183, 233 n. 1
Hocart, A. M., 82
Hoebel, E. A., 124, 127, 131, 132

Iamonte, N., 174
Ianni, F., 20
Iannò, N., 174
Ierardo, M., 117
Ierinòs, 145
Imbergamo, F., 210
Imerti, A., 88, 89
Imerti-Condellos, 60
Ingroia, A., x, 204, 209, 219
Inzerillo, S., 136
Inzerillo, V., 194

Inzerillos, 88, 136, 146
Ishino, I., 77

Jacob, M., 104
Jacobs, J. B., 4, 5, 6, 7, 9, 11, 10, 215, 225, 232 n. 9, 230 n., 234 n. 3
Jamieson, A., 205, 231 n. 3, 243 n. 12
Jones, M., 105
Joutsen, M., 226

Kefauver, E. C., 3
Kelly, R. J., 9
Kenney, D. J., 230 n. 2
Kerner, H. J., xi, 223
Kertzer, D. I., 67
Knight, S., 105
Korneck, P., 244 n. 2
Koselleck, R., 104, 108

La Barbera, G., 201, 232 n. 10
Labate, A., 75
Labate, Paolo, 50
Labate, Pietro, 50, 103
Labates, 153, 163
La Duca, R., 184
La Fiura, G., 15, 142
La Fontaine, J., 73
La Licata, F., 243
La Marmora, G., 116
La Mattina, N., 58, 146
Landesco, J., 7, 9, 243 n. 9
Lane, F., 172, 173
La Rosa, F., 236 n. 13
Lasco, F., 218
Laslett, B., 103
Latellas, 215
La Torre, P., 203, 204
Laudanis, 29
Lauro, G., 50, 88, 89, 174, 179, 198
Lavanco, G., 21
Lestingi, F., 17, 19, 34, 40
Lèvi-Strauss, C., 89
Lewis, R., 216
Libri, D., 49

NAMES INDEX

279

Libris, 49
Licandro, A., 176, 199
Li Causi, L., 66
Ligato, L., 176
Liggio, L., 45, 46
Light, I., 226
Lima, S., 194, 195, 196, 201, 202, 236 n. 17, 242 n. 6
Lipari, P., 176
Llewellyn, K., 124
Lodato, S., 12, 32, 63, 64, 74, 100, 148, 159, 161, 169, 170, 192, 212, 216, 230 n. 5, 243 n. 11
Lo Forte, G., x, 118, 171
Lombroso, C., 34, 68, 69
Lonardo, A., 232 n. 9, 234 n. 3, 235 n. 9, 237 n. 21
Lorenzoni, G., 37, 74, 75, 78, 81, 147, 150, 161, 181
Lo Schiavo, G., 163, 189, 239 n. 14
Lo Zito, A., 213
Lucchese, G., 120
Lucentini, U., 192, 243 n. 11
Luckmann, T., 66, 67, 96, 119, 221
Lugli, W., 218
Luhmann, N., 64, 114, 150
Lunardi, P., 219
Lupo, S., 14, 16, 33, 35, 39, 41, 104, 128, 142, 150, 156, 174, 194, 238 n. 6, 239 n. 15
Lupscha, P. A., 7
Lynch, G. E., 229 n. 2, 230 n. 2

Maas, P., 4, 5, 7, 40, 232 n. 9, 234 n. 3, 237 n. 21, 238 n. 7
Mack, J., 223
Mackenzie, N., 67, 102
Macrì, A., 60, 96, 115, 162, 168
Macrì, V., x
Madonia, F., 43
Madonias, 169, 170
Magatti, M., 174, 174, 205
Maggi, M. A., 217
Magliuolo, L., x
Maine, H., 52, 76

Malafarina, L., 15, 48, 49, 59, 69, 70, 84, 108, 112, 113, 236 n. 18
Malinowsky, B., 123
Mammoliti, S., 154, 201
Mancini, G., 167, 243 n. 8
Mangiameli, R., 36, 189
Maniscalco, M. L., x, 119
Mannoia, F. M., 27, 42, 44, 51, 99, 108, 137, 146, 152, 159, 163, 241 n. 5
Marcenò, C., 46, 59, 67, 69, 73, 91, 239 n. 11
March, J. G., 99
Marchese, A., 80
Marchese, G., 70, 80, 235 n. 12
Marino, Girolamo, 56
Marino, Giuseppe, 25, 56, 110, 181, 183, 184
Marmo, M., 75, 235 n. 7
Marsala, V., 74
Marsalas, 85, 138, 139
Martino, P., 73
Massari, M., 231
Mastropaolo, A., 192
Masuccis, 160
Matacena, A., 200, 213
Mattarella, P., 201
Mauss, M., 89
Maviglias, 242 n. 4
Mazzaferro, G., 201
Mazzaferros, 46, 91, 145
Mazzini, G., 103, 116, 238 n. 10
McClennan, J., 3
Melari, F., 238 n. 4
Meligrana, M., 239 n. 15
Mendelson, E. M., 110
Messina, L., 28, 41, 42, 54, 56, 72, 90, 91, 117, 118, 141, 166, 167, 193, 233 n. 12, 237 n. 2
Messina Denaro, F., 93, 138, 139
Michels, R., 43
Mignosi, E., 192
Milazzo, V., 56
Minore, S. (Totò), 28, 56
Minores, 56, 88
Mintz, S. W., 77, 83
Mirimovitsch, I., xii
Misasi, R., 199

Molès, 214
Mondani, P., 198, 200
Monnier, M., 232 n. 8
Montalbano family, 36
Montalto, S., 38, 128, 129
Montanaro, S., 194
Montanelli, I., 111, 178
Monzini, P., xi, 160, 230 n. 3, 232 n. 8
Moore, S. F., 124, 223, 225
Morabito, G., 27
Morabito, S., 91, 132
Morabitos, 145
Morgan, G., 143
Mori, C., 161, 239 n. 14
Morisi, M., 205
Morris, N., xi
Mosca, G., 82, 150, 186
Murat, J., 237 n. 1
Musolino, A., 15
Musolino, R., 153
Mutolo, G., 65, 98, 105, 135, 139, 193

Natoli, L. (W. Galt), 184, 185, 242 n. 3
Navarra, M., 45, 188
Naylor, R. T., 92, 217
Nelken, D., 143
Nelli, H. S., 3, 5, 6, 7, 8, 9, 229, 231 n. 6, 242 n. 1
Nicaso, A., 36, 39, 40, 59, 86, 121, 185, 232 n. 8, 238 n. 4
Nicastro, S., 103
Nicotri, P., 80, 230 n. 5
Nirta, A., 63
Nirtas, 60
Nisticò, V., 193
Novacco, D., 182
Nozick, R., 171
Nunn, S., 241 n. 2

Orlando, L., 204, 211
Ownby, D., 76, 226
Owtram, N., xii

Palmeri, G., 104
Panarella, C., 4, 9, 10, 215, 230 n. 2

Pannella, M., 208
Pansa, A., xii
Paoli, L., 12, 14, 17, 30, 32, 76, 92, 149, 216, 217, 222, 225, 240 n. 1, 243 n. 1
Parini, E. G., 206
Parisio, 33
Patti, A., 85, 138
Patty, J., 234
Pecorelli, M., 205
Pellegrini, A., x, 71
Pelliccia, A., x
Pennino, G., 195, 201
Pennino, G. (nephew of the above), 201
Pennisi, R., 200
Peristiany, J. G., 73
Perrow, C., 19, 143
Pesces, 145
Peterson, V. W., 7
Pezzino, P., xi, 16, 24, 25, 33, 36, 65, 86, 101, 103, 104, 105, 110, 142, 144, 180, 182, 186, 231 n. 4
Pigliaru, A., 239
Pillera-Cappellos, 29
Piromalli, Girolamo (Mommo), 49, 60, 115, 116
Piromalli, Giuseppe, 49, 201
Piromallis, 31, 60, 115, 168, 170, 214, 218
Pirrello, P., 174
Piselli, F., 31, 191, 242 n. 5
Pistone, J. D., 20 (D. Brasco)
Pitrè, G., 25, 109, 110, 111, 238 n. 3
Pitt-Rivers, J., 73, 77, 82
Pizzorno, A., xi, 15, 142, 196
Poggi, G., xi, 171, 172, 173
Polifroni, C., 59, 208
Popitz, H., 52, 57, 63
Portanova, M., 231 n. 3
Pospìsil, L., 124
Prestifilippo, G., 120
Principe, S., 199
Provenzano, B., 56, 63, 64, 99, 176, 202, 214
Puccio, V., 80, 120
Puglisi, A., 243 n. 12

NAMES INDEX

281

Pulvirenti, G., 28
Puzo, M., 3

Raith, W., 244 n. 2
Ramella, F., 243 n. 12
Ramirez, R., 153
Rampolla, C., 189
Rappaport, J., xii
Ravano, E., 218
Re, K., 209
Recupero, A., 36, 101, 103, 142
Reina, M., 136, 201
Renda, F., 24, 36, 105, 181, 189, 243 n. 12
Reuter, P., xi, 6, 8, 9, 20, 175, 225
Rey, G. M., 152, 174, 218, 221
Riall, L., 36, 40, 180
Riccobono, R., 92, 93
Riina, S. (Totò), 45, 46, 53, 54, 55, 56, 57, 58, 63, 64, 70, 80, 99, 117, 118, 119, 120, 130, 132, 136, 137, 138, 139, 140, 148, 159, 202, 205, 209, 214, 233 n. 12, 236 n. 17, 239 n. 12, 13, 240 n. 22
Rimi, V., 56, 82
Rimis, 56, 88
Rizzo, W., 29
Rizzotto, G., 24, 40
Roccuzzo, A., 192
Roddy, K. P., 230 n. 2
Romano, A. M., x
Romano, S., 18, 121, 122, 123, 239 n. 15
Romano, S. F., 36, 187
Romeo, P., 199, 200, 201
Romeo, V., 193
Romolas, 145
Roniger, L., 77, 89, 92
Rossi, L., 243 n. 11
Roth, G., 45
Rotolo, A., 146
Ruggeri, F., xi
Ruggiero, V., xi, 217
Ruotolo, S., 194

Sabella, S., x
Sabetti, F., 162
Sahlins, M. D., 17, 81, 86

Salerno, T., 234 n. 3
Sales, I., 230 n. 3
Salvemini, G., 187
Salvo, I., 70, 195, 202, 236 n. 15, 17
Salvo, N., 70, 195, 236 n. 15
Salvos, 196
Sangiorgi, A., 35, 39, 41, 42, 128, 149, 156
Santapaola, B., 28, 29
Santapaolas, 29, 85
Santino, U., xi, 15, 36, 141, 142, 170, 195, 240 n. 1, 243 n. 12
Santoro, M., 66, 73, 240 n. 1
Satriani, L., 116, 241 n. 7
Savatteri, G., 56, 205
Savoca, G., 146
Savoca, N., 29
Sbriccoli, M., 21
Scalone, F., 213
Scarpinato, R., 152
Scavuzzo, P., 163
Scelba, M., 197
Schelling, T., 156, 159, 160
Schneegans, A., 34, 171
Schneider, J., xi, 15, 25, 39, 66, 74, 147, 161, 186, 204, 243 n. 12
Schneider, P., xi, 15, 25, 39, 66, 74, 87, 147, 161, 186, 204, 243 n. 12
Schumpeter, J., 173, 177
Schwab, B., xii
Sciacca, A., 29
Sciarrone, R., 168, 218, 231 n. 3
Sciascia, L., 236 n. 16
Scopelliti, A., 233 n. 13
Scordato, C., 192
Scott, R. W., 143
Scriva, F., 30
Scriva, P., 90, 121, 125, 129, 155
Sereni, E., 173, 180
Sergi, P., 129
Serraino, F., 153
Shelley, L., xi
Siebert, R., 91, 174, 243 n. 12
Signorini, L. F., 234 n. 5
Signorino, D., 170
Siino, A., 148, 176

Siino, F., 35
Silvestri, F., 49
Simmel, G., 46, 83, 107, 112
Sindona, M., 237 n. 22
Sirchia, G., 81
Smith, D. C., 3, 222, 223
Smith, M. G., 16, 52, 151, 240 n. 16
Smuraglia, C., 231 n. 3
Snyder, F., xi, 240 n. 17
Sonnino, S., 33, 141
Sorci, A., 149, 194
Spadaro, T., 58, 146, 149
Sparaino, S., 163
Spataro, A., 209
Spero, J. E., 237 n. 22
Stajano, C., 162, 192, 237 n. 22, 243 n. 7
Sterling, C., 147, 224
Stille, A., 12, 192, 243 n. 11
Stilo, Don, 189
Strange, S., xi
Strati, D., 50
Strati, S., 38, 69, 72, 151, 189
Szakolczai, A., xi

Tarrow, S. G., 191
Tefft, S. K., 102
Tegano, G., 89
Teganos, 89
Tegnaeus, H., 76, 82
Teresa, V. C., 234 n. 3
Terranova, C., 136, 203
Tescaroli, L., 205, 207, 210
Tessitore, G., 14, 20, 24
Tilly, C., 172, 179
Tinnirellos, 160
Tino, P., 167, 168
Titone, A., 139
Titone, V., 35
Tönnies, F., 89
Tonry, M., xi
Torrio, J., 9
Traina, A., 160
Tranfaglia, N., 206, 242 n. 5
Trapani, G., 194
Travaglio, M., 207, 211, 212

Trigilia, C., 84, 243 n. 12
Tripodo, D., 50, 60, 115, 174
Turner, V. W., 66, 68, 80, 81, 93
Turone, G., 167, 204
Turriello, P., 181
Tursi Prato, P., 200

Ulizzi, A., 234 n. 5
Unger, R. M., 131, 132, 133, 136, 138

Valachi, J., 40, 232, 234 n. 3
Vannucci, A., 174, 205
Varano, A., 176, 179
Vasile, V., 195, 242
Veltri, E., 211
Vigna, P., 207
Villari, P., 34, 150
Violante, L., 206
Violi, P., 23
Virga, V., 56
Vitale, L., 14, 208, 219
Vizzini, C., 111, 149, 178, 183, 188, 189
Volpi, G., 211, 218

Wagman, R. J., 5, 234 n. 3
Warren, C., 103
Weber, M., 16, 17, 41, 42, 44, 45, 49, 53, 54, 59, 63, 65, 76, 77, 80, 83, 84, 89, 95, 124, 151, 154, 155, 170, 171, 196, 236 n. 14, 240 n. 18, 241 n. 3
Webster, H., 110, 171
Wikan, U., 74
Williams, P., 147, 224
Wolf, E. R., 77, 83
Woodley, R., 20
Worthnington, J., 4, 9, 10, 215, 230 n. 2

Yates, F., 104

Zagari, A., 31, 59, 83, 112, 113, 117, 126, 134, 232 n. 7
Zagari-Violas, 62
Zaza, M., 58
Zito, S., 199
Zubios, 34

Subject Index

Alleanza Nazionale (AN, National Alliance party), 213
AMGOT (Allied Military Government of the Occupied Territories), 189
anti-mafia government initiatives
   in Italy, 10–12, 26–27, 205–207, 208–212, 214–215, 243 nn. 8, 10, and 13
   in the United States, 10–12
   See also anti-mafia pool, Palermo; *maxiprocesso*
anti-mafia movement
   in Italy, 12, 203–205, 210–211, 243 n. 12
   in Palermo, 204, 243 n. 12
anti-mafia pool, Palermo, 13–14, 146, 196, 203–204, 243 n. 11
arms trade, 91–92, 217
Aspromonte mountain, 29, 37, 38, 59, 61, 73, 87, 145, 153, 192, 193, 234

bacchiaggiu, 112–113, 237–238 n. 3
banditry, 35–36, 147
Beati Paoli, 184–185, 242 nn. 2–3
bootlegging, 9–10, 231–232 n. 6

Bourbon kingdom, 179–180, 182–183, 237 n. 1
brigantage. *See* banditry
brotherhood ties
   in mafia associations, viii, 7, 17, 80–83, 85–94, 150–151, 235 nn. 10–11, 236 n. 15
   in premodern groups, 78–80, 236 n. 14
   See also fraternization contracts

camorra, 36–37, 40, 229 n. 1, 230 n. 3, 232 n. 8, 235 n. 7
Carabinieri, x, 21, 49, 106, 112, 135, 136, 181, 193, 205, 240
Carboneria, 101, 103–104, 237 n. 1
Catholic religion and church
   attitude toward the mafia, 192, 193
   as independent legal order, 122
   symbols used in mafia ceremonies, 68, 237 n. 2, 238 nn. 9–10
Christian Democracy. *See* Democrazia Cristiana
cigarette smuggling. *See* tobacco smuggling

285

Clean Hands investigations, 10, 174–175, 212
clientelism, 187, 191–192, 242 n. 5
Communist Party. *See* Partito Comunista Italiano
construction industry, 166–168, 174–176
Corleonesi, 134, 155, 176, 203, 207, 216
   break of mafia rules by, 94, 118–119, 136–140, 239 n. 12
   increase of Cosa Nostra's patrimonialism and secrecy due to, 45, 53–57, 70, 117–119, 233 n. 12
   rise of, 53–57, 88, 148
Cosa Nostra, American
   activities of, 7–9
   ceremony of initiation in, 5, 234 n. 3
   commission of, 4–5, 232 n. 9, 233 n. 15, 238 n. 8
   decline of, 10–12, 225, 243 n. 9
   dimensions of, 5–6
   internal organization of, 4–7, 230 n. 4, 231–232 nn. 5-6
   investigations of, 10–12, 20
   labor racketeering of, 8–9
   origins of, 242 n. 1
   recruitment criteria and process of, 11, 235 n. 9, 237 n. 21
   relationships with government representatives and officials, 8, 243 n. 9
Cosa Nostra, Sicilian
   ceremony of initiation in, 5, 17, 65–70, 72, 234 n. 6
   commissions of, 4–5, 16, 52–58, 145, 232 n. 232
   decline of, 10–12, 214–219
   dimensions of, 5–6, 26–29
   entrepreneurial transformation, 9–10, 94–98, 148–151, 221
   expansion out of Sicily, vii, 32, 231 n. 3
   forerunners of, 33–36, 38–40
   internal organization of, 16, 40–46, 51–58, 62–64, 230 n. 4, 231 n. 5, 233 n. 12
   investigations of, 10–12, 205–207, 208–212, 214–215
   multifunctionality of, 18, 143, 172–177, 220–221
   normative system of, 18, 93, 120–121, 124–140, 237 n. 2, 240 n. 21
   and other Sicilian crime actors, 27–29, 158–161, 231 n. 1
   political dominion of, 8, 141, 155–177, 240 n. 1, 241 n. 5
   and politics, 188–189, 190–198, 201–202, 205–207, 212–214, 242 n. 5
   recruitment criteria and process of, 11, 90–92, 110–111
   reserved affiliation to, 70, 239 n. 13
   signs and rituals of recognition, 113, 238 nn. 4–5
Criminalpol. *See* Direzione Centrale della Polizia Criminale

Democratici di Sinistra (DS, Democrats of the Left party), 208
Democrazia Cristiana (DC, Christian Democracy), 136, 176, 208, 212
   and clientelism, 192
   and Cosa Nostra, 193–197, 201–202, 205, 207, 242 n. 6
   and 'Ndrangheta, 189–190, 198, 200–201, 207
Direzione Centrale della Polizia Criminale (Criminalpol), 26–27, 29–30
Direzione Investigativa Antimafia (DIA, Antimafia Investigative Directorate), ix, x, 21, 27, 28, 30, 141, 142, 144, 145, 147, 151, 184, 194, 199, 200, 205, 216, 219, 230, 236, 243
Direzione Nazionale Antimafia (DNA, Antimafia National Directorate), x, 243
Direzioni Distrettuali Antimafia (DDAs, Antimafia District Directorates), 205, 243
   Catanzaro DDA, 30
   Palermo DDA, x
   Reggio Calabria DDA, x, 144, 198

double morality
  in Italy, 84
  in mafia groups, 83–85, 236 n. 16
drugs, drug trafficking
  Cosa Nostra and 'Ndrangheta's involvement in, 10, 58, 61, 91, 95, 96, 144–149, 215–217
  mafia traditional prohibition of, 7, 60

extortion, 10, 164–170, 185–186, 218–219, 222, 241 n. 8

Fascist regime, 121, 161, 188, 239 n. 14, 242 n. 4
Federal Bureau of Investigations (FBI), 6, 20, 234 n. 3
feudalism
  public and private in, 173, 176
  disintegration of in Southern Italy, 179–182
Forza Italia (FI, Go Italy party), 211–213
Fratellanza, 34, 40, 68, 81, 104, 231
fraternization contracts, 17–18, 66, 76–78, 89–90, 236 n. 14
Freemasonry, 179, 237 n. 1
  Cosa Nostra and 'Ndrangheta's involvement in, 116, 198–199, 207, 238 n. 10, 242–243 n. 7
  influence on the development of mafia associations, 101, 103–104, 116
  original functions and decay, 104–105

gambling, 7
Guardia di Finanza, 149

honor, code of, 5, 11, 67, 72–75, 94, 96, 156, 162–163, 181, 235 nn. 7–8

kidnappings, 59, 60, 61, 115, 116, 145, 243 n. 10

La Cosa Nostra. *See* Cosa Nostra, American

law, theories of
  in legal anthropology, 123–124, 240 n. 17
  in legal positivism, 123–124, 239–240 n. 16
  Santi Romano's institutionalist theory and its reception, 18, 121–123, 239 n. 14–15
LCN. *See* Cosa Nostra, American

mafia
  associations in nineteenth century, 16, 25–26, 33–40
  debate on, 14–15, 24–25, 66, 90, 141–143, 173–174
  delegitimation of, 94–98, 139–140, 192
  enterprises, 144–148, 154–155, 222
  legitimacy of, 67, 75 182–186, 188–193
  restraints of research on, 20, 230 n. 5
  and state-building process in Southern Italy, 178–182
  and symbolic action, 65–67, 233 nn. 1–2
  and women, 88–89
  See also Cosa Nostra, American; Cosa Nostra, Sicilian; 'Ndrangheta
maxiprocesso (maxi-trial), 13, 203–204, 236 n. 17
Mezzogiorno. *See* Southern Italy
modernization
  and consequences for mafia associations, 94–100, 192, 203, 221
  of the Italian society, 192, 203, 221
money laundering, 92, 152–154, 237 n. 22

narcotics. *See* drugs
'Ndrangheta
  ceremony of initiation in, 17, 65, 67–72, 232 n. 7, 234 n. 4, 234 n. 6
  commission of, 16, 58–62, 233 n. 13
  decline of, 10–12, 214–219
  dimensions of, 16, 29–31, 159
  entrepreneurial transformation, 9–10, 94–98, 148–151, 221
  expansion out of Calabria, vii, 32, 214
  forerunners of, 36–40

SUBJECT INDEX

287

'Ndrangheta (*continued*)
  internal organization of, 16, 46–52, 58–64, 232 n. 8
  investigations of, 10–12, 205–207, 208–212, 214–215
  multifunctionality of, 18, 143, 172–177, 220–221
  normative system of, 18, 112, 120–121, 124–135, 240 n. 20
  political dominion of, 8, 19, 155–177, 240 n. 1, 241 n. 4
  and politics, 189–191, 193, 198–201, 205–207, 212–214, 242 n. 5, 243 n. 8
  ranks of, 46–49, 112, 114–118, 234 n. 4, 239 n. 11
  recruitment criteria and process of, 11, 90–91, 110
  signs and rituals of recognition in, 113, 238 nn. 4–5

Oblonica, 34, 38, 128
omertà, code of, 5, 11, 109–110. *See also* secrecy
organized crime
  in China, 225–226
  debate on, 222–227, 243–244 nn. 1–2
  in Japan, 226, 233 n. 14

Parliamentary Anti-mafia Commission, 139, 141, 197–198, 200, 206–207
Partito Comunista Italiano (PCI, Italian Communist Party), 189–190, 203, 204, 208, 242 n. 4
Partito Democratico della Sinistra (PDS, Democratic Party of the Left), 208
Partito Socialdemocratico Italiano (PSDI, Italian Social Democratic Party), 200, 201
Partito Socialista Italiano (PSI, Italian Socialist Party), 190, 198, 243
pentiti (mafia witnesses)
  contribution to knowledge of the mafia, 13, 20–21, 24, 27–31, 40–42, 44, 46–48, 50–55, 57, 59, 61, 65–72, 74–75, 79–81, 83–85, 87–88, 90–91, 93, 95, 97–98, 110–111, 114–116, 118, 121, 128–130, 134–135, 141, 148–149, 155–156, 159, 161, 163, 166, 169, 179, 185, 190, 202, 205, 207–208, 212, 230 n. 4, 231 n.5, 232 n. 9, 233 nn. 12 and 15, 234 n. 3, 235 nn. 9 and 11–12, 236 n. 15, 237 nn. 19, 21, and 22, 240 nn. 20–22, 240–241 n. 2, 241 nn. 4–5
  controversy about, 208–210, 243 n. 8
  forerunners of, 14–15
  growth in the 1990s, 99–100, 205
  precautions in dealing with, 21–23, 230 n. 5
Pizza Connection case, 10, 215
power, as key goal of mafia action, 151–154, 240–241 n. 2
Prohibition, 9, 231–232 n. 6
prostitution, 7, 217, 229 n. 1
protection. *See* extortion
public contracts bid rigging, 10, 12, 148, 167–168, 174–177, 216, 218–219, 222

racket. *See* extortion
RICO (Racketeer Influenced and Corrupt Organizations Act), 11, 229–230 n. 2
rituals
  of fraternization, 76–85
  of installation, 42, 44, 234 n. 6
  of passage, 67–75
  of purification, 236–237 n. 18, 237 n. 19
  of recognition, 113, 238 n. 5, 238 n. 6
  of separation, 112–113
  See also Cosa Nostra, American; Cosa Nostra, Sicilian; mafia; 'Ndrangheta
Rognoni-La Torre Act, 204
  See also anti-mafia government initiatives; anti-mafia pool, Palermo; *maxiprocesso*

Santuario della Madonna di Polsi (Sanctuary of Our Lady of Polsi), 29, 59, 87
Savoia Kingdom of Italy, 179–181, 183, 186–189

secrecy
- as a gradual property, 102–103
- in mafia associations, 18, 105–112, 114–120
- and violence, 18, 101–102

sicilianismo, 25, 184

Southern Italy
- measures to foster development of, 167–168, 211
- nineteenth-century backwardness of, 39, 82, 178–182
- persisting gap vis-à-vis northern Italy, 210–211

status contracts, 16–18, 65–66, 72–73, 78–80, 89–90
- mafia members' duties descending from, 17, 72–75, 78–83, 108–112, 235 nn. 9 and 12, 235–236 n. 13
- *See also* fraternization contracts

Stoppaglieri (or *stoppaghieri*), 34, 38, 86, 101, 104, 128

tobacco smuggling, 50–51, 58, 95, 148–149

trasformismo, 187

trust
- created by mafia brotherhood ties, 17, 89, 108, 146, 150–151
- denied in mafia daily life, 92–94, 97–100, 118–120
- lack thereof in Southern Italy, 150–151, 165, 180

violence
- as equalizing factor in mafia groups, 43–46, 49–51, 231–232 n. 6
- as means of mafia entrepreneurship, 153, 154–155, 172, 175–176
- as means of mafia political dominion, 155, 203–204, 207
- as open resource in nineteenth-century Southern Italy, 181–182
- and secrecy, 18, 101–102
- *See also* extortion

SUBJECT INDEX

289

www.ingramcontent.com/pod-product-compliance
Ingram Content Group UK Ltd.
Pitfield, Milton Keynes, MK11 3LW, UK
UKHW022230230426
12048UKWH00016BA/1173